P9-EEF-683

WESTWARD VISION

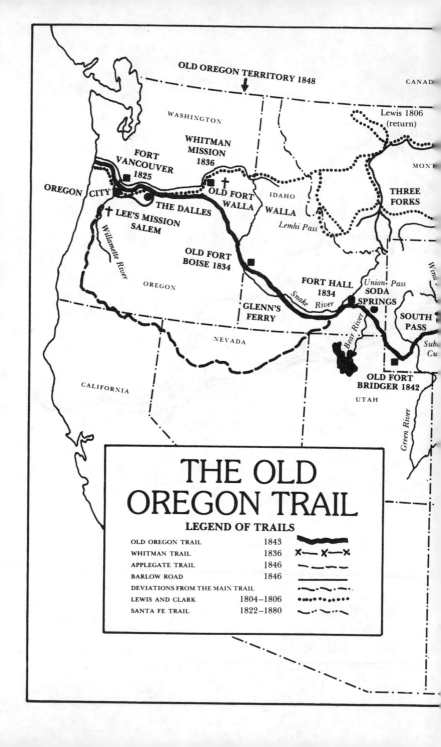

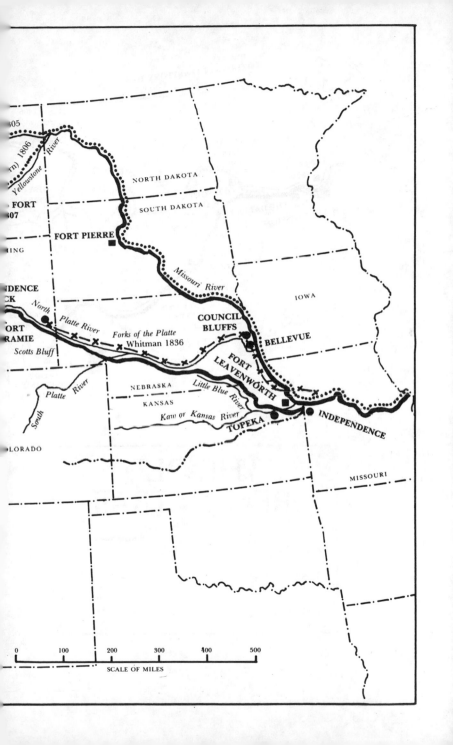

805

(rn) 1806

Yellowstone River

NORTH DAKOTA

FORT
807

SOUTH DAKOTA

ING

FORT PIERRE

Missouri River

NDENCE
CK

IOWA

North

Platte River

COUNCIL
BLUFFS

ORT
RAMIE

Forks of the Platte
Whitman 1836

BELLEVUE

Scotts Bluff

FORT
LEAVENWORTH

NEBRASKA

Platte River

Little Blue River

KANSAS

South River

Kaw or Kansas River

TOPEKA

INDEPENDENCE

LORADO

MISSOURI

0	100	200	300	400	500

SCALE OF MILES

978
LAV

WESTWARD VISION

The Story of the Oregon Trail

David Lavender

with illustrations by Marian Ebert

University of Nebraska Press
Lincoln & London

LARAMIE HIGH SCHOOL
LIBRARY/MEDIA CENTER

To Val and David,
Larry, Shannon, Davy, and Martha

Copyright 1963 by David Lavender
All rights reserved
Manufactured in the United States of America

First Bison Book printing: February 1985
Most recent printing indicated by the first digit below:
2   3   4   5   6   7   8   9   10

Library of Congress Cataloging in Publication Data
Lavender, David Sievert, 1910–
    Westward vision.
    "Bison."
    Reprint. Originally published: 1st ed. New York :
McGraw-Hill, 1963. (American trails series) With new
prologue.
    1. Oregon Trail. 2. Overland journeys to the Pacific.
3. West (U.S.)—Description and travel. I. Title.
F880.L39 1985   978   84-20815
ISBN 0-8032-2866-X
ISBN 0-8032-7915-9 (pbk.)

Prologue to Bison Book Edition, copyright 1985 by the
University of Nebraska Press.

Contents

BC# 10177

Prologue to the Bison Book Edition:
A Sense of Place

Go west, young man, and grow up with the country. But, in the absence of such allures as gold, where in the West?

On leaving home behind, most of the restless migrants in the colonies and, afterward, in the young republic simply traveled a few score miles into an adjacent territory and settled there. By contrast, the Oregon pioneers decided, almost overnight it seemed, to cross two thousand miles of plains and mountains inhabited by potentially hostile Indians and seek out living space in an area dominated by representatives of a foreign power with which their nation had already fought two wars.

Why?

Several studies have sought to explain America's westward expansion by examining the characteristics of the movers themselves, and of course it was within each person's private self that the decisions were made. Still, the lure of destination, the "sense of place," that unshackled those private motives and put the wheels to rolling is also worth attention. That will be the burden of this book.

What's in a Name?

First, of course, was curiosity. What marvels lay hidden in the interior of North America? What riches? How many miles separated the Atlantic from the Pacific? Were there waterways—Northwest Passages—through or around the continent that would shrink traveling time to the lucrative commerce of Asia?

Of the various schemes designed to answer these questions, the first that concerns us sprang from the fertile imagination of Major Robert Rogers. An authentic hero of the French and Indian Wars of 1754–63, Rogers became, shortly after peace was made, governor of Michilimackinac, a fur-trading post that stood beside the strategic strait linking Lakes Huron and Michigan. That was pretty far west—far enough, perhaps, for a contingent of soldiers financed by the triumphant British government to continue on to the Pacific. After establishing a camp beside the western ocean, the explorers would move on north to find the outlet of the fabled Northwest Passage, for whose discovery the Admiralty had already offered a reward of £20,000.

Mixed with this ambition were fur-trade schemes involving another ex-soldier, Jonathan Carver. (See the summary on pages 50–64.) Carver did take trade goods as far off as the northern reaches of the Mississippi before both plans collapsed. It was a profitable experience, nevertheless. From it Carver drew material for a book, *Travels through the Interior Parts of North America,* that went through thirty or so editions between 1778, when it was first published, and 1796.

The *Travels* included a map of North America. Some of it represented land Carver had seen. Some he drew from the talk of traders and Indians. And some he plagiarized from the work of theoretical geographers who wished to impose a pleasing symmetry, including the standard Northwest Passage, onto this continent they had never traversed. Among the notable features of Carver's rendition was a continental divide formed by a single ridge of north-south hills. Running westward from the divide was the usual Great River of the West. It was not there because any European had actually seen it, but because it created an aesthetic whole. The Mississippi flowed south; the St. Lawrence went east; the Red-Winnipeg-Nelson system (Carver called it the Bourbon) wandered north into Hudson Bay. Clearly there had to be a comparable river in the West.

Since places are not real until named, Carver and Rogers invented Ourigan, or Ouragon, or Aurigan, or, as it eventually became, Oregon. Rogers said, as of course he had to, that it was an

Indian name. Possibly it was, though no investigator has reported a Native American word closer to it in sound than the Shoshonean *Oyer-Un-Gon*, which is said to mean "Place of Plenty." Very nice, but it is unlikely that either Rogers or Carver ever encountered a Shoshoni from the Far West. And if phonetics is the criterion, what of Ouragan, which in French, a language both men knew, means "hurricane," or, by extension, "great trouble"? So meaning may not have been involved in the choice. Just the romantic suggestiveness of its long, liquid sounds. The sounds of reality.

Thomas Jefferson and thousands of others saw Carver's map. Just looking at it turned the West into a true place—and also raised questions in a few prophetic minds. Pioneers were already pouring over the Appalachian Mountains toward the Mississippi. Might not their descendants continue on and on, establishing new republics separate from Washington because of distance but unshakably linked to America by shared ideals? Surely foresight required that the parent nation gain control of the Great River of the West for the sake of the progeny.

Rites of Possession

In 1778, the year Carver's *Travels* was published, England's famed navigator, Captain James Cook, sailed two ships north up the Pacific looking for that tantalizing Northwest Passage through or around North America. He did not find it. His sailors, however, learned they could trade such trinkets as metal buttons off their jackets to the Indians of America's Northwest Coast in exchange for lustrous sea-otter pelts that commanded fabulous prices in China. The word spread and soon ships from several nations were scouring the region's convoluted inlets and islands. During the constant tacking back and forth, English mariners fell into a squabble with the Spanish, who claimed territorial rights in the area by virtue of earlier explorations. Sovereignty, the English said, could not be established Spanish style by simply landing and going through a ceremony. National ownership and the exclusion of other powers had to be based on actual occupation.

The dispute reached the heads of government and very nearly precipitated a war before Spain agreed to press her claims no farther northward than her already viable colonies in California.

As a follow-up to the sword-rattling, England sent three ships under Captain George Vancouver to the Northwest to conduct a new, detailed study of the area. On April 29, 1792, Vancouver's little fleet met, somewhere near the Strait of Juan de Fuca, an American trading ship, the *Columbia,* commanded by Robert Gray. This was Gray's second trip into the area; the first had been something of a triumph. In spite of being loaded with trade goods that did not suit the tastes of the natives, he had managed to obtain enough furs to merit sailing to Canton, China, where he had swapped the pelts for tea and nankeen. He took this cargo on around the world to his home port of Boston. Cannon salutes and cheering throngs greeted him, and during the excitement the notion of an American actually standing on the far side of the continent took on a vividness it had never before possessed. Now, loaded with a better assortment of goods, Gray was back to harvest more furs from places his rivals had not yet found.

He and some of Vancouver's officers exchanged pleasantries, then went their separate ways. Vancouver worked into what he named Puget Sound and reveled not in its fur-bearing animals, which failed to interest him, but in its magnificent vistas. He spent two months there and grew so entranced that on June 4, 1792, he landed near the site of present-day Everett, Washington, and took possession of the region for Great Britain by means of a ceremony like those his nation had disdained during its recent quarrel with Spain.

Meanwhile Gray had continued south to test some muddy waters and strong currents he had noted earlier. On May 11, 1792, he crossed a dangerous bar into a broad bay and sailed another few miles upstream. Convinced by the behavior of the Indians that they had never before seen a vessel like his, he decided he was the discoverer of the stream and named it for his ship, *Columbia.* If he associated the river with Carver's Oregon (which, indeed, he may never have heard of) he made no mention of the fact in his log. No matter. Coincidence had triumphed.

PROLOGUE: A SENSE OF PLACE

The Great River of the West was *there,* proved so by a citizen of the United States.

A rough-and-tumble sea dog, Gray had no more interest in diplomatic niceties than Vancouver had in fur. During the ten days he spent trading inside the river's mouth, he conducted no ceremony of possession in the name of the United States. The English were not so negligent. Using the dubious excuse that Gray had not sailed far enough upstream to claim effective discovery, one of Vancouver's officers, William Broughton, took a small vessel to within sight of Mt. Hood, which he named. There he landed, and by moonlight asserted the sovereignty of Great Britain. He let Gray's name for the river stand, however, and ever afterward British documents spoke of the river as the Columbia and the surrounding region as the Oregon—always *the.* Americans, on the other hand, coppered their bets, speaking of "the river Columbia or Oregon," just in case Carver had been right and his earlier name, the reputed Indian name, was the one to use in discussions about sovereignty.

During the years when the sea-otter trade was developing, beaver hunters of Canada's aggressive North West Company had pushed so far overland that supplying their posts with canoes from their base on Lake Superior became increasingly difficult. Hoping to find a Pacific approach that could be used instead, one of the company's partners, Alexander Mackenzie, in 1793 managed with infinite labor to lead a small party through present-day British Columbia to the ocean. The ordeal convinced him that the Columbia River, which no one had yet traversed, would probably turn out to be the only suitable approach to the interior.

Mackenzie presented his arguments in the final chapter of a book he wrote about his experiences. As an added inducement he stated that the Columbia valley was "the most northern situation fit for colonization, and suitable for the residence of a civilized people." If the government, he said, would end certain trading monopolies in the Orient, British merchants operating from the river's mouth could drive the Yankees out of the North Pacific.

The British government, influenced by the North West Company's bitter rival, the Hudson's Bay Company, responded coolly.

Still, these were the last hot days of European imperialism, when dreams of power swept across whole continents, and who could say what dramas might yet be enacted in that far-off land to which the infant United States had staked but so controversial a claim?

Cross Country

Oregon. Columbia. No matter what visions the name awoke in patriots, it was not possible to forget either the enormous land-mass or the foreign power, Spain, that separated the United States from that still half-unbelievable region beside the Pacific. And a foreign nation, unlike the land, was a frustration at which it was possible to grow angry. By holding Louisiana Territory, which stretched from vaguely defined Texas north to Canada and from the west bank of the Mississippi River to the unknown mountains of the continental divide, Spain was in a position to throttle further expansion by America's ever-restless pioneers. Yet destiny lay westward. Convictions born during nearly two hundred years of Atlantic crossings decreed it. So did the young nation's assurance to pioneers that the communities they built beyond the Alleghenies would not be treated as inferior colonies but would either be taken into the Union as full-blown states or recognized as worthy allies. Surely these promises were not to end at the Mississippi.

Foreseeing that the blockade might eventually force the United States to embark on drastic adventures, Thomas Jefferson had tried on four occasions before the turn of the century to gather information about the western lands by urging small groups to scout the area for him. For the most part the efforts failed. New urgency came when he learned, shortly after assuming the presidency in 1801, that Napoleon had wrested Louisiana from Spain as a part of a plan to reestablish New France in North America. Many dangers, including involvement in a war between France and England, might evolve from that. More than ever it behooved the president to learn, with due caution, all he could about the potential battlefield.

To lead a small expedition composed mostly of military men,

Jefferson chose two army officers who were also wilderness experts, Meriwether Lewis and William Clark. He arranged for Lewis to sharpen his powers of observation by taking a crash course in practical science. His instructions to the pair were as broad as his own interests in the natural history of North America and the future safety of his own country. He wanted the party to win the regard of the Indians (who might be useful allies in case of war) and to learn whether the flow of the Missouri and its tributaries would let furs, a vital item of frontier commerce, be diverted down that stream to American rather than to British dealers. He wondered whether goods could be taken in small boats to the head of the Missouri and then transported across a short portage to the "Columbia or Oregon." In particular, he desired information about the soils, minerals, vegetation, growing seasons, animal life, and climate of the whole stretch of the continent, for clearly he did not expect the Mississippi to be a boundary forever.

By stating that scientific inquiry was the expedition's sole object, he obtained money for it from Congress and passports from France and England. Then, just as the men were starting down the Ohio, he learned that Napoleon had given up his New World ambitions and had abruptly sold Louisiana to the president's envoys in Paris for $15 million. Lewis and Clark would be studying American, not foreign, land! And beyond the continental divide lay Oregon, the title to which would be immeasurably strengthened if they traversed the western river's full length. In the excitement, how was it possible not to speculate about the continent's farthest rim?

The expedition, which lasted two and a half years (it started up the Missouri in May 1804 and returned late in September 1806) was, in the words of one enthusiast, "incomparably the most perfect achievement of its kind in the world." The lone fatality resulted from appendicitis. The single scuffle with Indians brought no loss of life to the explorers. All objectives were achieved, two negatively: the Rockies were not the single chain that Carver's map showed but a knot of mountains across which a successful commerce could hardly be sustained. There was no practical way to divert furs from Canada, but as if in compensation, the West's own cold and coiling streams teemed with beaver. To those conclusions the explorers added volumes of data about the physical realities of the West.

A wondrous land indeed, easily visualized now, and yet the Americans nearly lost it—would have lost it if the British had been able to develop a vision of Oregon as a home for their own settlers rather than as a source of profit for stockholders in a trading monopoly.

England Takes Over

The first extensive project to arise from the Lewis and Clark adventure was John Jacob Astor's Pacific Fur Company, and it died in infancy during the second war between England and the United States, 1812–15. Convinced by a party of Nor'Westers that they were soon to suffer a naval attack, Astor's men sold to the Canadians the post, Astoria, that they had built at the river mouth. When a small naval sloop appeared later, nothing remained for the captain to do but hoist a flag over the station and change its name to Fort George.

The war having ended in a draw, the Treaty of Ghent decreed that all captured territory was to be returned to its original owners. But who had owned Oregon? Unable to decide, the peace commissioners compromised. For the next ten years, beginning in 1818, both countries should have, under a supplemental Treaty of Joint Occupation, equal rights of trade and settlement. Curiously, however, the negotiators decided that since Astoria had been captured rather than purchased, the post should be turned back to Astor. A pointless formality. By then the Nor'Westers had spread so many posts throughout the region that Astor chose not to compete with them. Astoria stayed in British hands.

Later, in 1821, the Hudson's Bay Company absorbed the North West firm and embarked on a calculated policy of stripping the country of beaver and thus deterring American trappers from entering. Not the least of their steps was the building of a powerful bastion on the north bank of the Columbia about ninety miles above its mouth. This they named Fort Vancouver in direct reference to the exploration and claims of that English mariner and his men. The chief factor in charge of Fort Vancouver was John McLoughlin, a canny, hardworking manager whose generosity was, on most occasions, as expansive as his body was herculean. Before long, HBC fur brigades—some boasters said the initials stood for "Here Before Christ"—were sweeping into every nook and cranny of the country. Simultaneously, maritime trading posts appeared to challenge American trading ships.

Joint occupation by one occupant! Some of the sheen disappeared from the concept *Oregon*. But there was resentment, too, for there were many Americans who firmly believed that Lewis and Clark had made the region wholly theirs, to be developed along whatever republican lines circumstances dictated.

Oregon Fever

Out of the nature of things and not through conspiracy or concerted planning, American expansionists evolved a strategy for countering Britain's de facto domination of the Oregon country. First they would focus national attention on the disputed region and then make it appear so desirable that groups of people would suddenly start wanting to go there as soon as the old adversary in two wars was pushed out of the way.

The first shot was fired by Representative John Floyd of Virginia, who in 1821 and again in 1822 introduced bills in Congress to organize the entire Columbia River drainage as Oregon Territory. He described the region as a treasure house of furs and timber and predicted that a great commercial city would one day arise at the mouth of the river. Although neither bill came to a vote, this was yeasty stuff and launched hot arguments as to whether or not so distant a region could really be governed from Washington. The talk, of course, gave new firmness to the entire concept of Oregon as a place, a destination.

The Monroe Doctrine, though aimed at Russia, added more visibility by declaring that no part of the American continents were to be colonized by European nations. Shortly thereafter the administration signed, without consulting Britain, a treaty setting the southern boundary of Russian Alaska at 54°40'. Monroe also recommended that Congress order the placing of a military post at the mouth of the Columbia. The House committee that was appointed to study the idea issued bellicose reports that further delighted American jingoists with their twistings of the lion's tail. Oregon, oh, Oregon!

The agitations upset the Hudson's Bay Company, which wanted the boundary issue settled so that it could go ahead with its developmental plans. Yielding to its pressure, the British government asked for and obtained a new series of talks. Gradually the area under dispute narrowed. The British would accept as a boundary the Columbia River as far upstream as the 49th parallel. (The Hudson's Bay Company believed it needed the stream as a line of communications to its posts in what is now British Columbia.) The United States countered with a demand for a line along the 49th parallel. This would place the magnificent harbors of Puget Sound in the hands of whatever U.S. territory or independent, American-style republic took shape in the Northwest.

When neither side would yield on its demands, the negotiators compromised again, saying that the Treaty of Joint Occupation would be extended indefinitely, with either country having the right to abrogate it by giving a year's notice in advance. The delay played squarely into American hands. A few fur trappers and maritime traders at last managed to penetrate the area. Crushed quickly by the mighty Hudson's Bay Company, they carried their outrage home to Congress and their local newspapers. Excluded from land they had every right to be in! A beautiful land, moreover, with boundless potential for fisheries, agriculture, and stock raising as well as for furs. It was easy to get there, too, by avoiding the Indian-plagued Missouri and striking up the Platte and Sweetwater rivers to a broad saddle in the continental divide called South Pass.

Availability! A fuzzy-minded New Englander, Hall Kelley, proposed to march three thousand emigrants westward to what he described as "the loveliest and most envied country on earth." The expected thousands stayed away, but he did stir the imagination of an adventurous trader, Nathaniel Wyeth, into attempting to place fishing and trading posts almost within the shadow of Fort Vancouver itself. Failure again. However, a few of his men did settle in the Willamette Valley, south of the Columbia, where a few retired employees of the Hudson's Bay Company had established farms. And so a new name began to sound—Willamette. *That* was the place for settlement to begin, Wyeth reported on his return home with two Indian boys he wanted to train as interpreters.

By chance the lads appeared just at a time when enthusiasm for converting America's own pagans was cresting in missionary societies throughout the East. During the next few years, several zealots established widely scattered stations throughout Oregon. Many of the divines, notably Marcus Whitman, took their wives with them. That completed the picture. Homes! And land! Land to farm! Land to speculate with as demand grew and prices rose! Land that some Congressmen proposed to give free to pioneers who risked crossing the dry High Plains and shaggy mountains to reach the new Eden.

Sensing the danger that was building up, the Hudson's Bay Company persuaded a handful of people to settle with two priests north of the Columbia, to serve as magnets for an influx of Britons. It didn't work. There was no overflowing reservoir of population in eastern and midwestern Canada to draw on, and the company's rigid paternalism was no match for the motives that inspired the Americans, who were now envisioning, under the rising sun of Manifest Destiny, a continental United States and not a collection of separate republics.

The trickle that began with Joel Walker's family in 1840 swelled into a flood—800 or more migrants in 1843, almost twice that many in 1844, close to another doubling the next year, and 4,500 in 1847. Easy? No. Some movers endured real hardship and danger. At best it was "a tedious and tiring trip," as one man described it, adding, "but I think we are well paid for our trouble." So was the nation, which used the influx to obtain, without a third war against England, the boundary it wanted.

It was a mass migration without precedent—a leap across half a continent to reach one special place, the feeling for which had been building in the nation's consciousness for decades. Soon gold would perform a similar service for California in the span of a year or two. Not until then would the migration turn and flow back eastward to help fill in the empty places it had skipped by on the initial exhilarating move toward the setting sun.

WESTWARD VISION

PROLOGUE: THE LONG QUEST

The story of the Oregon Trail begins in one very real sense with Columbus. Somewhere to the west, supplanting the ancient caravan routes which heathen Turks had blocked, lay a new road to man's old hopes—to the Orient and the fulfillment it symbolized. Dreams as bright as that die hard. For centuries after the geographic fact of America had forced itself onto the Old World, yearners kept insisting that somewhere a passage to Cathay wound through or around the interrupting continent. Simultaneously, the inconvenient land mass was found to have values of its own. Lured by these riches, the Spanish, the French, and at last the English strove with tiny forces to control an enormous future.

Circumstance gave the explorers of each of those peoples a different goal. Incredible troves of gold and silver in Peru and Mexico led the Spaniards to search for still more mines as they groped into what is now the southwestern part of the United States. Staunch Catholics, accompanied everywhere by their priests, the searchers believed that the Indians, while useful in performing forced labor, also possessed souls worth saving. This principle kept the Indians at least partly human in Spanish eyes, permitted intermarriage, and helped bring about in Mexico a considerable population of mixed bloods who sustained a culture of more variety, intelligence, and artistic accomplishment than other nationalities would attain elsewhere in the New World during the next several generations.

3

Farther to the north, meanwhile, the French found themselves conditioned by another tremendous geographic truth—the St. Lawrence River. Its broad flood opened to their canoes an arduous but usable water highway through a land that otherwise was clogged by dark forests and shaggy mountains, the Appalachians. A road to the Orient? French explorers groped eagerly up the river into the Great Lakes and on to the Mississippi. They encountered no Chinese, but they did discover Indians possessed of lustrous furs that could be bought for trifles in cloth, hardware, muskets, and other manufactured trinkets.

Like the Spaniards, the French and their black-robed priests accepted the Indians on terms of somewhat equal respect. But fur-gathering did not require as much crop land or as many manufactories for its support as did the Spanish mines. As a consequence, the tiny hamlets along the St. Lawrence—Montreal, Quebec, Three Rivers—remained less than self-supporting and French Canada never attracted sufficient population to give reality to her vast ambitions.

Both nations were well planted before the English came. Santa Fe was founded in New Mexico about 1610; Champlain gazed longingly westward from the eastern shore of Lake Huron (1615–16) before the Pilgrims touched Plymouth Rock. Furthermore, the English seemed pinned to the Atlantic coast by the mountains. Only one river system, the Hudson and its tributary, the bloody Mohawk, offered a useful way to the interior—and at first the Dutch, who were no real threat to France, kept the English out of that riverway.

The English did not seem to mind. Their early energies were devoted to clearing farms in rocky New England, plantations in the South. This was something new to the New World: none of the other colonists had been interested chiefly in land for its own sake. Instantly the Indians recognized the threat. They also sensed the contempt in which the average Englishman held them, as though the red men were first cousins to the wolves, fit only to be exterminated. Aided by the French, the Indians struck back furiously. Partly because of this and partly because of the unfriendly geography, the English advance was snail-slow; only a rash prophet would have supposed that the rainbow trails to the

West might eventually become the heritage of the thirteen seaboard colonies.

Yet all this long while—for nearly two centuries after the defeat of the Spanish Armada in 1588—the energies of Spain and France had been waning, those of England increasing. Futilely Spain and France tried to check the island nation's headlong growth to maritime supremacy; and Europe's wars stirred dreadful echoes in the New World. England always won. In 1713-14 the French lost the Canadian provinces of Newfoundland and Acadia (Nova Scotia) and the rich fur territories draining into Hudson Bay. In 1763 she surrendered the rest of Canada and also Louisiana, as the entire Mississippi basin was then known, though in an effort to confine England's ambition the treatymakers gave the unexplored area west of the great river to Spain.

It was too late. By 1763 no power, certainly not Spain, could have confined the western surge of the Anglo-Saxon peoples. With growing momentum they breached the Alleghenies and floated down the Ohio, sweeping aside both the native inhabitants and the tiny outposts of the French. Some of their dreams were the same as the ones the French had followed—a usable way to the Orient, a bountiful harvest of furs. But mostly the men who came on the heels of the fur-gatherers were farmers eager for a piece of tillable soil. Land, to their way of thinking, could best provide a poor man the security he needed for working out his destiny in his own way.

Impossible dreams fizzed through this ancient quest for self-sufficiency. At times the yearning created monsters of selfishness; often it was aborted by its own blunders. But unbelievable adventurings rescued it just as often; hope regenerated itself on the renewed promise of better lands somewhere out beyond. England's own folly in trying to check the advance through the Quebec Act of 1774 helped bring the United States into being.

No check—Indians, nature, or politics—ever lasted. In each generation someone always managed to go one step farther west. Eventually the gropings coalesced into what we now call the Oregon Trail. Yet in one sense the name is misleading. Men were looking for the way before ever they heard that strange word *Oregon*, plucked from heaven knows where. The search was full-blown in the Mississippi Valley when the French still dreamed of controlling a continent with hardly enough men to play a modern game of football; when Spain's haughty dons in Mexico were determined to puncture the insane ambition; when scarcely a handful of English hunters had yet ventured into the foothills of the Alleghenies; and when the United States, inheritors of the dreams of each of those nations, had hardly been thought of. Yet the very emergence of the new country as an independent nation guaranteed that the long search would succeed and that men would stand at last beside the sea of their desiring. In time there even came to be a name for the inevitability—Manifest Destiny. And that is what this book is about.

ONE

DREAMERS & SCHEMERS

THE FABULOUS LAND

In 1719 the French court bubbled with speculation about the fabled lands of the American West. Much of the excitement sprang from the New World schemes of a handsome Scot named John Law, who at the age of twenty-three had had to flee England for killing a man in a duel. For twenty years after the slaying, Law had wandered from one of Europe's capitals to another, living luxuriously out of his winnings as a gambler and now and then soliciting various governments to set up and let him manage a national bank.

By and large, Law's ideas about banking were sound. Fiscal ministers declined to heed him, however, until in 1716 he caught the ear of the Duke of Orléans. To Law, the duke granted letters patent authorizing him to establish a Banque Générale in Paris, the first institution of its kind in France.

No country ever stood in greater need of a financial wizard. The extravagances of Louis XIV, topped by the War of the Spanish Succession (called Queen Anne's War in the American Colonies), had mired the nation in appalling debt. The Peace of Utrecht (1713–14) had stripped from her some of her most lucrative fur-producing and potential farmlands in Canada—Hudson Bay, Newfoundland, and Acadia. When the once-dazzling king at last died in 1715, his heir was a boy of five. The government passed into the hands of a regent, the Duke of Orléans, and French prestige sagged lower than it had been for many years.

9

Even the country's specie was distrusted, and the value of coins fluctuated erratically.

Law's bank inspired immediate confidence by redeeming its notes with the same weight of metal that had originally been paid for them. His paper soon commanded a premium, and within a year the government was accepting his banknotes in payment of taxes. Delighted by this new stability in the country's economy, the Duke of Orléans lent a ready ear to Law's next scheme—a trade monopoly embracing all of Louisiana, a name for the entire drainage system of the Mississippi River. At the time no one in France, or in America either, realized how enormously the territory stretched—but small matter. Law was deemed capable of handling it all.

His *Compagnie d'Occident,* more informally called The Mississippi Scheme or The System, was launched in August 1717. Circulars were issued showing the prairies black with bison and the rivers teeming with beaver, as indeed they were. Colonists were recruited to till lands whose fertility was described in ecstatic hyperbole. Money poured in. In headlong zest the *Compagnie d'Occident* absorbed other trading monopolies. Soon most of France's non-European trade lay within its grip. To reflect the expansion, Law in 1719 changed the company's name to *Compagnie des Indes.* Speculators continued to call it The System.

In 1718, Law's Banque Générale became the Royal Bank of France. His *Compagnie des Indes* assumed management of the mint. Blandly he proposed to pay off the entire national debt by accepting in payment for shares in the *Compagnie* those royal obligations which the government itself could not redeem. The rush to convert these obligations into stock sent prices rocketing. Shares issued at 500 livres each sold within two years for 10,000 livres. On January 1, 1720, the *Compagnie* declared a 40 per cent dividend. The price of stock thereupon zoomed to 18,000 livres, and speculators grew absolutely frantic.

As might be expected, Paris developed fresh interest in the romantic American West, whose resources were (in large measure) to guarantee the *Compagnie's* continued growth. To satisfy the curiosity, several extraordinary frontiersmen were paraded before the periwigged *haut monde.* What these men said and the actions they proposed reflected two centuries' accretion of igno-rance. Since the briar patches growing out of these deep-rooted mistakes later plagued even the efforts of the United States to open communication with Oregon, it is useful to pause here for a glance at what Frenchmen in 1719 supposed they might find if they succeeded in penetrating the unknown of Louisiana as far as the Western Ocean.

Very soon after Columbus' voyages, sea and land adventurers in the employ of Spain had learned the shape of Central and South America. Magellan's circumnavigation of the world had revealed the width of the central Pacific. In spite of these discoveries, a wistful belief persisted that in the unvisited North the continents of Asia and North America leaned together—as, of course, they do. If they actually joined, theoretical geographers reasoned, then perhaps the bleak coasts of Newfoundland were nothing more than the edges of a peninsula extending eastward from the Orient.

Men can always find "evidence" for believing what they wish to believe. When Jacques Cartier returned to Paris in 1534 from his venture into the New World's huge Gulf of St. Lawrence, he brought with him two savage lads named Taignoagny and Do-magaya. This pair reported that far up a great river that emptied into the bay lay a kingdom called Saguenay, rich in copper and gold. Cartier's second expedition the following year pressed up the St. Lawrence to stockaded villages of Iroquois long houses and the mountainous island where Montreal eventually would stand; but the nearest the explorers came to Saguenay was another kidnaped Indian who in Paris spun even more fabulous tales: one-legged men, flying men, pygmies, and (equally entrancing) ordinary men in woolen clothes who raised cinnamon and oranges and who pos-sessed great stores of gold, copper, rubies, and other rich things.

In 1535 such yarns did not seem fanciful. Only fifteen years ear-lier Cortez had marched through the wilderness of Mexico to the savage treasures of the Aztecs. Rumors were trickling back to Europe of Pizarro's equally fantastic conquest of the Incas. Why couldn't there be other empires equally rich somewhere in the misty North? In 1540 Coronado marched from Mexico as far as the plains of central Kansas, hunting first for the opulent Seven Cities of Cibola and then for Quivira. He was still wandering

across the limitless prairies when Cartier returned (1541) to the
St. Lawrence for the third time. On this trip the Frenchman led
with him boatloads of colonists for establishing a way station to
the Orient.

Both efforts failed, and permanent settlements in North America
would not take shape for another two-thirds of a century. The lure
of Asia, or at least of a rich Oriental offshoot located somewhere in
North America, in no wise faded, however. In an attempt to retain
the dream and at the same time account for such wisps of knowledge as were beginning to float out of the wilderness, library
cartographers produced several fantastic maps. Although various
in detail, most of the charts embraced one of two hypotheses: first,
of a waterway *around* North America or, second, of a waterway
through the continent. A few maps went whole hog and showed
both features. Some managed not only to include these new theories but to retain as well the old idea that North America was a
mere extension of mysterious China.

These refinements emanated in the main from English merchant adventurers eager to locate markets and trade routes not yet
dominated by Spain or Portugal. In their minuscule ships the
Elizabethan sea dogs tried, among other things, to grope around the
north of Russia to the Orient. This failing, they speculated about
the possibility of skirting North America. One of the most capable
of their number, Sir Humphrey Gilbert, spent a decade studying
every traveler's tale on which he could lay hands. His conclusions,
published in 1576 as *Discourse of a Discoverie for a New Passage
to Cataia,* declared that America was an island and that through
her "Northern Sea the Passage Lyeth." He urged that England
as a matter of self-preservation find this waterway and build forts
along its shores.

In the year the *Discourse* was published, Martin Frobisher began twisting among the icebergs beyond Greenland in search of
the passage's eastern end. Drake may have been looking for its
western end three years later when he rounded South America,
plundered a Spanish galleon off Panama and fled north perhaps as
far as Oregon before abandoning his arctic cast and striking on
westward across the Pacific. If Drake also abandoned the waterway theory, as his ship's chaplain Francis Fletcher suggested

("... wee conjecture that either there is no passage at all through these Northerne coasts ... or if there be, yet it is unnavigable"), he was one of the few who did. For two more centuries the will-o'-the-wisp distorted the world's thinking.

Sometimes men called the mythical waterway The Northwest Passage; sometimes the Strait of Anian. The Spanish searched for it through the deserts of the American Southwest, the Russians from the inhospitable shores of Kamchatka. The intensity of the yearning inevitably produced opportunists who asserted that they had already discovered the strait. Most notable of these liars, because he left his name permanently in our geographies, was old Juan de Fuca. Juan was a Greek. He adopted his Spanish pseudonym, he said, in order to please the viceroy of Mexico, in whose service he had sailed for twenty days through the passage to the Northern Ocean, past lands that in the standard folklore of the time were "very fruitfull, and rich of gold, Silver, Pearle, and other things, like Nova Spain." [1]

The second will-o'-the-wisp of the theoretical geographers showed waterways through the unknown lands. In their most modest form, these channels were ordinary rivers heading near each other and flowing in opposite directions. Since no one had yet glimpsed the Rockies, it was deemed that travelers could cross from one stream to the other by means of a simple portage across an unpretentious "height of land." For really feverish imaginations, however, this inconvenience was too much. Their maps showed a huge inland sea with rivers flowing out of it in both directions. One simply sailed across the sea without the bother of a portage. Cartographers who liked the idea of America being a peninsula attached to Asia declared that Oriental frontiersmen had already settled on the Asiatic side of the inland sea and that trade could be opened simply by reaching the far shore.

This marvelous inland sea was a hangover from a conclusion to which one Giovanni da Verrazano had jumped in 1524. While Verrazano's tiny *Dauphine* had been coasting along a sandspit

---

[1] By coincidence an actual strait, now called Juan de Fuca, lies between the state of Washington and Vancouver Island, at almost the latitude the Greek claimed for his mythical passage. One can still start discussions in the Pacific Northwest about whether or not old Juan actually saw the opening that bears his name.

outside Chesapeake Bay or perhaps farther south along Pamlico Sound, his masthead glimpsed water on the spit's far side. Too wary of Indians to land and investigate, the explorers decided without more ado that they had found an isthmus narrower than Panama and that the ocean beyond "without doubt reaches to the extremities of India, China, and Cathay."

Later, as men began to suspect the width of the American continent, Verrazano's sea retreated westward but never quite disappeared. Beguiled by thoughts of finding it, George Weymouth sailed up what is now called the Penobscot River; Henry Hudson tried the stream that bears his name; John Smith examined the James, the Chickahominy, the Potomac. And when Champlain at about the same time went with the first permanent French colonists up the St. Lawrence and heard of huge inland seas to the west, he was convinced, so he urged his king, "that the means of reaching easily the kingdom of China and the East Indies" lay within his country's grasp.

By pushing up the Ottawa River, Champlain found the Great Lakes. Unable because of administrative duties to cross them himself, he sent Jean Nicolet in 1634 into the dim reaches of Green Bay, a westward-trending arm of Lake Michigan. Convinced even here on the shores of reality that he had reached the Orient, Nicolet carefully donned a robe of Chinese silk before stepping from his birchbark canoe to meet what turned out to be several more half-naked red men.

Ah, but just a little farther! For Nicolet learned from the Indians that by traveling from Green Bay up the Fox River a man could reach a short portage that led to a western-flowing stream, today's Wisconsin. The Wisconsin would bring the traveler to a still mightier river, the Mississippi.

Nicolet had no reason to connect his Mississippi with the stream which the Spaniards far to the south called Espíritu Santo. The Frenchman had come a vast distance from the mouth of the St. Lawrence. Surely the "height of land" dividing the Atlantic and Pacific drainages could not be far away; perhaps it was the very Fox–Wisconsin portage the Indians had told him about. If so, the great river would flow into the Vermilion Sea of the Spanish— that is, into the Gulf of California.

The deduction wasn't reasoning, exactly; it was faith. The Great Lakes had failed as a way to China (or to the Pacific, depending on the theory); ergo, the Mississippi must be the key. Besides, there were political considerations that fostered belief. If the Mississippi did flow into the Pacific, an advance from posts on the Great Lakes would enable the French to outflank the Spanish in New Mexico. It certainly would enable them to pinch off the English from any considerable westward advance. Accordingly, the government eventually got around to advising Jean Talon, *intendant* at Quebec, that "since nothing is so important for the colony as the discovery of a passage to the South Sea, his majesty wishes you to give this your attention."

Talon assigned the enormous task to Louis Jolliet, a divinity student turned fur trader. With him Jolliet took Père Jacques Marquette, a Jesuit missionary stationed at bleak St. Ignace on the Strait of Michilimackinac between Lakes Huron and Michigan. In a pair of fragile canoes manned by five *voyageurs* the explorers crossed the Fox–Wisconsin portage, and on June 17, 1673, "with a joy which I [Marquette] cannot express," entered the Mississippi.

The joy faded as they passed fearsome cliffs painted by the Indians to resemble monsters. Even more alarming was the debris-laden flood of the muddy Missouri that roared out of the west across their path. "I have seen nothing more dreadful." To avoid it they paddled cautiously along the eastern bank of the Mississippi.

As the combined rivers continued persistently southward, disappointment grew. Somewhere in what is now Arkansas they began hearing of traders from New Spain. Fearful of capture and certain by now that their river was the Espíritu Santo of the Spanish and hence would not open into the Pacific, they turned back.

So the will-o'-the-wisp retreated one more step westward. If the Mississippi would not open the fabled gateways, then surely the Missouri would—or so Jolliet and Marquette understood from the Indians while they labored up the Mississippi and then turned into the Illinois as an easier approach to the lower end of Lake Michigan.

Given a fair chance, their great contemporary Robert Cavelier, Sieur de la Salle, might have done something about the muddy river that poured out of the West. He too yearned to find the way to the Orient. He talked so much about it that the rapids by his seigneury above Montreal were called derisively La Chine, a name they still bear. His more immediate desire, however, was to strengthen unbreakably France's hold on the Mississippi Valley by building a string of posts from the Great Lakes to the mouth of the river.

Jealousies, misunderstandings, and bald-faced lies kept him from succeeding. He did solve the geography of the present Illinois country and built forts there; he gave Louisiana Territory its name and took possession of its millions of square miles for his king. By following the Mississippi to the Gulf, he confirmed what Jolliet and Marquette had surmised about the river's course. But when he returned to France to seek aid for furthering his projects, he saw his plans vitiated by the intrigues of a renegade Spaniard named Diego Dioniso de Peñalosa Briceno.

An adroit and handsome fortune hunter from Peru, Diego Peñalosa had worked his way up the slippery ladder of favoritism to the governorship of New Mexico. There he tripped. Because of a quarrel with church authorities he was seized by the Inquisition and exiled from the New World. Burning for revenge, he eventually landed in Paris. The idea he propounded there was for him to recruit freebooters among the discontented inhabitants of the West Indies, establish them at an ostensible trading colony near the mouth of the Rio Grande, and when one of the periodic wars between Spain and France broke out, sally forth and seize New Mexico for the French.

When La Salle arrived in Paris proposing an honest colony at the mouth of the Mississippi, the court warped it out of shape by incorporating into it some of Peñalosa's piratical ideas. To gain any support whatsover, La Salle had to agree. The outcome was failure all around. Peñalosa was shunted aside; and although in 1684 La Salle did go farther west than he had originally intended and founded a settlement near Galveston, Texas, he was murdered by one of his own men while crossing overland to Illinois. Most of his pioneers were lost.

Activity in the North meanwhile kept pace with La Salle's efforts in the South. In 1680, even before reaching the Gulf, La Salle had ordered a Franciscan priest named Louis Hennepin and two *voyageurs* to win the natives to France by establishing a trading post somewhere on the upper Mississippi. Sioux Indians captured the trio, tortured them a bit, and then wandered with them through much of present Minnesota. During the peregrinations, Hennepin saw and named the Falls of St. Anthony within the present city limits of Minneapolis.

While the captives were languishing in a Sioux village at Lake Mille Lacs, Minnesota, another of France's incredible lords of the wilderness, Daniel Greysolon, Sieur du Lhut (Duluth) was preparing to push off toward the Western Ocean. To clear the way for his explorations Du Lhut several months earlier had brought a truce to the continual wars between Sioux and Chippewa and Assiniboin and had won each touchy tribe to French allegiance. While doing it he had heard of salt water twenty days' journey to the west. The Sea, which his superior Frontenac had already urged him to find! Now he could do it. Du Lhut located the trail which eventually would develop into the canoe route between Lake Superior and Lake Winnepeg; then just as he was about to start his eager *voyageurs* along it, he heard that the Sioux were holding three Frenchmen captive.

The honor of France—or, more crassly, the prestige of the French fur traders—demanded that the whites be freed. With two *voyageurs* paddling him in a single canoe through the sinuous waterways, Du Lhut reached Lake Mille Lacs, stormed into the lodge of the chief, and by sheer force of personality won his country's victory. But his own yearning died in the doing. By the time he had returned Hennepin and the others to the safety of Michilimackinac (more commonly Mackinac), the season was too late for him to venture westward. For a variety of causes he was never able to start again.

Father Hennepin returned to France and in 1683 published a book that became a phenomenal best-seller, *Description de la Louisiane*. His observations were sound, his maps good for the time, his lies relatively minor. Bedazzled by his success, he attempted to repeat it ten years later with other books. In these he made himself the hero of expeditions he had not accompanied. He plagiarized from the accounts of others, and when facts palled he indulged in soaring fancy. He made money doing it; the unending literary exploitation of the West had at last begun.

Other scribblers recognized a good thing. Among them was the Baron de Lahontan, a marine who served in various of Canada's frontier posts and who in 1688 or thereabouts ventured an unknown distance west of Michilimackinac. In 1703, Lahontan followed Hennepin into print with *Nouveaux Voyages dans l'Amérique Septentrionale*. Like Hennepin, the baron was a good reporter; but, again like Hennepin, he found truth confining. Nevertheless he was effective. His Indian sages, discoursing learnedly on "the natural man," exerted a marked influence on eighteenth-century European philosophy. He tangled American geography for years with his Rivière Longue flowing out of the mysterious West. He claimed to have wintered well up the Long River, a sluggish stream, easily navigable except where it poured in cataracts out of the mountains. Toward its source it widened into a lake (the inland version of the Western Sea again). Lahontan modestly admitted that he had not seen the lake in person, but said that Indians assured him that the Tanuglauks inhabiting its shores owned boats big enough to hold two hundred persons. Beyond the lake was a stream that (as usual) flowed to the Western Ocean. Variants of all this appeared on maps for almost another century.

Balancing the fabricators were actual explorers. One was Jacques de Noyon, who reached Lake of the Woods and in time heard of a western sea that eventually proved to be Lake Winnepeg. Very shortly thereafter Henry Kelsey of Hudson's Bay Company reached the rivers beyond Lake of the Woods—no one knows exactly which rivers—and brought back tales of bison, grizzly bears, and enormous plains where not a single tree grew; yarns that sounded as fanciful as other men's stories of golden-shod dwarfs.

So it went, grains of fact gathered by the antlike searchers of immensity, and with each fact came encrustations of legend. Where nothing is known anything can be believed: stones that shine at night, mountains of salt, vague relatives of the *gougou*—a tree-tall monster of the early St. Lawrence that carried in its pouch human victims on which to lunch as desired. Somewhere

18

in this never-never land were wandering Welshmen, the Lost Tribes of Israel, the descendants of Tartars. Just across the horizon, in the next village, was an Indian who owned a Japanese dagger or a Chinese silver coin or an axe made of a metal not iron—obvious proof that by some route or another the savages had opened trade with men from the Orient. And always, steady as the thrum of water, was the unruffled voice of eighteenth-century rationalism declaring that since canoes already had followed rivers and lakes so far west to so many beaver, they soon could push on a few more miles to the rainbow's end.

Much slower than fancy, a few settlements took form in the Mississippi Valley. In 1699 Cahokia was founded on the east bank of the river, a little below the mouth of the turbid Missouri. A few leagues farther south and a little later in time came Notre Dame de Cascasquios, or Kaskaskia. A more significant settlement, also dating from 1699, was Biloxi, founded in what is now the state of Mississippi by Pierre Le Moyne, Sieur d'Iberville. Tenuously but certainly La Salle's great dream was taking shape; Louisiana was becoming a political reality rather than just a pretentious name.

With Iberville to Biloxi came his extraordinary younger brother (by nineteen years), Jean Baptiste Le Moyne, Sieur de Bienville. They were natives of Canada, sons of a former governor. Both had fought the English with gallantry and dash on the North Atlantic and in Hudson Bay. Now both were eager to contain the English in the East and launch absorptive drives toward the Spanish in the West.

Young Bienville pushed explorations up the Red River of the South, hoping it would lead either to the mines of Mexico (which the avaricious French placed farther north than they really were) or to the Southern Sea. More prosaically but of more immediate benefit to the new colony, he also mastered the local Indian dialects.

After the older brother's death from yellow fever, Bienville assumed charge of all Louisiana—that is, of the entire Mississippi drainage. His star alternately dimmed and brightened as favoritism in the French court put other administrators over him and then removed them. The capital was shifted from Biloxi to Mobile. Other probes, some now lost to our knowledge, searched along the lower tributaries west of the river for the Spaniards who were rumored to be trading with Indians just beyond the next hill. And of course if one reached New Mexico, then California and the way to the Orient were but a step farther.

Throughout these slow casts toward the setting sun, the great flood of the Missouri continued to challenge imagination. More and more frequently, memorials to the court mentioned it as the way west. The discussions were epitomized in an elaborate *Mémoire pour Découverte du Mer de l'Ouest,* prepared and presented in April 1718 by Bobé, "Priest of the Congregation of Missions." France, Bobé declared, was in a better position than any other nation for discovering "the sea"—whether the Pacific or the mythical inland Western Sea or both is not clear. He elaborated on six routes, derived from an omnivorous study of manuscripts and maps by authors who knew little more about the West than he did. Of these six possible routes, Bobé recommended two. One went west from Lake Superior, the other up the Missouri, whose geography in Bobé's mind was thoroughly mingled with that of Lahontan's Rivière Longue. From the Missouri (or from various other streams the father listed) there was a short portage to a west-flowing river that would lead to a sea from whose sandy shores Indians easily garnered fortunes in gold dust.

These hopeful miasmas of ignorance, lighted by only occasional gleams of information, were current in the French court when John Law's comet soared, dragging the *Compagnie d'Occident* behind it as a dazzling tail. On being granted monopolistic trade rights to Louisiana, Law asked that Bienville again be named governor of the vast area and be responsible henceforth only to the company.

In those palmy days Law got whatever he wanted. Bienville became governor and immediately prepared to extend The System's influence throughout the unmapped reaches of his province. To prepare for an influx of colonists he laid out in 1718 a new capital, New Orleans.[2] Since the *Compagnie* was now military guardian of Louisiana, he also readied expeditions against

[2] Although work on the post began in 1718, New Orleans did not formally replace Mobile as administrative headquarters for Louisiana until 1722.

the Spaniards. The dons too were expanding. A Frenchman named St. Denis had alarmed them by crossing from Louisiana into Mexico; as a counterthrust the Spaniards were inching into Texas. Bienville ordered the commanders of his minuscule "armies" to chase away any foreign traders they encountered and to erect barriers against further encroachments by forming treaties of alliance with the Indians. The French were also directed to be alert for information about routes to the Western Sea.

In 1719 two of these expeditions marched into the plains. Neither was as big as a twentieth-century baseball team. The first, consisting of half a dozen mounted men under Claude du Tisne, left Cahokia, Illinois, in the spring; by bluffing or dodging several bands of hostile savages, they reached as far as what is now central Kansas. The second numbered seven whites and the Negro slave of their commander, Bénard de la Harpe, who was a particularly eager exponent of the theory of riverways across the continent. Starting from the French outpost of Natchitoches, in the west-central part of today's state of Louisiana, La Harpe's army pushed up the Red River to a mat of driftwood fifty or so miles long, the so-called "raft" under which the stream gurgled impassably. The Frenchmen wallowed around this *embarras* for a time, turned northward and incredibly reached as far as eastern Oklahoma.

Neither expedition found any Spaniards or any certain news of the Western or Southern seas. However, the Spanish heard of the enemy "armies" and the next year hurried forth from Santa Fe a retaliatory force led by Pedro de Villasur. Villasur chased phantom Frenchmen as far as the Platte River in Nebraska. There, in August 1720, his column was almost annihilated by Pawnee Indians.

While La Harpe and Du Tisne were exciting the Spaniards with their armies, Bienville took to Paris with him an even more fabulous frontiersman—Etienne de Bourgmont, who had spent most of his life leaping from one scrape into another. One uproar had forced him to flee France, where his father was a respectable doctor. Another had driven him from the outpost of Detroit, where he served briefly as commander *pro tem.*, to an island in Lake Erie, to which he was followed by his paramour, a Madame Tichenet.

When the authorities closed in on him there, he fled with some Indians to the distant Missouri River. By 1712 he had extended his trading activities to the mouth of the Platte. From the Missouri Indians he picked up (so secondhand reports said) the usual fantastic tales: Far up the Missouri on the shores of the inevitable lake dwelt a race of fierce dwarfs with large protuberant eyes and shoes of gold. Et cetera. But at least Bourgmont knew more about the river's realities than did any other white man. Overlooking his earlier peccadillos, Bienville took him to Paris to spin his yarns and have him appointed commander of the Missouri district.

Before Bourgmont was well started, John Law's spectacular career flamed to an end. Speculators cashing in on their quick profits and more conservative financiers growing dubious about the soundness of The System drove stock prices down even faster than they had soared. Law was ruined and exiled. His *Compagnie,* however, was too interlocked with the French government to be allowed to expire without a few gasps toward reorganization. Bourgmont in 1723 went ahead with the building of Fort Orleans near where the Grand River enters the Missouri (roughly the central part of present Missouri). The next year he advanced perhaps as far as the Kansas–Colorado border. There he dazzled the still-unsophisticated Indians of the High Plains with what then seemed wonderful gifts of beads and knives and cloth, and with an awesome pageantry of gunfire, fluttering pennants, and gleaming armor.

It was France's last brave gesture at penetrating the continent from the south. As the Spanish threat receded, so did the energies of Louisiana. This was France's true finish in the West, for without the vitality that springs from faith nothing could be accomplished. No advance, for example, could reach far into the unknown without supplies of trade goods and ammunition for the Indians. But forcing loaded pirogues up the Mississippi was desperately hard and expensive, while bringing them down the river from the Great Lakes was extremely dangerous because of the hostility of the Fox Indians. In the Missouri difficulties intensified. The implacable flood crushed the spirits of the *voyageurs* as relentlessly as it did the fragile ribs of their bark canoes. Distances were dismaying; the Indians unpredictable, especially the Sioux. The treeless plains, devoid of birch for canoes or gum for their repair, demanded new techniques of existence that the forest-dweller would have to spend years mastering. The second decade of the century was too early for the attempt to succeed. Energy withered. Fort Orleans was abandoned and Bourgmont returned permanently to Paris. Behind him he left only a handful of shadowy traders to slip from village to village with their trinkets, going no one knows how far. Probably it was not as far as the romantic today likes to think.

In the North the efforts lasted a little longer. In a sense these too were offshoots of the roseate dreams generated by Law's New World schemes and by the memorials pouring into the court, Bobé's included. Was there no kernel of truth anywhere in the accounts? To learn, the Duke of Orléans sent into the West, Pierre François Xavier de Charlevoix, a learned and polished Jesuit, teacher of a promising lad named Voltaire.

Charlevoix had been in America before, from 1705 to 1709, as an instructor in the Jesuit college at Quebec. Lest Spain or England consider his new assignment nothing more than spying (he was supposed to determine the boundaries of Acadia as well as discover the way west), Charlevoix pretended to be inspecting the Jesuit missions on the frontier. He reached Quebec late in 1720 and spent the winter pumping every man he could find who had ventured beyond the Great Lakes. The next spring the provincial government placed two canoes and eight *voyageurs* at his disposal and directed a succession of French army officers to accompany him and speed his passage from post to post.

Charlevoix visited Detroit and the famous center of the northern trade, Michilimackinac, not yet moved from the shores of the strait to the island of the same name. He reached Green Bay and planned to go on over the now-classic Fox–Wisconsin portage to the Mississippi. The warring Fox Indians blocked the route, however, and he had to circumvent them by skirting the shore of Lake Michigan to the St. Joseph–Kankakee passage through the Illinois country. He stayed several weeks in the Illinois settlements and then floated on through the chill of winter to New Orleans, arriving early in 1722.

Some of the tales Charlevoix heard on his journey flabbergasted him. Living in the West, he wrote in his journal, seemed to unfit men for telling the truth: "They make no difficulty substituting some romance . . . in the place of the truth which they do not know." But he could not ignore one name which again and again cropped up in answer to his queries about proper routes to the far seas—the Missouri.

As far away from the river as Green Bay he talked to Sioux who insisted that travelers could cross from the Missouri to another stream that discharged into salt water. When he saw with his own eyes the turbid thrust of the western stream he was awed and wrote that this was "the finest confluence of two rivers that, I believe, is to be met with in the whole world. . . . The Missouri is by far the most rapid of the two and seems to enter the Mississippi like a conqueror, carrying its white waters unmixed quite to the opposite side." And in Kaskaskia, a squaw of the Missouris declared to him that "the Missouri rises from very high and bare mountains, behind which there is another large river, which probably rises there also and runs to the westward."

Was Charlevoix, a shrewd observer and conscientious reporter, hearing at last of the Rocky Mountains and of the Columbia River? Or is his generalized description just one more lucky fable that by chance would turn out to coincide with reality, as Juan de Fuca's mythical strait corresponded to a true opening north of Washington? A study of Charlevoix's full report indicates that he was simply compounding the errors that had gone before him. For instance, he has the Missouri, Minnesota, and Mississippi rivers heading within walking distance of one another. Still, his easy generalities were instinct with a tremendous future: "I have good reason to think that . . . after sailing up the Missouri as far as it is navigable you come to a great river which runs westward and discharges into the sea." Lewis and Clark would later act on that exact premise.

Charlevoix recommended that the king finance an expedition to explore the route. He knew, however, that the odds lay heavily against acceptance of the proposal. The French government had already sent out two patrols which had doubled as exploring parties (Du Tisne's and La Harpe's) and was preparing a third (Bourgmont's). Meanwhile Law's beautiful System had exploded. Western talk was suddenly unfashionable, and Charlevoix shrewdly sensed that the court wits probably would have nothing but barbs for a recommendation that involved spending more money chasing faded rainbows through the blank spaces of Louisiana. Accordingly he offered an alternative plan: The westward push should link itself to the fur trade and pay its own way.

The principle was not new; beaver pelts and exploration had interacted since the days of Champlain. As Charlevoix surely had learned on passing through Quebec, the commingling had been officially extended in 1716 by the governor of New France and his *intendant*. The pair had asked the home ministry for the right to license posts west of Lake Superior on the ground that such a step would further the discovery of the Western Ocean. Enthralled still by Law's magic West, Paris agreed—but with the niggardly proviso that "these establishments would cost nothing to the king, while commerce should indemnify those by whom [the posts] were founded."

The plan scarcely got off the ground. One brigade leader, Zacharie de la Noüe, did reach Rainy Lake and another ventured among the Sioux, but both soon retreated in the face of hostile savages. In spite of these failures, however, Charlevoix used them as models for his alternative suggestion. Let the government help modestly with the establishment of a combined trading post and Jesuit mission on the upper Mississippi near the Sioux Indians, who then inhabited Minnesota and seemed to know more about the western mystery than did any other available tribe. The Sioux would bring to the post Indians from still farther west. The missionaries could then learn the language of the distant tribes. Using information and guides thus obtained, traders and Jesuits could push self-sustaining posts deeper and deeper into the unknown. The method obviously would take time, but at least it was no drain on the king.

Again fancy speculates "If. . . ." If the court had adopted Charlevoix's first proposal to send a government-financed party up the Missouri, might Frenchmen have reached the Pacific Northwest via Lewis and Clark's route three-quarters of a century ahead of the Americans? It seems unlikely. Bases capable of launching the effort did not then exist at the mouth of the Missouri. The extent of the journey was infinitely greater than anyone realized, including Charlevoix; the very endlessness of the march might have defeated the explorers' spirits. Still, though such speculations are idle, it is not idle to note the pattern: little aid to western trail-finding ever came from any government. The routes were worked out almost entirely by fur traders paying their own way. It was a trader, Alexander Mackenzie, who first crossed the northern part of the continent to the Pacific. A few years later, Meriwether Lewis and William Clark did duplicate the feat with an official government party somewhat farther south. But there was no effective follow-up to the Lewis and Clark effort, despite continued cries in Congress for support, nor was their route ever used by later emigrants. The workable road to the West, the Oregon Trail, was laid out step by step by self-supporting fur traders.

As the tales of their effort mount—tales of cruelty and greed and treachery, of courage and faith and sacrifice—one cannot help wondering at the source of this irresistible urge to go just a little farther toward what proved in many cases to be only despair. The possibilities of profit will not explain it in full; too many men ruined themselves with their reaching. Curiosity, adventure, vanity, and a desire to escape the restraints of ordered society played their part, but it was hardly a conclusive part. A deeper need to leave footprints that others could follow, to give names to the unnamed, to found new towns for new hopes—in varying degrees these creative urges were present in each birchbark canoe, later in the keelboats, still later in the canvas-topped wagons. But at critical moments in the history of the western migration even that does not seem quite enough to explain what perhaps can never be caught in words. In the end one is tempted to conclude that the westward surge was a human instinct, like the need to love or to taste spring air and believe again that life is not a dead end after all.

The time would come, during the 1840s, when individual yearning swelled to group migration, when every village in the land felt the tug. Henry David Thoreau seldom moved very far from Massachusetts ("I have traveled a great deal in Concord," he wrote), but even within those circumscribed limits he knew which way he headed. In his essay "Walking" he declared:

> I turn round and round irresolute sometimes for a quarter of an hour, until I decide, for the thousandth time, that I will walk into the south-west or west. Eastward I go only by force; but westward I go free.... I should not lay so much stress on this fact if I did not believe that something like this is the prevailing tendency of my countrymen. I must walk toward Oregon, and not toward Europe. And that way the nation is moving, and I may say that mankind progresses from east to west.

Where did you go? West. Why? Just because. Magic. A thing of the spirit. The *gougou* vanished— as did the dwarfs with protruding eyes, the gilded man, the lost Welshmen, the Wandering Tartars. But the magic stayed. Thoreau said it again, quoting with relish the words a governor-general of Canada had applied to the entire continent but which Thoreau attached to the westward urge: "The heavens of America appear infinitely higher, the sky is bluer, the air is fresher, the cold is intenser, the moon looks larger, the stars are brighter, the thunder is louder, the lightning is vivider, the wind is stronger, the rain is heavier, the mountains are higher, the rivers longer, the forests bigger, the plains broader...." "Will not man," Thoreau then asked, "grow to greater perfection intellectually as well as physically under these influences?"

The hyperbole was not necessarily believed when spoken. Mainly it was an attempt to clothe in metaphor the stirring in the viscera. The Oregon Trail was part of that stirring. Most of the other highways of the nation have been responses to specific conditions—to the gold of California or to the liberated trade of Santa Fe. In a large sense the Oregon Trail was also a route to a material goal, to the lush farmlands along the Willamette River. But it was more. It was Manifest Destiny made visible in wheel tracks. It was, as Thoreau recognized, a culmination of Occidental man's age-old instinct to follow the setting sun to the blessed isles, to the gardens of the Hesperides.

Charlevoix felt the tug at the mouth of the Missouri. But the court in Paris did not feel it. The administrators chose the cautious plan, the cheap one of building a combined trading post and mission on the upper Mississippi. Comparable chains would drag at men's feet for decades. But there were always a few who saw past the narrow vision, who kept on straining to break free, out and beyond.

THE MOUNTAINS THAT SHINE

Hostility among the Sioux and Fox Indians of the upper Mississippi was so implacable that until 1727 private enterprise declined to risk the post Charlevoix recommended. In that year the government at last offered the temporary protection of a few soldiers. Heartened by this, a few traders decided to undertake the venture. The two Jesuit Fathers, Guignas and Gonner, long since appointed to the mission, at last had an establishment to go to.

The flotilla left Montreal on June 16, threaded the lakes to Green Bay, crossed the portage to the Wisconsin River, and so reached the Mississippi. Turning north, on September 17 they reached a widening of the river named Lake Pepin. Cautiously they landed on the north (Wisconsin) shore near a jutting point since called Maiden Rock. Four days of energetic chopping in the dense forest felled enough trees to build a stockade one hundred feet square and twelve feet high. Bastions were added at two opposite corners and three small houses were built inside, each sixteen feet wide but varying in length from twenty-five to thirty-eight feet.

The post was named Fort Beauharnois in honor of the new governor of Canada; the mission was called St. Michael the Archangel. The whole was dedicated on Governor Beauharnois' birthday, November 4, but the actual celebration had to be delayed until a belated shipment of rockets arrived. These were shot off on November 14 to shouts of *"Vive le Roy! Vive Beauharnois!"* Smugly the reporter added, "What contributed much to the amusement was the terror of some lodges of Indians who were at that time around the fort. When these poor people saw the fire-works in the air, and the stars fall down from heaven, the women and children began to fly, and the most courageous of the men to cry for mercy and implore us very earnestly to stop the surprising display of that wonderful medicine."

The pioneers needed an amusing memory. The winter was so long and severe that the surrounding forest was considerably thinned by the shivering woodchoppers. Game was hard to kill. In the spring, flood waters drove the inhabitants from their huts. Profits were so slim meanwhile that the fort's commandant begged the government to lend additional support until the traders felt justified in taking over the full running of the outpost.

These reports and pleas were carried east in the summer of 1728 by the mission's junior priest, Father Gonner (sometimes spelled *Gonor*). He traveled by way of Michilimackinac. At that teeming rendezvous of the fur brigades he encountered a stern forty-three-year-old ex-soldier who during the next dozen years would chip out of the granite of the western wilderness an enduring fame as one of North America's great explorers: Pierre Gaultier de Varennes, Sieur de la Vérendrye.

Vérendrye was the son of the governor of Trois Rivières, a fur-trading town on the St. Lawrence halfway between Montreal and Quebec. He had joined the colonial troops at the age of twelve and a few years later had participated in the brutal winter march with the French and Indian troops that had ended in the vicious massacre at Deerfield, Massachusetts. Transferring to Europe, he fought as a lieutenant in the War of the Spanish Succession. At Malplaquet in 1709 he was shot through the body, hacked by sabers, and left for dead. Reviving, he was taken prisoner, endured captivity for fifteen months and then escaped. Too poor to maintain himself as a lieutenant in France, he returned as an ensign to a colonial regiment in Canada. There he married and began a large family. Peace closed the slim opportunities for advancement the army held. Restless and ambitious, Vérendrye turned to the fur trade. By 1726 he was in charge of the post at Lake Nipigon, a short distance due north of the humped top of Lake Superior.

Sometime before this he had caught the western contagion. The first germ may have been yarns he heard spun during his youth by

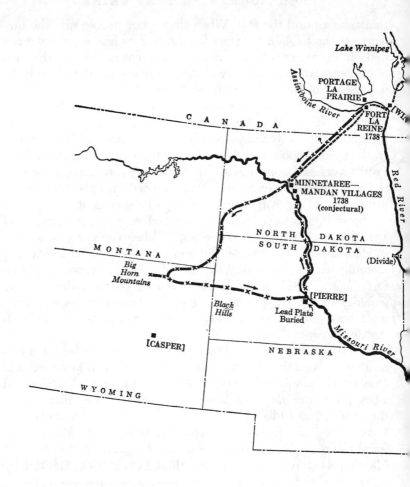

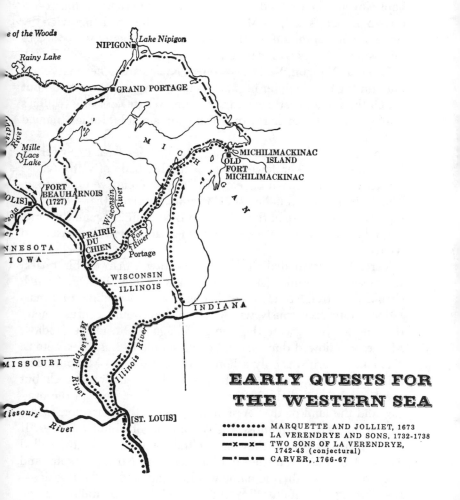

EARLY QUESTS FOR THE WESTERN SEA

•••••••• MARQUETTE AND JOLLIET, 1673
▬▬▬▬▬ LA VERENDRYE AND SONS, 1732-1738
▬x▬x▬ TWO SONS OF LA VERENDRYE,
1742-43 (conjectural)
▬•▬•▬ CARVER, 1766-67

a fellow townsman and predecessor at Nipigon, Jacques de Noyon. In 1688 or thereabouts Noyon had found the portage from Kaministiquia on the northwest side of Superior over a height of land to the maze of rivers, tarns, and bogs that lead to Rainy Lake. Perhaps Noyon even reached as far as Lake of the Woods at the northern tip of today's state of Minnesota. He had come home with the standard Indian tales of dwarfs and of rivers flowing westward to salt water, of ships with cannon, and so on.

Later, at Nipigon, Vérendrye must have heard other marvelous tales during bitter winter nights when there was nothing to do but watch the fire and let one's fancy roam. Whatever the infection's source, its real clincher came from an amiable Indian named Ochagach.

Ochagach told the trader of a great lake far west of Superior. From this lake a river flowed west to another body of water whose surface rose and fell—an ocean tide, or so Vérendrye understood. The Indian was probably speaking of the river that does flow northwest from Lake of the Woods to Lake Winnipeg, and Winnipeg's broad shallow waters sometimes are lifted by sustained windstorms.

Vérendrye persuaded the savage to draw a map on birchbark. It was seriously crude. The string of lakes west of Superior (which should have trended northwest) look like the vertebrae of a mastodon. More disastrously wrong, since they would confuse men's thinking for years, were the rivers. Ochagach's St. Pierre (today's Minnesota) flowed due east out of its source in Lake des Tetons. The lake in turn was only a hop and skip from the Missouri. The Mississippi bent around so sharply that its headwaters all but overlapped those of the Missouri. Beyond them, beyond the prairies and the land of the "Assiniboins," were the marvelous *Montagnes de pierres brillantes,* the Mountains of Shining Stones. If these meant anything, they meant the rounded hills now called Turtle Mountains on the border between North Dakota and Manitoba; eventually the name would be applied to the Rockies— the Shining Mountains. Beyond the Shining Mountains was an even more dazzling name, La Rivière de l'Ouest, the Great River of the West, flowing toward the setting sun.

The Great River. It was always there: Charlevoix had heard of it too. But to each new listener it had the glow of Paradise newly created. So it was with Vérendrye. He summarized the stories in a report, added a copy of Ochagach's map, and carried the papers from Nipigon to the rendezvous at Michilimackinac. There he met Father Gonner. They talked. One of the stalwarts at Fort Beauharnois was a favorite nephew of Vérendrye's, Christophe Dufrost, Sieur de la Jemeraye. Vérendrye no doubt asked about Jemeraye's health and then, knowing the purpose behind the fort, inquired what progress was being made toward the Western Sea.

None, the father said. In fact, Gonner was inclined to deprecate the entire setup. The Sioux were implacable, the waterways uncertain—a dubious place, all in all, as a jumping-off point to anywhere.

Vérendrye unrolled his map, told his tales. He fired the priest with his own enthusiasm. Indeed yes; the lakes and rivers west of Superior looked like much the better way.

Would Gonner present the memorial to the governor? The Father not only agreed, but in Quebec added favorable arguments of his own. Vérendrye meanwhile gathered fresh information at Nipigon and two years later brought it himself to Quebec. What his fervor now dreamed of was a force of a hundred men, equipped and paid by the king, which he could lead to the sea.

The response was similar to that which had met Charlevoix's Missouri recommendation half a dozen years earlier. Although Governor Beauharnois urged the plan on his superiors, the French court gave Vérendrye nothing more than a license to build posts in the West. He was instructed to explore but warned that the effort must cost the government nothing. Even this sop was granted chiefly on the strength of his assurance that by extending French posts across the plains he could intercept Indian hunters bound for the English at Hudson Bay and divert their pelts to Montreal.

At this point men who were merely ambitious would have quit. But by using his trading monopoly in the West as security, Vérendrye was able to equip fifty men at ruinous rates of interest. He must have sensed the dichotomy that would plague the rest of his days: if he devoted too much time to trading, the government might revoke the license extended him on his promise to

explore; if his returns in beaver suffered because he was wandering away after western chimeras, his creditors would certainly
grow clamorous. Nevertheless, in 1731 he pushed off in high
spirits for Kaministiquia on the far shores of Lake Superior. With
him went his nephew Jemeraye, veteran of the atrophying fort on
Lake Pepin, and three of his sons—later a fourth would join the
family search for the western gleam.

It is not germane to follow here the labors of the next years—
the untangling of the waterways; the pushing of one post on ahead
of another; the harrying by creditors in Montreal and by per-
fumed ministers in Versailles, contemptuous because results came
so slowly. There were emotional shocks as well. In 1736 Jemeraye
died, an irreparable loss. The same summer the oldest son paid
dearly for a Hobson's choice. Two years earlier a howling mob of
Monsoni and Cree Indians had asked for French guns and powder
and leadership in a war party aimed against the Sioux. Denying
them might have raised an immediate danger. So Vérendrye
joined their war dances, showed the Indians his old war wounds,
and sent his oldest son along to fight their enemy. The Sioux remembered. Two years later they surprised young Vérendrye and
twenty others on an island in Lake of the Woods and slew every
man. The whites wanted beaver, did they? Very well, they should
have it. The savages cut the head from each corpse, wrapped it in
a temptingly fine pelt, and left the symbols for the traders to find.
Cocky with triumph, the Sioux then placed so much pressure on
the fort at Lake Pepin, the one which had been built to open the
way to the sea, that it had to be burned and all Minnesota abandoned to the Indians.

By this time Vérendrye had reached the southern end of Lake
Winnepeg and had built a post near where the Red River of the
North flows into it. (The Red River rises in what became the
United States and forms the boundary between Minnesota and
North Dakota.) He learned that Lake Winnepeg was not the sea
of his desiring and that its outlet river, the Nelson (he called it
the Bourbon) flowed into Hudson Bay. Where then was the River
of the West?

He asked ceaseless questions of the Indians. He heard of three
great rivers—the giant Saskatchewan, flooding out of the West into

the upper parts of Lake Winnepeg; of the main western fork of the Red, the Assiniboine; and of an especially intriguing river off to the south. The last was the Missouri, but Vérendrye did not associate it with the turbulent branch that entered the Mississippi near Cahokia, where he had never been.

Confusion was inevitable. Talk through an interpreter, much of it signs, was bound to be fuzzy. Furthermore, Vérendrye, for all the blunt directness of his soldier's imagination, was filtering what he heard through the litmus of his own dreaming. Naturally it came out colored, particularly since Indians had a way of saying what they sensed the man wanted to hear. He thought for a time that the Missouri flowed *to* the West, not *from* the West. Later he rectified the mistake to the point of realizing that the stream went due south, but he did not realize that this course held only through part of the Dakotas and that the eastward trend then resumed. Hearing garbled talk of white men at the river's mouth, he decided that the river must empty into the Spanish Sea somewhere near California. Actually, of course, he was picking up dim rumors of the tiny French settlements in the Illinois country.

Equally intriguing were stories of a people called Mandans who dwelt on the banks of the mysterious river. The Mandans were said to be light-skinned. They tilled the earth, lived underground in fortified cities. Their country was full of rich ore. No, the Mandans were not regular Indians.

These exciting tales, plus the more solid satisfaction of fourteen canoeloads of furs, Vérendrye took back to Quebec in 1737. He found the government impatient. Stories were not enough. Why hadn't he found anything useful? Was he waxing rich and soft as a trader while he ought to be exploring?

Actually he was tens of thousands of livres in debt, and he realized that the time had arrived when he must make a spectacular effort. He held off his creditors with his furs and managed to rake together the supplies he would need for an overland push to the enticing river in the South.

Back the foaming waterways he went, through the lakes, over the portages. In September 1738 he reached his fort near Lake Winnipeg. From there he toiled up the swift, shallow Assiniboine into the treeless prairies, speckled with unbelievable herds of buffalo and deer. At the Assiniboine's closest approach to Lake Manitoba, he found a great crossroads of the Indian trade. From the stream, with its heavy water traffic, a portage led north to Lake Manitoba, Lake Winnepegosis, and the huge country tapped by the Saskatchewan. Up from the South came a heavily beaten trail (still visible in spots) over which the Mandans carried their surplus pumpkin meal and dried corn for trade in the North and down which the northern tribes traveled when visiting the Missouri.

At this strategic intersection Vérendrye and his men built Fort La Reine. Then on a brisk fall day, October 18, 1738, accompanied by two of his sons, several traders, twenty *voyageurs,* and two dozen Assiniboin Indians, he started south to see the Mandans for himself and learn what they could tell him of the farther country. They marched afoot. Horses had not yet reached that far north and the Frenchmen's skimpy supplies and presents for the Mandans were packed on big, wolfish Indian dogs. The trail was good, but the Assiniboins refused to be hurried. They veered here and there to visit; one of the villages they encountered grew so excited about the trip that they decided to go along for the fun. By now six hundred or more persons were hiking along with the French. They traveled in three orderly columns, the aged and lame in the middle row, protected by guards in the van and at the rear. The women managed the impedimenta; the warriors carried only their bows and lances. When scouts signaled that buffalo were in sight, every able male ran out to help surround the herd on foot and perilously kill the next day's meal. Firewood for cooking was carried on the baggage dogs, supplemented at the nightly camp by *bois de vache* (dried buffalo dung), and no one went hungry. In spite of the efficiency, however, Vérendrye estimated that his Indian companions stretched what should have been a sixteen-day journey out to more than six weeks.

The Assiniboins knew that the Mandans had not yet seen white men, although the Missouri tribes occasionally received European artifacts through barter with other Indians. So this arrival was a great event, and the Assiniboins wished to wring all the prestige possible out of it. They sent runners ahead to suggest that the Mandans meet the visitors with a committee appropriate to the

978
LAV

occasion. The Vérendryes of course awaited these greeters with keen anticipation.

On November 28 about thirty Mandans appeared. The French were no great surprise to them. Vérendrye had sent them tokens by other Indians some years before, and the savages' inordinate love of gossip had rapidly carried word of the new French posts in the North far and wide across the plains. But to Vérendrye the Mandans were a shock and a bitter disappointment. He had been prepared for a race of at least semi-civilized whites. The men grinning amiably in front of him were just more Indians, carelessly draped in buffalo robes without even a breechclout beneath. "I knew," he wrote dejectedly in his report, "that from that time we had to make allowances for all we had been told."

The chief of the welcomers led the new arrivals to his own village, one of six Mandan towns located near and on both sides of the Missouri. Just where on the Missouri is uncertain. Some authorities suggest the neighborhood of Bismark, others the site fifty or sixty miles up river where Lewis and Clark later wintered; the government's official Vérendrye National Monument is a hundred miles beyond that.[1] Time and disease have shrunk the towns. The one visited by the Vérendryes held 130 lodges and the Frenchmen got lost wandering from house to house. Decades later, after smallpox brought by traders had decimated the tribes and they had fled on up the river, the towns held half that many lodges and had decreased in number from six to two.

Throughout the migrations another tribe stayed consistently upriver from the Mandans. These were the Gros Ventres (Big Bellies) also called Minnetarees and Hidatsa. In the time of Lewis and Clark the Gros Ventres occupied three villages; the same number may also have existed when the Vérendryes reached the river. These earthen villages were duplicates of the Mandan settlements; but in other respects the whites considered the Big Bellies grumpier, dirtier, and far less trustworthy than their neighbors.

Whatever the locale of the Mandan village, the Frenchmen approached it in style. Vérendrye started one of his sons ahead

[1] The historic drift of the Mandans has been up the Missouri from a point not known. The tribe probably had not reached the site of the government's marker by the date of the Vérendryes' visit.

BC# 10177

with a flag. Then, as the visitors neared the log stockade, the Indians lifted each man onto their shoulders and carried them ahead with a great shout. At the edge of the pickets Vérendrye managed to get his people back onto the ground and lined up with such Assiniboins as possessed guns. At his command they fired three volleys, to the astonishment of the villagers crowded on the ramparts and along the moat circling the town.

As Vérendrye looked over the waiting crowd he saw at last that there was reason for what had been told him. The Mandans amazed all visitors. When artist George Catlin was preparing to travel up the Missouri in the 1830s, a century after the Vérendryes' visit, William Clark told him that he would "find the Mandans a strange people and half white." Catlin agreed. "A stranger in the Mandan villages," he declared in his famous *North American Indians*, "is first struck with the different shades of complexion and various colors of hair which he sees in a crowd around him; and he is disposed to exclaim that 'these are not Indians.' Amongst the women particularly, there are many whose skins are almost white, with the most pleasing symmetry and proportion of features; with hazel, with gray, with blue eyes." One very odd mutation was "hair of bright silvery gray," found among both sexes, but especially women, and among every age group from infancy on. Completely intrigued, Catlin finished "I am fully convinced that they have sprung from some other origin than that of the other North American tribes, or that they are an amalgam of natives with some civilized race."

Catlin was wrong. The Mandans were ordinary Indians. But, beginning with the Vérendryes, the physical peculiarities of these river savages would lead to wild theorizing as amateur anthropologists among the fur traders sought to explain the mutations. The feeling of strangeness was increased by other differences. Most Indians of the plains, being primarily hunters, were nomadic. The Mandans were agriculturists and hence sedentary. They grew a kind of corn, pumpkins, beans, and sunflowers—the seeds of which they pounded into meal and mixed with fat for a high-energy pemmican useful on journeys and war parties. Women cultivated the crops, save for a poor-quality tobacco farmed by the men in the belief that women were too unclean for anything so important to ritual as smoking. Until traders introduced a few iron hoes toward the end of the century, cultivation was by means of the flat shoulderbone of a buffalo attached to short sticks. Sentries guarded the women as they worked, and near the gardens stood forts into which the hoers could flee when raided by their inveterate enemies, the Arikaras, Pawnees, or Sioux.

At harvest time the vegetables were dried on long racks in front of each lodge. Surplus was traded over amazing distances with the nomadic tribes north and south of the river. Other articles of barter in which Mandan craftsmen excelled were colored buffalo robes and deerskins tanned as soft and white as cloth and handsomely decorated with porcupine quills.

The circular villages were surrounded by a broad dry moat and a tall stockade surmounted by movable steps that could be hauled inside during a siege. A large plaza formed the center of the town, its dominant object a wooden hogshead taller than a man—the ark that held the tribal mysteries and medicines. Around the plaza and facing it clustered the dome-shaped, earth-covered huts of the residents.

Mandan mythology said that in the beginning the tribe lived beside a subterranean lake and reached the earth's surface by climbing the roots of a grapevine. The story may well reflect the cavelike nature of the dwellings. In preparing one of the lodges, the builders first dug a circular pit about two feet deep and fifty or more feet in diameter. Upright posts were set side by side, touching each other, around the rim of this pit. Earth was heaped against the outside. Long beams were run from the side walls to a higher framework formed by four uprights set in a square around the pit's center point. These beams were overlaid by a thick mat of willow branches. A square smoke hole was left in the center (rain could be excluded to some extent by a willow screen) and the mat was covered by one or two feet of hard-packed earth.

The sunny roofs were favorite resorts for persons engaged in decorating robes or making arrowheads, in gambling, wooing, gossiping, or in contemplation. Dogs joined the loungers. Sleds and bowl-like bullboats made of buffalo hide stretched over a frame of willow were often dragged onto the housetops to be out of the way. The porticoed doorways were often marked by tripods bearing the owners' shield and medicine bag. More spectacular were long upright lances to whose tops were affixed, amid fluttering decorations, the long-haired scalps of enemies slain in battle.

The lodges were cool in summer and warm during the congealing cold of the plains winter. Each sheltered several families and, a few years after the Vérendryes' arrival, the best horses. Cupboards and bedsteads screened by painted buffalo robes lined the curving wall. Beds stood two feet off the ground and were covered by buffalo hides, stretched hair side out while fresh, on a pole frame; drying, they shrank tight to the stead. More robes and mats of rushes served as seats around the sunken, stone-lined fire pit. The lodge floors were packed so hard and swept so clean, says George Catlin, "that they have almost a polish and would scarcely soil the whitest linen." Unlike their nomadic neighbors, the Mandans understood how to make fire-resistant pottery and could boil their food directly above the blaze rather than by dropping hot rocks into a vessel of water.

The villages seem to have been cleaner than the camps of the plains Indians, who simply moved on when a site grew offensive. The Mandans were personally clean as well. Trader Alexander Henry speaks of men and women bathing together morning and night. Catlin, whose descriptions incline toward romanticism, says the women bathed alone at sunrise, "running and glistening in the sun, whilst they are playing their innocent gambols and leaping into the stream." Both men and women wore their hair long, often to the calf of the leg and, Catlin says, "in such profusion as to conceal the whole figure from the person walking behind them." It was oiled to a gloss and the part, as with all western Indians, was painted red. Great attention was paid to headdresses of horn and feather and quill; the plumes of a single choice eagle tail would bring a good horse in trade.

Other customs struck white visitors as less picturesque. For instance, the Indians smeared themselves with bear grease to ward off mosquitoes, which in spring were a dreadful harassment, and to prevent colds, which they believed were taken through the pores. Even more distressing was putrid buffalo meat. During the spring thousands of the animals drowned on falling through the weakening ice of the river. The natives liked the decomposed meat that washed by during the break-up. According to an English trader, Charles Mackenzie, "When the skin is raised you will see the flesh of a greenish hue and ready to come alive at the least exposure to the sun, and so ripe and tender that very little boiling is required. The stench is absolutely intolerable, yet the soup made from it, which comes bottle green, is reckoned delicious." Young Mandans, stark naked, leaped nimbly across the ice floes to the "nauseous carcasses" and towed them ashore. The women meanwhile were dragging in driftwood that they would dry and use for fuel or building material. Both sexes were excellent swimmers, employing a flashing crawl stroke rather than the more sedate breast or side stroke then prevalent among the whites.

They were a hardy race, enduring dreadful self-torture to prove their prowess. A young man performed his sacred rite by going naked in below-zero weather to a hilltop. There without food or sleep he danced and howled and lacerated himself with arrowpoints, often for as long as a week. When he returned, his friends ran as many wooden skewers under his skin as he had spent days in the open. Each skewer was attached by a cord to the heavy head of a buffalo bull. For as many days as there were heads, so Alexander Henry relates, the youth dragged the burden around and around the village. If he fainted he was revived and set going again as soon as possible.

There were comparable group tortures. At the end of the annual religious festival, young men who had gone without food or sleep for three days were skewered under the skin of breast and shoulders and hoisted off the ground by cords hanging from the roof of the medicine lodge, the main building fronting the plaza. They dangled and swung, blood streaming, until they fainted. Then they were lowered. As soon as each novice recovered, his little finger was struck off with an axe.

A dead person was dressed in his best attire, wrapped in wet buffalo robes that shrank on drying, and placed with his hunting implements and a supply of provisions on a scaffold on the prairie immediately behind the village. These scaffolds, built of poles laid on four posts, were higher than a man or wolf could reach. Hundreds of them stood in ranks near each village. Relatives

41

frequently lay under the scaffold of a family member and cried and moaned and slashed themselves with knives to show their grief. When the scaffolds finally collapsed, all bones save the skulls were buried. Bleached by the prairie sun, these were placed in circles of a hundred or more, each eyeless face looking toward the center.

The Mandans were polygamous. Because of fatalities from the continual wars and the dangerous hunting of the plains, women outnumbered men and had to be provided for. Also, the man who possessed the most wives to grow crops and dress hides for him was the one who could trade for the greatest number of goods. Mandans were generous with their women. As many primitive people do, a host offered his guest a bedfellow as a matter of course. Whites who wrote reminiscences found, or pretended to find, the morals of the three sedentary tribes along the river quite shocking. The humbler *voyageurs* were not so troubled. When David Thompson, the great geographer of the North West Company, wanted to walk with dogsleds scores of miles through sub-zero weather to the villages in 1797 in order to obtain their latitude and longitude for his map of the West, he had no trouble obtaining recruits. "The curse of the Mandanes," he wrote, "is an almost total want of chastity; this, the men with me knew, and I found it almost their sole motive for making the journey thereto."

In spite of such customs, French and English and American traders in succession found the tribe to be genial, intelligent, and helpful in its own way. The Mandans were one of very few groups who never made war on the whites. As the Vérendryes immediately learned, it was almost impossible to escape from one of their lodges without being feasted to the point of physical distress.

Yet even Mandan hospitality had its bounds. The inroads made on their larders by the six hundred Assiniboins who accompanied the first Frenchmen finally compelled the hosts to resort to a stratagem. First they traded their fancy robes to the visiting Indians at exorbitant rates for guns, powder, ball, iron kettles, knives, and awls. Having thoroughly fleeced the nomads, they spread a rumor that a Sioux war party was coming. The Assiniboins, who were terrified of the Sioux, fled in panic only three days after their arrival.

Unfortunately for Vérendrye, his Cree interpreter had become enamored of an Assiniboin squaw. When she fled, the Cree followed. In a sense he was no great loss. To communicate through him, Vérendrye had to give the question he wanted answered to a son who spoke Cree. The interpreter then passed on the words in Assiniboin, a smattering of which language was known to several Mandans. The answers returned through these channels were probably garbled. Yes, the Mandans said, white men did live near the mouth of the river—the Illinois settlements of which Vérendrye had already heard. But he kept hoping for New Mexico or California. Before he could make the Mandans understand what he wanted, however, the interpreter vanished and now the explorer had nothing but sign language to rely on. Though surprisingly fluent, the device nevertheless had limitations. For a frustrating day Vérendrye did what he could with it, meanwhile sending his sons to a neighboring village in the hope that a fresh start in a new environment might produce something.

The efforts netted only a few vague repetitions of what they had already listened to. Rather than waste more time at this fruitless pursuit, Vérendrye decided he had better return to his forts and the endless chore of obtaining enough beaver to satisfy his creditors. To his unsuspecting hosts he presented a French flag and an engraved lead plate that said he was taking possession of their country for his king. To prepare for a return trip, he ordered two of his men to stay for a year in different villages, learning the language and the geography. One of the pair was his own servant, a "prudent, God-fearing man" and useful to his master. But Vérendrye, though fifty-three years old now, wanted information more than convenience.

Just before departure he fell violently ill. Although still sick five days later, he was too worried to delay longer. Weakly he plodded out into December gales so furious that soon he and his men had to crawl into sheltering gullies and dig holes for themselves in the snow. The *voyageurs* wanted to give up and retreat, but mile by mile Vérendrye forced them on until they reached an Assiniboin village. There he collapsed. He sent his sons on to Fort La Reine with the men but he himself was unable to follow for two more months.

In the fall the pair who had stayed at the Mandan village returned with a report of horse-riding Indians who came annually out of the southwest to trade. These nomads told of bearded whites who lived beside a huge lake of undrinkable water. Surely that was the sea! But the search had to wait. Vérendrye was still sick; his creditors were clamoring; the Indians whom he thought he had converted to peace were fighting again. Not until 1741 was he able to smooth these tangles enough to spare his eldest living son, Pierre, for a return trip to the Mandan villages with two *voyageurs*.

The trio returned dejected. The horse Indians had not appeared that year and the Mandans refused to venture into the unknown to look for them.

There *had* to be a way west. Even Governor Beauharnois was impatient by now and Vérendrye's creditors were downright ugly. Only a solid achievement would bring him respite. Accordingly, in the spring of 1742, two other sons, Louis-Joseph (called the Chevalier) and François, accompanied by two *voyageurs*, made a last effort. On May 19, after a hike of three weeks, the quartet reached one of the earthen villages along the Missouri. How far up the Missouri is not known, and that makes a difference in trying to reconstruct their next advance. Wherever the town was, they sat around in it for two months, waiting for the Horse Indians. None appeared. Desperate, the brothers finally prevailed on two Mandans to lead them to the Gens de Cheveaux.

Although the Missouri River Indians now possessed a few horses, the Frenchmen could not obtain mounts for their trip. They had to walk. In the skeleton report the Chevalier later wrote in an effort to convince the government that they had tried to do the job, he says they marched twenty days west-southwest. He states (in translation) that they passed "soils of different colors, as azure, a sort of vermilion, grass-green, shining black, a white as of chalk, and also the color of ochre"—a description which suggests the badlands along the Little Missouri River and hence a departure from a Gros Ventre village. Yet the brothers specifically

name the Mandans, so immediately a determination of routes begins to break down.

In any event, twenty days of walking was enough for the Mandan guides. They refused to go farther. Though the brothers
needed a discovery as soon as possible, they were now constrained
to build a small hut and wait for someone to find them. One Mandan gave up and went home. Finally, on September 18, 1742, the
explorers saw smoke and traced it to a village of people the Chevalier calls in his account the Beaux Hommes. None of the tribes
he names can now be identified with confidence. These may have
been Cheyennes or Crows.

The remaining Mandan left. The brothers and the *voyageurs*
sat around the village of the Beaux Hommes for three more weeks,
learning bits of the language. At last they were able to communicate well enough to persuade some guides to take them on toward
the Horse Indians.

So it went—an advance southwest to a new village, a pause,
another start. They secured horses, but this probably did not speed
things much. They were journeying with an entire village now
and on each traveling day had to endure the pandemonium of
breaking an Indian camp, packing the travois, and dragging the
awkward vehicles off in chaotic disorder through the increasing
cold.

In November they met the tribe they sought, the Gens de
Cheveaux, groaning because their enemy, the Gens du Serpent,
had lately wiped out some of their villages. With the Horse Indians, the four Frenchmen wandered on into the country of the
Gens de l'Arc. En route they picked up evidence that trade goods
were passing to these tribes from Spanish settlements, probably
in New Mexico. This made them fear that the undrinkable lake
they had heard of was a part of the Southern Ocean, already
known to the world. What they needed to bring to their father,
so that he could overwhelmingly awe the government and his
creditors, was word of the fabled Western Sea—whether inland
water or an unknown opening off the upper reaches of the Pacific
was now immaterial. A new approach to an old area was not
enough. The eternal glint of hope tugged them on, however, and
they wandered deeper into mystery.

The cavalcade turned into a war party of several allied tribes aimed at the Gens du Serpent. The French were urged to participate: "Do not be afraid to come with us, you have nothing to fear, and you will be able to see the sea that you are in search of." They drifted on, uncommitted still and wondering whether they shouldn't be getting back to their father at Fort La Reine. But they could not resist. Besides, they had traveled so far that now they were reluctant to try making their way back to the Missouri without help from the natives.

On New Year's Day, 1743, they glimpsed in the far distance a thread of blue peaks cold on the winter horizon. At this point, the Chevalier reports, two thousand fighting men and their families had joined the column. The hubbub was monstrous. "Every night songs and yells filled the air and the men kept coming and weeping over our heads [an old Indian custom, not effeminate] begging us to accompany them to the war. I always refused, saying that we wanted to create peace, not discord." But always the will-o'-the-wisp: "I had a strong desire to behold the sea from the top of the mountains."

On they went. Deciding on January 9 that the enemy was near, the warriors made a camp for the women and children. Here the Vérendryes left their baggage. One brother stayed behind to guard it. The Chevalier and the two *voyageurs* rode on with the warriors, most of them mounted. "Finally on the twelfth day, we arrived at the mountains."

What mountains?

No one will ever know—except that they certainly weren't the coast range and no sea lay beyond them. Various theories have been offered. Most of the conjectures, one finally decides, spring out of local patriotism. Generally they are supported by ingenious computations of numbers of days and rates of travel, neither of which can be more than approximated. Occasionally there are strange explanations of why the brothers, trained wilderness explorers, really didn't travel in the direction the Chevalier said they went. One theory has them reaching the vicinity of present Calgary; another favors Helena, Montana. Some commentators have them sighting and even crossing the main chain of the Rockies in Wyoming, now known as the Wind River Mountains. Still others contend that they ended somewhere near modern Casper, Wyoming. A considerable body of opinion maintains that they went no farther than the Black Hills of South Dakota, while an even greater number of historians feel that the mountains they saw were the Big Horns of north-central Wyoming.

The Chevalier's description of the hills is no help. He says only that they were for the most part "well wooded with timber of every kind and appear very high." The description seems inadequate for the imposing, ice-toothed peaks of the Wind River Mountains, or even of the bald, glaciated, snow-crowned major summits of the Big Horns. But perhaps the adventurers saw only the lower northern spurs of the Big Horns. Or perhaps the Black Hills really are the farthest they went.

At this point an analogy may be useful. In 1805, when François Antoine Laroque of the North West Company was trading in one of the Minnetaree villages, a group of Crow Indians, splendid horsemen, arrived from the southwest to barter, as was their regular custom. Laroque returned with them to their home territory. After traveling with them for a time comparable to that spent by the Vérendryes and at a rate which must have approximated theirs, Laroque reached the Big Horns. The similarities are far too vague really to prove anything but they at least show that the Big Horns are not an unreasonable conjecture, which is more than can be said for most of the other guesses except the Black Hills.

At the foot of the Big Horns—or the Black Hills—the war party with which the Chevalier rode came on a camp recently and hastily abandoned by the enemy Gens du Serpent. With Indian illogic, the two thousand invaders decided that the Serpents had rushed away in order to circle their flanks and massacre the women and children who, for safety's sake, the attackers had left behind. Pell-mell they wheeled back. The Chevalier galloped disgustedly at their heels until he realized that his *voyageurs* had been outdistanced. Returning for them, he frightened off some would-be attackers with a gunshot. But now the reunited trio was lost. The frozen prairie held no tracks they could follow. For two days they wandered, then by sheer luck stumbled on the undisturbed baggage camp.

A blizzard immobilized the cavalcade for a time. After the storm had blown itself out, the wanderers struggled eastward through snow two feet deep in places. Emerging into an easier area, the whites joined still another tribe and eventually reached another earthen village two hundred miles or so below the Mandan towns. This village was inhabited by Arikaras.

Identification of sites is now at last possible. Throughout their wanderings the young Vérendryes had carried with them a rectangular lead plate eight and a half inches long by six and a half deep. At the time of its manufacture the plate had been stamped with an inscription in Latin which translates: "Pierre Gaultier de la Verendrye deposited this in 1741, the twenty-sixth year of our most illustrious Seigneur Louis XV, in the time of his Viceroy, Monseigneur the Marquis de Beauharnois." Pierre, the father, had not been able to make the projected trip in 1741, however, and now the date was March 30, 1743. With an awl his sons scratched onto the back of the plate their own names and those of the *voyageurs,* and corrected the date. Building a pyramid of stones, the brothers placed the metal in it, secretly lest the Arikaras take umbrage.

We can be fairly certain that the cairn stood in the vicinity of what became Pierre, South Dakota; in 1913 a Pierre schoolgirl stumbled onto the plate and took it home to her father. It is mere coincidence that the town happened to have the same name as that borne by both the elder Vérendrye and his oldest surviving son.[2]

Discouraged and with no good news to report, the quartet drifted back up the river to the Mandan villages and eventually, after a brush with the Sioux, reached Fort La Reine on July 2, "to the great joy of our father, who was very anxious about us." They had been gone fourteen months.

The tale of their travels did not impress the court. Vérendrye lost his monopoly to another trader. The fellow proved totally ineffective, however, and after two years Vérendrye, at sixty-two, was allowed to try again. Abandoning the Missouri—by now he was fairly certain it entered the Mississippi—he turned northward to the Saskatchewan, which also had been discovered by his fam-

[2] Pierre, South Dakota, grew out of Fort Pierre, a trading post of the American Fur Company, christened in 1831 in honor of Pierre Chouteau of St. Louis.

ily and on whose banks they had already built a post at The Pas, Manitoba, in the watery country west of Lake Winnepegosis. How far beyond The Pas one or another of the sons may have pushed his canoes is uncertain, but the same old stories trickled tantalizingly back with them—lofty mountains and beyond the peaks salt water. In the fall of 1749 Vérendrye prepared for a last gigantic effort. He never made it. Before the year ended, he died.

His sons asked to be allowed to carry on his work, but his estate was bogged in debt and the monopoly was handed to Jacques Lagardeur de Saint-Pierre. Saint-Pierre ordered the brothers to stay out of the West. Defiantly François (who had guarded the baggage near the western mountains) tried to slip through to the Saskatchewan with a single laden canoe. At Michilimackinac he was arrested. Forced to return to Montreal, he wrote the court, "I venture to appeal to you for relief. To find ourselves excluded from the West would mean to be cruelly robbed of our heritage, to realize for ourselves all that is bitter and to see others secure all that is sweet."

Nothing happened. Saint-Pierre, with orders to search out the Western Sea, never got past the Vérendryes' Fort La Reine on the Assiniboine. A subordinate, the Chevalier de Niverville, reached The Pas, fell ill, and sent ten men on up the Saskatchewan. They claimed they ascended far enough to see the Rockies, though no one can say up which fork of the river they traveled or whether they really did glimpse the Continental Divide. It does not matter much. Time was running out for New France. The mother country's intermittent war with England erupted again in America in 1754 and in 1756 spread to Europe. Vérendrye's son, Pierre, who had made the 1741 trip to the Mandans, and François, who had been turned back at Michilimackinac, served under Montcalm. In 1759, at the siege of Quebec, François was killed. Pierre drowned when a ship carrying refugees to France sank in the St. Lawrence.

France too went under. The Peace of Paris stripped her American possessions from her and handed the trans-Mississippi West to Spain. England acquired Canada. If any further search was made for a trail to the Pacific, it would have to be done by men of a different nation.

THE GREAT RIVER OURIGAN

England's colony of North Carolina had little interest in the war that eventually cost France her New World possessions. Why should southern farmers waste money over the embroilments of Albany fur traders? But North Carolina's governor, Arthur Dobbs, just over from Ireland, said the farmers had to be interested. By sheer vehemence—Dobbs was an inordinately persistent man—he managed to pry out of the colonial legislature "for the common defense" more funds and more soldiers than might otherwise have been granted. He also inadvertently prepared the way for Robert Rogers' bold scheme of finding the Northwest Passage to the Pacific.

Dobbs, who had been born in Ireland in 1689, was wealthy and well educated. One of his early treatises was a speculation about the nature of the Aurora Borealis. As a member of the Irish House of Commons he made serious, if somewhat futile, efforts to improve Ireland's stagnant trade. He simultaneously developed a notion that a seaway to the Orient opened out of Hudson Bay. This passage, he proclaimed during the next eighteen years (1731–49), had not been made available to English merchants because of the conniving of the Hudson's Bay Company. Its officers, he charged, did not want outsiders snooping around and opening chinks in the company's monopoly over the enormous area that drained into the Bay. He urged Parliament to transfer the firm's privileges to someone who would search more energetically for a waterway to the riches of Cathay.

The Company of Adventurers had indeed been lethargic during those years. But it was also sure that no such passage existed. One of its own governors, James Knight, had become infatuated with the same idea; and in 1719 the company had given him two ships to "find out the Streight of Anian in order to discover gold, and other valuable commodities." After Knight and his entire company died in the barrens (their bodies were found in 1722), the company lost interest. But Dobbs' needling coincided with a political trend against monopolies, and as a matter of expediency both the government and the Hudson's Bay Company decided to make a gesture. In 1741 Christopher Middleton, one of the organization's former maritime captains, sailed off to settle the matter.

Middleton reported negatively. Unconvinced, Dobbs charged that the company had bribed him to hide the truth, and the two men began an acrimonious war of pamphlets. As a by-product of the dispute, Dobbs issued *An Account of the Countries adjoining Hudson's Bay* in 1744. The monograph was designed (its subtitle said) "to shew the great Probability of a NORTH-WEST PASSAGE, so long desired." His sources of information were his reading and stories recounted to him by a half-breed named Joseph La France, who had reached England in 1742 after a series of remarkable trips which La France says he took through the Canadian interior.

Partly as a result of Dobbs' agitation, the English Admiralty now offered a reward of twenty thousand pounds to any private individual who found the passage. The Dobbs Company was formed to try. Its two ships were named, optimistically enough, *Dobbs* and *California.* They did not reach California, and Dobbs finally gave up. His next pamphlet, issued in 1750, was entitled "Bees, and the mode of Taking Wax and Honey."

In 1754, the year in which General Braddock sailed to America to begin his disastrous march against Fort Duquesne, Dobbs, now sixty-five, was named governor of North Carolina. The conflict which developed after his arrival in America rekindled his interest in the lands to the north; when he met, shortly after the capitulation of Canada, one of the war's most romantic heroes, Robert Rogers, they had much to talk about.

An athletic frontier farmer six feet tall, possessed of phenomenal endurance, daring, and ingenuity, Rogers had been the one sparkling figure in the Champlain Valley theater, where incredible British bumbling had more than offset British numerical superiority over the French. At Fort William Henry, Rogers forged his semi-autonomous, green-clad rangers into a rapier that filled the French with terror but excited the jealousy of England's regular Army officers. His culminating effort was a dazzling march by two hundred men across a hundred fifty miles of enemy-held wilderness to destroy the Indian stronghold of St. Francis on the St. Lawrence River. When the survivors of the successful attack reappeared with dramatic suddenness at the British outposts, victory bells pealed throughout New England.

After the capitulation of Montreal in September 1760, Rogers marched west to accept the surrender of Detroit. Tumbled ice floes and howling winds kept him from repeating the pageant at Michilimackinac. Turning homeward in the dead of winter, he led his troops through Ohio and Pennsylvania to heroes' welcomes in Philadelphia and New York. He was not yet thirty years old.

Victory bells paid no debts, however. Under pressure of circumstance he had been careless about his vouchers and the Army disallowed several of his claims, amounting to several thousand pounds. At the same time that this financial morass opened under him he married, and so found himself doubly in need of lucrative employment.

A peacetime military assignment in the Carolinas brought him into contact with Governor Dobbs, who recommended to the English ministry that Rogers be appointed Superintendent of the Southern Indians. The job did not materialize. Desperate for money, Rogers decided to try hack writing and in February 1762 advertised for subscriptions to a four-volume series that would recount his personal adventures, describe Britain's new North American possessions, and offer "some proposals for the Discovery of the North-West Passage by Land."

The phrase *by Land* was novel. Dobbs had urged exploration by sea. Rogers, who had reason to be confident of his own abilities to make long journeys overland on minimum supplies, planned instead to march to the Pacific and then turn northward until he found the passage's western end.[1] He seems never to have doubted the existence of a passage. That faith, as well as the bold hope of crossing an entire continent to find the outlet, can be attributed directly to the fanatical influence of Arthur Dobbs.

[1] This is an assumption. The particular four-volume set he proposed in 1762 never appeared, but the plan described above was the one he proposed to Parliament in 1765. Probably it had taken shape in outline at least by the time of the advertisment.

The bloody Indian uprising known as Pontiac's Conspiracy interrupted his plans. Of the western outposts only Fort Pitt and Detroit, both heavily besieged, escaped destruction. Rogers joined a relief party hurrying to Detroit. When his commander ordered an ill-judged attack on the enemy, the corps was almost annihilated. Rogers rallied thirty men in a farmhouse, fortified the building with bales of beaver pelts that had been stored there, and held off two hundred savages with the loss of only two soldiers. At last the survivors managed to reach the stockade and the siege dragged on for more months until the Indians lost patience and drifted away.

Back in New York, Rogers was imprisoned for debt. Soldiers who had served under him stormed the jail and released him, a move that did not impress the city's creditor class. Harried on all sides, Rogers fled to London to see what he could do. There he published at his own expense two books instead of the four he had promised in North Carolina. The first was autobiographical; the other was descriptive of the interior of North America. Neither mentioned the Northwest Passage, but their immense popularity did prepare the ground for a petition he presented to Parliament in 1765. In that document he proposed that the government spend £36,182 equipping an expedition of two hundred men, commanded by Robert Rogers, that would cross "from the Great Lakes towards the Head of the Mississippi, and from thence to a River called by the Indians Ouragan which flows into a Bay that projects North-Eastwardly into the Country from the Pacific Ocean." From that bay the explorers would probe northward until they proved or disproved the existence of the passage's western end.

So far as is known this is the first printed use of the word that soon became *Oregon*. Where Rogers picked it up is uncertain. George Stewart suggests in *Names on the Land* that it derives from a spelling error made during the preparation of a map for Lahontan's *Mémoires de l'Amérique Septentrionale*. When copying the name Ouisconsink, an early phonetic form for the Wisconsin River, the cartographer first changed a few letters and then hyphenated, so that the word came out *Ouracon-sint* with *sint* on a separate line. From there to Rogers' Ouragan, Stewart argues, is no great jump. Except that the Lahontan map clearly shows its Ouracon-sint as flowing into the "Missippi" from the east, and it seems strange Rogers would appropriate for the unknown river the name of a stream by then familiar to the frontier. But no other guess about the name's origin is any better, including the one that suggests it derives from a peripatetic Irishman named O'Regan.

The English government was intrigued by Rogers' proposal. The notion of searching for the passage's western end, rather than for its baffling eastern approach, was not new. Drake may have been looking for it nearly two centuries before. A few Spanish mariners had edged cautiously up the foggy coasts, hunting for the opening. Juan de Fuca claimed to have found it. Vitus Bering and Alexi Cherikov had had it in mind during their desperate journey to Alaska for the Russians in 1741. While Europeans had been fighting each other in eastern America during the French-Indian War, Russian otter hunters had been inching their murderous way along the Aleutian Peninsula, and quite possibly word of their encroachment on what the Peace of Paris said was English land may have reached Britain's ministry. They would have liked to learn more. But after an expensive war it was politically inexpedient to risk thirty-two thousand pounds to look for a passage which some people were beginning to believe did not exist.

As a sop for the refusal, the government appointed Rogers commander of Fort Michilimackinac and Superintendent of Western Indians at a salary of ten shillings a day. He accepted the post with his usual optimism. At least he could gather more information while he was in the West. He might even send out a private expedition which, if it succeeded, could claim the reward of twenty thousand pounds which the Admiralty had offered for discovery of the passage.

Arthur Dodds, coincidentally enough, died in North Carolina in 1765, the year that Rogers, now thirty-four, started across the Atlantic for the Northwest.

Preparations for the leap to the frontier and still another hearing on his old claims against the Army delayed the would-be explorer in New York for several months. It was March before he could hurry to New England, where his wife had remained during his sojourn in London. While in Boston, he sought out one of his former ranger captains, James Tute, and prevailed on him to come along to the frontier. Probably he dangled before Tute the Admiralty's promise of twenty thousand pounds for whoever found the Northwest Passage.

At about the same time Rogers was approached by another veteran of the French-Indian War, fifty-six-year-old Jonathan Carver, whom Rogers may have known during the conflict at Fort William Henry in the southern part of the Champlain Valley. What they talked about can only be guessed at. Thirteen years later and without mentioning Rogers, Carver states (*Travels Through the Interior Parts of North America in the Years 1766, 1767, 1768;* first published in London in 1788) that ever since the war he had wanted to go West to learn the nature of the huge territory which England had so recently acquired. He felt, he says, that the French charts and accounts of the area were deliberately misleading. To be able to correct these deceptions he taught himself surveying and mapmaking. Then, as soon as he learned the facts about the upper Mississippi Valley, he planned "to ascertain the Breadth of that vast continent, which extends from the Atlantic to the Pacific Ocean." If he succeeded in his crossing he would propose that England establish a settlement near the Straits of Anian to facilitate the discovery of the Northwest Passage.

The plan sounds remarkably like Rogers' scheme. In his book, however, Carver mentions Rogers only in passing as governor of Michilimackinac and never mentions Tute at all, though Tute and he traveled many hundreds of miles through the wilderness together. Probably Rogers hired Carver merely to be mapmaker for whatever expedition developed. Why should he have intended the man to be anything more? Carver was fifty-six at the time of his employment, an age at which the senior Vérendrye, a trained frontiersman with a burning desire to explore, had felt obliged to leave the more rigorous expeditions to his sons. If Rogers had needed a young wilderness leader in addition to James Tute, he could have found one. Nobody in America was better acquainted with first-class woodsmen than was Robert Rogers of the Rangers. But perhaps Carver felt that by promoting himself he could promote the sales of his book. If so, he's part of a numerous company.

Having hired both Tute and Carver, Rogers returned to New York. There he again lost an appeal for reimbursement of his old claims; and when he and his wife started for Michilimackinac he was in as desperate need as ever for some stroke that would restore his solvency. On August 10 the couple reached their new home on the south shore of the narrow strait between Lakes Huron and Michigan. A small log stockade surrounded a drab collection of about thirty homes, a few warehouses and public buildings, and a Roman Catholic church. During summer Mackinac hummed with energy. Hundreds of canoes manned by Indians and French *voyageurs* congregated there from the country beyond Lake Superior, from present Michigan and Wisconsin, and even from the lesser-known streams beyond the Mississippi. The odorous furs they brought with them were sorted, graded, beaten clean, and repacked for shipment to either Montreal or Albany. Trade woolens and hardware imported from those same two centers were being broken out of bales and made up into outfits for shipment to the Indian country. Savages from hundreds of miles of unmapped forest pitched their lodges outside the stockade and, while waiting to hold councils and receive presents, weighed the new white claimants who had supplanted the French.

Rogers faced a tense situation—more tense than he knew. Although Pontiac's revolt had failed three years earlier, the Indians were restive still and he must assemble chiefs from the most remote districts to listen to his harangues and smoke the pipe of peace. The local merchants were even more touchy. Edicts of the new government stated that they could operate only under license and from fixed posts; they could no longer follow the Indians to their villages and hunting grounds. This was an absurd order, the traders roared. The distant Indians simply would not come hundreds of miles to the fixed post at Mackinac but would sell their skins to unlicensed *coureurs de bois* or to Spanish traders and French smugglers hanging around Prairie du Chien, a settlement of Indians and half-breeds near where the Wisconsin River flowed into the Mississippi. By the time Rogers arrived several traders already had gone defiantly into the wilderness, and out of what seemed to him ordinary fairness he issued licenses wholesale to those still wandering disconsolately around Michilimackinac.

It was a gesture that would bring trouble. Jealousies seethed through the post. The old French resented the upstart English. Traders working out of New York were locking in an underground struggle for power with those from Montreal. Rogers' superior as Indian Superintendent was Sir William Johnson, the skillful, domineering feudal baron of the Mohawk Valley who naturally favored the Albany traders. Both Johnson and General Gage, Rogers' military commander, were his enemies because of clashes during the war. They had objected to his appointment as commander of Michilimackinac, and when he seemed to them to side with the Montreal crowd, he guaranteed himself future trouble.

He did not sense the undercurrents at first. His immediate problem, so he thought, was to assemble the Indians for a great council the following spring and to familiarize himself with his district. As part of this project he instructed Jonathan Carver, under orders dated August 12, to map the Indian country between Lake Michigan and the Mississippi. Carver was to winter near the Falls of St. Anthony on the upper river and in the spring drop to the Illinois and return to Michilimackinac via lower Lake Michigan. One possible exception only was noted: "Should you receive Orders from me to March farther to the Westward with any other Detachment that I may send this fall or winter you are to do it." None of this is mentioned in Carver's book.

Rogers' vague maybe-so planning (and there is no telling how much Carver understood of the order's possible implications) grew suddenly firmer with the arrival of letters from the ministry in London indicating that the discovery of a route to the Western Sea would be considered an important development. When Tute followed Carver toward the Mississippi fifteen days later, his instructions were specific. He too was to winter near the Falls of St. Anthony, pick up Carver to be his mapmaker, and then go to "Fort La Parrie" on the Saskatchewan, where supplies would be sent to him. He was to pass his second winter at Fort La Prairie, then travel westward and "do your endeavor to fall in with the great River Ourigan." At its forks "you will find an Inhabited

Country and Great Riches," including gold on the north fork and a populous town from which "the Inhabitants carry their Gold near Two Thousand Miles to Traffic with the Japancies." Interestingly enough, Tute was warned away from the Missouri. "You must take care not to be deceived by the Rivers Missisure" or those falling into Hudson Bay or the Gulf of California.

As second in command Rogers named Tute's clerk, James Goddard. Carver was third in line of succession. And just in case Tute wondered about Rogers' source of information or thought that perhaps he was being handed a large order, he was exhorted in writing: "Believe in it like a Man that is Devoted to his king and Brave out every difficulty and you may be sure of success."

In company with several traders, Tute's party left during the bright dawn of September 17 in a "Bark Canoe with Goods & proper necessities." Circling via Green Bay, the Wisconsin, and the upper Mississippi was a roundabout route to the Saskatchewan. But they had to find Carver, the only cartographer available; and, more important, they had to make sure that a sufficient number of Indians traveled to Rogers' great council the next spring. They were also supposed to trade for as many pelts as possible during the winter and send the fur to Rogers to help him meet his expenses.

They mismanaged everything. They did not overhaul Carver, who had left Michilimackinac on September 2, only fifteen days ahead of them. They did not go to the Falls of St. Anthony as instructed, but wintered instead somewhere south of Prairie du Chien. They did not send any pelts to Rogers. Bribing Indians to go to the spring council required more presents than anticipated. To obtain the goods from the rapacious traders at Prairie du Chien, Tute drew heavy drafts on Rogers. When the bills reached the commander, they astounded him and led him to suppose that Tute was buying equipment for the Western adventure —a disastrously wrong assumption, as matters developed.

Carver meanwhile had parted company near Prairie du Chien with the traders he had accompanied from Michilimackinac. In a single canoe manned by a French-Canadian and a Mohawk Indian, he moved slowly up the Mississippi, between steep wooded hills, among islands, past alternating precipices and "verdant plains." While paddling through Lake Pepin, he saw the ruins of Fort Beauharnois, founded forty years earlier as a jumping-off place for the West. Above the mouth of the Rivière St. Pierre— the St. Peter's or Wattapaw Menesotor of the Sioux, today's Minnesota River—the Mississippi was choked with ice. Afoot in the company of a young Indian, the aging mapmaker hiked sixty miles upstream, past the roaring cataract of St. Anthony's Falls. No other white man, he said, had ever gone so high.

Returning to open water, he put a peace pipe on the bow of his canoe and a flag on its stern. By his own account he went two hundred miles up the ice-free St. Peter's to the country of the Sioux. He lived with a village of these Indians for five months. He learned their language perfectly, as he tells it, and picked up from them many hitherto unknown details of western geography.

In April 1767 Carver persuaded some of the Sioux chiefs to visit Rogers at Michilimackinac. He went with them as far as Prairie du Chien to see if any instructions had arrived for him. On May 6 he met James Tute's party at the settlement and learned of his new assignment. After starting as many Indians as they could toward the council (rival traders from St. Louis lured several away), the explorers struck back up the Mississippi toward distant Fort Prairie. The party consisted of Tute, Goddard, Carver, an interpreter, eight *voyageurs*, a Chippewa chief, and a guide. Carver's book mentions only Goddard (by indirection) and gives himself as leader rather than third in the chain of command.

At the mouth of the Chippewa River, which runs into the lower part of Lake Pepin and points toward the underside of Superior, the Indians balked. Continuing farther up the Mississippi would bring them into the territory of their enemy, the Sioux. The whites did not press. They were desperately short of food. Game was scarce and they had no goods to trade for provisions. So they turned up the Chippewa, hoping to reach Grand Portage on the northwest shore of Lake Superior in time to intercept the supplies supposedly being sent to Fort La Prairie by that route. Having replenished their larders, they would continue to the Saskatchewan with the supply brigades.

On July 19, after a hard, starving trip, they reached Grand

Portage. The canoes from Mackinac had not yet arrived. While the explorers waited, Carver picked up more geography from a group of Cree and Assiniboin Indians who had come out of the plains to meet the brigades. On August 2 the flotillas began appearing. On the seventh the man they were expecting arrived, François Le Blanc. His ten canoes were loaded solely with his own goods. For Tute he had nothing but a letter from Rogers, complaining about the lack of peltries from Prairie du Chien and stating that the heavy drafts they had drawn "convinces me ... you must have now Goods enough with you to compleat your Expedition." He urged them to push on to Fort La Prairie. As early as possible the next year he would send them supplies for the trip to the Pacific.

The failure to receive goods was disconcerting enough. To make matters worse, the explorers learned from the newly arrived traders that Rogers was out of favor with his superiors. Under the circumstances it seemed inadvisable to push blindly and hungrily westward. A hastily convened conference voted to abandon the project and the party returned around the north shore of Lake Superior to Mackinac. They arrived August 29. Rogers was dumfounded to see them, and they in turn were furious to learn that his drafts were no longer being honored and he could not pay them for their year's work.

Things reached such a pass that during the winter Rogers was imprisoned on a flimsy charge of treason. When the little supply schooner *Gladwin* sailed from Michilimackinac for the east next summer, 1768, Rogers, in agony from ill-fitting irons, traveled ignominiously in the hold on the ballast stones. Above decks went Jonathan Carver. He had passed the winter, he says, very pleasantly.

To secure the wages due him for his mapping and to promote himself as the leader of the transcontinental expedition Rogers so long had dreamed of, Carver once more kissed his wife and five children goodbye and sailed to London. He never saw his family again. Without benefit of divorce he remarried in England, stayed there, and begot more children.

In Montreal, Rogers was acquitted of the charge of treason. But he was not reinstated at Michilimackinac. To justify himself and to rebuild his career as best he could, he too went to England. Creditors periodically had him clapped into debtors' prison. During intervals of freedom he and Carver effected a reconciliation and worked together on their western plans.

In 1772 Rogers submitted a new petition to Parliament for aid in finding the Northwest Passage. The route proposed was different from that outlined in his petition of 1765. Presumably the changes were the result of Carver's geography lessons with the Sioux Indians on the Minnesota River and the Crees and Assiniboins at Grand Portage. The modified plan stated that the explorers would ascend the Minnesota to its source and thence would portage to a branch of the Missouri. They would ascend the Missouri to its head. Another portage, this one thirty miles long, would bring them to the "Great River Ourigan." At the Ourigan's mouth they would establish a base camp and, as Rogers had proposed in his first petition, the party would search northward from it for the passage's western end.

Nothing happened. Rogers was put into debtors' prison again, was released, and returned to America. When the Revolution broke out, he joined the Loyalists, skidded downward, turned to heavy drinking, and died in wretched circumstances. Carver fared little better. A member of Parliament, according to Carver, was about to underwrite the plans for the expedition when the war with the colonies "put a stop to an enterprize that promised to be of inconceivable advantage to the British dominions."

Brought to this dead end, Carver turned not to drink but to book-writing and produced his famous *Travels*. His geography is askew and he claims all credits for himself, but so long as he sticks to straight reporting it is a useful and entertaining book. The public loved it. The *Travels* went through thirty editions in various languages, but for Carver the fame came too late and he also died in penury.[2] Yet because he had felt the magic, two of the place names he plagiarized acquired new force and through him became forever fixed in the American consciousness.

The first was Oregon, which received its final spelling in the

[2] James Tute, the third member of the western cast, stayed in the Northwest. As a trader he finally did reach the Saskatchewan, but died in the wilderness of smallpox in 1781.

Travels. Carver almost certainly learned the word from Rogers. The land in which he blithely headed the river was hopelessly wrong, however. Indian stories and maps convinced him, he wrote, that the highest part of the American continent rose a short distance west of the headwaters of the Minnesota River. Here occurred a phenomenon observable nowhere else in the world—the birth of four great rivers, each flowing toward a different compass point, "viz, the St. Lawrence, the Mississippi, the River Bourbon [today's Nelson, which empties into Hudson Bay] and the Oregon, or the River of the West."

Oregon: the name stuck. When the *Travels* crossed the Atlantic to the newly free United States of America, it was read eagerly by a combination minister and writer of school textbooks, Jedidiah Morse, metaphorical father of American geography and actual father of Samuel F. B. Morse, inventor of the telegraph. Morse applied the name to a westward-flowing river in his *American Gazetteer.* That is probably where schoolboy William Cullen Bryant saw it a little before he used the word in his precocious poem "Thanatopsis," once memorized by thousands of restive students. Bryant meant the river. Well before he had composed the poem, however, a ship captain named Robert Gray discovered an actual River of the West and named it after his vessel, the *Columbia.* Partiotism helped rivet that term unshakably. Thus displaced, the word *Oregon* should have withered and died. It didn't. Partly thanks to Jonathan Carver, it had come to stand for the glow of man's desiring. Leaving the Columbia, it attached itself to an entire area and waxed even greater than if it had stayed where it began.

The other name Carver made permanent was *The Shining Mountains,* so-called "from an infinite number of crystal stones, of an amazing size, with which they are covered and which, when the sun shines full upon them, sparkle so as to be seen at a very great distance." Carver stole this term too—from maps stemming from the Vérendryes. His own chart in the *Travels* shows The Shining Mountains beginning at about the point where Vérendrye and the Indian Ochagach placed them, near the Assiniboine River. On this chart they are an east-west chain stretching almost to the Pacific, with the River of the West lying just to the south of them.

In his text, however, Carver propounded a different thesis, that The Shining Mountains were part of a south-north chain extending from Mexico far into the north.

For the first time an American was hearing of the Rockies— not of North Dakota's Turtle Mountains, which was what Vérendrye's Shining Mountains represented. To be sure, Carver erred wildly in placing the north-south range. He seemed to think the mountains ran through western Minnesota, and he probably envisioned timbered hills like the Adirondacks he knew rather than snow-clad peaks. Later explorers finally got the facts straight; yet even then Carver's name stuck—The Shining Mountains. The Rockies are not so designated on any map—true places are never on a map, says Melville in *Moby Dick*—but anyone who writes or reads very much about the Continental Divide sooner or later picks up the term. *Rockies* does not say enough; *Shining Mountains* somehow has the touch. Jonathan Carver tried to put it in words:

> Those mountains [he wrote], I believe surpass any thing of the kind in the other quarters of the world. Probably in future ages they may be found to contain more riches in their bowels, than those of Indostan and Malibar, or that are produced on the Golden Coast of Guinea; nor will I except even the Peruvian Mines. To the west of these mountains, when explored by future Columbuses or Raleighs, may be found other lakes, rivers and countries, full fraught with all the necessaries or luxuries of life; and where future generations may find an asylum, whether driven from their country by the ravages of lawless tyrants, or by religious persecutions, or reluctantly leaving it to remedy the inconvenience arising from a superabundant increase of inhabitants; whether, I say, impelled by these, or allured by hopes of commercial advantage, there is little doubt their expectations will be fully gratified in these rich and unexhausted climes.

The song the Sirens sing: the better land somewhere out beyond. Carver's avid reader, Jedidiah Morse, heard it too. In his *American Geography*, published in the year of George Washington's inauguration, 1789, while Spain still claimed the entire trans-Mississippi West, Morse predicted, "The period is not far distant, when the AMERICAN EMPIRE will comprehend millions of souls, west of the Mississippi." And "The Mississippi was never designed as the western boundary of the American Empire."

These were reckless words in 1789. Moreover, it should be noted that Morse was not speaking of a single nation. By *American Empire* he meant several autonomous countries resembling the United States but prevented by distance from being linked politically to her. Another half-century would pass before many men dared call for one nation, indivisible, stretching enormously from sea to sea. Actual wheels would have to roll along the Oregon Trail before the full span of the continent could be welded into a political as well as a geographic unit. But already the mountains were shining, already the great river beckoned.

THE STRANGLING OF SPANISH LOUISIANA

When Jonathan Carver paddled up the Minnesota River in the fall of 1766, he was violating Spanish territory. So was Peter Pond, of Connecticut Colony, who followed Carver onto the Minnesota in 1773 and 1774. Both must have realized what they were doing, yet in his reminiscences neither mentioned the illegality. Spain's hold on the territory parceled out to her by the 1763 Peace of Paris was too flimsy, in the minds of frontiersmen, to merit the dignity of words.

The Spanish ministers did what little they could to remedy the weakness. Lacking citizens in America who were tough and experienced enough to administer the new country, they turned to the French already established there. It was a pair of Frenchmen, Pierre Laclède Liguest and his thirteen-year-old stepson, René Auguste Chouteau, who founded the post that became administrative headquarters for upper Louisiana—St. Louis. As at New Orleans, Frenchmen filled most of St. Louis' minor administrative offices and many of the major ones, including at times the governorship. The Spanish lacked an instinct even for the West's major economy, the Indian trade. In general it was the French bourgeois and his French *voyageurs* (many of whom had crossed the Mississippi to escape British rule) who laboriously carried a few boatloads of goods to the rendezvous at Prairie du Chien or who each year forged a little farther along the lower Missouri and its tributaries.

Aided by these French, Spain played such politics as she could in the Mississippi Valley. During the Revolution, she lent useful aid to the brilliant maneuvers by which George Rogers Clark secured the American rear from flanking attacks through the Ohio country. Stung, the English commander at Michilimackinac assembled 750 or more Indians at Prairie du Chien, floated down the Mississippi, and late in May 1780 launched a disorganized attack on St. Louis. The townspeople had been warned in time to build a "tower" for defense and fortify it with a cannon. Anchoring themselves to this strongpoint, 29 Spanish soldiers and 281 hastily impressed French militia beat back the attackers. Clark simultaneously repulsed a feeble thrust toward Cahokia, and that ended the British threat.

It did not end Spain's anxieties, however. Peace brought to the east bank of the Mississippi a vigorous young nation less likely than England to stop there. Almost at once, expansionists like Jedidiah Morse began talking of American empires beyond the river. Overt moves accompanied the rhetoric. In 1790, Secretary of War Henry Knox instructed General Harmar to send out soldiers disguised as Indians and accompanied by Indians to explore the Missouri. The attempt was assigned to Lieutenant John Armstrong. He reached St. Louis, copied some maps, and then gave up for want of proper equipment and Indian guides. Three years later a prominent botanist, André Michaux, backed by Secretary of State Thomas Jefferson and the American Philosophical Society, started west to collect botanical and zoological data along the upper Missouri and on to the Pacific. Michaux, it developed, was involved in a harebrained French conspiracy to use discontented American backwoodsmen in an attack on New Orleans. When the United States government learned of the plot, it ordered Michaux stopped.

How much Spain knew of these and of other imperialistic moves involving Americans is uncertain, but it was enough to make her profoundly suspicious. Wanting to keep the United States weak, she closed the mouth of the Mississippi to American commerce, fostered intrigues designed to split Kentucky and the South away from the Atlantic states, and pushed explorations of her own up the Missouri.

Even greater energies were aimed toward the Pacific Northwest. There Russian sea-otter hunters were working ruthlessly southward from the Aleutian Islands. To counter the imperialism that might follow these wild and bloodthirsty *promyshlenniki,* Spanish soldiers and padres strung presidios and missions up the coast of California. Culmination of their effort came in the year of the American Declaration of Independence, when Juan Bautista de Anza led a group of trail-blackened colonists into San Francisco. The same summer Silvestre Vélez de Escalante and Padre Francisco Domínguez tried to open communication from Santa Fe to the Golden Gate through Utah. Their tiny force rode within a few miles of the Great Salt Lake, of which Indians told them (the Western Sea at last?); later their cartographer showed a river running from the lake to the ocean. But the nip of winter and perhaps their own timorousness kept these explorers from trying to check on the fantasy. They swung back south, and that was the limit of Spanish thrusts out of Mexico by land.

By sea they reached farther. Ordered to sail north until he found the Strait of Anian, Juan Pérez in 1774 discovered a lovely mountain-locked, forest-girt harbor that would turn into a hotter spot than Spain could handle—Nootka Sound on the west coast of Vancouver Island. Two years later Bodega y Cuadra reached southern Alaska and claimed it for Spain. At almost the same time Bruno Heceta (with Juan Pérez serving as his chief pilot) felt such currents off the fog-shrouded coast of northern Oregon that it caused "me to believe that the place is the mouth of some great river, or of some passage to another sea." A tremendous discovery at his fingertips—but Heceta's crew was too ravaged by scurvy for him to follow through. Sunk in the lassitude of their disease, they let the ship drift southward. Another eighteen years would pass before the world learned that by ironic coincidence there really was a Great River of the West entering the ocean at about the point where the mythmakers had long insisted it lay.

The English Admiralty meanwhile dispatched Captain James Cook to the Pacific with two ships to settle once and for all the question of the Northwest Passage. Cook sighted American land in 1778, missed the Columbia River in the usual mists, and like Pérez put into Nootka Sound. The natives, daubed with red paint and tossing feathers by way of welcome, swarmed out in their huge war canoes to welcome the whites, presumably much as they had welcomed Pérez. With this difference—the English struck up a trade that the Spanish either overlooked or forgot to mention.

The Indians were clad in downy sea-otter cloaks. Knowing they were bound for the Arctic, the English sailors offered bits of metal in exchange for the furs. To the savages these brass buttons, tin candlesticks, iron bureau handles, copper cooking pots, and the like were priceless. They divested themselves on the spot. During the month the ships stayed in Nootka, rewatering and fitting new masts, every detachable piece of metal on them disappeared. When at last Cook continued north, his humblest sailors were sleeping on fur beds for which Chinese mandarins would pay fantastic prices.

At the 60th parallel, Cook found an estuary that for a time he hoped might lead to the elusive passage. It proved landlocked. He named it Cook's Inlet, speculated that a large river perhaps flowed into it, and sailed on north until he ran into ice. Retreating, he wintered on one of the Sandwich (Hawaiian) Islands, where he was stabbed to death by natives during a quarrel over his ship's cutter. His successors made one more sortie northward and then started home, convinced that no passage existed. At Macao, below Canton, the English ships paused for refitting. Chinese fur merchants got wind of the sea-otter pelts, hard used by now, and bid for them in a frenzy.

Various journal-writers noted the phenomenon, including Lieutenant James King, who was keeping the official account, and John Ledyard, a corporal of marines from Connecticut. Ledyard's account reached print first. After the expedition had returned to England, the Yankee was transferred to a man-of-war and sent against his native country during the closing days of the Revolution. Jumping ship, he made his way to the home of an uncle in Connecticut and there in the spring of 1783 dashed off an account of his travels. A year later King's and Cook's three-volume account was released. Immediately the accounts gave new impetus to the westering urge of Canadian fur traders.

During the later 1770s, merchants working out of Montreal had found a route from the Saskatchewan River into the wild and watery lands that tip toward Lake Athabaska. This was rich fur country, but it posed fearsome problems in transportation—upwards of three thousand canoe miles along sinuous rivers punctuated by more than two hundred rapids and one hundred portages. Food as well as trade goods rode human pack horses across these portages; *voyageurs* straining to cover three thousand miles during the open weather of two short summers had no time for hunting and fishing. To keep moving they needed enormous supplies of pemmican, dried buffalo meat and dried berries pulverized and solidified in fat. Most of this was prepared along the Red River of the North, near or even in Spanish territory, and shipped far and wide throughout the Northwest by canoe.

The capital required by the gigantic effort led to various combinations of individuals that finally became stabilized as the North West Company. One of the company's early partners and the first white man to reach Athabaska was Peter Pond, the irascible genius from Connecticut. In an effort to solve the Nor'Westers' transportation problems, Pond began speculating about supply depots on the Pacific. A navigable river from that ocean to the interior would save incalculable time, effort, and money. And surely, considering how far west of Montreal Athabaska lay, surely the remaining distance to the Pacific could not be very great.

His arguments convinced his partners. In 1781 one of them, Alexander Henry the Elder (originally of New Jersey), suggested that England's Royal Society finance an expedition to find the desired river. Again nothing developed; as usual the traders would have to work out their own salvation. An epidemic of smallpox among the tribes of the Saskatchewan retarded their efforts for a few years, but new vigor sprung from Pond's visit to Montreal and the United States during the winter of 1784–85. He encountered a copy of Cook's *Voyages;* avidly he read about the sea-otter pelts of Nootka Sound and of the Russian incursion into the trade farther north. He grew excited. The English—and the North West Company—must have a share in this commerce on the edge of their own continent. The river of which he dreamed would be the key to it.

He hurried with Cook's maps back to Athabaska and asked hundreds more questions of the Indians. Their answers persuaded him that Lake Athabaska's outlet stream flowed northwest into Great Slave Lake. The huge outlet river of Slave Lake, the Indians said, struck due west. More questions, and Pond became convinced that the waterway entered the Pacific at Cook's Inlet.

He had no chance to learn. Competitors found their way into the district he had opened. Their leader, John Ross, was killed in a scuffle with some of Pond's men. It was the third slaying to involve the hot-tempered Nor'Wester. As a youth in Detroit he had killed a rival trader in a duel; later, in 1782, he had been tried for and acquitted of the murder of one of his erstwhile partners, Jean-Etienne Waden. Fearful now of a government inquiry that would hurt everyone's trade, Pond's company and Ross' associates hastily combined. To keep an eye on the far-western situation, this new company sent out to Athabaska with Pond a twenty-four-year-old, stiff-necked, extraordinarily capable Scot named Alexander Mackenzie.

Pond welcomed the youth. He sensed that Ross' murder might mean agitation for his recall from the wilderness. Besides, he was old for the herculean trips he envisioned. His best work now might be to prepare another man to pursue his dream.

During the long below-zero nights in their mud-daubed cabin Pond talked and talked and talked to the dour youth. He explained his notes and traced out by the flickering firelight the maps he had made from Indian information. There was ice water in his young companion's veins—and yet by spring Alexander Mackenzie had caught the fever.

Pond was recalled, as he had feared. Methodically Mackenzie reorganized the Athabaska department and brought in a cousin to administer affairs while he followed the lake's outlet river, wherever it led. He started with a handful of men in June 1789.

The breaking ice of Great Slave Lake almost crushed their fragile craft. They wormed through and for three hundred miles the hissing current drove them westward. Then the granite wall of the Rockies reared across their path and the river bent north into the Arctic Sea. Bitterly disappointed, Mackenzie spent five hazardous days exploring the stream's vast delta (it would henceforth be called the Mackenzie River) and turned back.

He had found one of the greatest rivers of the continent, yet he and the North West Company partners considered the exploit useless. The sense of failure made Mackenzie more determined than ever to reach the Pacific. Perhaps, as Pond once had speculated, a man might push up the roaring Peace River to its headwaters, locate a portage over the Rockies, and so reach a westward-flowing stream. It would be a dreadful labor, but perhaps not so dreadful as paddling all the way from Montreal. One would never know without trying.

Doggedly Mackenzie worked two more years setting his district in shape to leave again. He spent his vacation, the winter of 1791–92, in England, studying reports of new maritime discoveries on the northwest coast and teaching himself how to determine latitude and longitude. During the summer of 1792 he traveled from Montreal back along the interminable rivers. By the spring of 1793 he was high up the Peace, ready to strike out afresh.

For his trip he prepared with infinite care a special birchbark canoe twenty-five feet long and four feet nine inches in beam. It was light enough for two men to carry on their shoulders three to four miles an hour, yet it was capable of transporting 3000 pounds of provisions, trade goods, extra birchbark for repairs, ten men (Mackenzie, his clerk Alexander McKay, six *voyageurs*, two Indian hunters) and a dog. The roaring torrents of Peace River Canyon almost battered the craft to pieces. The men rebuilt it again and again. They poled it into the foam, dragged it by ropes, waded and carried it. Finally they left the water altogether, lugged the canoe to the canyon rim and marched with it through dense bramble bushes. Returning to the stream, they finally gained the headwaters and from there crossed a portage of 817 steps to the Pacific slope.

An even worse river now pummeled them. This was a tributary

of what later would be known as the Fraser, after the fur trader who first ran its full terrible length in 1808; but when Mackenzie felt the brown surge of its main stream he called it by its Indian name, Tacoutche-Tesse.

The Tacoutche-Tesse flowed west at the point Mackenzie encountered it. Soon, however, it bent south through a resounding canyon. It persisted in going south as steadily as the Mackenzie had persisted in going north. Wild Indians whom the Scot enticed into talk told him (correctly) that the lower canyons of the Tacoutche-Tesse could not be navigated and (incorrectly) that it did not run into the sea. Mackenzie began to fear that it was only a branch of the Great River of the West, Carver's Oregon, and that he might not have time to reach its mouth before winter. Meanwhile he learned that by crossing another range of mountains to the west he could gain the sea in a relatively short time.

He led his now-despairing men back to the Blackwater. They followed this to the limits of navigation, then staggered afoot under heavy loads over a barren pass, through marshes, and among enormous trees to the Bella Coola. From coastal Indians whose paddling skill amazed these trained paddlers they obtained canoes. They outfaced hostility, outlasted the gnawings of hunger and the chill of drizzling rains. At last they tasted salt water. On a huge rock their leader wrote in vermilion mixed with grease (one can still decipher the words) "Alexander Mackenzie, from Canada, by land, the twenty-second of July, one thousand seven hundred and ninety-three."

Save for Cabeza de Vaca's blind wanderings through Texas and northern Mexico (1528–36), this was the first crossing of North America. But although the route might become famous historically, it obviously was too rugged for commercial transportation. So far as the North West Company's problems were concerned, Mackenzie's two epic journeys proved only that if a useful river route existed anywhere, it must be to the south.

The river was there, all right, its mouth hidden in the mists of the Oregon coast. Heceta had suspected it, but for years navigators overlooked it. Cook once again unleashed the forces that led to its discovery. For when English traders operating in the Orient learned of the fantastic prices his sailors had received in Canton for the pelts they had acquired on the Northwest coast, and when peace let commercial shipping move again, a few captains set sail at once for remote Nootka Sound.

At first English ships dominated the trade. Americans soon followed. There was an eager demand in the newly free country for Oriental teas and silks. Unfortunately, the United States possessed limited amounts of the silver and ginseng root the Chinese preferred in exchange for their products. The publication of Cook's and Ledyard's books indicated a third commodity, however, sea-otter fur. Why could not a bold captain take Indian goods to the Northwest and swap them for otter pelts, trade the fur in Canton for tea, and bring the tea home to New York and New England?

Six merchants of Boston, Salem, and New York subscribed $49,000. With this money they fitted out two ships: the *Columbia* of 212 tons burden, commanded by John Kendrick; and as a tender for the *Columbia,* the 90-ton sloop *Lady Washington,* commanded by Robert Gray. They loaded the ships with the kinds of trinkets that inland traders out of Albany sometimes used—snuff-boxes, rat-traps, jew's harps, cooking pots, iron tools, pocket mirrors (only the last three moved well on the Northwest coast), and in October 1787 the two ships left Boston on a stormy voyage. Heavy gales parted them off Cape Horn. Scurvy crippled the crews. Kendrick had to put in at the Spanish island of Juan Fernández for help; when Gray landed on the Oregon coast for water and for fresh berries to fight the disease, he lost one man in a scuffle with the Indians.

Gray reached Nootka in September 1788, Kendrick a little later. The captains of the English ships already there smugly told the newcomers that they had arrived much too late to trade that season and then sailed off to winter comfortably in China and the Sandwich Islands. The Americans built huts for shelter and gloomily sat out the rainy winter. In the spring the English returned one by one—four ships in all. Their chief entrepreneur, who this year had stayed in China, was John Meares, an egregious yet oddly engaging scoundrel who soon came as close as any single private citizen can to precipitating a world war.

Spain had belatedly decided to halt Meares' trade—and everyone else's on the Northwest coast. Nootka was hers, she felt, on the basis of the landing by Juan Pérez in 1774. When rumors reached Mexico City that Russia planned to establish colonies at Nootka, the viceroy ordered two warships north to establish garrisons and stand off the threat.

No Russians were about when the vessels arrived—only English and Americans, who during the next several weeks stood in and out of the harbor on trading trips along the coast. The division of strength played into the hands of the Spanish commander, Estévan José Martínez. One by one he pounced on the English. One of Meares' four ships, the smallest, he appropriated and manned with Spanish sailors; another he ordered back to China; two he seized and took as prizes to Mexico, their crews imprisoned below decks. The Americans he did not bother. Perhaps he thought the young and remote United States too insignificant to be worrisome. Perhaps he was kept placated by John Kendrick, who with strange indolence lolled around Nootka while Gray busily traded throughout the coastal sounds in the little *Lady Washington*.

After the seizures, Kendrick sent Gray home via Canton in the *Columbia* while he himself remained on the coast with the *Lady Washington*. Gray carried to China with him a few English sailors and 215 pelts belonging to Meares' company. The Yankee did not trade to advantage in Canton. He was green at the game and the market was depressed. Furthermore, half the tea he did buy was spoiled by weather during the trip to Boston. Still, he was accorded a hero's welcome on his arrival—the *Columbia* was the first American ship to circumnavigate the globe—and his principals immediately outfitted him with more suitable trade goods for a return trip to the Northwest coast.

Meares in the meantime had rushed to London to demand his government's help in recovering his ships. The ministry decided to make the affair a test of Spain's claim to the Northwest. To rouse public opinion it printed the *Memorial* in which Meares listed his grievances, and Meares added to the clamor by publishing his *Voyages Made in the Years 1788 and 1789 from China to the Northwest Coast of America ... and Observations on the Probable Existence of a North West Passage.* The last part of the title rose from a superficial glance Meares had taken at the Strait of Juan de Fuca between Vancouver Island and present Washington state. "Its extremity," he decided, "could not be at any great distance from Hudson's Bay." Alexander Mackenzie, who read Meares' book in London, knew that the geography was foolish; but the account of the sea-otter trade helped intensify the Scot's desire to find his western river.

A great many other Englishmen also read Meares' book and roared their disapproval of Spain's presumption. Spain retorted by mobilizing and calling on France for help. England voted a war chest of a million pounds and invoked the aid of her allies in the Triple Alliance. But France was already being eaten by the cancer that shortly would break forth as the French Revolution. She dragged her feet; Spain had second thoughts and backed down. On October 28, 1790, she signed the Nootka Convention, which amounted to an abandonment of her territorial pretensions in the Northwest. Anyone could trade there until the unpredictable tracings of history determined the possession of the land.

Robert Gray learned of the surrender more than a year after his departure from Boston on his second trip. During that year he had traded northward in the *Columbia* as far as the maze of islands off the southern tip of Alaska and southward as far as Oregon. Competition from other traders was fierce, and he began looking for some hitherto untouched sound or river mouth where the unsophisticated natives would be ripe customers for the first trading ship to reach them. At latitude 46°10′ he felt strong currents and saw turbid water. The signs surely meant a river mouth somewhere behind the fogbanks, but squally weather kept him from pressing the search. He wandered northward a bit and dropped anchor outside an Indian village he had visited previously. It was April 28, 1792; Alexander Mackenzie was just starting his long journey from Montreal to Athabaska, eager to discover the River of the West.

Two English ships hove into sight. They were commanded by George Vancouver, who had been dispatched to receive from a Spanish emissary the plot of land at Nootka which Meares claimed to own, and to explore the coast for the Passage whose ghost Meares had raised. Some of Vancouver's men visited the *Columbia*. They told Gray about the Nootka Convention and pumped him for useful geographic information. He told them he believed that there was a river to the south, but they brushed by the suggestion. They were more interested in what he had to say about the Strait of Juan de Fuca to the north.

After they had sailed on, Gray discovered the harbor off the Washington coast which still bears his name. Dissatisfied with his reception there, he sailed south for another look at his supposed river. This time, on the blue-and-silver spring morning of May 11, 1792, using his pinnace for a guide, he groped across the seething bar into "a large river of fresh water, up which we steered." During his tours of the coast he had used up on other discoveries the names of all his backers and associates. The only thing he had left for the river was the name of his ship—*Columbia's River,* he wrote it.

Although many natives swarmed around his vessel, trade again was disappointing. For that reason he explored only a few miles upstream and stayed only until May 18, although it took him until the afternoon of the twentieth to escape back across the murderous bar. Trading recklessly northward, he fought more Indians, grounded himself on a rock, managed to work free, and at last put back into Nootka. Vancouver was there. With some smugness Gray told the Englishman that a huge river certainly did lie at 46° 10′.

In the fall, one of Vancouver's men, Lieutenant Broughton, crossed the bar for a belated look. He found a tiny English vessel there, the *Jenny,* commanded by James Baker; in a pinnace he sailed a hundred miles or more up the Columbia, making rough sketches and naming, among other things, the dazzling white cone of Mt. Hood. Later, some English would insist that Broughton's examination rather than Gray's perfunctory visit constituted effective discovery and that England's claim to Oregon was therefore more valid than the United States'. The question would not be settled until the Oregon Trail was deep with ruts. That, not arguments over who saw the river first, would make the difference.

Spain did not care about sea-otter pelts. What she wanted to guarantee with her claim to California and the Northwest coast was protection for the feeble settlements along the Rio Grande and, more particularly, the silver mines in northern Mexico. The close of the Revolution brought restless Americans pushing dangerously against the eastern bank of the easily navigable Mississippi. Immediately thereafter the noose began to squeeze from the northwest. Noting the advent of Gray and Kendrick in the Pacific, the Viceroy of Mexico in December 1788 wrote Madrid in warning: "We ought not be surprised that the English colonies of America, being now an independent republic, should carry out the design of finding a safe port on the Pacific and of attempting to sustain it by crossing the immense country of the continent. . . . It is indeed an enterprise for many years, but I firmly believe that from now on we ought to employ tactics to forestall its results."

England was a more immediate threat, however. First the Nootka Convention stripped Spain's northwestern flank bare. Word of the surrender had scarcely reached St. Louis when information arrived that English traders were infiltrating upper Louisiana from posts on the Assiniboine River and from Prairie du Chien.

The dismaying word about the Missouri was brought down the river from the Mandan villages in 1792 by a trader (a Frenchman, of course) named Jacques D'Eglise. D'Eglise had ventured that far up the river because the administration in St. Louis had been having trouble with the surly Indians on the lower Missouri. The government's way of punishing the savages was to withhold trade goods from them. This was hard on hand-to-mouth traders who lacked capital enough to wait out the interdict. To stay in business they had to find new customers among tribes not already licensed to someone else. Driven thus, D'Eglise had labored farther up the tumultuous Missouri than anyone else had yet gone from St. Louis.

The Mandans had changed location since Vérendrye's time. After smallpox had killed half the tribe about 1781, the panicked survivors had fled sixty miles upstream to a point near the mouth of the Knife River and had settled in two new villages. English traders had reached them there as early, evidently, as 1785. By the time the St. Louis trader arrived, a small but regular commerce was flowing toward the Assiniboine.

Jacques D'Eglise reported the intrusion to the lieutenant-governor in St. Louis, Zenon Trudeau. The upper river abounded with furs now going to Montreal, he said. Furthermore, the Mandans possessed Spanish bridles and horses wearing Spanish brands.

Zenon Trudeau jumped to the conclusion that the Mandans were in direct contact with Santa Fe, although actually the goods trickled slowly to the Missouri from tribe to tribe. But if the Indians had made direct contact, then what was to prevent an English army from marching against New Mexico from a landing in Hudson Bay?

The geographic misunderstanding was colossal, but the countermeasure based on it was logical enough. To protect New Mexico's entire northern arc, Spain must string forts up the Missouri, over the "height of land," and down the great River of the West to the sea. (This was still the mythical River; word of Gray's discovery had not yet reached beyond the ships hovering along the Northwest coast.) Although the forts might serve some military functions, their main usefulness would be to secure, through trade, the allegiance of the western Indians, who would then do Spain's fighting for her. Since traders would benefit, they should pay—the same old fallacy that had hampered western exploration for centuries.

Trudeau sent D'Eglise's data about the English invasion of the upper Missouri—"as much as I have been able to find out about this trip from an ignorant man who made no observations and who hardly knows how to speak his own French language"—to Baron Carondelet, the governor in New Orleans, on October 20, 1792. The following July, Carondelet drew up new trade regulations designed to exclude foreign citizens from the river and to divide its trade more equitably among authorized applicants, who might be either naturalized or native-born citizens.

On receipt of these regulations, Trudeau called a meeting of traders to discuss the rules in conjunction with forming a new company which, in return for monopolistic privileges, would promise to explore westward. During the rest of the winter of 1793–94 St. Louis buzzed with talk of the project. When the time came for actually putting up cash, however, the Chouteaus and others of the town's more powerful fur merchants held back. They were doing well enough with the monopolies they had, and the long shot upriver looked far too risky. In the end, nine lesser traders, led by Jacques Clamorgan, banded together to form La Compagnie de Commerce pour la Découverte des Nations du haut du Missouri—more briefly, the Missouri Company.

They were so sure that the government would approve their formal request for a ten-year monopoly that they dispatched their first expedition before an answer came from Governor Carondolet. They were safe; expediency demanded his authorization. Carondolet not only granted the request but added a promise of a 2000-peso reward to the Spanish subject (native or naturalized) who first reached the Pacific.[1] To collect the money, the claimant need only bring back a note written in Russian by one of the Russian commanders on the coast. The Governor of Louisiana obviously had little idea of where Alaska was.

On paper the Missouri Company's plans were sound. The first expedition, which left St. Louis in May 1794, was to be followed by two more in 1795. Each was to be bigger than its predecessor. Each was to build posts and garner information that would help its successor push farther on toward the Pacific. It was still pretty much of a blind push, however. Correspondence as late as July 1795 mentions Nootka as a destination, which suggests that word of the Columbia River (Gray was back in Boston by July 1793) was strangely slow in reaching responsible authorities in St. Louis.

The first expedition was commanded by Jean-Baptiste Truteau, a name confusingly similar to that of Zenon Trudeau, the lieutenant-governor. Truteau, who had served briefly as the first schoolteacher in St. Louis, was a trader of wide and varied experience, but he lacked adequate material for this enterprise. The company started him up the yellow flood of the Missouri with only two pirogues loaded with a picayune assortment of goods worth 20,000 pesos. He was expected to use some of these for bribing his way through the tribes of the lower river and still have enough left over to please the Mandans.

Accompanying Truteau along the lower reaches of the river went Jacques D'Eglise. Urging rights as discoverer of the Mandans, D'Eglise had requested a private monopoly of the trade

[1] Carondolet in turn acted without authorization, which did not arrive from Madrid until 1796.

with them. The monopoly had gone to the Missouri Company instead, but he was allowed to continue his own venture although not a member of the firm. He did carry some guns for the company on this trip. When he forged ahead of Truteau, the Poncas pounced on him up near the border between present Nebraska and South Dakota and seized the weapons—or so D'Eglise said. Truteau, who later paused to recover the company property, thought cynically that D'Eglise had used the guns as a bribe to obtain his own safe passage. If so, the misappropriation got him only out of Ponca territory. A little later the Arikaras halted him and held him.[2]

When Truteau came toiling along behind him, he was stopped by the Sioux. They bullied what they wanted out of the traders and delayed them so long that Truteau had no chance of reaching his goal, the Mandan villages, before winter. To escape his oppressors he dropped downstream and built some huts. From frying pan into fire; along came a band of Omahas under their arrogant chief, Blackbird, who reputedly bought arsenic from unscrupulous St. Louis traders and used it, along with appropriate mumbo-jumbo, to convince his rivals that his boast of controlling life and death was not empty rhetoric. Blackbird practiced still more extortion on Truteau before allowing him to continue in the spring to the Arikaras. It was as far as the first expedition ever reached. Truteau stayed there perforce for a year, waiting fruitlessly for the second expedition to rescue him.

About the time of Truteau's arrival among the Arikaras in the spring of 1795, D'Eglise started downstream with his load of pelts. En route he met, among the Pawnees, two deserters from the English trading posts among the Mandans. He took the pair

---

[2] This was getting to be an old story. In 1793, before the founding of the Missouri Company, D'Eglise had tried to return to the Mandans. He had been stopped then also, either by Arikaras or possibly by Sioux. The blockaders wished (a) to carry goods to the farther tribes and so reap the trading profits for themselves and (b) to make sure guns did not reach their enemies upriver.

In 1793 the Arikaras lived near Grand Detour, central South Dakota, in earthen villages even more elaborate than those of the Mandans. The next year, however, the Arikaras gave way before Sioux pressure and migrated farther up the Missouri, settling finally near the mouth of Grand River, a little south of the boundary of North Dakota.

on to St. Louis. There they were interviewed by both the lieutenant-governor and the two principal men of the Missouri Company, Jacques Clamorgan and A. Reyhle. The deserters told what they had learned from the Indians about western geography—garbled rumors of the Yellowstone River and of the Great Falls of the Missouri, which they shifted from their proper location far back into the mountains and swelled to a thunderous cataract three hundred feet high. Of more immediate concern, however, was their confirmation that the Mandans possessed Spanish goods and that the English were now actually building forts (small trading huts) on the upper river.

The government's fear of a British attack on Santa Fe sprang alive again. Clamorgan and Reyhle sought to make capital out of it for their company. On July 8, 1795, they wrote Zenon Trudeau, for transmission to Madrid, that "an invasion menaces all that extent of land which separates us from the Pacific Ocean." The government should dispatch soldiers to meet the threat. The company would gladly garrison the troops in its posts if the government granted a subsidy. Consider, they said, what the company was already doing. Just that spring (1795) it had sent a second expedition after Truteau with twice as many goods as he had carried. A third, equipped with four pirogues, was about to follow the second. One of these four boatloads was destined for the Arikaras and one for the Sioux, "whom it is necessary to flatter in order not to risk being beheaded." The remaining supplies were to please the Mandans and to enable the explorers "to go overland to the Far West." The cost of this third expedition was stated to be 200,779 pesos, "enormous capital the repayment of which ought to be favored by the Governor-General."

The quoted cost seems about double the true amount. Even so, the risk was considerable. Meeting it called for a leader of more than ordinary ability. The man whom the company proposed to hire was a naturalized Scot and erstwhile English trader, James Mackay.

Mackay, well-born and well educated, fluent in both Spanish and French, was a trained surveyor. He had emigrated to Canada about the time of the American Revolution. He had traded, explored, and mapped westward toward the Rockies—perhaps even to them. In 1787 he had visited the Mandan villages, while the trade was still novel enough for the Mandans to honor white visitors by loading them onto buffalo robes and carrying them in an excited parade into the earthen towns. A few years later, Mackay had wandered into St. Louis and, to secure the trade privileges reserved for citizens, had sworn allegiance to the Spanish government. The Missouri Company thought enough of his capabilities to offer him not only a salary of $400 a year but also a share of the profits. In urging that Carondolet make the appointment official, Trudeau wrote, on July 15, 1795, ". . . since no native of the country has been found with sufficient intelligence to be entrusted with the important management of the discoveries that are proposed and the control of their interests, [the company] have suggested to me Mr. Mackay, a Scotchman but a naturalized Spaniard, whom I have approved because of his honesty and intelligence."

Carondolet sent no troops. But he did authorize Mackay's appointment and he increased the reward for reaching the Pacific via the Missouri from two thousand to three thousand pesos. Six months before this authorization reached St. Louis, Mackay was on his way with the four pirogues manned by thirty-three men.

In October he turned the big bend of the Missouri toward the north. He bluffed through threatening Otoes. Reaching the truculent Poncas, he learned why the second expedition had never reached the waiting Truteau. In the face of the Poncas' demand for tribute, the morale of the whites had collapsed and they had made no effort to go on. Mackay blamed the debacle on the incompetence and licentiousness of their leader, Lécuyer, who, according to Mackay, "has no less than two women since he arrived and who has given away a large number of things belonging to the company."

Mackay was stopped in his turn by cold weather. Settling among the Mahas, or Omahas, a little north of the mouth of the Platte, he ran head-on into the dispenser of arsenic, Chief Blackbird. Blackbird and his bully-boys bled Mackay white, taunting him meanwhile with remarks about the superiority of English goods and the fine character of the English traders who were coming in increasing numbers out of Prairie du Chien across

Iowa. One party leading twelve packhorses, the Blackbird told the Scot, had crossed the ice of the Missouri the preceding winter and had built a post on the Platte River. Gloomily Mackay wrote in his journal that intrigues by the English among the Missouri tribes had reached such proportions that Spain must adopt prompt countermeasures "unless we desire to see ourselves exposed to abandon this magnificent country." He began building a fort, convinced that only by force could the river be kept open for commerce. He appealed to the government for troops and armament and to Clamorgan for more goods. Reaching the Pacific, he was beginning to think, might cost far more than anticipated. What was worse, he felt he must stay among the Mahas until tensions were resolved.

Still, some gesture toward the West had to be made. Believing mistakenly that Jean-Baptiste Truteau was with the Mandans and could furnish supplies for an overland crossing, Mackay delegated the responsibility for the journey to a Welsh dreamer named John Thomas Evans.

The whole romantic fuzz of the frontier is epitomized in the unlikely character of John Evans. He had been born near Caernarvon, Wales, in 1770. His father and brother were Methodist preachers and he carried some of their zeal with him wherever he went. As a youth he had visited London and there joined a convivial, romantic, literary, and intensely patriotic Welsh group called the Caradogion Society. The Caradogion Society at the time of his arrival had been enthralled by a theory that Prince Madoc, legendary son of an actual Welsh king named Owain Gwyneed, had crossed the Atlantic to America in 1170 with three hundred colonists in ten ships. The group multiplied in the New World. Offshoots from it accomplished wonders, including the establishment of the Aztec empire. In spite of their abilities, however, the transplanted Welshmen had been forced by Indians to retreat into the unknown. Discussions about finding their descendants and reconverting them to Christianity became a popular pastime in the Caradogion Society. An enterprising poet named Iolo Morganwg, perhaps promoting a free trip to America, offered to look for the lost nation if the Society produced enough subscriptions to finance his journey.

Iolo was forty-six, married, and the father of several children. When subscriptions fell short of his expectations, he developed second thoughts. John Evans, then only twenty-two, offered himself as a substitute. Armed with letters of recommendation to Dr. Samuel Jones, founder of the school that later became Brown University, he sailed for America in the fall of 1792. He was boastful, high-handed, stubborn, fearless, and capable. Although Jones told him that the quest was folly, Evans remained unconvinced. To finance his passage, he worked for a time in a Baltimore counting house and then made his way to St. Louis. There he learned of the light-skinned Mandans and decided that they were the descendants of Madoc's Welsh colonists. Hearing of Mackay's expedition up the Missouri, he signed on.

He must have possessed instinct for the wilderness. Out of thirty-three possible choices to undertake a trip of incredible magnitude, Mackay selected John Evans. In the dead of winter with a party of only three or four men, the twenty-five-year-old Welshman was supposed to cross several hundred miles of frozen plains to the Mandan villages. If he saw English traders anywhere, he was to drive them out. Having procured supplies from Truteau, he was to advance to the Pacific either by the Missouri or by any of its western branches that appeared to offer success. En route he was to make maps and keep a journal. In case he ran short of ink for these he was to use gunpowder, "and for want of powder, in the summer you will surely find some fruit whose juice can replace both." Meanwhile he was to claim all the territory he traversed for Charles IV, King of Spain, and for the Missouri Company, carving their names on trees and stones as a proof of his journey.

He set out in bitter February weather and got to about the White River, a distance of perhaps 250 miles. Sioux spotted his party and gave chase for twelve or fifteen miles. Luckily a storm blew up that night and the whites escaped, but that was fright enough for the moment. Back they went to Mackay's new Fort Charles. Furious, Mackay sent messengers with presents to the Sioux chiefs, asking that they visit him at the Maha village. At last they drifted in and after an interminable harangue agreed to let Evans go on up the river in June.

83

He and his small crew spent six weeks poling and cordelling their pirogue seven hundred miles to the Arikara villages. It does not appear that Evans saw Truteau there or anywhere. And the Arikaras were as jealous as ever. It took the Welshman until September to persuade them to let him continue with his men to the Mandans, carrying a pathetic little package of goods and a few medals to distribute among the chiefs as symbols of their Spanish father's love and strength.

He took possession of the English trading post and ran up a Spanish flag. When traders appeared on October 8 he told them to clear out. Amazingly, they went, fearful perhaps that Evans' superior might be following with force enough to make the expulsion stick.

As winter dragged on, Evans spent his time working over a map of the river. He began to get some glimmer of how distant the mountains were; finding the Missouri to be 500 *toises* wide (about 3200 feet), he decided that its source must be much farther off than earlier reports had indicated. He also decided sorrowfully, as Vérendrye had before him, that the Mandans were only Indians after all.

During the icy, blizzard-torn winter the English traders on the Souris and Assiniboine rivers to the north maintained a polite but watchful contact with him. Deciding at length that Evans was bluffing, they let their notes to him grow curt. In March they sent out a party headed by René Jessaume to win back the Indians and kill the rival white man.

Jessaume was an old hand among the Mandans. Nearly every reminiscence mentions him—none favorably. Alexander Henry the Younger, who encountered Jessaume at the villages in 1805, says ". . . his principles, as far as I could observe, are much worse than those of the Mandanes; he is possessed of every superstition natural to those people, nor is he different in every mean, dirty trick they have acquired from intercourse with the set of scoundrels who visit these parts—some to trade, others to screen themselves from justice."

According to Evans' own story, the Mandans warned him of Jessaume's "horrid Design." Nevertheless the Welshman was almost trapped. "*Jussom* [Evans' italics] came to my house with a number of his Men, and seizing the moment that my Back was turned to him, tried to discharge a Pistol at my head loaded with Deer Shot but my Interpreter having perceived his design hindered the Execution—the Indians immediately dragged him out of my house and would have killed him, had not I prevented them."

Faced by such enmity, undermanned, destitute of goods and with little prospect of receiving more, Evans gave up the quest for a usable route to the Pacific. In the spring of 1797 he returned to St. Louis. Mackay too gave up that year. The Missouri Company was sinking. In an effort to find a financial transfusion that would revive it, Clamorgan linked himself to Andrew Todd, a Montreal merchant who had come down the Mississippi from Michilimackinac to see about setting up a supply house in New Orleans. But Todd died of cholera and that hope ended. The partners of the Missouri Company fell to quarreling among themselves and the organization dwindled to being just one more bartering concern on the increasingly crowded river.

Knowledge proved less fragile. Details that must have come from Truteau's, Mackay's, and Evans' journals and from their maps found a way to Washington. There they fell into the hands of Thomas Jefferson, who for years had been fascinated by the thought of western exploration and of the boon a transcontinental waterway would be to the United States. Even at this late date, perhaps he could find someone stalwart enough to locate a practical trade route to the Columbia.

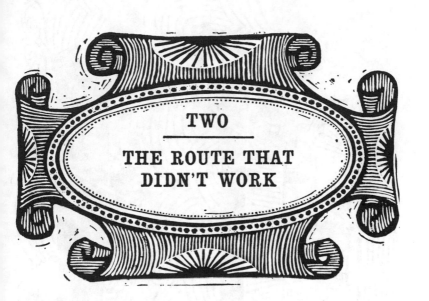

TWO

THE ROUTE THAT DIDN'T WORK

5

THE AMERICANS TRY

When Thomas Jefferson was fourteen years old he attended a school kept by the Reverend James Maury. Thirty years later, when Meriwether Lewis was fourteen, he went to school under James' son, the Reverend Matthew Maury. The small coincidence spreads. Jefferson's teacher, James Maury, subscribed fully to the belief that the American colonies could acquire a rich Oriental trade by opening a waterway up the Missouri and down the River of the West to the Pacific. Maury took particular interest in an expedition proposed by a neighbor of his, Dr. Thomas Walker, who wanted to explore the Missouri "to discover whether it had any such communication with the Pacific Ocean." The French-Indian wars aborted the plan, but no doubt it caused talk in the family. And one of Dr. Walker's sons-in-law, Nicholas Lewis, was the uncle and legal guardian of Meriwether Lewis.

Jefferson's youthful interest in the West soon vaulted out of schoolroom romancing to intensely practical considerations. First as a member of Congress, then as Minister to France, Secretary of State, Vice-president and finally President, he realized that the United States could not afford to let a strong nation occupy the west bank of the Mississippi. His first fear was England. As early as 1783, the year the Treaty of Paris confirmed American independence, he picked up from some source not identified a rumor that a British expedition planned to explore the unknown lands between the Mississippi and California. The project was presented to him as purely scientific. Jefferson suspected an attempt at colonizing, however, and felt that the threat should be forestalled by an American advance in the same direction. On December 4, 1783, he wrote of his fears to George Rogers Clark, leader of the American wilderness forces beyond the Alleghenies, and added, "some of us have been talking here in a feeble way of making the attempt to search that country. but I doubt whether we have enough of that kind of spirit to raise the money. how would you like to lead such a party?"

Neither the British nor the American expedition materialized. But Jefferson stayed concerned enough that in 1786, when he was Minister to France, he furthered John Ledyard's harebrained scheme of hiking alone across two continents. Ledyard was the book-writing marine who had been at Nootka with James Cook. He thought, as did Peter Pond and Alexander Mackenzie, that great riches awaited the discoverer of a feasible route for linking to the Orient the sea-otter trade of the coast and the fur trade of the interior. But Ledyard's vision was not grounded in reality. He proposed to locate the way single-handed. After failing to obtain passage to his starting point, Nootka, by an American or English trading ship, he decided to walk across Siberia, talk himself aboard a Russian vessel at Kamchatka, and reach the Pacific coast that way. From there, accompanied only by a faithful dog, he would travel eastward from one Indian tribe to another until he reached civilization. Jefferson listened to all this in Paris with skepticism. Ledyard, he wrote, "is a person of ingenuity & information. Unfortunately he has too much imagination." Nevertheless he helped Ledyard obtain a Russian passport, though when Catherine the Great learned what the man was up to (a revolutionary from the radical new United States, spying out her Pacific establishments!) she had him arrested and dragged back from the middle of Siberia. So ended that scheme.

André Michaux's scheme of botanical exploration up the Missouri and on to the coast was another fantasy. Yet until the expedition became involved in political intrigue against Spain, Jefferson, as a member of the American Philosophical Society, supported it with money and prestige. Meriwether Lewis, the son of a family friend of the Jeffersons, wanted desperately to go on Michaux's journey, but the lad was not yet eighteen (it was the spring of 1792) and Jefferson declined to recommend him. It was just as well; that trip aborted, too.

Meanwhile the British were pressing against Spanish North America from all directions. The Nootka Convention was an official indication of her interests in the Northwest. In the Northeast her traders encroached unofficially but brazenly on the upper Missouri. Obviously the two sections were not going to stay separated forever. The next transcontinental move came in 1800, when the North West Company decided to send their best mapmaker, David Thompson, from the headwaters of the Saskatchewan across the tremendous mountains of present Banff and Jasper parks to the Columbia. Perhaps some of Thompson's *engagés* actually did see the western river with a party of Kootenai Indians who had come timorously over the mountains from the far slope to buy guns for fighting the Blackfeet. Thompson himself seems not to have succeeded, however. High water and vast precipices blocked a horseback probe he made with Duncan McGillivray. The next summer, 1801, his Indian guide landed him in a cul-de-sac and he had to turn around. After that, his company's energies were absorbed by a feud with its own defecting partners, including Alexander Mackenzie, who set up a rival concern called the XY Company. Nonetheless, the westward probe, once started, would inevitably be continued sooner or later—and the government of Great Britain would be asked to support it.

This became clear with the publication, late in the fall of 1801, of Alexander Mackenzie's reminiscences, *Voyages from Montreal ... to the Frozen and Pacific Oceans.* In the concluding pages of the book, Mackenzie, who naturally but erroneously assumed that his Tacoutche-Tesse and Gray's Columbia were the same stream, proposed a plan whereby Britain could dominate the fur trade of North America. England, he said, must control the Columbia watershed as far south as the 45th parallel. A giant depot at the mouth of the river would receive supplies destined for the interior and pelts intended for China. Since these pelts could not be brought out of the interior via the Peace River, a workable route to the Columbia must be found via the headwaters of either the North or the South Saskatchewan. (David Thompson's efforts to find that route were even then ending in failure.) Posts strung along this route and at strategic points on the coast would assure Britain not only of the inland trade but would also drive the sea-otter "adventurers" from the United States off the ocean.

There were hurdles. To make the plan fully effective, the Hudson's Bay Company would have to grant other fur-trading companies transit rights across jealously guarded Hudson Bay to the navigable rivers of the interior. The South Sea and East Indian companies would have to relax their monopolistic claims to all trade in the Pacific and the Orient. As Mackenzie recognized, government intervention would be the surest way to force such a yielding, and in the end the English government proved reluctant to tamper with the vested interests. Nonetheless the proposal, appearing boldly in public print, served to alert Thomas Jefferson.

Two could play at this game of dominating the commerce of the wilderness. Mackenzie might urge England to assert her rights over the Columbia watershed, but Gray's discovery had given the United States a prior claim to the area. An American expedition that pushed up the Missouri and on to the coast would fortify this claim. Indeed, the Missouri might very well offer a better gateway through the mountains than did the Saskatchewan, which because of its location would be frozen much of the year. If navigable tributaries of the Missouri ran up toward the Saskatchewan, then Americans could bring English pelts down those streams for transshipment either west to the Columbia and China or east to the Mississippi and the United States.[1]

Entrenched trading monopolies were the obstacles to Mackenzie's plan. Spanish Louisiana blocked Jefferson's counter project. Before any secure commerce could flow between the Atlantic states and the Pacific coast, the United States must possess the intervening territory. Jefferson must have been aware of this need when he began making definite plans for a transcontinental expedition—and that was at least as early as February 1801, a month before his inauguration, for in February he appointed Meriwether Lewis his private secretary. Lewis, who had spent most of his

[1] In his secret message to Congress asking authority for the expedition, Jefferson naturally stressed the second alternative.

manhood with the Army on the frontier, was not qualified for secretarial tasks. But he did have a passion to explore. He was young (twenty-six when appointed), flexible, vigorous, self-reliant. More important, he was intelligent enough to familiarize himself with some of the processes involved in scientific observation and discreet enough to be trusted with the political problems inherent in exploring someone else's land.

As for securing that land, Jefferson probably had no other plans than to move as the expediencies of the moment dictated. Napoleonic Europe was in a turmoil; one had to be ready for anything. In May 1801, only four months after Lewis' appointment, Jefferson learned that through the secret Treaty of San Ildefonso, signed the previous October, Bonaparte had forced Spain to return to France the huge western territory wrested from her by the Treaty of Paris in 1763. Spanish Louisiana no longer existed. It was French Louisiana, though because the treaty was secret Spanish officials in St. Louis and New Orleans still pretended to be running their districts—and in some cases probably thought they were.

What did Napoleon's gesture mean? Was this a flanking movement in another of his attacks on the British Empire? If so, England would surely strike back through the Mississippi Valley. Whichever power won, a strong nation would hold the West. There would be no hope of uninterrupted communication overland between the United States and the Columbia or of luring Canadian pelts into American commercial channels. Of more immediate concern, commerce on the Mississippi River would be at the mercy of foreigners far stronger than Spain—and the Spanish had already caused enough trouble to the trans-Allegheny settlements by her arbitrary closings and openings of the vital artery.

Jefferson (and his private secretary too, no doubt) watched anxiously as Napoleon massed troops in the West Indies. About the same time, Spanish officials made another move toward closing the Mississippi at New Orleans to American trade. Warhawks in the West and in Congress began to cry. Simultaneously word reached Jefferson that an epidemic of yellow fever was crippling the French army in the Indies. If the debacle proved complete enough, Napoleon might call off the New World adventure. Then perhaps he would listen to an American offer to buy New Orleans. Jefferson instructed Robert Livingston, American Minister to France, to start negotiations. Later, as the full extent of the disaster in the Indies became known, Monroe was sent to France to support Livingston.

Those moves were improvisations. Meanwhile the plan for an expedition to the Columbia went steadily ahead. In November 1802, pretending politely that he knew nothing about the Treaty of San Ildefonso, Jefferson asked the Spanish Minister in Washington, the Marqués de Casa Yrujo, whether Yrujo's country would object to a small United States expedition exploring for "a continual communication .... by water" to the Pacific. Yrujo, continuing the pretense, said that his country most certainly would.

In spite of the warning Jefferson summoned Congress to a secret meeting on January 18, 1803, and asked an appropriation of $2500 for sending an Army group of ten or twelve men to the Columbia on a "literary" venture—*literary* being in those days an elastic enough term to embrace scientific as well as humanistic investigations.[2]

The request was granted and Lewis was appointed commander. He finished his studies in navigation and then spent most of the spring in Philadelphia and Lancaster buying equipment—camp gear, tools, clothing, drugs, arms and ammunition, astronomical instruments, and geegaws to use as presents for the Indians. To transport this paraphernalia and his men, he ordered built in Pittsburgh a keelboat fifty-five feet long, manned by twenty-two oars, and two pirogues. If these were the same pirogues that he took up the Missouri, one was propelled by seven oars and was painted red; the other, driven by six oars, was white.

---

[*] Twenty-five hundred dollars surely was not adequate. By the time Lewis reached St. Louis, he knew that ten or twelve men were too few. Four times that many were needed to push the expedition up the Missouri to the Mandan villages; three times that many went on to the Pacific and back. Lewis spent $2160 on supplies in Philadelphia alone. Even granting that his men accepted much of their pay in the form of land bounties, the cash outlay for the trip must have exceeded the sum authorized. Scholars, however, have not been able to discover how much the expedition actually cost or from what government fund the money was taken. Obscure public bookkeeping is not, evidently a recent innovation.

The expedition was of course perilous. To help guarantee its completion in case anything happened to him, Lewis selected as his co-captain an Army officer four years older, under whom he had served for a brief time on the frontier. This was William Clark, redheaded youngest brother of George Rogers Clark. Lewis extended the offer with a promise that Clark was to be his military equal. The War Department demurred, however, and commissioned Clark a second lieutenant. No one on the expedition, other than the two leaders, ever knew of the slight. Both signed papers and were addressed as captain. In three years of often arduous living together, Lewis never once pulled his rank on Clark or countermanded one of his orders. From beginning to end the adventure was truly, if not technically, the Lewis and Clark Expedition.

Before Lewis left Pittsburgh he learned that Napoleon had startled Jefferson's emissaries by offering to sell not part of Louisiana Territory but all of it. The disaster to the French army in the West Indies had chilled the Emperor's New World ambitions. His restlessness was shifting toward the Orient, and he needed money. If war with England developed, he did not want her to obtain Louisiana, yet he was not prepared to defend the territory. Accordingly, he offered the huge wilderness to the United States, mainly to keep it from Britain. The price was roughly $11,250,000 and the assumption by the United States of France's debts to American citizens, an amount estimated at $3,750,000. Litigation, interest and so on later raised the sum another $8,221,320, so that the total cost of Louisiana Territory's 909,000 square miles came to $23,213,567—about four and one-fifth cents an acre.

Aware, as Jefferson was, of what this acquisition might mean to their young country, the American envoys promptly accepted. If the Senate swallowed the unconstitutional assumption of power and ratified the purchase, one more duty would be added to the proliferating chores of the expedition: the captains would now have to convince the unruly and skeptical Indians of the West that they owed allegiance to a new Great Father. As events developed, the treaty was ratified, after considerable senatorial grumbling, in October.

On August 30 Lewis started down the Ohio with seven soldiers and three young civilians who had volunteered to go along and were on trial. At Louisville, Kentucky, nearly a month later, he picked up Clark, Clark's Negro slave York, and eight or nine men whom Clark had recruited. At Fort Massac near the mouth of the Ohio they acquired a veteran hunter, George Drouillard, whose name became more or less stabilized in the *Journals* as Drewyer. Sent into Tennessee to recruit, Drouillard picked up another eight men. Two tough Army regulars, Sergeants John Ordway and Patrick Gass, were requisitioned at Army posts in Illinois. After a season of hardening, the men not already members of the Army were formally sworn in, save for Drouillard. In addition, a civilian boat crew of French *voyageurs* was later hired in St. Louis to help transport supplies as far as the Mandan villages.

Lewis had planned to winter in one of the small settlements a few miles up the Missouri from its mouth. The Spanish commander in St. Louis had received no word concerning the transfer of the territory, however, and declined to grant permission. Winter quarters accordingly were established on the Illinois side of the Mississippi. While Clark managed the camp, Lewis gathered supplies and information. Most of the traders in St. Louis proved cooperative.[3] In addition, Jefferson somehow obtained and sent to the expedition material and maps gleaned from John Evans and Jean-Baptiste Truteau of the dying Missouri Company. Clark evidently talked to James Mackay in person. As a result the explorers started out well acquainted with the lower river and the Indians along its banks.

The trip began on May 14, 1804. A few of the soldiers and hired boatmen had encountered the river before, but probably even their stories did not fully prepare the others for the ordeal they faced. Twenty-five hundred miles of collapsing clay banks had loaded the spring flood with silt. Indians called the river Smoky Water, whites The Big Muddy. To one traveler it looked like bad

[3] Not all, however. The Spanish trader Manuel Lisa and a "Mr. B" put so many obstacles in Lewis' way that he exploded, "I think them both great scoundrels, and they have given me abundant proofs of their unfriendly dispositions toward our government . . . these puppies are not unacquainted with my opinions." Or perhaps it was a private animosity. Lisa, at any rate, became a United States citizen and rendered his new country useful services during the War of 1812. See pages 168–169.

coffee colored with condensed milk. To everyone it sooner or later became sullen, unpredictable, treacherous. The light canoes which had mastered the eastern and northern rivers would not have worked on the Missouri, even if birchbark had grown along its bottomlands for building the fragile craft. This tumultuous river demanded force, not delicacy.

The expedition's keelboat and pirogues carried square sails, but the wind seldom sat for long in the right quarter. Oars sufficed only in relatively slack water. To dodge the full surge of the twisting current, the boats crept from one bank to the other at nearly each of the innumerable bends. Even so the downstream sweep was generally so insistent that headway could be made only by human muscles straining on towropes.

The men floundered through prickly underbrush on the banks or up to their waists in the water and mud of the river margin. They chopped leaning trees out of the way, dragged themselves ahead by willow branches. Snakes were a danger, burrowing woodticks a torment, the blazing sun on the water an agony. An even worse ordeal was mosquitoes. Pierre-Antoine Tableau, who was on the river when the Lewis and Clark Expedition labored upstream, described the tortures of his own *voyageurs* thus:

> During the whole day the boats were enveloped as in a cloud and the engagés who were compelled by the extreme heat to keep the body naked, were covered with blood and swellings. Often our hunters, not being able to endure them, returned at full speed to throw themselves into the boats. What is more they could not aim their weapons when covered with these insects. . . . In short, the mosquitoes, not leaving the crew at liberty to take its food in the evening or its rest at night, exhausted it as much as did all the work of the day.

Sudden squalls added danger to discomfort. Just below the sandy mouth of the Platte (Clark writing) "the atmispr. became Sudenly darkened by a black and dismal looking Cloud." A blast of wind threw the keelboat against an island where she would have been "dashed to pices in an Instant, had not the party leaped out on the Leward Side and kept her off with the assistance of the anker & Cable . . . In this Situation we Continued about 40 Minits, when the Storm Sudenly Seased and the river became Instance-taniously as Smoth as Glass."

The high water of spring swept away entire islands, or made new ones by cutting off wooded points. Clark was amazed that the pirogues were not crushed by falling banks. Sometimes travelers felt their campgrounds crumbling away beneath them. A collapsing tree twelve feet in circumference once almost swamped Tabeau's keelboat.

Sometimes floating trees caught against the bank. Logs and mud packed in the branches. The solidifying tangle, called an *embarras*, reached out into the stream like a dike. The confined current escaped around its point so swiftly that often a boat could not progress against it. Then the cursing *voyageurs* had to land on the *embarras* and chop a passage through its inner end.

Planters were trees whose earth-laden roots caught in the river bottom and left the top protruding like the tilted mast of a sunken derelict. Treacherous brother of the planter was the snag, which kept its teeth hidden beneath the turbid surface. Even more dangerous was the sawyer. In the words of explorer David Thompson,

> The sawyer is generally a Tree of large dimensions broken about the middle of its length, it's roots are in the mud . . . but not so firmly as to keep the broken tree steady, the strong current bends the tree under as much as the play of the roots will permit, the strain on which causes a reaction, and the tree rises with a spring upwards above the water and with such force as will damage or destroy any vessel.

There were compensations. Until after the expedition crossed the Continental Divide, the men ate regally and regularly—waterfowl, deer, elk, bear, and—once they had reached the plains—buffalo. The camp cooks were good; often whiskey was issued all around to relax aching muscles; and the squaws of most of the tribes they visited proved not just complaisant at the offering of meager trifles but even, with the full consent of husbands and brothers, downright eager.

It was an amazingly harmonious and hence effective force. Occasions for disciplinary measures were few, quarrels among the men rare. During the first summer one hired boatman and one soldier deserted; one soldier was dismissed for insubordination. Infractions after that were minor. One man, Sergeant Floyd, died of natural causes on the outward journey and was buried near what is now Sioux City, Iowa. The only clash with Indians that reached the point of bloodshed was Lewis' fight with Blackfeet on Maria's River during the homeward trip. Adroit dealings kept other potentially dangerous encounters within manageable bounds.

The captains chose a high bluff some fifty miles north of the shallow Platte as the place to begin their conferences with the Indians. Here trade routes, in 1804 still used primarily by Indian merchants, struck westward into the plains. Here the once-belligerent Otoes, Omahas, and Poncas had exacted tribute from the traders of Spanish St. Louis. Although smallpox had crippled the tribes in 1802, the shadow of their power still had to be reckoned with. On a bluff far enough above the river that the prevailing wind swept away the mosquitoes, the expedition created a bower of sorts by spreading the keelboat's square canvas sail across some wooden posts. Runners brought in a few minor chiefs—the main parts of the bands were off hunting buffalo—and Lewis arranged them picturesquely under the awning. He harangued them about their new American Father, passed out medals and a bottle of white man's milk (whiskey), and demonstrated a patented airgun that shot almost as powerfully as a musket and, while pressure lasted, much more rapidly. The gathering was not impressive, but it gave a name to an entire area that soon became an important center of the Indian trade—Council Bluffs.

The Sioux came next. A Yankton band, whom the captains harangued at the mouth of South Dakota's James River, proved genial. Not so the dread Tetons. The collision with them came at Bad River (the explorers called it the Teton), not far from the spot where Pierre Vérendrye's sons sixty-one years earlier had buried a lead plate claiming the land for France. Warned by traders who had been victimized by the piratical band, Lewis and Clark were prepared for trouble. Although only a few Tetons were in sight when the keelboat dropped anchor on the evening of

September 24, a heavy guard was posted and two-thirds of the men spent the night on board so that the entire force could not be caught by a surprise attack.

The next morning the Indians began to congregate. As many of the principal men as the space would hold crowded under the usual awning. One old Frenchman among the *voyageurs* knew enough sign language and dialect for rudimentary communication, but attempts at oratory foundered into grunts and baffled shrugs. Dumb shows were possible, however. The soldiers paraded martially; medals were handed around; and the main chief, Black Buffalo, was given "a red coat & a cocked hat & feather &.C."

Unimpressed, the Indians demanded more. The captains countered by inviting five chiefs aboard the keelboat to see some "Curiossities." As an additional gesture of good will, Clark writes, "We gave them ¼ a glass of whiskey which they appeared to be verry fond of, Sucked the bottles after it was out & Soon began to be troublesom, one the 2d Cheif (called the Partizan) assumeing Drunkness, as a Cloake for his rascally intentions." To show disapproval, Clark and a boat's crew rowed the five ashore. As the pirogue nosed into the bank, warriors seized its cable. The chiefs began shoving Clark. The Partizan's "justures were of Such a personal nature I felt My self Compeled to Draw my Sword." Lewis loaded the swivels on the keelboat; the soldiers sprang to arms. "I felt My self warm," Clark wrote, "& Spoke in verry positive terms." The Indians backed off. To show that they intended to move about as they pleased, the captains now ordered the little flotilla a mile farther up the river to a small "Willow Island."

During the next two days, while still more Indians rode into the camp, the Tetons changed tactics and put on an elaborate show of friendship. They placed each captain on an "elegent painted" buffalo robe and lugged him into the center of the village of conical skin tepees. They solemnly passed the peace pipe, presented the expedition with four hundred pounds of fresh buffalo beef, and treated Lewis and Clark to a feast of dog meat and pemmican. At dark (Clark again) "all was Cleared away   a large fire made in the Center, about 10 Musitions playing on tambereens (made of hoops & Skin stretched), long Sticks with Deer & Goats Hoofs tied so as to make a gingling noise, and many others of a Similer Kind, those Men began to Sing, & Beet on the Tamboren, the Women Came forward highly Deckerated in their Way, with the Scalps and Tropies of War of their fathers Husbands Brothers . . . . & proceeded to Dance the War Dance which they done with great Chearfullness. . . ."

The cheer was false. Certain Omaha prisoners of the Sioux warned Peter Cruzatte, who had traded among their nation during previous years, that the Tetons had no intention of letting the whites continue up the river. When departure time came, chiefs who were lounging on the keelboat ordered the craft not to cast off. Warriors seized the mooring rope. Lewis drew a sword to cut the boat free. Clark aimed a swivel. Under the prompt show of force, the chiefs again backed down and, saving face, said all they really wanted was a little tobacco. Clark contemptuously tossed them some and the boats moved on up the river.

Even a bluff that works is less dramatic to report to one's superiors than is a battle. Yet Lewis and Clark had dared not fight. A running skirmish with the Sioux conceivably might have cost so much in men and matériel that the expedition could not have continued. Certainly a fight would have subjected every other white party on the river to retaliatory attacks for years to come. On the other hand, an eagerness to curry the favor of the Partizan and his bully-boys would have increased their arrogance and so have led either to retreat or bloodshed. The captains avoided both traps with remarkable coolness. What the doing cost their nerves shows inadvertently through Clark's journal entry for September 28, when at last the four days of taut alertness were over. "I am," he scribbled beside the campfire, "verry unwell for want of Sleep."

The triumph over the Sioux was not lost on the neighboring tribes. When the expedition reached the three Arikara villages, the Indians and the St. Louis traders living with them greeted the Americans effusively. They feasted the enlisted men and gave them bedmates. They listened solemnly to Lewis' harangues, agreed to let a chief go to Washington, provided information, and sent an emissary on upriver with the explorers to make peace with their enemies, the Mandans and Minnetarees.

The laboring boats reached the five scattered villages of those allied tribes toward the end of October. Lewis and Clark held an elaborate council and then searched for a suitable site for establishing winter quarters. It was high time. The days were short; wild geese flew overhead, ice formed on quiet water at night.

Three miles below the lowest village they found an ample wood supply in a grove of leafless cottonwood trees at the base of a high clay bluff. Here they built a triangular post which they named Fort Mandan. To help them glean from the Indians information about the West and about the unknown lands on either side of the Missouri they hired as one of their interpreters the René Jessaume who once had tried to murder John Evans. As another interpreter they hired Touissant Charbonneau. A notorious lecher, the aging Charbonneau had at the time two wives. One was a Shoshone girl sixteen or seventeen years old and pregnant; her name was Sacajawea. Charbonneau had won her in a gambling game with Minnetarees who had seized her during a battle with her people up toward the foot of the mountains.

The winter passed quickly. Wood-gathering and hunting filled many hours for the men. The blacksmiths were kept busy making iron axes to trade for Indian corn. In their spare time the soldiers constructed dugout canoes and stitched up extra supplies of buckskin clothing and moccasins. For amusement they danced with each other to the rollicking squeak of Peter Cruzatte's fiddle. Sometimes they gyrated in the villages for the entertainment of the Indians; after all, the savages showed off their dances to the whites, didn't they? Afterwards there were squaws aplenty. By spring Clark was noting in his journal that most of the men had "Venerials Complaints."

The Sioux caused two alarms during the winter. First they raided a group of village Indians; later they pounced on four of the expedition's hunters, stealing some of their horses and weapons but not harming the men themselves. Pursuit proved ineffectual, and American prestige suffered.

This was unfortunate, for by now English traders (most of them were of French descent) had arrived from the Assiniboine for their regular winter's business. Rather haughtily Lewis told them the United States would permit the trade, which Spain in theory had not, but the English must not tamper with the loyalties of American red men. The traders acquiesced; after all, an appearance of politeness cost nothing. Actually they took these emissaries from the United States no more seriously than they had taken John Evans' pronouncements on behalf of Spain. Neither did the Mandans, who of course were used to the English but had no idea whatsoever of the United States. By spring Lewis and Clark realized that in order really to impress the Mandans they would have to take one or more chiefs to Washington with them on their homeward journey and let the savages see for themselves the reality of their new Father.

Learning the expedition's destination, the leader of the Canadian traders, François Antoine Laroque, asked to go along. The captains demurred. It would not do to have a responsible British citizen along while they searched for routes into the heart of Britain's best fur country. No doubt their refusal made Laroque suspicious. Under pretense of needing new supplies, he made a midwinter trip to Fort Assiniboine and reported to his superior, Charles Chaboillez. Chaboillez already knew the expedition was bound for the Pacific; on arriving at the Mandan villages Lewis had sent his passports and a polite note to the English post. After listening to Laroque, the Nor'Wester decided that his company had better send its own expedition at least as far as the Rockies and win over the Indians before American influence became established.[4]

Naturally Laroque told the Americans none of this when he returned to the Missouri. But he did tell them something that perhaps served as an even sharper warning. The XY and North West companies, he said, had amalgamated. The implications must have been obvious to the Americans. With the feuding between the companies ended, Mackenzie's policy of thrusting posts across the continent and laying claim to the Columbia would probably become dominant again. In short, Lewis and Clark must not

[4] Leadership of the Nor'Wester project was assigned to Daniel Harmon. He fell ill, however, and Laroque took his place. Traveling mostly with Crow Indians, during the summer of 1805 Laroque skirted the northern flank of the Big Horns and reached the lower Yellowstone River, the first white man to see that valley.

fail. If they did, years might pass before another expedition could be dispatched, and by that time the British might be immovably established on the Columbia.

While the captains waited for the Missouri to open, they collated their natural science data, compiled Indian vocabularies, and wrote long reports for Jefferson. But mostly, by assiduously questioning the Mandans and the farther-ranging Minnetarees, they tried to find out what lay ahead. By spring they had some concept of the Missouri's upper reaches and of the multiple ranges of the mountains. They surmised at last that the Pacific was farther away than anyone had hitherto supposed. They hoped nevertheless to return to the Mandan villages by fall. They clung to a hope that rivers navigable to small boats would carry them most of the way to the ocean. The portage from the Missouri across the Divide to the Columbia was represented as short, and they fondly believed that by using packhorses they could move from one waterway to the other within half a day.

Where were they to get the horses? According to the Minnetarees, great herds of the animals belonged to Indians who lived just beyond the mountains, the Shoshone and Flatheads. Men of those tribes frequently slipped across to the eastern slope to hunt buffalo with bow and arrow (they had no guns; the Minnetarees enjoyed ambushing them), and the Americans might be able to find one of their hunting camps and get horses there.

Shoshone—suddenly Charbonneau's young wife became important. Sacajawea was a Shoshone. Perhaps she could point out the campgrounds her people favored. In any event, she could interpret. It meant burdening the expedition with the baby boy who had been born to her February 11 after severe labor, but the soldiers would just have to put up with the unexpected inconvenience. They didn't ask Sacajawea, of course. They asked Charbonneau. He agreed after a small show of temperament. Why not? He was the one who went down on the rolls as interpreter and who drew the pay.

By April the river was free of ice. On the seventh Corporal Warfington went downriver in the keelboat with the personnel no longer needed by the expedition and with reports and nine cases of specimens for President Jefferson. The same day the main party started upstream in two pirogues and six clumsy dugouts hollowed from cottonwood trees. In addition to Lewis and Clark, there were three sergeants, twenty-three privates, the hunter Drouillard, Charbonneau, his wife and infant son Baptiste (Clark called the boy Pomp), Clark's Negro slave York (the amorous delight of Indian women along the entire route), and Lewis' huge Newfoundland dog Scammon. So far they had been following the tracks of men who had risked the dangerous river ahead of them. From here on they would be entirely on their own.

WISHFUL THINKING

The river soon turned straight west. The landscape grew austerely beautiful. Broad floodplains stretched endlessly on one side; on the other towered gray and yellow and red and greenish clay bluffs, spectacularly eroded. The Yellowstone poured in from the south. The captains made "the necessary observations to determine its position," marveled at the buffalo, elk, and antelope, noted the suitability of timber, and decided that this would be an ideal location for a trading post, as time proved it to be. On, endlessly endlessly on—shivering in the night frosts, bloodied by insects, buffeted by winds so hard that at times they had to lie to, eating well but finding more excitement than they desired in huge grizzly bears—a "verry large and turrible looking animal, which we found verry hard to kill."

Labor increased as they ascended. "Proceeded on by means of the Cord" (towrope) becomes a regular entry—"using oars mearly to pass [cross] the river in order to take advantage of the shores." Save for one hemp rope reserved for the white pirogue, their lines were now homemade affairs of elkskin, which stretched badly when wet and sometimes snapped. When a break occurred the towed craft swung broadside to the current and, in rocky stretches, was in instant danger of being overturned. "We observed great caution at those places." Sometimes the rope-pullers struggled in ice water "even to their armpits," sometimes in "mud so tenacious that they are unable to wear their mockersons," and sometimes on "sharp fragments of rocks which tumble from the clifts." "In short," Lewis observed, "their labor is incredibly painfull and great, yet these faithfull fellows bear it without a murmur."

The leaders kept eying northern tributaries which (Lewis again) "might furnish a practicable and advantageous communication with the Saskashiwan river .... that productive country of valuable furs exclusively enjoyed at present by the subjects of his Britanic Majesty." The matter became critical when, halfway across present Montana, they reached a flood-swollen stream that Lewis named Maria's River, after his cousin Maria Wood.[1]

Which stream led to the mountains? Which was the tributary? A mistake that threw the expedition off course for any appreciable length of time would be fatal.

The men unanimously believed muddy Maria's to be the main fork of the Missouri. The captains, on the basis of their long winter talks with the Minnetarees, inclined toward the now-limpid fork coming from the left. After a week spent examining both branches their opinion remained unchanged, in spite of the forebodings of the men.

To relieve themselves of part of their burden, they dug a cache near the mouth of Maria's River. In the jug-shaped hole they buried provisions, salt, tools, powder and lead, and at least three traps, to be picked up on their homeward journey. The red pirogue being no longer necessary, they tied it to trees on a small island and covered it with branches so that Indians would not find it. On July 11 they entered the clearer fork. To reassure the

---

[1] The name soon lost its apostrophe, becoming Marias River. Although the stream rises east of the Rockies, one branch does point to Marias Pass, the gentlest declivity in the Continental Divide north of Wyoming's South Pass. Lewis and Clark never knew of the low saddle. No Indian mentioned it. The route was infested by Blackfeet; other tribes avoided the area. As a result Marias Pass was not generally known until 1889, when engineer John F. Stevens found it for the Great Northern Railroad. The curious blank spot probably made no difference to our early history. Marias Pass was so remote and its summers so short that it would not have been practical for emigrant wagons rolling toward Oregon.

men, Lewis pressed ahead on foot with four companions to find the Great Falls, which were known to be on the main stream. Along the way he was seized by severe cramps and a high fever. He purged himself with a black bitter tea made from boiled choke-cherry twigs and staggered on. On June 13 they heard the distant roar of a cataract and soon saw columns of mist. The Falls! He and Clark had been right.

They needed horses now, to portage around the falls and its bracketing rapids. Since leaving the Minnetarees, however, they had not seen a single Indian, though Indians almost certainly had been watching them. To make matters worse, Sacajawea, their best hope of establishing contact, was desperately ill. Clark bled her, applied bark poultices, and physicked her with fetid water from a mineral spring. Who took care of her four-month-old baby during her periods of delirium no one bothered to say.

While Clark staked out a carrying route around the cataracts —it turned out to be eighteen miles long—Lewis directed the felling of the only cottonwood tree in the region large enough (twenty-two inches in diameter) to furnish truck wheels. The men sawed out four sets and made axles from the mast of the white pirogue, which was then cached. After a dreadful pitch up a hill bordering the river, the route became fairly level. But it was carpeted by cactus the spines of which their moccasins could not turn. The ordeal ate up a month of precious time. Buffalo, grizzly bears, and rattlesnakes were a continual threat. Flash floods swept the gullies; one almost drowned Clark and the recovering Sacajawea. Vicious hailstorms hammered some of the men off their feet. The crude carriages on which they transported the heavy dugouts and goods broke down continually. Once in a great while they found relief by hoisting a sail and letting the wind push the ponderous vehicles. But mostly, Clark wrote,

> the men has to haul with all their strength wate & art, maney times every man all catching the grass & knobes & stones with their hands to give them more force in drawing on the Canoes & Loads, and notwithstanding the coolness of the air in high presperation and every halt, those not employed in reparing the course, are asleep in a moment, maney limping from the soreness of their feet some

become fa[i]nt for a fiew moments, but no man complains all go chearfully on. to state the fatigues of this party would take up more of the journal than other notes which I find scarcely time to set down.

On July 15 they were back in water. The change brought scant relief. They wanted to go west but now the river was taking them due south. Without horses for carrying their equipment, they had no choice but to follow the stream. As the mountain current became swifter and shallower, progress became possible only by dint of hellish labors on towropes and poles.

The days fled alarmingly. Unless they soon found horses, they risked being trapped in the wilderness by winter. In a desperate effort to find a village of Sacajawea's people (she was beginning at last to recognize landmarks), Clark, Charbonneau, and two others walked ahead of the toiling canoes. Every man's feet were raw. Clark had fiery boils on his ankles. Like Lewis, he fell ill but nevertheless kept on. They reached a place where the river split bewilderingly into three branches. Later, looking up stream from Three Forks, the captains named the left branch Gallatin, the middle Madison, the right Jefferson. Clark believed the Jefferson was the one they should follow, but to make sure limped up it for twenty miles alone (the other men collapsed) and then cut overland to the Madison. He came back to Lewis "very sick with a high fever on him and much fatiegued and exhausted." He had seen no fresh Indian sign.

On July 30, after a two-day rest, they started up the Jefferson. The river frayed into coiling, shallow channels choked by brush and beaver dams. Mountains pinched close on either hand. The dugouts grated on stony riffles; the exhausted men slipped and fell, bruising themselves sorely on the rocks. Swampings wet the cargoes. Finally they abandoned one canoe entirely. As a thin comfort, Sacajawea assured them that they were nearing the headwaters and that her people were probably at a summer camp just beyond the Divide. In desperation Lewis determined, on August 8, to press ahead with three men until he had found the Indians.

Three days later he spotted a lone Shoshone riding bareback, but before he could entice the savage into talk, Private Shields blundered up with a rifle and startled the man into flight. Glumly they plodded on.

The next day, August 12, they reached "the most distant fountain of the waters of the Mighty Missouri in search of which we have spent so many toilsome days and wristless nights.... one of those great objects on which my mind has been unalterably fixed for many years." To show his triumph over the once-overwhelming stream, Private McNeal exultantly put one foot on either bank. Lewis sipped the "pure and ice-cold water." They crossed the divide at what is now Lemhi Pass (west of Armistead, Montana) and descended "to a handsome bold runing Creek of cold Clear water." Here Lewis repeated his symbolic ceremony, tasting "the water of the great Columbia river." [2] Americans at last stood on the Pacific slope, on land whose title had not yet been allotted to any nation.

The following day, several miles down the Lemhi, they frightened off three more Indians, then overhauled an old crone and a girl of twelve or so. By signs and gifts of beads, pewter, looking glasses, and vermilion, Lewis convinced the trembling pair that he did not intend to slay them on the spot. Through them the whites reached a poverty-stricken, almost foodless village presided over by Chief Cameahwait. The pipe was passed, a dance performed. The amenities observed, Lewis the next day began, through Drouillard's sign language, the delicate job of persuading the highly skeptical Shoshones that it would be to their advantage to produce horses for these white strangers.

The Shoshones feared that the visitors were setting up an ambush by Blackfeet. Lewis impugned their courage with just the right amount of scorn. The braver ones began moving; but then the women wailed as though this were the end of everything and the trip degenerated into a face-saving crawl interrupted by fits of panic. Brief reassurance came when Drouillard killed two deer for the starving marchers; the savages fell on the carcasses like "famished dogs... blood running from the corners of their mouths," and worse. Then fear swelled again and Lewis had to

[2] He drank from the Lemhi. The Lemhi runs into the Salmon, the Salmon into the Snake, the Snake into the Columbia.

allay it by surrendering his rifle to Cameahwait, leaving himself defenseless. It was no help to reach the assigned meeting place with Clark and find that the expedition had not yet arrived. Suspicion flared again. Lewis tried to prove that all was well by saying again that a Shoshone woman was traveling with the whites. This information they shrugged off. But they were interested in his tales of a black man with short, kinky hair (the only hair they knew was long and straight) and of the merchandise Lewis promised in exchange for horses. But they wanted to see the goods before they would produce as many horses as the expedition needed.

The next day Clark's group arrived. A council assembled under a willow bower and Sacajawea was sent for to interpret. "In the person of Cameahwait she recognized her brother." They embraced and wept. Sacajawea "resumed her seat, and attempted to interpret for us, but her new situation seemed to overpower her, and she was frequently interrupted by her tears." She helped carry the point, however. After the main warriors had received some medals, a uniform coat, shirts, knives, awls, beads, and so on, plus a promise that American traders would soon bring guns for fighting the Blackfeet, the Shoshones agreed to return to their campgrounds and round up the necessary pack stock.

While Lewis and a group stayed behind to cache the canoes and some of the goods and make saddles out of rawhide thongs and boards, Clark went ahead with eleven men to explore the Salmon River, into which the Lemhi flowed. The Salmon coursed alluringly westward, but the Indians said it was unnavigable. They were right. After Clark's group had clambered for some distance among the boulders of the canyon bottom, they were willing to believe what the Indians told them: farther down "the Mountains close and is a perpendicular Clift on each side.... the water runs with great violence from one rock to the other on each side foaming & roreing ... so as to render the passage of anything impossible." The expedition must perforce rely on the thirty indifferent horses (for packing, not riding) that Lewis was prying with infinite patience out of the vacillating Indians.

In early September they led the pack train over "emence hils" from the Salmon watershed to the Bitterroot. An unseasonable snowstorm frightened them. "Several horses fell," Clark wrote.

"Some turned over, and others Sliped down Steep hill Sides, one horse Crippeled & 2 gave out. with the greatest dificuelty risque &c we made five miles & Encamped." The trail, he thought, was the worst "that ever horses passed." But he soon had occasion to revise the estimate.

In the lovely, north-trending Bitterroot Valley they heard from Flathead Indians of a trail that would have brought them over the Divide from the Missouri in four or five days, compared to the fifty-two days which their own strenuous, U-shaped route had required. To explorers searching for the best transcontinental route to the Oregon country, the information was exciting. But right then they had no time to check. Snow was shining on the peaks and they must reach the ocean before winter closed the land.

Just below their camp the Bitterroot flowed into a tempting stream which the party named Clark's Fork of the Columbia. But the Flatheads warned them not to embark on it. Clark's Fork was roundabout and interrupted by a dreadful waterfall, a statement corroborated by the absence of salmon in the stream. Accordingly the expedition purchased eighteen more horses from the Flatheads and turned up Lolo Creek along a trail nearly seven thousand feet high which Nez Percés Indians from farther west reputedly used in reaching buffalo country along the Missouri.

In "those tremendous mountains," William Clark later wrote his brother George, "we suffered everything which hunger cold and fatigue could impose." For food they had to use precious horses. Pack animals fell over cliffs. The men, already exhausted by their ordeal on the upper Missouri, began to collapse. In scattered groups the strongest tottered down to a Nez Percé village on the Clearwater River. The first to arrive sent back dried salmon and camas root to eat and horses for the weakest to ride.

Everyone became violently ill from the unaccustomed diet, but as soon as they could drag themselves around they began chopping down huge yellow pines and burning out the centers to form dugouts. They left their thirty-eight surviving horses with Nez Percés, who promised to care for the herd. On the morning of October 7, 1805, they launched their new craft down the Clearwater. The river, low and crystal-bright under the fall sun, bubbled merrily westward to the Snake; the powerful Snake bored strongly through deep, gray-brown canyons of lava toward the Columbia. Because the season was "far advanced and time precious with us," they ran rapids more recklessly, Clark admits, than they should have, but survived with only minor upsets. They lived on dried salmon until they hated it, bought dogs for stewing from the river Indians, and occasionally managed to shoot a few ducks.

On October 16 they saw the great blue glitter of the Columbia. They portaged goods around Celilo Falls, its edges hung with ramshackle stages from which the Indians fished, and lined their canoes through a channel the savages pointed out. At the Short Narrows, or Dalles, a little farther on, "this great river is compressed into a chanel ... not exceeding *forty five* yards wide ... swelling, boiling & whorling in every direction." Because the banks were not suitable for an easy portage, the tired men simply shot through the "agitated gut ... to the astonishment of all the Indians ... who viewed us from the top of the rock." The ferocious Cascades, where Bonneville Dam now stands, they circumvented by a portage of "940 yards of bad slippery and rockey way." Save for the penetrating mists and the thieving of the pestiferous, slope-headed, flea-ridden, water-adept Indians who bobbed in and out of nearly every camp, the worst was now over. On November 7 they heard the roar of the ocean. Clark, his notebook open on his damp knees, wrote impulsively "O! the joy."

After several miserable, rainswept days spent creeping around the north shore of the estuary, they crossed to the south side, where elk were plentiful. On tributary Lewis and Clark River they felled trees that split readily into "the streightest & most butifullest logs." Working in daily rain, they built seven cabins for dwellings and one for storage, facing each other across a street twenty feet wide. The outer walls of the cabins were joined by a heavy stockade, and the whole was named Fort Clatsop.

In these quarters, while the men hunted (they grew as tired of elk as they had of dried salmon) or went to the ocean to make salt or dallied with the singularly unattractive, venereal-tainted Chinook squaws, the captains repeated the routines of the previous winter. Lewis compiled scientific notes. Clark drew a master map from the running charts he had kept each day and from information gleaned by sign language from the Indians they had encountered. What is extraordinary about his intuitive geography —his map boldly embraced almost the entire West though he had threaded only a tiny part of it—is not that a few points turned out seriously wrong but that so much eventually proved correct.

As the chart took form, the captains grasped at a thin hope. The distance and labors of the circuitous route they followed through the Rockies precluded its ever being the commercial water route that President Jefferson desired. But a land portage directly across the mountains from Great Falls to the Clearwater might be an adequate substitute. Clark was sure it would. On February 14, 1806, the day on which "I compleated a *map* of the Countrey through which we have been passing," he declared flatly to his journal, "We now discover that we have found the most practicable and navigable passage across the Continent of North America."

Pack animals for the long land interval were no problem. Writing in his own journal the next day, Lewis described the Indian horses of the interior Northwest as:

> lofty eligantly formed active and durable . . . marked much like our best blooded horses in virginia which they resemble as well in fleetness and bottom . . . . An eligant horse may be purchased from the natives in this country for a few beads or other paltry trinkets which in the U' States would not cost more than one or two dollars. This abundance and cheapness of horses will be extremely advantageous to those who may hereafter attemt the fir trade to the East Indies by way of the Columbia river and the Pacific Ocean.

After the wet boredom of the rainy winter, the expedition was eager to start back up the Columbia on March 23. Two magnificent Indian canoes supplemented the battered pine dugouts they had built on the Clearwater. One of these new craft they obtained from the Chinooks in trade for Lewis' gaudy dress-uniform coat. The other they simply appropriated "in lue," said Lewis, "of the six Elk which they stole from us in the winter."

The upriver journey was wet and hungry. They left Fort Clatsop before the salmon run began (partly from restlessness and partly to reach the Nez Percés before those Indians wandered off hunting with the horses) and they had almost no trinkets left for purchasing dog meat. The Indians who helped them portage around the Cascades stole impudently, even trying to make off with Lewis' Newfoundland, Scammon. Farther upstream, the Narrows and Celilo Falls were such a tumult from spring floods that they decided to shift to horses. Obtaining them was a mortification. The whites were so poor by now that the Indians insulted them grossly —"tanterlized me," Clark wrote indignantly. But patient haggling finally brought enough bony animals with which to make a start. At the mouth of the Walla Walla they secured more. This enabled them to avoid the canyons of the lower Snake by riding up the Walla Walla and then cutting overland across the vast rolling swells of endless grass to the Clearwater.

The Nez Percés returned all but two of their horses in reasonably good condition. Now the whites were rich in animals—sixty head. After being turned back once by snow on the Lolo Trail, they finally made the crossing during the last week of June. In the north end of the Bitterroot Valley, near present-day Missoula, Montana, they split forces. Clark was to retrieve their caches on the Jefferson, then cut east over what is now Bozeman Pass to the Yellowstone River and explore the lower reaches of that stream. Lewis was to investigate the direct route over the mountains and then try to determine whether the Marias River really did extend far enough northward to be a route for tapping the fur trade of Canada.

Helped by one of Sacajawea's rare bits of guiding, Clark's group avoided the "emence hils" between the Bitterroot and the Salmon, reaching the Jefferson instead by a shorter, easier trail through the Big Hole Valley of western Montana. The men had been without tobacco since March and when they reached the caches "they became so impatient to be chewing it that they scarcely gave themselves time to take their saddles off their horses before they were off to the deposit." By horse and canoe, chewing happily, they then coasted downstream to Three Forks.

Here the party again divided. Sergeant Ordway led nine men in the canoes to Great Falls. Clark took eight, plus Charbonneau and his family, to the Yellowstone, reaching it near Livingston.

As soon as they found adequate timber, they built two dugouts, each twenty-eight feet long. The horses were entrusted to Sergeant Pryor and three men for delivery overland to the Mandan villages. Before the riders were well started, Crow Indians slipped into their camp at night and stole every animal. Chagrined but undismayed, the soldiers shot two buffalo, stretched the hides over frames of willow branches, waterproofed the seams with tallow, and bobbed precariously down the Yellowstone after their captain. They overtook him on August 8.

Lewis and his nine men meanwhile had crossed the Divide to Great Falls as easily as the Indians had said they could. On July 18, while the others worked to refurbish the hidden pirogue and the goods in the cache (partially damaged by water), Lewis turned overland through excessive heat toward the Marias, taking with him Drouillard and the Fields brothers, Joseph and Reuben.

Storms blew up. He could not take adequate shots of the sun to determine position, but he soon became unhappily sure that the stream did not extend "as far north as I wished and expected." As the quartet started back toward the Missouri they ran, on the twenty-sixth, head-on into eight Indians, some Gros Ventres of the Prairie and some of the Piegan tribe of Blackfeet. The groups approached each other gingerly. Each was afraid that the others were outriders of a larger party somewhere out of sight. But a council relaxed suspicion somewhat and they camped together.

Lewis took the night's first watch, then turned the duty over to Joseph Fields. Toward dawn, Joseph laid his rifle on the ground. A watchful Indian pounced on it. The others thereupon dove for the rest of the guns. In the ensuing scuffle, Reuben Fields stabbed one Indian to death. Unaware of the killing and trying to prevent bloodshed that would rouse the entire Blackfoot tribe to revenge, Lewis ordered his men to hold their fire. But when the retreating Indians tried to run off the whites' horses, Lewis himself snapped a shot through the darkness and killed one of them.

The six survivors fled wildly, leaving some of their own horses behind. Fearing a retaliatory attack not only on themselves but on others of their party traveling the Missouri, the whites rode hard to the mouth of the Marias. Pausing only once for rest, they covered the 120 miles in little more than twenty-four hours.

Near the mouth of the Marias they rejoined, with "unspeakable satisfaction," the rest of Lewis' party and the detachment Ordway had led down from Three Forks. Hastily they dug up the caches they had left in the vicinity the year before. Some of the goods, including furs belonging to the men, had been damaged; and the red pirogue which they had concealed on an island was too decayed to use. One small puzzle arose: "we . . . recovered every article except 3 traps belonging to Drewyer which could not be found." Lewis does not speculate on the disappearance. Yet where did the traps go? If they were pilfered, who but a white trapper would take those items and nothing else? The matter is possibly suggestive, as the text will later indicate.

In the white pirogue and five canoes the group paddled rapidly downsteam. A few days later Lewis nearly lost his life, not to aroused Blackfeet but to one of his own men. He and one-eyed Peter Cruzatte wounded an elk. They separated to search for it. While Lewis was rustling in his elkskin clothing through the willows, a gun banged and "a ball struck my left thye about one inch below my hip joint"; it sliced clear across "the hinder part of the right thye; the stroke was very severe." He yelled for Cruzatte. No answer. Fearing Indians, he staggered to the pirogue, classically determined "to sell my life as deerly as possible."

There were no Indians. Peter Cruzatte, seeing among the willow leaves what looked like an elk to his single eye, had shot his own captain in the rear and in terror over what he had done had not answered Lewis' hail. The accident turned out to be merely ignominious and painful, but it might easily have been the one fatal wounding of the entire trip.

On August 12, after encountering two trappers bound for the virgin grounds near the mountains, they overtook Clark's group. On August 14, the reunited expedition joyfully returned to the neighboring villages of the Minnetarees and Mandans. As a step in winning these Indians to the United States, they now endeavored to persuade several chiefs to go with them to Washington. But at a council called for this purpose chief after chief stood up and said no, he could not go. Their people were at war with the Sioux and those terrible scourges would massacre any

Mandans or Minnetarees who ventured into their lands. Clark held out "bountifull gifts" and promised full protection—to no avail, until at last René Jessaume, who was still in the villages, prevailed on She-he-ke or Big White, so called for his complexion. She-he-ke was not a principal chief. Furthermore, he (or perhaps Jessaume) imposed conditions. He "would go," Clark grumbled to his journal, only "if we would take his wife & son & Jessoms wife & 2 children [which] we wer obliged to do."

Accompanied by these not entirely welcome passengers, they swiftly coursed the 1600 miles of river still separating them from St. Louis. On September 23, 1806, the entire village turned out to welcome them. "I sleped but little last night," Clark confessed in his journal the next morning, but even so they were up early. A post bound for the East had been halted across the river at Cahokia so that they could send dispatches to the President. Only after the letters had been composed did the captains take time out to dine with Auguste Chouteau and then visit a store to purchase some of the clothing they so badly needed.

They were elated. They had strengthened their country's claim to Oregon; they had brought back the first definite knowledge of how huge and varied and rich that northwestern land was; they had begun—with far more success than their countrymen would finish it—the long and tragic process of dealing with the savage inhabitants of that country. And although they had not found a way to tap the fur trade of Canada, they did point out that a comparable commerce was available to Americans within their own borders. The headwaters of the Missouri, Lewis wrote Jefferson, were "richer in beaver and Otter than any country on earth."

This compact wealth, Lewis continued, together with British pelts from the country adjoining the Missouri, could be taken readily by horseback and bateau to a depot on the Columbia and from there shipped to Canton in less time than Canadian furs were sent via Montreal to London. Most Oriental goods, he conceded, would probably still be carried around the Horn or the Cape of Good Hope by sailing vessel; but articles not perishable, bulky, or "brittle" could be handled on the Columbia route. Sloops would move them 183 miles up the Columbia to the rapids; after a portage, smaller boats would carry the merchandise to the

Clearwater. Pack trains which had transported furs across the mountains could then return to the Missouri with the goods from China. To facilitate the exchange there would have to be posts first on the upper Missouri and later west of the Divide (where the United States' title was not yet clear, though Lewis did not mention the point). True, the commerce he outlined was not the sweeping trade Jefferson had hoped for. But it was no mean substitute, as John Jacob Astor would immediately realize.

To this outline Lewis added a pair of predictions. One concerned the British fur traders and was, if anything, too restrained. The other ventured a forecast about travel to Oregon and was dead wrong.

During the winter at the Mandan villages the captains had learned of the union of the North West and XY companies. On their return trip they had heard of Laroque's exploration toward the Yellowstone. On the basis of this evidence Lewis suggested to Jefferson that the British traders would try to "ingroce" the fur trade of the upper Missouri. The company's strides, he said, must be "vigilently watched" and "spedily opposed."

Actually the Nor'Westers were taking even longer strides than Lewis realized. Inspired in part by the American expedition, one company partner, Simon Fraser, had already gone from the Tacoutche-Tesse (after 1808 it would be called the Fraser River) up the Nechako into British Columbia, where he and his men built three posts. While Lewis was writing his letter to Jefferson, another North West Company partner, David Thompson, was preparing to cross the Divide well south of Fraser's Peace River route. The following spring (1807) Thompson succeeded because, he wrote, "the murder of two Peagan Indians by Captain Lewis of the United States drew the Peagans to the Missisouri to revenge their deaths; and thus gave me an opportunity to cross the Mountains by the defiles of the [North] Saskatchewan River, which led to the headwaters of the Columbia, and there we builded Log Houses." Thus within months after the American expedition reached St. Louis, the British were established on the Pacific slope in exactly the sort of post Lewis was recommending to his president.

His own toils considered, the captain's other prediction was much rosier than the first and far less justifiable. Carried away by an understandable exaltation over the expedition's successful return, Lewis declared without qualification that "in the course of 10 or 12 Years a tour across the Continent by this rout will be undertaken with as little concern as a voyage across the Atlantic is at present."

It was wishful thinking. A trail to Oregon by way of the upper Missouri simply would not work. During the next seventeen years a great deal of money and blood and incredible suffering would go into the learning of that truth and into the painful working out of a better way. As usual the job was done not by government but by private fur traders—or rather, because of a little-noted but revolutionary upheaval of the system, by their more glamorous successors, the mountain men.

7

THE FIRST MOUNTAIN MEN

August 12, 1806, was a day of significant meetings. Meriwether Lewis had been shot in the seat of the pants less than twenty-four hours earlier. In great pain after a sleepless night and eager to overtake Clark, he ordered his little fleet on to the Missouri at dawn. Toward 8 A.M., somewhere between the White Earth and Little Missouri rivers in western North Dakota, the bowsman spied two American trappers, Joseph Dixon and Forest Hancock, camped on the northeast bank of the stream. Lewis ordered his pirogues ashore.

The encounter is duly noticed in most summaries of the expedition. Less frequently is adequate attention given to the revolutionary change in fur-gathering which had brought Dixon and Hancock so far up the dangerous river.

Since the discovery of the New World, Indians had been the primary gatherers of pelts, particularly beaver. Hunting the amphibians during summer, the Indians set up log deadfalls baited with bark. If the beaver gnawed on the bait, the "saumier" was released and dropped onto the victim. Or dams might be cut to drain the ponds. As the beaver emerged from their mud-and-log houses to see what was wrong, they entered alleyways prepared of stakes driven into the mud. These channeled them to the waiting hunters. At other times dogs were used to smell out the weakest spot in the lodge and indicate it by scratching. The Indians then blocked the exit, broke through the lodge roof, and killed the inhabitants with spears.

Winter hunts, when fur was prime, were more difficult. Using heavy iron chisels fastened to long wooden handles—the Hudson's Bay Company imported enormous quantities of the instrument for trade—the Indians cut holes around the beaver lodges through ice that was often two feet thick. They dropped nets through these holes. With other iron tools obtainable only from white men, they then chipped an opening through the frozen mud of the lodge. As the frightened beaver fled, they became entangled in the nets and drowned or were pulled out and dispatched with a blow on the head. Those that escaped to burrows in the bank were tracked down by dogs.

To obtain the pelts so laboriously gathered, white traders set up at strategic spots log-cabin posts, often called forts since they were designed to resist attack. The more pretentious of these posts might consist of several small buildings surrounded by a stockade. Potato gardens and sometimes dairy cattle supplemented the routine wilderness diet of fish, game, waterfowl, tallow, pemmican, and the wild rice that grew lushly around the Great Lakes and the headwaters of the Mississippi.

In theory, the Indians brought skins from their hunting grounds to these posts and exchanged them for cloth of various kinds, kettles, tools, awls, guns, lead and powder, mirrors, and such decorative items as earbobs, beads, vermilion, and tiny hawk bells. Practice, however, led to destructive variations in the pattern. The Indians quickly became dependent on manufactured goods. To obtain what they needed for their livelihood, they bought from the trading posts on credit. They were supposed to repay the debt with pelts on their return from the beaver streams. Many hunters were reliable. Others were not. To secure the debts, the head trader sent runners, often half-breeds related to the tribe, out to the hunting camps to claim the furs, to forestall rivals, and to obtain, if possible, pelts that were rightfully pledged to a competitor.

The chief inducement used to draw Indians to the trading posts or to the runners' temporary camps was "high wine." This was nearly straight alcohol. It was easy to transport because of its concentration and could be heavily diluted before use. When a group of savages arrived to barter, the white traders opened proceedings with a round or two of "free" drinks that dimmed Indian caution. Sometimes the savages would part with every pelt they had for more and more watered alcohol. They whooped and vomited and fought. Occasionally they attacked the white men who had unleashed the debauch, especially after they had exhausted their credit and, penniless, were refused both liquor and necessities.

The governments of Canada and the United States tried to restrain the worst offenses. Before entering the Indian country traders had to obtain licenses and post bonds as guarantees of good behavior. The sale or gift of alcohol to Indians was prohibited. White men were not permitted (on paper) to buy land from the native tribes, to hunt on their grounds, or follow them to their hunting camps. In an effort to keep prices in line, the United States set up its own posts, called factories, in direct competition with private enterprise. For reasons beyond the scope of this work, the factories enjoyed only limited success and were abolished by Congress in 1822. The other restrictive regulations were blandly ignored; adequate enforcement was almost impossible in the wilderness. Canadian traders restrained themselves somewhat for the sake of the future; those from the United States rarely did.

This centuries-old trading system was radically altered west of the Mississippi by the invention of a simple mechanical device, the spring-powered iron trap. According to David Thompson, iron traps were first used in the Canadian West in 1797 by Nipissing, Algonquin, and Iroquois hunters. The first bait was green aspen

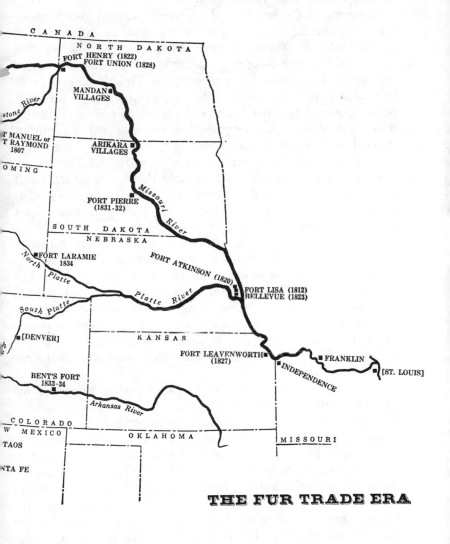

THE FUR TRADE ERA

twigs and produced indifferent results. But then, so an ancient Indian told Thompson, the Great Spirit Weesaukejauk revealed the magic of the craft—castoreum.

Castoreum is a secretion of the beaver's perineal glands and is voided, apparently, as a kind of calling card, analagous to dog custom with trees. The trapper mixed this "medicine," as he called castoreum, in secret proportions with various pungent substances such as oil of juniper and gum of camphor. To hide his own smell he waded upstream several yards, dipped a twig into his scent bottle, thrust it into the bank, and placed a trap in the water beneath it. When a beaver paused to see who had come by, it stepped onto the trap's release pan, preferably with a hind foot. Caught, it dove for deep water. The trap chain, held by a stick thrust through a ring in its end, brought the animal up short and it drowned. Sometimes, if the trap was poorly placed, the animal reached shallow water. In that case it generally gnawed off its paw and escaped.

Sadly the Indian who had told Thompson about the discovery of castoreum finished, "We are now killing the Beaver without any labor, we are now rich, but shall soon be poor, for when the Beaver are destroyed we have nothing to depend on to purchase what we want for our families, strangers now over run our country with their iron traps and we, and they will soon be poor." But at least in most of Canada, Indians remained the principal hunters. In the western United States they were superseded by whites.

The nomads of the plains were not so readily subverted by goods sold through fixed trading posts as the Indians of the eastern forests and rivers had been. Except for the earthen towns of the Arikaras, Mandans, and Minnetarees, there were few stationary villages a trader could visit. Save for guns and ammunition, the Indians could obtain from the endless buffalo herds nearly everything they valued—clothing, lodge coverings, boats, sinew, utensils, ceremonial objects, and what not. They took to drink slowly. Furthermore, according to Pierre-Antoine Tabeau, who was on the Missouri when Lewis and Clark ascended it, a Sioux could obtain from the traders as much for a buffalo robe as for a beaver pelt. So why hunt beaver? Digging into burrows along the river bank (the Missouri beaver did not build lodges) or wading in cold water with heavy iron traps was a drudgery fit only for squaws. Hunting buffalo on horseback was exciting—a warrior's calling. Let white men demean themselves if they wished. Indians wouldn't.

In time perhaps they could have been lured to the calling, as the Canadians lured many of the northern tribes. But the fur merchants in St. Louis were too impatient. As soon as traps became available, Regis Loisel, for one, equipped during the winter of 1803-4 ten of his men working out of Isle of Cedars in central South Dakota with fifty of the newfangled implements. In the spring of 1805, three of these trappers accompanied Lewis and Clark as far into North Dakota as the mouth of the Little Missouri. The expedition's personnel also had brought traps with them, private property for fleshing out their Army pay of five dollars a month. But so far as our records go, and that most certainly is not far enough, the first men who tried to take the invention into the wilderness, unsupported by a major company or by the government, were the pair Lewis met on August 12, 1806—Joseph Dixon and Forest Hancock.

The two trappers had left Illinois in the summer of 1804. Probably the factor that set them in motion was the Louisiana Purchase, which freed the river of interference from Spanish authorities. Their luck was next to incredible. Indians farther downstream had turned back larger, better-equipped parties. They had robbed this pair also and had shot Dixon in the leg during a scuffle. In meager compensation for their toil the pair had caught only a few beaver and were woefully short of supplies. Nevertheless they were still headed upstream, hopeful that a fortune was waiting just around the bend.

Lewis "gave them a short description of the Missouri ... and pointed out to them the places were the beaver most abounded. I also gave them a file and a couple of pounds of powder and some lead. these were articles which they assured me they were in great want of." And that might have been the last mention of the matter, had not two privates of the expedition, John Collins and John Colter, just then come paddling downstream in a dugout.

Colter and Collins had been lost for two weeks. Shortly after returning to the Missouri from his encounter with Blackfeet near the Marias, Lewis had sent the pair ahead of his party to hunt. While their canoe had been beached in a willow clump, the group they were to supply had overshot them. They were just now catching up.

Presumably Colter too exchanged words with Dixon and Hancock. Then Lewis ordered his party on. That evening, with a burst of yelling, they overhauled Clark's group, and the reunited expedition traveled together to the villages of the Minnetarees and Mandans. While they were halted there, persuading She-he-ke to go with them to Washington to meet the Great Father, Dixon and Hancock reappeared.

The trappers had refined their plans. If beaver were as numerous as Lewis had told them, should they not stock up enough supplies for an extended stay in the mountains? And would it not be wise to strengthen themselves with a man who knew something of the fabulous country at the head of the river?

The hunter they fastened onto was John Colter. He was from Virginia originally but had signed with Lewis at Maysville, Kentucky. Thomas James, who trapped with Colter three years later, described him as then being a little more than thirty years of age, a little less than six feet in height, of unquestioned integrity, and formed by nature "for the hardy indurance of fatigue, privation, and perils." During the transcontinental expedition's first winter on the Illinois shore, opposite the mouth of the Missouri, he had been disciplined for hunting too frequently in the vicinity of a convenient grog shop. After that he had settled down and became, through his ingenuity, willingness, and phenomenal marksmanship, one of the stalwarts of the crossing and one of the few enlisted personnel singled out by Thomas Jefferson for special praise.

Although Colter had been two and a half years away from the allurements of St. Louis, he decided to return with Dixon and Hancock to the beaver grounds. His commanders agreed to give him an honorable discharge provided that no other member of the expedition ask a similar favor. The men not only consented but pooled their scanty resources to outfit the three adventurers with knives, powder horns, hatchets, powder, lead, and other articles for a two-year hunt. They also added enough heavy traps that the trio started upriver with twenty of the irreplacable mechanisms. Colter may have paid for the equipment out of wages accrued to him at five dollars a month or with beaver skins he had collected during the expedition's journey.

This trio were the precursors of the fabled mountain men of our folklore. (Colter, indeed, would soon create a large share of that lore.) They were also outlaws. The government trading licenses, which every white fur-gatherer was supposed to obtain before venturing onto Indian lands, gave permission to barter only. The privilege did not include the right to hunt or trap, pursuits prohibited by an act of 1802.

Colter, Dixon, and Hancock may not have known of the interdict. If they possessed a trading license (the men from Illinois may have obtained one before starting upriver, or Lewis and Clark may have presumed to issue them one, though no record says so), they perhaps supposed it covered all their activities. Or, more likely, since they did not intend to trade at all, lacking the necessary goods, they may have thought they needed no license whatsoever. Certainly the mountain men who roamed the Rocky Mountains unrestrained two and three decades later assumed that trapping was their inalienable right and were indignant when told otherwise.

They may not have known: but Lewis and Clark did. Only two years earlier the captains had instructed the British traders among the Mandans about United States laws governing the fur business. Shortly after returning to civilization Meriwether Lewis would state in an "Essay Concerning Indian Policy" that white hunting on Indian lands annoyed the natives and would recommend that it be restrained—with one exception. The Indians above the Mandan villages, he said, did not know how to trap and hence did not appreciate the value of furs. White trappers were needed to help them learn—"a very necessary link in the chain which is to unite these nations and ourselves in a state of commercial intercourse," is the way Lewis put the matter.

Until that happy state of sophistication arrived, he suggested, new treaties entered into with the mountain Indians should concede hunting privileges to the fur merchants.

No such privileges were on the books, however, when Lewis and Clark permitted their men to trap during the transcontinental trip. They were not officially allowed when Colter and his two partners went back up the river. They had not been made legal two and a half years later when William Clark and Lewis' brother Reuben joined the St. Louis Missouri Fur Company, whose purpose, in Meriwether's own words to Secretary of War Eustis (in a letter dated July 15, 1809), was "... to hunt and trade." They never were made legal throughout the entire era when the West was being opened by the fur brigades.

During that long period many individuals, both red and white, protested the trespasses. But there is no indication that anyone who really wanted to trap was ever dissuaded by the objections or by the laws, or that anyone was ever given more than token punishment for violation. Winking at inconvenient statutes is an old American custom.

Born illegally, the mountain man held himself apart from nearly every other civilized standard as well. Reverting easily to semi-savagery, he mastered the wilderness even more skillfully than the Indians did. His defiance of standards—freedom, in one sense of the word—has led to his being almost as overglamorized in our escape yarns as has been the cowboy with his "law" of the six-gun. Actually, like the cowboy, the mountain man was, economically speaking, the manipulator of a very limited organism, the iron spring trap in place of the longhorn steer. Still, after the slurs are in and noted, the fact remains that the fur trapper was largely instrumental in determining the history of the early American West, including unraveling the best way and means of reaching Oregon. In the face of that reality it is perhaps gratuitous to keep insisting, as this account will, that legally speaking he should not have been there at all.

No one knows for sure where Colter and his companions went. Lewis had recommended the Three Forks of the Missouri, which could be reached most directly by avoiding the Great Falls and going instead up the Yellowstone and over Bozeman Pass, reversing the route Clark had just followed. Anyway, the slaying of the two Blackfeet near the Marias had created a danger of reprisal along the circuitous Missouri. Colter's latest biographer, Burton Harris, believes accordingly that the trio went up the Yellowstone and wintered on Clark's Fork of that stream, north of present Cody, near the boundary between Wyoming and Montana. This guess, based on rather circumstantial evidence, is of course impossible to refute. And yet, in speculating on the trappers' whereabouts that winter, one inevitably wonders also about the most tantalizing mystery of the early Rockies, the affair of Zachary Perch and, or, Jeremy Pinch.

In the summer of 1807, David Thompson of the North West Company finally made his long-delayed crossing of the Continental Divide in Canada. First he sent off up the North Saskatchewan five men under Finan McDonald, a giant Scot, six feet four inches tall with wild red hair and an unkempt red beard. On May 10 Thompson followed with ten packhorses, his half-breed wife (whom he had married in 1799 when she was fourteen), and three small children aged six, two, and one. A road of sorts had been prepared the summer before by half-breed Jacques Finlay —a poor job, "no where cleared any more than just to permit Jaco and his family, to squeeze thro' it with their light baggage and it is the opinion of every Man with me as well as mine that Jaco Finlay ought to lose at least half of his wages for having so much neglected the Duty for which he was so expressly engaged at 150 pounds pr. year, besides a Piece of Tobacco & Sugar, & a Clerk's Equipment."

The wretched trail led to Howse Pass, "stupendous a solitary Wilds covered with eternal snow, a Mountain connected to a Mountain by immense Glaciers, the collection of Ages." Foaming Blaeberry Creek led them down the other side to what was the Columbia River, though at first Thompson did not recognize it as such. This stream surged north; he knew that the Columbia entered the ocean well south of where he was. Without suspecting the elbow bend which the stream makes around the Selkirk Mountains of eastern British Columbia, he built a canoe and turned upcurrent toward the lovely lakes near the river's head, reaching them in mid-July.

As his handful of men hewed timbers for a trading house, a band of Kutenai Indians rode in to greet them. The savages had known since the previous summer that a trader from the North West Company was coming to them, bringing guns that would let them slip eastward across the mountains to hunt buffalo and fight off, on equal terms, raids by their inveterate enemies, the Indians of the plains. No doubt they had spread the exciting word among the tribes of western Montana and northern Idaho. This (or the gossip of British traders in the Mandan villages far to the east) may be the means whereby knowledge of Thompson's doings reached a party of Americans—forty-two of them, the Kutenais said, repeating hearsay picked up from other tribes. These Americans, the Indians went on, had crossed the mountains three weeks earlier and intended to build a military post, as Thompson interpreted the tales, at the junction of the two "most southern & considerable Branches of the Columbia." They already had lured the Flathead Indians southward to trade with them.

Giving body to this news was a letter which had been passed on to the Kutenais by a "more southerly Tribe." It contained a rough summary of United States regulations concerning the Indian trade. Its concluding paragraph belligerently asserted America's claim to "the Columbia River with all its branches" and declared that Great Britain had no right to any of the area's commerce.

This extraordinary document, appearing out of nowhere, was addressed to "the Foreigners who may at present be carrying on a Traffic with the Indians within our Territories." It was dated July 10, 1807, at "Fort Lewis, Yellow River, Columbia." It was signed by "James Roseman Lieutenant" and what appeared to be "Zachary Perch Captain & Commanding Officer."

Thompson did not deign to answer. The Kutenais wandered off and evidently reported what they had seen to the writers of the letter. Back came another curt note, this one addressed to the "British Merch. Trafficking with the Cabanaws" (Lewis and Clark had called the Kutenai tribe the Cattanahaws). The writer complained of Thompson's disrespect in not answering the first letter and ordered him to leave the Columbia watershed "with a good grace" before American military patrols threw him out. This letter, which Thompson received in December, was dated September 29 from Poltito Palton Lake. It was signed by "Jeremy Pinch Lieut." The signature Zachary Perch of the first letter had been smudged and perhaps should have read Jeremy Pinch. Or perhaps the writer of the second letter did not recall accurately the name and rank he had invented for the first missive.

Someone was trying to bluff Thompson out of the country. The American government never built a Fort Lewis anywhere on the Missouri, Yellowstone, or Columbia rivers. The only military expedition it dispatched into that area at that period was Lewis and Clark's. A search by scholars through Army records has revealed no officers of the time named Zachary Perch, Jeremy Pinch, or James Roseman.

Yet someone who was close enough to Thompson to know about his activities did write the letters. Who? And from where?

It is incredible that forty-two American trappers could have gone into the area without leaving some mark in written records. But a handful might have—for example, Dixon, Hancock, John Colter, and the suppositious persons who perhaps lifted Drouillard's three traps from the cache near the Marias (see page 116).

Other conjectures point toward Colter's association with the letters. For example, the names Poltito Palton Lake and Yellow River, Columbia. The Palouse Indians, relatives of the Nez Percés, were called by Lewis and Clark the Pelloat Pallahs and, again, the Pallotepallers. This tribe occupied parts of what is now southeastern Washington and contiguous sections of Idaho. Thompson suggests they may have ranged even farther south; his map of the West, now in the British Museum, calls the Salmon River of central Idaho the Pallahtopallah.

As for Yellow River, Columbia, the usual explanation is the Yellowstone. This ignores both "Columbia" and the fact that by 1807 Yellowstone was a familiar enough name that the writer would hardly have dropped the final syllable. An alternative suggestion is available. Just south of the Palouse nation (the Pallotepallers) lived the Cayuses, main branch of a tribe which Lewis and Clark called Yelletpo. The Yelletpo's main river (into which the Palouse River of Washington flows) is today's Walla Walla. The Walla Walla, which members of the expedition might well recall as the Yelletpo, does flow into the Columbia, which accounts for that part of the address.

The phonetic similarity of these Indian names to the addresses given in the Perch-Pinch letters does not mean that the writer had actually moved very far down the Columbia. He may even have been east of the Rockies. But if, for the sake of his bluff, he was pretending to be on the Columbia, he would want to use names with an authentic Columbia flavor. Where did he pick them up? From Indians? Or from the only white man in the region who could possibly have heard them—John Colter, a member of the Lewis and Clark expedition, who would have only his memory of sounds to help him when it came to transcribing the Indian words to paper? [1]

Thompson did not bluff. He wrote back to Jeremy Pinch for delivery by the Indians a note saying that he would refer the American's letter to the directors of the North West Company. "If prior discovery forms any right to a country," he said, "Lieutenant Broughton of the British Navy many years ago explored the Columbia for 120 miles." Calmly then he pushed his company's posts deeper into what eventually became territory of the United States.

No more was heard from Perch-Pinch. The mystery probably has no ready solution. It is important mainly as indicating that the new race of mountain men, born overnight of the iron trap,

[1] The speculation is subject to problems in timing. The letter from Yellow River was dated July 10, 1807. On that day Colter was on the Missouri, near the mouth of the Platte. There he met a party of traders with whom he returned to the Yellowstone, arriving late in October, whereas the letter reputedly from Poltitio Palton Lake was dated September 29. All this seems to preclude Colter as the writer of the letters. But someone was still in the mountains. The evidence that Manuel Lisa in 1807 hired Hancock and perhaps Dixon on the upper river is too sketchy to be conclusive. And what of the persons who perhaps stole Drouillard's traps? If those men met Colter, they might have been implementing their bluff on Thompson by using names which Colter alone could have repeated to them. The conjecture strains credulity, but the whole episode is fantastic.

had quickly reached the Rockies in greater numbers than our written records indicate.

Why Colter separated from Dixon and Hancock in the spring of 1807 is not known. Cabin fever engendered by the piling snow and below-zero cold of the mountains may be the reason. They may have found trapping less rewarding than they had hoped; Colter descended the Missouri with very few pelts, but he may have sold the bulk of his take to British traders at the Mandan villages. All we really know is that suddenly he appeared, alone in a small dugout canoe, at the mouth of the Platte River. There he met two keelboats (possibly only one; accounts vary) commanded by an old hand on the lower Missouri, a Spaniard named Manuel Lisa.

Lisa had been born in New Orleans in 1772. He started trading on the Wabash River. Toward the end of the century he shifted to St. Louis and the Missouri. He challenged, without success, the old Missouri Company headed by Jacques Clamorgan. With better luck he wrested from the powerful Chouteaus a monopoly they had hitherto enjoyed among the Osage tribe of western Missouri.

He was not universally loved. St. Louis court records show that he was continually embroiled in lawsuits. Meriwether Lewis once described him as a puppy. Thomas James, soon to be associated with him on the upper river, recalled venomously that "Rascality sat on every feature of his dark-complexioned, Mexican face— gleamed from his black, Spanish eyes and seemed enthroned in a forehead villainously low." His men so hated him, James avers, that one of them swore to kill him if he ever caught the Spaniard straying alone from camp. Nevertheless, during the next decade Manuel Lisa was the single towering figure on the Missouri River.

The Louisiana Purchase upset the old trading monopolies and opened the upper river to exploitation. Lisa, moreover, was aware of the revolution which traps were bringing to the acquisition of beaver pelts. Pierre-Antoine Tabeau, a trader among the Arikaras, had already recognized the impossibility of depending on plains Indians for hunting. Such pelts as the tribes did produce, Tabeau suggested, could be garnered at a post among the Mandans and another on the Yellowstone. But the main reliance above the Mandans should be on white hunters working the various tributaries by means of packhorses. To avoid being pillaged by the savages, Tabeau added, the whites should work for peace among the tribes and meanwhile travel in strong parties.

The expedition Lisa prepared during the winter of 1806-7 followed Tabeau's views so closely that one must suppose that the Spaniard was familiar with them. He raised $16,000 for his strong party by forming a partnership with William Morrison and Pierre Menard of Kaskaskia, Illinois. Another Spaniard, Benito Vasquez, was second-in-command. Thirty-seven of the forty hired hands were French-Canadians. The other three were Americans who had been with Lewis and Clark—John Potts, Peter Wiser, and George Drouillard, the last of whom represented by proxy the interests of Morrison and Menard, who that year stayed at home.

The group started up the river in April. In May one Canadian deserted. Lisa ordered Drouillard to bring the man back dead or alive. Taking the orders literally, Drouillard wounded the fellow so severely that he died while being transported to the nearest settlement for treatment. (On their return to St. Louis more than a year later, Lisa and Drouillard were tried for murder and acquitted.) The dead man's place was taken by a twenty-year-old youth who soon became notorious in the literature of the West, Edward Rose, of mixed white, Indian, and Negro blood. Rose had already engaged in enough brawls as a boatman on the Mississippi (a pirate, Washington Irving says) that the end of his nose was missing to someone's teeth and his forehead was lividly scarred.

In July the little flotilla paused near the Platte, where the last hardwood grew, and cut extra masts for the keelboats from ash trees. There they persuaded Colter to return to the mountains with them and labored slowly on, the monotony broken by one Jean-Baptiste Bouché, who was flogged for various derelictions and who tried to wreck the boats in revenge.

They found the Arikaras in a dangerous mood. A chief who

had been persuaded by Lewis and Clark to visit Washington had died on the way home. The Indians suspected the whites of murdering him—and at the same time wished to keep the river trade within their own grasp. As Lisa's boats drew near, two or three hundred warriors swarmed to the bank and ordered him ashore. Those with guns emphasized the directions by firing across the bows.

Two stories are told about what happened next. Lisa's friends said he calmed the Arikaras by resolutely loading and aiming the little swivel cannon on the keelboats. His enemies declared that he bought his way free by treachery. He gave the Indians goods, including guns and ammunition, and told them that another group rich in booty and bearing one of their ancient foes, a Mandan chief, was toiling along behind him. With guns they could pick off the party easily.

This second group consisted of two boats. One held thirty-two men under Auguste Pierre Chouteau, who intended to trade. The other boat was manned by several soldiers under Nathaniel Pryor, who had been a sergeant with Lewis and Clark and was now an ensign in the regular Army. Pryor was responsible for returning to their villages, first, several Sioux chieftains who had been in Washington and next the Mandan She-he-ke, interpreter René Jessaume, and their wives and children.

Earlier in the spring, Chouteau and Pryor had hoped to join forces with Lisa for mutual protection. But waiting for them (Lisa had promised Acting Governor Frederick Bates he would do so) would have let a rival trader reach the upper river at the same time he did. Besides, Lisa had a long way to go to the Yellowstone before winter and felt he could not afford delays. Off he had rowed, in violation of his own word.

In spite of this defection, Pryor delivered the Sioux to their unpredictable people without incident. At the Arikara villages matters at first seemed equally peaceful. But a Mandan squaw, prisoner of the Arikaras, whispered to Pryor that the villagers were planning a sneak attack. He sent his interpreters, Pierre Dorion and René Jessaume, to arrange a council if possible and meanwhile readied the keelboat holding She-he-ke and the women for defense. Fighting erupted before the council could assemble.

The Arikaras dived into a clump of willows and began shooting. The whites sprayed the flimsy cover with rifle fire and with scatter shot from their swivels, at the same trying frantically to cast off from the exposed river bank. Chouteau's boat grounded on a sandbar. His men leaped overboard to drag it free as bullets churned the water around them.

After a running fight with Indians who followed howling along the bank, the boats escaped. White casualties came to four dead and ten wounded, including Jessaume, shot through one thigh and shoulder. Indian casualties must have been higher; willow brush does not furnish effective protection against bullets. The men were furious at Lisa, whom rightly or wrongly they blamed for the attack. And the Arikaras were furious at all Americans, a developing hostility that in time would drive mountain-bound trappers completely from the river.

While Pryor and Chouteau limped back to St. Louis, American prestige drooping at half mast, Lisa continued upstream. He passed the Mandans by using a mixture of gifts and defiance, and terrified a truculent encampment of Assiniboins by firing his swivels over their heads. He turned through the frosty fall days up the Yellowstone's swift current, his men gasping at the towropes, and late in October reached the mouth of the Big Horn. There, racing winter, the men built a log post named Fort Raymond after Lisa's young son. More generally, however, it was referred to as Manuel's Fort.

Somehow Lisa secured a few horses. These were packed with samples of merchandise and sent south under young Edward Rose to lure Crow Indians to the post for trade. Colter, carrying his supplies on his back, was sent afoot toward the Rockies to look for beaver streams and talk to whatever Indians he met. His biographers generally assume he went without white companions. If so, it was a staggering achievement.

During the trip, made in the worst of the winter months of 1807–8, Colter covered about five hundred mountain miles. His general route has long been known; refinements were added in 1952 by Burton Harris from a close study of manuscript maps drawn by William Clark in St. Louis after talks with Colter and George Drouillard of the Lisa expedition. As Harris points out, we cannot be certain whether Colter traveled his ragged loop in a clockwise or counterclockwise direction. The assumption is that he went clockwise; that is, south, then west and north before returning to Fort Raymond. Either way, the circle embraced the Absaroka range and parts of Grand Teton and Yellowstone national parks.

He walked up Pryor's Fork to the Pryor Mountains and through them to Clark's Fork of the Yellowstone and the upper Big Horn Basin, where he probably met Indians, for it was a favorite wintering ground. He passed the site of Cody; and in the canyon of the North Fork of the Stinking Water River (since prettied to *Shoshone*) he skirted the travertine deposits, rumbling hot springs, erupting geysers, and sulphurous gas vents that trappers later called Colter's Hell—not Yellowstone Park, as park tourists are frequently told. Still keeping southward, he found a pass through the Owl Creek Mountains to the headwaters of Wind River. From there Two-gwo-tee Pass opened a way across the Continental Divide to Jackson Hole, backed by the stupendous lift of the Teton Peaks.

From today's viewpoint, Colter's next move is strange. By the time he reached Jackson Hole he must have been short of supplies. He had explored as far from Lisa's Fort Raymond as Indians were likely to venture for trade. Teton Pass, which pierced the southern reaches of a huge range ahead of him, must have been clogged at that time of year (probably January) with tremendous snowdrifts. Nevertheless he pressed ahead, undoubtedly on homemade snowshoes. Perhaps, as Harris suggests, he had heard from Indians about the Spanish settlements in New Mexico and was looking for a river (the Green) which might lead toward their villages. If so, he missed it and found instead a branch of the Snake. Or (for the sake of another conjecture) perhaps he was looking for the trappers he may have met with Dixon and Hancock, the ones who had written the bogus Perch-Pinch letters to Thompson and whom Colter may have supposed to be, as Thompson had reported Indian rumor, on one of the "most southern & considerable Branches of the Columbia"—which is exactly what the Snake River is.

On the western slope of Teton Pass, just inside the Idaho border, he found a chunk of rock that vaguely resembled a human head. While waiting out a blizzard or while hiding from Indians, he chipped this block into a more recognizable profile. On one side he scratched "John Colter," on the other side "1808." A farmer plowed up the relic in 1931 and swapped it for a pair of second-hand boots to a man who presented it to the museum in Grand Teton National Park. It is generally considered authentic.

Whatever Colter was looking for west of Teton Pass he did not find. Turning back, he next worked his way northward through Yellowstone Park, traveling perhaps with Indians—it seems impossible he could have threaded those mountains alone. He crossed Cooke's Pass to Clark's Fork of the Yellowstone and for some reason worked back into the Big Horn Basin before returning to Fort Raymond in the spring of 1808. He may have seen signs of George Drouillard in the Big Horn area. The hunter was also exploring the region that spring.

At about this time Edward Rose returned empty-handed from the Crows, who had inveigled his goods from him without anything tangible in exchange. This caused a violent altercation with Lisa. At the end of it Rose tried to blow his boss and the keelboat out of the water with a swivel gun. The first shot did only small damage. Bystanders prevented a second, the keelboat went its way to St. Louis, and Rose returned to the Crows to live as an Indian. Meanwhile, three other men, who may have started into the Big Horn area with Drouillard, continued southwest over the Continental Divide to the Spanish, or Green, River, which Colter had missed. Save for Colter, they are the first privately supported Americans who are known to have reached Pacific drainage. Their names are not recorded.[2]

A richer area than any of these lay around Three Forks. As soon as spring allowed the setting of traps Lisa's men pressed toward the region. Colter, needing no rest from his winter trip, went with

[2] Deduced from a letter (used by courtesy of the Missouri Historical Society) written in French by Lisa's partner, Pierre Menard, to one Langlois on October 7, 1809, from the Mandan villages. The letter summarizes, in rather ambiguous fashion, the events of the preceding year. I may be wrong in my reading of the times as they relate to one another, and the crossing of the three unnamed trappers to the Green may have occurred in 1809. In any event, they were the first Americans to see that important stream.

them. On the Gallatin, the easternmost of the forks, he ventured out of camp alone, either trapping independently or as an emissary looking for friendly Indians. Or perhaps a few companions which our folklore has forgotten were with him. At any event, according to Thomas James, he fell in with eight hundred Crow and Flathead Indians.

Fifteen hundred Blackfeet attacked them. Though wounded in the leg, Colter helped beat off the aggressors. For an Indian fight, the slaughter was fearful. James, who saw the battlefield two years later, reports that "skulls and bones were lying around on the ground in vast numbers." The Blackfeet saw at least one white man (possibly more) contributing to the havoc. It did nothing to allay the hostility which Meriwether Lewis' party had initiated near the Marias.

In the fall (1808) the whites were back at Three Forks—or perhaps they had camped there all summer. By October, writes Lisa's partner Pierre Menard, they had made twenty packs of beaver—about one ton of choice fur. In the manner of trappers, they risked the streams in small parties, and it was perhaps during this hunt that Colter had his legendary race with death.

He and John Potts were trapping the westernmost fork, the Jefferson, in small canoes. To avoid Indians they hid by day and worked at dusk and dawn. In spite of the caution Blackfeet surprised them. Details vary with the account one reads. This much seems definite: Potts was shot and mutilated, but killed one attacker before dying. After confiscating the trappers' furs (the pelts later were bartered to Alexander Henry the Younger in Canada), the Indians stripped Colter for torture. They started the ceremony by ordering him to run for his freedom naked through brush and over rocky, cactus-strewn ground. He was sturdier than they anticipated. He started like an antelope over a high ridge toward the central fork, the Madison. Straining his heart until blood gushed from his nostrils, he outdistanced every pursuer but one. He turned abruptly on this one and killed the Indian with the savage's own spear. Gaining the Madison, he dived under a log jam, found an airhole, and lay in the icy water while enraged Blackfeet clambered above his head looking for him. In the numbing cold of night he emerged. Either the other trappers had left the country or he dared not try to reach them. He wormed up a sheer cliff and headed for Fort Raymond, more than two hundred miles away. Cactus lacerated his bare feet. Insects and sun ravaged his naked skin. For food he had only roots and bark. But in seven days by one account, eleven by another, he reached the Big Horn.

Far behind him at the Three Forks the frustrated Blackfeet were feeling still more vengeful toward all whites.

The whites persisted. In the spring of 1809, Menard reports, they went again to Three Forks, where Blackfeet robbed them not only of their furs but also of their horses, traps, and firearms. Undeterred still, some of them went on over the Divide to the Flatheads on the Columbia watershed, and Menard hopefully expected them to make at least fifty packs. Others of the attacked group went southward to the Green. Still more went into the Big Horn Basin to trade with the Crows. By summer's end, the main outlines of the Northern Rockies were pretty well known.

During these eventful months Lisa had been busy in St. Louis. He had arrived there during August 1808, seeking capital to expand his company, and had found competitors preparing to follow him to the mountains. After what must have been uneasy maneuvering, the antagonistic merchants banded into a single corporation called the St. Louis Missouri Fur Company. Menard, Morrison, and Lisa continued as partners. Among their new associates were such figures as William Clark; Pierre Chouteau, Senior; Reuben Lewis, the brother of Meriwether; and a tall, wiry pioneer of the lead-mining district, Andrew Henry.

With the St. Louis Missouri Fur Company, Meriwether Lewis, now governor of Upper Louisiana (Missouri) Territory, executed on behalf of the United States an extraordinary contract for returning to the Mandan villages Chief She-he-ke, René Jessaume, and their families. In exchange for $7000, the fur company agreed to enlist a semi-military escort of 125 hands, forty of them to be "Americans and expert riflemen." Pierre Chouteau, Senior, was to command the group, with Reuben Lewis as adjutant.

It was the government's intent, Lewis wrote Chouteau, that "the aricare nation should be severely Punished for their unprovoked attack" on Nathaniel Pryor two years before. The Indians were to be forcibly taught that they were not to interfere in any way with navigation on the Missouri. Two hundred and fifty traders had promised to help administer the lesson; they would rendezvous with Chouteau at the mouth of the Cheyenne River. In addition, Chouteau was empowered to employ up to 300 friendly Indians as auxiliaries, promising them plunder in case of war or gifts of horses furnished by the repentant Arikaras in case those Indians capitulated without a fight. Altogether, said Lewis, this was "a force sufficient Not Onely to bid defiance to the Aricares, but to exterpate that abandoned nation if necessary."

The Arikaras could escape the blow either by surrendering those tribesmen who had actually killed whites during the attack on Pryor; or, if the killers were unavailable, by producing an equivalent number of other Indians who had been active in fomenting the trouble. "These murderers when delivered will be shot in the presence of the nation."

For various reasons mostly outside the scope of this work, Secretary of War William Eustis frowned on the contract. Pierre Chouteau, he said, was agent to the Osage Indians and should not have vacated the post to take command of the detachment. Lewis should not have authorized, in addition to the $7000 fee, another $500 to Chouteau for buying presents to win over Indian auxiliaries. And so on—but nothing about the Nazilike terms offered the Arikaras.

As events turned out, the contract may have helped kill Meriwether Lewis. He had made enemies in the turbid whirlpools of Missouri politics. Land speculations had put him heavily into debt. When the government declined to honor the $500 draft to Chouteau and Lewis could not make it good himself, his creditors swarmed out while his enemies watched in glee. During the summer he was totally stripped. Ill, worried, and melancholy, he started to Washington to straighten out his troubles. Part of the way he traveled over the Natchez Trace. At a grubby tavern he died violently, the victim of suicide—or of murder.[3]

The military expedition escorting She-he-ke left St. Louis early

[3] For a summary of the conflicting theories, see Jonathan Daniels, *The Devil's Backbone, The Story of the Natchez Trace*, American Trail Series (McGraw-Hill, 1962), pp. 165–84.

in June. The Sioux it met proved uncooperative. They said they had been promised cheap trade goods by the Americans and had not received them. They certainly were not going to help such a people make war on fellow Indians.

Unable to enlist them as warriors, Chouteau changed tactics and took six of their chiefs along as peacemakers. Later he picked up several Mandan dignitaries who had come down the river to meet She-he-ke. If white traders actually gathered at the mouth of the Cheyenne River to help cow the Arikaras, as Lewis had promised, Chouteau did not mention it. But even without reinforcements his detachment looked imposing enough that the Arikaras evacuated their villages of women and children and could be enticed into a council only with difficulty. There Chouteau told them grandly:

> I have orders to destroy your nation, but the chiefs of the sioux and mandan nations have United together and interceded for your pardon—at their particular request, I shall ground my arms untill new orders can be received from your Great father who alone can pardon or destroy.

For the moment the threat sufficed. She-he-ke was allowed to pass on up the river and regain his home, where his neighbors considered his tales about white civilization absurd lies. His mission accomplished, Chouteau returned to St. Louis.

The trading section of the expedition, commanded by Lisa, Menard, and Andrew Henry, left St. Louis a few days after the military. It was an imposing flotilla—thirteen keelboats and barges and canoes, and 172 men. A June departure was late for trappers hoping to reach the Yellowstone before winter. They pushed hard, pausing only to leave traders with the Sioux and Arikaras; they reached the Mandan villages in 97 days, compared to the 101 required by Chouteau.

In spite of the good time, it was an unhappy trip. Thirty-one *engagés* deserted; nine were discharged for disability or incompetence. Both Menard and Thomas James charged that the workers were ill-treated. James laid the blame on Lisa, who (he says) lolled and drank at his ease on the keelboat and declined to pass out sufficient boiled corn for rations. But Lisa left the party at the villages to return to St. Louis. "Thank God all this will end," wrote Menard to his friend Langlois. ". . . I have a good deal of faith in Mr. Henery [*sic*]. He fits in very well not only because of his humor but because of his honesty and his frank manner and his general behaviour."

From the Mandan villages Henry went overland to Fort Raymond (Manuel's Fort) at the mouth of the Big Horn with forty men and an equal number of horses. Menard, risking ice, continued up the river in some of the boats. A dozen or so men were detached to build Fort Lisa a little above the Minnetaree villages.

At both posts winter was a time of more discontent and of suffering from the below-zero cold. Spring was little better. Eager to escape the confinements of Fort Raymond's dreary cabins, a party deemed strong enough to resist Blackfeet went up the Yellowstone under Henry and Menard and over Bozeman Pass through heavy snow to Three Forks. There they built a crude headquarters post. It availed them little. The nature of their work demanded that the trappers leave shelter and scatter along the streams.

On April 12, 1810, the Indians struck. They killed two men outright. Three others vanished, almost certainly led off by the Blackfeet for death by torture. Menard organized a two-day pursuit that did not catch the raiders but did recover three strayed horses and forty-four traps which the Blackfeet had contemptuously tossed aside as of no value. At this point John Colter decided that he had strained his luck far enough. Bearing letters from Menard about the disaster, he and two men recrossed Bozeman Pass to Fort Raymond. There Colter hewed a small canoe out of a cottonwood tree and alone paddled two thousand hostile miles to the settlements he so long had ignored. He never risked the mountains again.

The trappers at Three Forks, cooped in their fort and plagued by bellowing grizzly bears whenever they slipped outside to hunt game or fetch water, grew restless again. Hoping that the Blackfeet had been satisfied by the earlier triumph and had left the region, they at last ventured onto the streams once more, still in small parties. Again the Indians struck, this time at Lewis and Clark's veteran hunter George Drouillard. He fought wildly from behind his horse until numbers overwhelmed him; when he fell the attackers were so furious at his resistance that they chopped off his head. Two Delaware Indian trappers who were with him were also slain.

At least the Blackfeet were impartial as to nationalities. That same summer (1810), David Thompson, needing dried buffalo meat for his posts west of the Divide, sent red-bearded Finan McDonald and two French-Canadians through Marias Pass to the plains with 150 Flathead Indian hunters. The Blackfeet attacked them too. The guns with which Thompson had supplied the Flatheads enabled them to hold the battle to a draw—a moral victory. This so enraged the insatiable Blackfeet that they pinched off Thompson's route up the North Saskatchewan to Howse Pass and forced him to find a safer crossing to the Columbia at chill Athabaska Pass, far north in present Jasper Park. And when the next year he sent two more of his men out to the plains with Flathead hunters, both were slain.

By now it was evident that Indians were rendering completely impractical the route which Lewis and Clark had declared "the most practicable and navigable passage across the Continent of North America." Completely discouraged by their attacks, Pierre Menard withdrew to the Yellowstone River. Andrew Henry, however, stayed resolutely near Three Forks with a party of indeterminate size. Some accounts say that during the ensuing summer he lost between twenty and thirty men in struggles with the old enemy. This is unlikely. He probably did not have that many men with him altogether; but matters were bad enough that in the fall he decided to find less risky ground. In so doing, he may inadvertently have stumbled, without realizing its significance, on what became the key to the Oregon Trail, South Pass at the lower tip of Wyoming's Wind River Mountains.

In retreating from Three Forks, Henry perhaps roughly followed Colter's old trail south through Yellowstone Park and west across Teton Pass into Idaho. Or he may have followed the Madison and crossed from its headwaters. Anyway, near the site of today's village of St. Anthony on what is now known as Henry's Fork of the Snake River, he built some small cabins.

In the spring of 1811, after a horrible winter of deep snow and scant rations, the group scattered. Some, it is said, worked south and reached the Spanish settlements in New Mexico. One lost his wits and wandered crazed through the wilderness of Idaho. Others worked eastward through the mountains to the Missouri. Three of them had succeeded in reaching the lower river by May. Henry, however, did not appear at the Mandan villages, where Lisa was waiting anxiously for him, until July.

No record survives to say with assurance where his mighty wanderings may have taken him. Possibly he trapped partway down the Green River with those men who reputedly reached the Spanish settlements. To his left he would have seen the Wind River Mountains slanting southeast into the interminable sage desert which in lower Wyoming breaks the barrier of the Rockies. He may have left the Green to skirt the base of those mountains, as Robert Stuart did less than two years later. If so, he almost inevitably found, between their southern tip and the rounded hills that fringe the northern part of the sage desert, the wide gray depression which later was called South Pass to distinguish it from Lewis and Clark's more northerly crossing.

Henry could have gone through this pass and turned north again to Wind River. By following the river around its hairpin curve and through the great canyon where it changes names and becomes the Big Horn, he would have reached familiar ground.

Did he?

Years later (1850) in a speech to the Senate advocating a Pacific railroad, Thomas Hart Benton, who knew Henry, declared flatly, "He was the first man that saw that [South] pass; and he found it in the prosecution of his business, that of a hunter and trader, and by following the game and the road which they made." It is the closest thing to evidence we have.

If Andrew Henry did discover the pass, his knowledge brought no one any good. From the Mandan villages he and Lisa hurried with such pelts as had accumulated there back to St. Louis. In spite of battle and death, they were ready to rush another party to the treasures of the mountains. They could not. Dissensions among their antagonistic partners were paralyzing the company. Dissensions between England and the United States had meanwhile resulted in an importation embargo on, among other things, the strouds and hardware upon which the Indian trade depended. Soon war would follow. Intrigues among the Indian tribes by both British and American traders would close the Missouri entirely, and another dozen years had to pass before Henry could join a new partnership and go back to the alluring, bloody grounds around Three Forks.

THE ORDEAL OF THE ASTORIANS

On July 17, 1808 (Manuel Lisa was traveling down the Missouri toward home), President Jefferson wrote a letter to Meriwether Lewis, governor of Upper Louisiana. A powerful new trading company, he said, "under the direction of a most excellent man, a Mr. Astor mercht of N. York long engaged in the business & perfectly master of it," was forming to move into the West.

This did not mean that Astor was going to the Pacific in person. Not since the German immigrant's early days in America, when he had tramped through the forests of upper New York state with a pack of trinkets on his own back, had John Jacob Astor dealt directly with Indians and frontier shopkeepers. He was the entrepreneur now, provider of capital for others to take afield, weaver of business threads through half the world. What Jefferson meant was that Astor was projecting, out of his own resources, expeditions large enough and bold enough to do immediately those things which Lewis and Clark had proposed be done more deliberately with government help—the location of trading posts in the interior, gathering of their furs at a depot on the Pacific, and the adding of this potentially enormous harvest to the otter trade Yankee shipowners were already carrying on, in somewhat random fashion, with Chinese merchants in Canton.

He was the only man in America who could have dared such a plan. Even the St. Louis Missouri Fur Company, sinewed by the strongest merchants in St. Louis, intended to move slowly and bring their furs to their warehouses in conventional pattern. But Astor was used to global operations. He had ample funds. His ships were already plying in the China tea trade. Very shortly he would send another vessel into the North Pacific to traffic with Russian fur-gatherers in Alaska—and, incidentally, to set up a zone-of-influence agreement under which the Russians promised to stay away from the Columbia. He had dealt for years with the North West Company partners in Montreal and their agents in London. He had heard directly from Alexander Henry the Elder Henry's dream of supply depots on the Northwest coast. Like Lewis and Clark, Astor was familiar with Alexander Mackenzie's proposal to stretch a chain of posts across Canada, corral the sea-otter trade and drive the Yankee "adventurers" off the ocean. Now, on the strength of Lewis and Clark's reports, he felt that times were ripe for Americans—that is, for John Jacob Astor—to adapt these plans to the latitudes of the United States.

Politics presented problems. Hostility between Great Britain and America had already resulted in trade restrictions. The area embracing the Columbia might easily become another cause of contention. Both countries laid claim to the territory, and at any moment Canadian fur interests might goad the home government into supporting Mackenzie's demand that the international boundary be drawn south of the river.

It was partly to protect himself against this possibility that Astor offered the North West Company a third interest in his Pacific scheme. They refused. Perhaps they hoped to corner the entire trade for themselves. After all, two of their partners, David Thompson and Simon Fraser, were already established on major rivers west of the Continental Divide. No responsible Americans were.

Undismayed (he may well have anticipated the rebuff), Astor went on with his plans. The Embargo Acts caused some delay in assembling adequate trade goods, but by the beginning of 1810 he felt ready to move. After reading of Lewis and Clark's struggles with the swift currents of the upper Missouri and with the precipitous trails of the Rockies, Astor had no illusions about sending supplies overland. His post at the mouth of the Columbia and others in the western interior would be built by workers carrying ample equipment around Cape Horn in a sailing vessel. Reinforcements of men and material would follow regularly in other ships. It was desirable, however, that an overland expedition be sent from St. Louis to find the best inland beaver grounds, locate strategic sites for trading posts, and placate the Indians by promising ample goods in return for their pelts.

To obtain experienced managers for these two expeditions, Astor raided the North West Company. Among the Canadians he hired were Alexander McKay, who had gone with Alexander Mackenzie on the first transcontinental crossing to the Pacific; elephantine Donald McKenzie, said to have weighed close to three hundred pounds; dour Duncan McDougall; amiable David Stuart; and David's nephew Robert Stuart, twenty-five-year-old son of a poor Scottish crofter. Likewise from Canada came most of the apprentice clerks and most of the *engagés*, the French-Canadian workhorses of one of the world's most arduous callings.

To balance these foreigners Astor wanted a few Americans, preferably ones who knew the Missouri River area and yet were not bound too closely to the jealous fur traders of St. Louis. The man he eventually settled on as his chief agent was Wilson Price Hunt, twenty-seven, originally from New Jersey but since 1804 a storekeeper and lieutenant of militia in St. Louis.

Hunt in turn approached Ramsay Crooks, actually a Scot but one who had been trading on the Missouri since about 1805; Crooks' partner Robert McClellan, who had been one of Mad Anthony Wayne's most daring scouts in the Ohio Indian campaigns; and irascible Joseph Miller, still another ex-officer of the American Army. When Hunt talked to Astor in New York in the spring of 1810, he could say only that the men "contemplated" going along. Nonetheless he signed the partnership agreements for them by proxy on June 23, and managed to swing each of them into line as he met them one by one later on.[1]

---

[1] One hundred shares of stock in the Pacific Fur Company were issued. Astor, who provided the entire financing, held fifty of these. McKay, McKenzie, McDougall, David Stuart, Hunt, and Crooks were allotted five each. McClellan and Miller held two and one-half each. Fifteen were reserved for future appointees. Robert Stuart, on joining the venture, acquired two of his uncle's five shares.

Both groups were scheduled to leave in September 1810, the sea party from New York on board the ship *Tonquin* and the overlanders by barge up the Missouri. Both, it was mistakenly thought, would reach the Columbia in 1811, the ship a few months ahead of the marchers.

A September departure from St. Louis allowed Hunt little time for lining up the thirty *voyageurs* he was authorized to hire. With Fat McKenzie (as Robert Stuart later called the Canadian) he hurried to Montreal, the great center of the fur trade, and began recruiting. It was a maddening experience. The boisterous, good-natured, simple-minded *voyageurs* were reluctant to step outside the familiar channels of the trade. When a few finally did sign on for the epochal journey to the Pacific, they demanded liberal advances on their salary, got howling drunk, and had to be bailed out of trouble before they could go to work.

Impatiently Hunt decided to finish the recruiting at Michili-mackinac Island, in the narrow strait between Lakes Huron and Michigan. There they encountered Ramsay Crooks, who earlier in the year had dissolved his partnership with Robert McClellan and had left the Missouri. Crooks agreed to take up the standing offer to go with the Astorians to the Pacific and then gave Hunt another shock. Thirty *voyageurs*, he said, were not enough. Though French-Canadians would labor as no American would to push a balky keelboat up a muddy river, they were generally useless in a fight. The expedition would need at least sixty hands, some of them American riflemen, to transport its goods and, if necessary, fend off Indian attacks. So the bartering, cajoling, and persuading had to be extended even farther than Hunt had anticipated.

September was at hand before the expedition reached St. Louis. There Hunt went about packing his trade goods and hiring American hunters and trappers. Manuel Lisa and his partners in the St. Louis Missouri Fur Company opposed him at every turn. They needed hunters for their own 1811 expedition; besides, a trading venture to the Pacific was too big for them to swallow. They were sure Hunt really intended to compete with them on the headwaters of the Missouri and was masking his scheme with this transcontinental braggadocio. In an effort to make sure, William Clark, one of Lisa's partners, wrote to Secretary of War

Eustis on September 12, 1810. "Mr. Hunt & McKinzey are at this place, prepareing to proceed up the Missouri, and prosue my trail to the Columbia. I am not fully in possession of the Objects of this expedition but prosume you are, and would be very glad to be informed."

Frightened by the unfavorable rumors which Lisa spread, reliable trappers held back. Fortunately Joseph Miller, another Missouri trader to whom Hunt earlier had offered shares in the company, appeared just then in the city. He accepted a partnership and was able to round up the necessary men.

On October 21 the party started upriver in three ponderous boats. It was a late launching, but if the overland party was to reach the coast by the following fall, as the sea group aboard the *Tonquin* expected, they must get as far west this year as possible. By the time ice stopped them on November 16, they had gone 450 miles to the mouth of the Nodaway, a little above present St. Joseph, in northwestern Missouri.

Here the company encountered Crooks' former partner, Robert McClellan. He was ripe for anything. Sioux Indians had recently robbed his post at Council Bluffs of three thousand dollars' worth of goods, and under the circumstances a trip to the Pacific sounded fine. "If I possessed anything more except my gun," he wrote his brother the night of the meeting, "I would throw it into the river or give it away, as I intend to begin the world anew tomorrow."

In January Hunt and several companions hiked 150 miles to Fort Osage, secured horses, and rode to St. Louis to obtain more men and equipment. Hunt was particularly anxious to sign on young Pierre Dorion, a half-breed Sioux interpreter who could help the expedition pass his dangerous tribesmen. In theory Dorion was bound to Lisa, but to escape what he considered Lisa's unjust liquor bill he signed on with the Astorians—even making Hunt agree to take along his Ioway wife Marie and their two small children. Lisa tried to stop him by having him arrested. Warned in time by a midnight horseback ride, Dorion hid in the forest until it was safe to go on with his new employer. Lisa did not forget.

Returning upstream, Hunt paused near Charette to talk with John Colter, who warned him against Blackfeet. On April 17,

1811, he reached the camp at the Nodaway and four days later put his force into motion. A bit less than a month later, as they were nearing Sioux territory, they were overtaken by a horseback messenger from Manuel Lisa.

The Spaniard had left St. Louis three weeks behind Hunt in a specially built twenty-oared keelboat to carry fresh supplies and men to his posts. He had hoped to overtake Hunt and join forces with him for mutual protection against the Sioux. But when he reached the Omaha villages four days behind Hunt, he despaired of overhauling the Astorians in time and dispatched an express asking them to wait.

On hearing the request, Crooks and McClellan flew into a passion. They had tried to go up the river in 1809 and had been turned back by Sioux. They were sure Lisa had prompted the Sioux in order to be rid of their competition. They now convinced Hunt that the Spaniard was up to some trickery out of pique over Dorion and that they should go ahead without delay. Hunt accordingly told the messenger that he would wait at the Ponca villages but actually rowed right by the rendezvous without pausing. Ethics were flexible on the river in those days.

A morning or two later, as they were eating breakfast on the shore, they saw three mountain men coming toward them in two dugout canoes. The trio turned out to be hunters who had crossed into Idaho with Andrew Henry the preceding year—John Hoback, Jacob Reznor, and Edward Robinson, the last of whom, now sixty-six years old, had been scalped long before in Kentucky and regularly wore a handkerchief around his head to protect the still-sensitive scars. Like Colter, they warned the Astorians away from Three Forks. When they said they knew a land route by which the Blackfeet could be avoided, Hunt promptly hired them as guides.

Presently the party had to wait for Lisa in spite of themselves. Three hundred and fifty Sioux halted them. As they were bluffing their way through with a mixture of gifts and threats, aided by Dorion's interpreting, Lisa's smaller party hove into sight, rowing prodigiously. So long as danger lasted, the groups continued together amicably. But near the Arikara villages in northern South Dakota the quarrel over Dorion erupted. In the heat of it Lisa and Hunt challenged each other to a duel, while Mc-Clellan offered to shoot the Spaniard without the delay of such formalities. Fortunately, John Bradbury, a naturalist traveling up the river with Hunt, and Henry Brackenridge, another tourist sightseeing with Lisa, were able to calm them down; and soon Hunt was offering to swap his boats to Lisa for some of the horses he would need for his overland ride across the mountains.

Crooks fetched Lisa's horses down from the Mandan villages, 150 miles to the north. Hunt purchased more from the Arikaras. There were eighty-two animals altogether, scarcely enough for packing the equipment. Only the five partners rode. The forty-five *engagés* and eleven trapper-hunters (including Edward Rose, whom they had hired at the villages) had to walk.

The westward march began July 18 across immense and naked prairies. Crooks fell so ill that he could not sit his saddle but had to be dragged behind his horse on a travois. A little later they found a camp of Cheyenne Indians and purchased another thirty-six animals. These were used to replace horses that had gone lame and to lighten the loads of the others.

As they skirted the north flank of the Black Hills and neared the country of the Crow Indians in Wyoming, a rumor reached Hunt that Edward Rose was fomenting mutiny. Aided by a small segment of the men, the mulatto planned to rob the others of horses and goods and rejoin the tribe which had adopted him after his violent parting with Lisa in 1808. Hunt moved first. When they met a band of Crows, he abruptly told Rose that the expedition needed him no longer, then took the sting from the dismissal by presenting the mulatto with a half-year's pay, a horse, three beaver traps, and various knickknacks. This so pleased the outlaw that he gave the Astorians directions for skirting the Big Horn Mountains and reaching Wind River.

For eighty miles they labored up that brawling stream. Two-gwo-tee Pass at its head would have taken them directly to Jackson Hole and the source of the Snake, but game had disappeared. Their guides thought they might find buffalo on the headwaters of the Spanish river, the Green. They therefore swung up a well-beaten Indian trail to the high, rolling, lake-dotted, spruce-freckled meadows now known as Union Pass. A trifle north of west they glimpsed awesome peaks that Andrew Henry's old trappers called the Tetons. Hunt more prosaically named the peaks Pilot Knobs. It was mid-September and the mouth of the Columbia was almost a thousand miles away.

They had to have meat. Turning their back on the Tetons, they dropped into a tributary of the Green and set up a hunting camp. Buffalo were plentiful. For five days the *voyageurs* were busy slicing four thousand pounds of beef into thin strips and drying it before slow fires into jerky for the days ahead. Hunt, McKenzie, and Crooks meantime found a camp of Snake (Shoshone) Indians. To establish friendly relations they paid the savages extravagantly for a dozen beaver pelts and promised to return later with more goods to open regular trade—one of the pilot operations they had been directed to launch.

On September 24 they crossed northwest from the Green to the swift, rugged Hoback River, named for one of their guides, and followed it to its junction with the Snake (or Mad River, as Henry's trappers had named it). Water all the rest of the way to the ocean! After 900 miles of herding the pack train the *voyageurs* were sick of horses. Now they could leave the hateful beasts and build canoes. Hunt was dubious; but partner Joseph Miller, afflicted with some bodily ailment that rendered riding distressful, agreed irascibly with the *engagés*. The only ones who really didn't care about the argument that developed were four hunters who were detached at the mouth of the Hoback to begin trapping operations.

Clerk John Reed was sent ahead to reconnoiter the river. After four days he returned with word that the narrow canyon by which it broke through the southern spurs of the Tetons was unnavigable. Hunt ordered the dismayed *voyageurs* back to their horses. They crossed spectacular Teton Pass to the north and on October 8, in a flurry of snow, reached the small cabins Andrew Henry had built on Henry's Fork of the Snake the preceding fall.

There they hollowed fifteen dugouts. For Joseph Miller the change came too late. He had grown disenchanted with the project. In a temper he tossed back his 2½ shares and joined four more trappers who were dropped out at this point—the guides Hoback, Renznor, and Robinson; and Martin Cass.

On October 17 the main party cached its saddles, entrusted its seventy-seven remaining horses to two Snake Indians who promised to guard the animals until traders returned, and launched their canoes. Soon they were on the Snake, 1800 feet wide, light-green water thrusting southward fast and smooth. Presently lava cliffs pressed closer and rapids began to toss them. The canoes kept upsetting. On the twenty-eighth Crooks' dugout smashed against a rock, destroying precious goods and drowning the steersman. The place was near today's town of Milner at the lowest point of the Snake's huge arc through southern Idaho.

The canyon had become hopeless—only sixty feet wide in places and roaring with waterfalls hundreds of feet high. The party cached its goods in nine holes and separated. Through cold fall rains McKenzie started north with four men across the lava plains, hoping to reach the Columbia. McClellan led a trio down the rim of the canyon on the tracks of John Reed and three others, who were exploring in that direction. Crooks and another pair started to walk two hundred miles back to Henry's Fork for the horses. Hunt and the remaining thirty-one, plus Dorion's squaw, now seven months pregnant, and her two children, moved soddenly back up the river to a better campsite and settled down to wait for the pack stock. They had nothing to eat but a little dried corn, a little jerky, a few fish they netted, and eight beaver they trapped.

On November 4 Crooks unexpectedly reappeared. The going was so rough that he had decided he could not possibly reach the horses and return before winter. Shortly thereafter two of Reed's men limped back with discouraging reports about the lower canyon. After a conference, the leaders decided to split the party in half, each leading a part, in the hope that small numbers might be easier to feed off the country. To his nineteen men Hunt added Dorion's family.

Crooks took the south side of the stream, Hunt the north. Canyon walls three hundred feet high kept them away from the river. Some of Hunt's *voyageurs* grew so frantic from thirst that they tried to drink their own urine. Rain saved them. Between today's towns of Caldwell and Payette, almost to the Oregon border, they encountered a few miserable Indian villages, stinking horribly of decayed salmon. They were able to purchase a few dogs to eat and finally a few horses to pack, one of which Hunt grew so fond of that he could hardly bear to part with it when starvation loomed again in December.

The river, flowing north now (so that Hunt was on the east bank) plunged into the snow-covered Seven Devil Mountains. Unable to cross their drifted summits, the group worked back down into the canyon bottom. The next morning, December 6, they were astonished to see Crooks' group on the other side of the stream. They too had been turned back by snow and by the deepening of one of the most tremendous canyons in America. During the last six days of their ordeal, nineteen men had shared as food one dog, one beaver, a handful of wild cherries, and the boiled soles of some worn moccasins.

Hunt had his men build a canoe from the skin of his recently butchered horse and ferry meat to the starving party. Crooks and an exhausted *voyageur* returned in the fragile craft to discuss the next move. They decided to reassemble and limp back to the Indian villages Hunt had passed. There they might be able to buy horses.

Crooks could not rejoin his men. The skin canoe drifted off during the night and he was unable, without tools, to build a raft strong enough to withstand the ice-choked current. The groups, still divided, straggled back on either bank. Crooks and his one *voyageur* were so exhausted that they fell behind. After making what provision he could for them, Hunt hurried on. Reaching an Indian village he wasted no time dickering but seized five horses. Butchering one, he sent some of the meat and a riding animal back for the stranded pair.

On rejoining the party Crooks was enraged to find that no supplies had been sent from Hunt's group across the river to his own famished party. He ordered a canoe built of horsehide and loaded it with meat. When everyone else declined to ferry the craft across the turbulent current, he struggled to do it himself but collapsed from sheer weakness. Shamed by his despair, Benjamin Jones finally did the job. One demented *voyageur* then tried to leave his own party for Hunt's side of the river, upset the hide boat and drowned.

John Day had a little better luck. Once an extraordinary woodsman and athlete, by his own admission Day had celebrated too hard too often. Forty years old now and broken by the hardships of the march, he thought he was dying and wanted to be with his old companion and boss, Ramsay Crooks. They hauled him across the river. Crooks got him into an Indian hut, told Hunt to go ahead with the men, who were already straggling away, and settled down to wait Day's death or recovery. An enfeebled *voyageur* named Dubreuil stayed with them.

Eventually the main groups managed to join on the west bank of the river. Three French-Canadians, terrified by the unknown dangers ahead, elected to stay with the Indians. The others, fortified by Indian guides and a few horses, floundered northwest along what became, with slight variations, the final lap of the Oregon Trail—up Burnt River's steep, narrow valley, along winding Powder River, and across the handsome swales of Grande Ronde.

At dawn on December 30 Marie Dorion gave birth to her child. In time many others would be born beside the trail, but this was the first with a touch of white blood in its veins. The father stayed behind with the augmented family for a day. On the thirty-first they rejoined the others. In Hunt's words, "His wife was on horseback with her newborn infant in her arms; another, aged two years, wrapped in a blanket, was slung at her side. One would have said from her air, that nothing had happened to her." But a week later, after they had dragged themselves across the pine-covered Blue Mountains, sometimes in waist-deep snow, the child died. At about the same time a sick *engagé* named Carrière wandered off with some Indians and was never seen again. They were the last casualties.

The party reached the Columbia near the mouth of the Umatilla. They still had three hundred miles to go. It was a nightmare of thundering rapids, thieving Indians, cold, and hunger. At last they obtained canoes and coursed the lower river in relative comfort. On February 15, 1812, they sighted the log palisades of Astoria. To their amazement they found that Mc-Kenzie, McClellan, Reed, and their eight men somehow had fallen in together. After desperate suffering they had crossed the

Idaho mountains that had stopped the others and had reached the fort a month ahead of Hunt's party.

Hundreds of miles behind, Crooks and Dubreuil sat for twenty days beside John Day. For a time Indians brought them food, then left. The trio sank into a torpor. Two wandering savages gave them a few morsels and went on. A wolf chanced by. It was Day who managed to kill it. The meat perked them up and they started feebly out along Hunt's trail. The three *voyageurs* who had left Hunt rather than risk the unknown joined them for a time, then dropped back again. Losing the trail, Crooks and the others wandered forlornly through the mountains, eating roots and horsemeat and sometimes only beaver skins. Dubreuil collapsed and was left with Indians. Finally Crooks and Day reached the Columbia, but near Celilo Falls savages stripped them of what little they had and drove them out of camp stark naked, without even flint or steel. For four days they subsisted on a handful of meal they made by pounding the bones of decayed fish. Then friendly Indians succored them with skins and horsemeat. Fearful of the savages who had used them ill before, they decided to return to St. Louis. Just as they were starting the hopeless journey, a flotilla of canoes hailed them. It was a group of trappers going downstream to Astoria.

On May 11 they rejoined their comrades at the post. What they heard there was almost as discouraging as their own experiences.

The *Tonquin,* a vessel of 290 tons commanded by Jonathan Thorn, had left New York on September 6, 1810. Aboard were thirty-three clerks and *voyageurs* and partners Duncan Mc-Dougall, David Stuart, and his nephew Robert Stuart. The hold was stocked with trade goods and equipment for building the fort on the Columbia. Thorn, on leave from the Navy, was a good seaman and kept scrupulous care of the property in his charge. But he was a hot-tempered martinet and did not get on with his passengers. When David Stuart and a group of sightseers did not return to the *Tonquin* promptly enough to suit him after a pause for water at the Falkland Islands, Thorn started to sail without them. Young Robert put a pistol to his head and forced him back. The Columbia's always dangerous bar was particularly tumultuous as the *Tonquin* crept toward it. Thorn nevertheless ordered a boat crew out to explore for a channel. The small vessel was never seen again. Thorn persisted, swamping still another boat. Eight men perished before the *Tonquin* finally gained the estuary on March 25, 1811.

The surrounding hills were rough, the forests dense. Duncan McDougall, in charge of the landing party, could not find a fort site that pleased him. Impatient to be off on a trading venture along the coast, Thorn finally all but dumped the fort-builders out on a spot just inside the tip of Point George, which embraced the southern side of the broad estuary. The ruins of Fort Clatsop, where Lewis and Clark had wintered six years earlier, were seven miles to the southeast.

In drizzling rains men unused to axes (including twenty-four Kanakas hired during a stop at the Hawaiian Islands) had to fell fir trees so huge that four people could chop on a single trunk at once. As soon as a warehouse began to take shape, Thorn hustled a small portion of the trade goods into it and on June 1 started north. He would return with the rest of the supplies, he said, later in the summer.

Work on the fort and on a little schooner, whose parts had been shipped aboard the *Tonquin,* continued dispiritedly. Original plans had called for an establishment 120 yards square. This quickly shrank to 75 by 80 feet. Lining opposite sides of the half-completed stockade were a single-story dwelling house and a double-story trading house, each 60 feet long.

On July 15 David Thompson of the North West Company arrived with a canoe full of *voyageurs* from a post which Finan McDonald and Jaco Finlay had recently built near the site of Spokane, Washington. En route Thompson had affixed to a stake at the junction of the Snake and Columbia Rivers a notice declaring "Know hereby that this country is claimed for Great Britain as part of its territories and that the N. W. Company of Merchants from Canada . . . do hereby intend to erect a factory in this place." But he told the Astorians that his company was belatedly accepting their employer's earlier offer of a one-third interest in the Pacific Fur Company. On the basis of that the men in the raw new fort embraced Thompson as a new associate. When he returned to

Spokane House, David Stuart and a small group went partway with him.

After separating from Thompson, Stuart built a post in north-central Washington, where the Okanogan River flows into the Columbia. From there he explored northward into British Columbia and liked what he saw. But at Astoria pessimism deepened. Indians brought word that savages at Nootka had massacred every man aboard the *Tonquin,* including partner Alexander McKay. There had been revenge of sorts, however. One wounded sailor had crawled into the hold and touched off four and a half tons of powder, blowing himself, the vessel, and an unknown number of celebrating Indians into fragments. But armament and goods designed to support Astoria until a supply vessel arrived were lost.

The arrival of the main part of Hunt's overlanders restored spirits somewhat. It was decided to reinforce David Stuart's post at Okanogan, send a party into southern Idaho to retrieve the goods which the overlanders had cached beside the Snake River on abandoning their canoes, and rush news about the misadventures to Astor. John Reed took charge of the dispatches, which for safekeeping he soldered into a bright tin box that he carried on his back. McClellan decided to go with Reed's party. He thought that the sufferings he had endured were worth more than two and a half shares. When the other partners at Astoria declined to increase his participation he surrendered his holdings and resigned in a huff.

The trip up the majestic gorge by which the Columbia breaches the Cascade Mountains was laborious. The goods destined for Okanogan had to be portaged around each of the rapids. Thieving Indians were so troublesome that the combined parties decided to slip past the Long Narrows (the Dalles) by dark. By dawn all but a small portion of the goods had been safely transported. Robert McClellan and John Reed stood guard over this remnant until *voyageurs* could return from the upper end of the rapids to pick up the material.

At that point the Indians realized what was happening. Several full canoes swarmed in and fell on the packages. At first the two whites tried to resist without shooting. Then one savage began wrestling with Reed for his gun. Another threw a buffalo robe over McClellan's head and struck at him with a knife. McClellan lunged free, killed his assailant with his rifle and with a pistol dropped another Indian who just then had knocked Reed senseless with an axehandle. Undeterred, others began hacking at Reed with a tomahawk. McClellan's guns were empty now, but he leveled them and charged so ferociously that the savages fled.

Rescuers from above came running at the sound of the shots. Reed was carried to a canoe and the voyage resumed. The defeated Indians slew two horses in their village, drank the hot blood for courage, and set out in pursuit. The whites forted up, and after a parley the trouble was settled by paying the savages three blankets and some tobacco for their dead.

Reed's tin box of dispatches had vanished during the melee. This loss and five tomahawk wounds led to the cancellation of his trip. For some reason the journey to Hunt's caches was also abandoned and the entire party went on up to Okanogan. As they were returning downstream a month later, they found Crooks and Day on the river bank.

Jut before they reached Astoria, the supply ship *Beaver* crept in across the bar. With renewed energy the leaders began to expand the fort and prepare trapping parties for the interior. Hunt was delegated to go on the *Beaver* to the Russian settlements in Alaska and open trade there. Reed, his wounds already healed, was appointed to retrieve Hunt's caches. The job of taking dispatches to Astor fell to Robert Stuart. Four employees, each of whom had crossed with the overlanders, were assigned to go with him—John Day, Benjamin Jones, André Vallé, and François LeClerc. McClellan joined the quintet for company, as did Ramsay Crooks. Like McClellan, Crooks had been so discouraged by his ordeal that he was withdrawing from the company.

In order to awe the Indians the different parties left Astoria together at the end of June 1812—fifty-one men in two barges and nine canoes.[2] It was soon evident that John Day was still unbal-

---

[2] David Stuart was bound for Okanogan. Other posts were to be established on the Spokane River and the Snake. After helping Donald McKenzie on the lower Snake, John Reed was to follow Robert Stuart's route as far as southern Idaho and retrieve Hunt's cached goods.

anced from his sufferings. He muttered darkly to himself, felt he was being persecuted by his companions, and raved at any Indian who inadvertently approached him. At the mouth of the Willamette River, Stuart had to make arrangements to send him back to Astoria.

Heavy guards watched the packaged merchandise at each portage and the travelers passed the scene of the earlier battle without incident. Reaching the barren, lava-brown interior a month out of Astoria, they began trading for pack stock. At the mouth of the Walla Walla, where the Columbia bends northward, they separated. Robert Stuart's six-man party rode due south through intense, waterless heat to the Umatilla, reaching it in the vicinity of modern Pendleton, then retraced Hunt's route into southwestern Idaho. There they encountered an Indian who the previous fall had crossed Teton Pass with Hunt's party. The fellow told a garbled tale about the misadventures of some of the trappers whom Hunt had left in the mountains and—much more to Robert Stuart's immediate concern—said he knew of a shorter trace across the Rocky Mountains than the one followed by the outbound overlanders.

Unless Andrew Henry had found the same gap a year and a half earlier, this was the first definite word of South Pass to reach white ears. Stuart immediately offered the Indian "a Pistol, a Blanket of blue Cloth, an axe, a knife, an awl, a fathom of blue beads, a looking glass, and a little Powder & Ball" to serve as guide. The grinning savage accepted—and vanished a day or two later, taking Stuart's horse along with him for good measure.

Guideless, the party rode on eastward, clinging as close to the river as the rough side gullies allowed. (Years later most emigrants to Oregon would avoid part of this crescent-shaped stretch by crossing the Snake at Glenn's Ferry, angling to the Boise River at about the modern city of Boise, and rattling down the Boise to another crossing of the Snake.) On August 18, twenty miles or so downstream from future Glenn's Ferry, on going to the river for water, Stuart's party were amazed to see a nearly naked white fisherman squatted in the shade of a willow bush. He was Joseph Miller, the partner who had withdrawn in pique from the company at Henry's Fort. A moment later three of the four trappers he had left with scrambled into sight—Hoback, Reznor, and Robinson.

They told a harrowing yarn. After leaving Hunt the four of them, plus Martin Cass, had trapped into the area where the states of Idaho, Wyoming, and Utah now join. Loaded with furs, they started east, probably below South Pass, nearer the present Colorado–Wyoming border. Somewhere around the Medicine Bow Mountains, Arapaho Indians raided them. They wolfed out the winter—and in the spring the same Arapahos stole the rest of their horses but let them repurchase two of the animals with half the ammunition the whites still retained. They wandered back westward, hoping to fall in with trappers from Astoria. Cass disappeared with one horse (later there was some suspicion that his companions may have eaten him during starving times) and Indians stole the second. Now here they were, utterly destitute, living on such salmon as they could catch in the river.

Stuart's party took them in tow and continued eastward. The canyon to their left constricted and they appreciated better why Hunt had quit the river. "Hecate's caldron," Stuart wrote in his journal, "was never half so agitated when vomiting even the most diabolical spells." He named the maelstrom "the Devils Scuttle Hole." [3]

To their astonishment, they found that six of Hunt's nine caches had been rifled. The thieves, although Stuart did not know it then, were the three *engagés* who, when Day had been sick, had dropped out to live with the Indians. The savages supported the trio for a time but grew restive. To calm them the whites took a group to the caches and outfitted a war party. Bravely the Indians and trappers set off to hunt buffalo on the headwaters of the Missouri. Blackfeet robbed them of everything they possessed and drove them back into Snake country. By chance they met some of the other trappers Hunt had detached, including Dubreuil, who for a time had been with Crooks and Day. Back to the Missouri the combined parties marched. This time Crows pounced on them, killed one man and sent the others scampering once more

[3] Modern dams and power developments have totally altered the thirty-mile stretch.

toward the Snake. John Reed later found them on his way to re-trieve the caches, and succored them.

On discovering traps and other equipment in the three caches that remained untouched, Hoback, Reznor, and Robinson de-cided to go back to their beaver-hunting. (Sixteen months later, they, John Reed, and several others would be massacred on the Boise River, less than two hundred miles away.) Miller, however, his "curiosity and desire of traveling thro' the Indian countries being fully satisfied," decided to return to St. Louis. Living on fish they caught, beaver they trapped, and dogs they traded for, the dispatch-bearers rode on eastward through a parched country of "Sage and its detested relations"—exactly the route that would become the Oregon Trail. Reaching the Portneuf River on September 7, they turned south up it and crossed to the Bear, still on the future trail and still heading toward the pass the Indian had told them about.

On the evening of the twelfth a few Crow Indians visited their camp. The next day they saw smoke signals on the mountains. Fearing that these presaged an attack, they turned eastward away from the Bear. Miller, who had trapped contiguous areas before, assured them that soon they would find a stream that would lead them where they wanted to go. Perhaps he meant one of the tribu-taries of the Green—Fontenelle Creek or LaBarge Creek—but if so the travelers swung too far north. After wandering uncertainly through mountains where aspen leaves were changing color with fall, they emerged onto a river (the Grey) which bore due north toward the Snake. Bewildered and fearful of the Crows behind them, they decided to continue to the Snake "and pass the first spur of mountains by the route of the party who came across the continent last year." Evidently, to judge from their later actions, they then hoped to go down the Green and resume their inter-rupted journey toward South Pass.

The Crows followed them to a camp near present-day Alpine, where the Snake roars out of Wyoming into Idaho. At dawn on September 19, a single Indian placed himself on a knob ahead of the white men's hobbled horses. Two others charged up behind the animals with a "diabolical noise" and stampeded them into following the Indian ahead. Despite their hobbles the terrified creatures ran "as if a legion of infernals were in pursuit." The whites seized rifles to give chase afoot, realized the hopelessness, and returned to defend the baggage. No more Indians appeared, though certainly more were about.

Hoping that on the plains below Henry's Fort they could meet Snake Indians who would sell them horses, the men put what they could carry onto their backs, built rafts a little later, and floated fifty miles or so back *down* the Snake toward the Columbia. En route they found an elk that had been wounded by a rifle ball. This made them fear that Blackfeet were in the vicinity. Finding no Snakes, they gave up that hope. Abandoning their rafts, they angled eastward toward Teton Pass. Fear of Blackfeet made them excessively cautious. In an effort to keep out of sight, Stuart chose such difficult routes that McClellan grew infuriated. Throwing down their one beaver trap, which it was his lot to carry, he said he would go his own way, and stalked off alone.

Crooks, who chose inconvenient times to fall ill, contracted a raging fever. The men wanted to abandon him. Stuart refused and forced Crooks to swallow all the castor oil they possessed. This "had the desired effect" but the invalid remained incapable of travel for four days, until they built a little wigwam of branches over him, tossed in hot stones, added water, and steamed him thoroughly. The next day, with others carrying his things, he was able to totter on for eight miles, most of it through swamps.

They crossed Teton Pass and labored up the Hoback River— "missing a single step you would go several hundred feet into the rocky bed of the stream." Game eluded them. They hoped for buffalo near the Green, but all they saw was a plume of smoke to the southwest. Hoping for friendly Indians with food, they sent LeClerc to reconnoiter. He returned the next morning saying that the smoke had been built by McClellan, who was in desperate straits from starvation. When Stuart's party reached the man "he was . . . emaciated and worn to a perfect skeleton, hardly able to raise his head or speak." But they inspirited him, added his possessions to their own packs, and coaxed him along for seventeen more miles.

That night one of the *voyageurs* proposed cannibalism by lot.

"I snatched up my rifle," Stuart wrote in his journal, "cocked, and leveled it at him . . . ; this so terrified the fellow that he fell instantly on his knees and asked the whole parties pardon, solemnly swearing he should never again suggest such a thought." The next afternoon they at last killed a buffalo, "and so ravenous were our appetites, that we ate part of the animal raw."

Leaving the Green, they veered southeast, parallel to the peaks of the Wind River Mountains on their left. In the desert country somewhat northeast of present Big Sandy, Wyoming, they encountered friendly Snake Indians. The band had just been robbed by Crows, however, and had nothing to trade the whites save one bony horse, some buffalo meat, "and leather mogasins, an article we much want." They were at this point scarcely a hundred miles from where they had been a month before on the Bear, though they had traveled a useless U 417 miles long, by Stuart's estimate, in getting there.

It was a great relief to load their packs on the new horse. Leading him and suffering greatly from thirst, they crossed South Pass on October 22, the first known traverse of the broad gateway to the West. But they kept too far south and so missed almost all of Sweetwater Creek, up which the emigrant wagons would later travel. They seem to have encountered this key stream a little above its debouchment into the fiery-red canyon of the North Platte. A few miles beyond that junction, near present Casper, they decided on November 1 to build a cabin and settle down for winter.

Game abounded and the days passed pleasantly. But on December 12 Arapaho Indians appeared. Though the visitors seemed friendly, the whites decided to play safe and moved farther down the North Platte to new winter quarters close to the present Nebraska border.

Early in March the river thawed. Hopefully the men built canoes, only to learn—as others would later—that the shallow stream was too full of sandbars to float even the lightest craft. Repacking their solitary horse, they hiked on through late snowstorms into a green spring teeming with waterfowl. On April 13, well down toward the Missouri, they reached an Oto village. Two French traders, just arrived there from St. Louis, told them that war had been declared between Great Britain and the United States.

To one of these traders they swapped their single horse for enough elk and buffalo skins to build a canoe, twenty feet long and four feet wide, on a willow-stick frame. In this shaky craft they floated to the Missouri and down it to the vicinity of modern Leavenworth, Kansas, where they found a wooden canoe on the beach. On April 30 they reached St. Louis, having traveled (by Stuart's somewhat inflated calculations) 3704 miles. Save for the northern detour and the final stretch along the lower Platte to the Missouri, this was the route which with only slight variations would grow into the Oregon Trail. Oddly enough, it was traveled for the first time not from east to west, but in reverse.

The little party gave a forecast of the trail. After an interview with them, the *Missouri Gazette* for May 15 declared:

> By information received from these gentlemen, it appears that a journey across the continent of N. America, might be performed with a waggon, there being no obstruction on the whole route that any person would dare to call a mountain in addition to its being much the most direct and short one to go from this place to the mouth of the Columbia River. Any future party who may undertake this journey, and are tolerably acquainted with the different places, where it would be necessary to lay up a small stock of provisions, would not be impeded, as in all probability they would not meet with an Indian to interrupt their progress; although on the other route more north, there are almost insurmountable barriers.

The estimates were reasonably accurate. The most difficult mountains the returning Astorians had encountered were those they climbed during their detour from the main trail. In comparison to the Blackfeet of the upper Missouri, the horse-stealers who most surely had interrupted their progress perhaps could be classed as a relatively mild impediment, one which larger, more vigilant parties could avoid. In any event, after the trip they had just completed (for all but Stuart a complete round trip), they were entitled to a few grand airs in front of the city reporters.

The day after the story appeared in St. Louis, Robert Stuart left on horseback with his dispatches for New York City. He arrived about June 23. He found Astor trying desperately to obtain a ship and government soldiers to send to the mouth of the Columbia. To reinforce his arguments Astor wrote the Secretary of Navy that Robert Stuart, just returned from the Pacific, believed that twenty-five or thirty men could defend Astoria against three or four hundred British. He added that Stuart "is of opinion that the jurney may be performed from the mouth of the Columbia to St. Lewis in 4 months that is after having some few establishments on this side of the Rocky mountains."

The predictions were correct, but nineteen years would pass before the Trail would be traveled again in its entirety in a single journey; twenty-one before American fur-trading "establishments," not government forts, sprang up beside the route; and twenty-eight before pieces of a wagon finally reached the lower Columbia. The War of 1812 was one cause of the delay. Although Astor at length was able to dispatch a supply ship, the *Lark*, it sank among the Hawaiian Islands. Nor'Westers, backed by their government—as Astor was not—closed in on the Columbia by land and sea. The Canadian partners at the fort, unable to gauge what was happening in the outside world, sold the buildings, supplies, and pelts to their former countrymen. Although the peace treaty closing the war left title to Oregon theoretically in abeyance, the area in actuality remained under control of the British fur traders. The disruption was so complete that as the West began to struggle out of the doldrums caused by the conflict, even South Pass had to be rediscovered—as usual by mountain men.

REDISCOVERY

Throughout the War of 1812 St. Louis felt naked. In the wild region between the upper Mississippi and the Missouri, red-haired Robert Dickson, one of the giants of the British Great Lakes trade, recruited hundreds of Indians on England's side. The tribes became so inflamed that Lisa's Missouri Fur Company had to abandon the upper river entirely, forsaking in the process trappers who were working south along the front range of the Rockies as far as Santa Fe. For a time Lisa tried to cling to the trade of the Arikara villages, but in March 1813 the slaying of several of his men forced him back to Council Bluffs. There, a few miles above Omaha, he built a private fort which was the only bulwark against a possible Indian advance down the Missouri.

The Mississippi route was equally insecure. The British seized the traders' strongholds of Michilimackinac Island and Prairie du Chien. Fort Dearborn (Chicago) was abandoned and its garrison massacred; Fort Madison, on the Mississippi at about the Missouri–Iowa border, was burned and forsaken. Periodic alarms that Dickson was leading a horde of savages toward the city along various of these routes swept St. Louis. To ease the tension, William Clark, then governor of Missouri Territory, determined in the spring of 1814 to recapture Prairie du Chien and build an American fort there.

Success was short-lived. A British counterattack easily retook Prairie du Chien, American prestige collapsed entirely, and the Indians on the western frontier became more dangerous than ever. To balance Dickson's influence and to secure for the United States Indian allies of her own, Clark turned to the two white men most at home among the Missouri tribes—Auguste Chouteau and Manuel Lisa.

Lisa, aided by $1335 worth of merchandise and the good will of a chief named Temaha, harangued 900 Yankton Sioux at the mouth of the James River so effectively that they slew twenty-seven hostile Iowas and thoroughly discouraged red talk of major raids on the Missouri settlements. When peace came, he performed even more valuable services by helping assemble the once-belligerent chiefs in a peace council at Portage des Sioux.

Trade nevertheless revived slowly. Workers were hard to find and markets were disrupted. The more distant tribes remained restive. Save for Lisa, the St. Louis merchants were afraid to risk capital among them. When in the spring of 1817 the Spaniard brought down from his post at Council Bluffs furs worth $35,000,

the other traders jealously charged him with misusing his pre-
rogatives as Indian agent to further his own ends.

Enraged by the talk, Lisa (whose salary as agent was $548 a
year) on July 1, 1817, sent an angry letter of resignation to William Clark:

> Manuel Lisa gets so much nice fur. Well, I will explain how I get
> it. I put into my operations great activity. I go a great distance
> while some are considering whether they will start today or to-
> morrow. I impose upon myself great privations. Ten months of the
> year I am buried in the depths of the forest, at a vast distance from
> my own house. I appear as the benefactor, not the pillager, of the
> Indian. I carried among them the seed of the large pumpkin from
> which I have seen in their possession fruit weighing one hundred
> and sixty pounds; also the large bean, the potato, the turnip; and
> these vegetables will make a comfortable part of their subsistence;
> and this year I have promised to carry the plow. Besides, my black-
> smiths work incessantly for them, charging nothing. I lend them
> traps, only demanding a preference in their trade. My establish-
> ments are the refuge of the weak, and of the old men no longer
> able to follow their lodges; and by these means I have acquired the
> confidence and friendship of the natives and the consequent choice
> of their trade.

Anti-British sentiment was meanwhile coloring government activity on the frontier. British citizens were denied the right to
trade among Indians living on United States territory. Military
forts were built wherever British influence had been strong during the war—at Chicago, Green Bay, Prairie du Chien, Rock
Island. As soon as John C. Calhoun became Secretary of War in
the fall of 1817 he formulated plans for pushing these forts even
deeper into the wilderness. One, Fort Snelling, was to be located
at the mouth of the Minnesota River—it eventually grew into the
twin cities of Minneapolis and St. Paul—and another at the junction of the Yellowstone and the Missouri.

The immediate purpose of the fort at the Yellowstone was to
protect the western fur trade by counteracting British intrigue
that supposedly emanated from posts along the Red River. But
there were longer range dreams as well. Writing to Colonel

Thomas Smith, commanding the 9th Army Department, Calhoun said, ". . . the glory of planting the American flag at a point so distant, on so noble a river, will not be unfelt. The world will behold in it the mighty growth of our republic, which . . . now is ready to push its civilization and laws to the western confines of the continent"—a direct voicing of the spirit of Manifest Destiny twenty-five years before that phrase was actually coined.

The western confines of the continent were too ambitious for a country still arguing with Great Britain over title to the Pacific Northwest. Calhoun had to readjust his goal to the Mandan villages. The frontier declined to accept the shrinkage, however, and continued to call the project the Yellowstone Expedition. Troop movements began August 30, 1818, when an advance detachment of 350 infantrymen started marching up the Missouri toward Council Bluffs, supported by six keelboats. Insisting that their destination was the Yellowstone, the St. Louis *Enquirer* trumpeted on September 4:

> The establishment of this post will be an era in the history of the west. It will go to the source and root of the fatal British influence which has for so many years armed the Indian nations against our western frontiers. . . . The North West and Hudson's Bay companies will be shut out from the commerce of the Missouri and Mississippi Indians; the American trader will penetrate in safety the recesses of the rocky mountains in search of its rich fur, a commerce yielding a million per annum will descend the Missouri, and the Indians . . . will learn to respect the American name.

Unfortunately for the expedition, the country was then in the grip of a tremendous to-do over steamboats. The first such vessel had reached St. Louis only the year before, 1817, reducing almost incalculably the labor hitherto required to move freight northward from the mouth of the Ohio, the great immigrant route, or from salt water below New Orleans. The more remote settlements were in a fever to share the boom. In the spring of 1819, accordingly, the *Independence*, loaded with flour, whiskey, sugar, and iron castings, thrashed up the snag-filled Missouri as far as Franklin, in the central part of the territory, where the ecstatic townspeople welcomed the captain and his intrepid passengers with an artillery salute and a civic banquet.

Enthralled by the general excitement, Calhoun decided to use steamers for moving the bulk of the new fort's soldiers and their equipment, "as it will give much more interest and éclat to the expedition and would probably impress the Indians and British with our means of supporting and holding intercourse with the remote posts of the Missouri." Without anyone's bothering to investigate the peculiar problems of navigating the Missouri, a fat cost-plus contract was awarded to one James Johnson, who agreed to deliver four steamboats to the Army at its Belle Fontaine post (near the confluence of the Missouri and Mississippi) by March 1, 1819, using them en route to haul the expedition's clothing and ordnance from Pittsburgh. The government itself simultaneously built a fifth boat, *Western Engineer,* for transporting to the frontier an exploring and scientific expedition headed by Major Stephen H. Long.

Wild rumors flashed into print. The *Missouri Gazette* cried on November 13, 1818, concerning the *Western Engineer:* "It is intended to take the steam boat to pieces at the mountains and rebuild her in [the Columbia]. The expedition is to traverse the continent by water!" Six months later a correspondent wrote from Fort Osage to *Niles' Weekly Register* of Baltimore, which had a national circulation, that if Johnson's steamboats succeeded,

> he will have done more for ... the whole union than any other man (except Jackson) ever did. He will have opened a safe and easy communication to China, which would give such a spur to commercial enterprise that ten years shall not pass away before we shall have the rich production of that country transported from Canton to the Columbia, up that river to the mountains, over the mountains and down the Missouri and Mississippi, all the way (mountains and all) by the potent power of steam—

a rebirth of the same unworkable idea that had been enthusiastically propounded by Lewis and Clark a bare thirteen years earlier.

Johnson's steamboats did not succeed. One of them proved unable to breast even the Mississippi. The others arrived late at Belle Fontaine. By then Johnson was so far in arrears on payments for supplies that the Bank of St. Louis sued out a writ of attachment against the property in the hold of one of the vessels. Asserting that the material was government property and could not be attached, Johnson asked the military commander at Belle Fontaine to provide him with troops for resisting the sheriff.

The request was refused. Johnson thereupon landed on the Illinois bank in order to be out of Missouri's jurisdiction. There the quartermaster made him unload the property for inspection. This and reloading took still more time. By now the troops, most of whom never did get a ride on the boats, had marched far ahead of their supplies. Their commander, General Henry Atkinson, ordered Johnson to provide certain equipment according to contract. Johnson said he couldn't. Atkinson retorted that in that event he would order the necessary stores in St. Louis and charge them to Johnson's account. Thus prodded, the contractor sent a pittance up the river by keelboat—then billed the government for freight at 16¼ cents a pound as against a normal rate for the same haul of 5½ cents.

During this exchange the government-built *Western Engineer* chugged jauntily by Johnson's immobilized steamers. She was an amazing little thirty-ton, shallow-draft vessel. Her bow, according to a St. Louis paper, resembled a rearing serpent, "mouth open, vomiting smoke, and apparently carrying the boat on his back." A paddlewheel at the stern dashed foaming water "violently along." Three brass cannon shone on the wheeldeck. An American flag rippled overhead. Beside it was another flag bearing "portraits of a white man and an Indian shaking hands; the calumet of peace; a sword." In spite of its dash, the *Engineer* came nowhere near the Columbia—nor was she intended to. On September 17 she landed half a mile above Lisa's fort and the engineers began setting up winter quarters preparatory to marching, the next summer, to the Colorado Rockies.

None of Johnson's steamers reached as far as Council Bluffs that season. One was abandoned below Franklin; two had to winter near the mouth of the Kaw River (present Kansas City). At Council Bluffs, more than two hundred miles farther on (and three miles above the engineers' cantonment) Atkinson ordered his footsore troops into winter quarters. Partly because of inadequate supplies, three hundred of them contracted scurvy before spring;

one hundred died. The affair became a national scandal. Calhoun's political enemies took joy, and an angry Congress refused any further appropriations for the extension of America's military might toward the mountains. The fort intended first for the Yellowstone and then for the Mandan villages was built instead at Council Bluffs, where the hamlet of Fort Calhoun, Nebraska, now stands, and was named Fort Atkinson in honor of its founder.

Fort Atkinson endured for only eight years. Still, it was not without effect. Because of the security the expedition promised, Lisa in the summer of 1819 took his wife and her companion to his Council Bluffs post, the first white females to venture so far west. He reorganized the Missouri Fur Company but died (August 12, 1820) before he could start its first expeditions upriver. The work was carried on by the company's new president, Joshua Pilcher. Pilcher established Fort Recovery on Cedar Island, South Dakota, where an earlier post had burned in 1810, and built Fort Benton at the confluence of the Big Horn and Yellowstone rivers. In the fall of 1822 these posts sent $25,000 worth of furs to St. Louis. The trade at last was perking up, thanks in part to the abortive Yellowstone Expedition.

The fiasco found another echo in a wild-eyed plan offered to Congress by Representative John Floyd of Virginia. Floyd wished to establish a United States post not on the Yellowstone but at the mouth of the Columbia itself. The situation there was as cloudy as ever. True, America's diplomats after three years of argument had won their contention that the trading post of Astoria had been the victim of military action and should be returned to its owner under the stipulations of the Treaty of Ghent re-establishing a prewar *status quo*. In 1818 a representative of the United States government traveled all the way around the Horn for a symbolic restitution of the property. Astor himself, however, made no attempt to regain the post his agents had sold to the North West Company, and their men stayed on undisturbed.

Reaffirming private rights to a single small log trading establishment was not the same as raising a public flag over hundreds of thousands of square miles of territory between Mexican California and Russian Alaska. Unable to agree about ownership of the Northwest, the weary diplomats on October 20, 1818, signed a convention of joint occupancy that gave citizens of each country equal rights of trade or settlement during the next ten years. This suited British fur men just fine. The Americans were not likely to assert their privileges in the immediate future. None of them was any closer than the lower Missouri. But Nor'Westers and their rivals from the Hudson's Bay Company were firmly established in a dozen scattered posts west of the Rockies, most of them on waters of the Columbia drainage.

To Congressman John Floyd the situation was outrageous. He had a personal interest in the West: his first cousin, Sergeant Charles Floyd of the Lewis and Clark expedition, had been the only fatality of the transcontinental crossing. This interest was further stimulated during the winter of 1819–20, when Floyd was living at Brown's Hotel in Washington. The freshman senator from the newly admitted state of Missouri, Thomas Hart Benton, also had quarters there. So did a pair of lobbyists who were in Washington to oppose the government Indian-trading factories—Ramsay Crooks, by then the field manager of the American Fur Company operations out of Michilimackinac, and fellow Astorian Russell Farnham, who had gone to the Columbia aboard the ship *Tonquin*. In between feeding statistics to appropriate congressmen, Crooks and Farnham regaled Floyd with tales about the Northwest. Because of this, Benton recalled in his memoirs, Floyd "resolved to bring forward the question of occupation." Throughout his efforts the Virginia congressman was enthusiastically supported by the senator from Missouri.

Floyd's first bill, to put a "small trading guard" at the mouth of the Columbia, was submitted to the House on January 25, 1821. His arguments supporting it mentioned whale fisheries, commerce with China, timber for ships, better grass for horses "than even Andalusia or Virginia," soil suitable for "turnips, potatoes, onions, rye, wheat, melons of various kinds, cucumbers and various species of pease." He touched upon the Indian problem.[1] But his most

---

[1] The Indians also furnished Benton a resonant tocsin when he viewed with alarm the British and Russians in the Northwest. Suppose, he cried in March 1825 during a Senate debate on one of Floyd's bills, that either of those nations secured the alliance of the Northwest's 140,000 savages. They were the best horsemen in the world. "The present age has seen the Cossacks of the Don and Ukraine, ravaging the banks of the Seine and Loire; the next may see the Cossacks of Oregon issuing

earnest oratory was reserved for the old Lewis and Clark thesis about the benefits which would accrue to the fur trade from a transcontinental highway along their route, from one "smooth and deep river" (the Missouri) over a portage of only two hundred miles to "another river equally smooth, deep, and certain, uniting it to the great western ocean." As for this two-hundred-mile portage (from Great Falls, Montana, to Clark's Fork of the Columbia), "the labor of ten men for twenty days would enable a wagon with its usual freight to pass with great facility."

The Yellowstone scandal was still too fresh in the nation's mind for Congress to give serious consideration to a bill that would put a military fort as far away as the Columbia. After glancing through a copy of Floyd's report, Secretary of State John Quincy Adams wrote in his diary that it was "a tissue of errors in facts and abortive reasoning. . . . There was nothing could purify it but the fire." The bill was brushed aside.

Undeterred, Floyd kept popping up with others. In January 1822, partly to embarrass Adams by making him seem uninterested in the West, he offered a bill that would have organized The Territory of Oregon, the first official application of the name to a land area rather than just to a river. This bill too did not pass, but the enunciation of the Monroe Doctrine gave him fresh hope. That statement of policy, aimed as much at the Russians in the Pacific as at Europeans in Latin America, made Congress more amenable to proposals about Oregon. Floyd's next bill to occupy the Columbia passed the House but was defeated in the Senate in spite of Benton's support.

The bill which passed the House shifted routes a bit to the south. Floyd (and Benton) spoke now of traveling up the Yellowstone to the Big Horn, following that river to its source, and crossing from there to the Lewis (Snake) branch of the Columbia. Conceivably Floyd's mythical traveler could have circled from the Big Horn River to the Snake via South Pass. Many trappers later did. More probably, however, Floyd meant (so far as he meant anything specific) a route approximating that used by

---

in clouds from the gorges of the Rocky Mountains, and sweeping, with the besom of desolation, the banks of Missouri and Mississippi"—unless, of course, the United States occupied Oregon.

Wilson Price Hunt's outbound Astorians in 1811—over either Union or Two-gwo-tee Pass. Whatever the land route, there is always in the background "smooth, deep and certain" river navigation.

All this is passing strange. Both Floyd and Benton name Ramsay Crooks among their sources of information. Crooks had very nearly died in the Snake canyons, which, although deep, were neither smooth nor certain. By contrast, he had returned safely by land through South Pass. He was one of those who had stated flatly in an interview with the St. Louis *Missouri Gazettee* "that a journey across the continent of N. America, might be performed with a waggon . . . the whole route . . . being much the most direct and short one to go from this place to the mouth of the Columbia river."

What had happened in the intervening decade to that direct and short wagon route? One is tempted to speculate that the orators did not see it partly because they did not wish to. Wagons were prosaic. Steamboats were new and exciting. So the sedentary travelers in the halls of Congress, blissfully unfamiliar with the true nature of the western rivers, soared on the new magic of steam up the Missouri and its tributaries, skittered with deliberate vagueness over the Rockies, and landed on another majestic steamer somewhere in untroubled canyons on the far side. If Crooks expressed doubts about the thesis, and it seems incredible that he did not, his pessimism was never permitted to reach the rostrum.

The government factories, or trading houses, against which Ramsay Crooks was lobbying when first he talked to John Floyd and Thomas Hart Benton, were abolished in 1822. To the frontier this victory was almost as exhilarating as steam. One newspaper editorialized that, thanks to the abolition, established traders "have increased their capital and extended their enterprises; new firms have engaged in it and others are preparing to do so. . . . The Missouri Fur Company, which alone employs upward of 300 men, has reached the mountains and will soon be on the Columbia river. Others have the same destination."

Chief among the others was William Ashley. A native of Virginia, Ashley had lived in Ste. Genevieve below St. Louis since about the time of the Louisiana Purchase. He was light of frame, had a thin face, a jutting nose and chin. He liked soldiering and enlisted consistently in the militia. During the War of 1812, which he spent mostly in the lead district of Washington County making gunpowder, he rose to be a lieutenant colonel. By 1822 he was a brigadier general. Well educated, possessing a sound practical knowledge of geology and surveying, he was primarily interested in politics. When Missouri became a state he was elected her first lieutenant-governor. To further his career, he needed money. The reawakening fur trade seemed to offer the speediest opportunity.

He carried the idea to Andrew Henry, an old friend whose marriage (it lasted eighteen days) he had witnessed in 1805. In 1809, it will be remembered, Henry had joined the St. Louis Missouri Fur Company and the following year had been driven by Indians from Three Forks across the Divide to a tributary of the Snake. On his way home he possibly had discovered South Pass. He spent the war as Ashley's neighbor in the lead districts; perhaps the turbulent years had dimmed his memory of the Blackfeet. He agreed to join Ashley in a new fur company and go back to the headwaters of the Missouri.

Half-measures would not suit the ambitions of either partner. They meant to invade the mountains with well over a hundred men and press on from there as far as their luck allowed—perhaps even to the mouth of the Columbia, or so the St. Louis *Enquirer* remarked after Henry's departure with the first keelboat on April 3, 1822. Pointedly the reporter added in italics, *"If the government of the United States . . . will not listen to the proposition of Mr. Floyd, the enterprise of the Missourians will, in the end, accomplish his great object."*

Benjamin O'Fallon, who was Indian agent at Council Bluffs (and whose wife was William Clark's sister), also noted Henry's progress. Dutifully he wrote to his superior, Secretary of War John Calhoun, that he had heard Ashley and Henry had been given a license not just to trade but also to trap and hunt on the Missouri. If so, he hoped that strict limitations would be placed on the latter two pursuits, for "nothing is better calculated to alarm and disturb the harmony so happily existing between us and the Indians in the vicinity of Council Bluffs." Probably this was lip service only. Calhoun referred the matter to O'Fallon's brother-in-law William Clark, then serving as Superintendent of Indian Affairs in St. Louis. Clark (who in 1809 had joined Andrew Henry in a company that openly trapped in defiance of the law) replied piously that his department had authority to issue trading licenses only and he presumed the new firm would confine itself to that. No effort was ever made to stop Henry or Ashley or any other of the trapper-traders in the West. Most of them probably felt no incongruity in their situations. But one wonders about Ashley. Two years later he would be campaigning for the governorship of Missouri on a platform that at least tacitly would advocate compliance with the laws of his country.

Although troubled by desertions and the loss of forty horses to Assiniboin Indians, Henry reached the mouth of the Yellowstone approximately on schedule. There he built a fort. The supply boat following him had harder luck. Somewhat below Fort Osage it broke off its mast against an overhanging limb, yawed broadside to the current, and sank with merchandise worth $10,000. Apprised in St. Louis of the disaster, Ashley promptly readied another vessel. This he took to the Yellowstone himself, then in the fall returned to St. Louis in order to start two more boatloads of men and supplies toward the mountains as soon as the weather opened in the spring of 1823.

The new company was not going to have the fur grounds to itself. In October 1822, Missouri Fur Company men went past Henry's new stockade to the mouth of the Big Horn, where they occupied Fort Benton on the site of Lisa's old Fort Raymond. Leaders of the party were Robert Jones and Michael Immel. In the words of Agent O'Fallon, Immel was "in some respects... an extraordinary man ... brave, uncommonly large, and of great muscular strength. When truly apprised of danger, he was a host in himself." He had been with Andrew Henry at Three Forks in the bloody days of 1810 and had crossed with him to Henry's Fork of the Snake. So Michael Immel knew what could be expected of Blackfeet.

During the winter he was reminded again. Thirteen of the company's men deserted; as they were straggling north toward the Missouri, Blackfeet killed four and robbed the rest. Nevertheless, driven by the knowledge that his former boss was pressing on his heels, Immel went back to Three Forks with his partner Robert Jones and thirty men as soon as Bozeman Pass was open in the spring. They collected twenty packs of glossy pelts and started single file down the Jefferson toward the pass and home. Indians ambushed them. Immel, Jones, and five more died. Four were wounded. Traps, horses, and pelts vanished.

As usual, the Blackfeet were impartial in their pillaging. A few days prior to the Immel-Jones disaster another band of them caught several of Henry's men a few miles above Great Falls. They butchered four. That made a total of fifteen deaths, plus woundings, heavy losses in material, and destruction of morale. Let the Blackfeet keep their beaver. Once more the trappers fled from the area. Another five years would pass before competition in other sections brought the white men back—to still more deaths. Despite Congressman Floyd's new enthusiasm for the old route, the upper Missouri was no more practical as a highway than it had ever been.

Farther south the Arikaras were underscoring the same point. Throughout 1822 they had been friendly enough to the various trapping parties moving up the river, but in March of the following year something set them off. They robbed six Missouri Fur Company *engagés* near Fort Recovery, then attacked the post itself. Two of their number were killed during the ensuing defeat and several wounded. When Ashley's two keelboats approached the ramshackle stockades that surrounded their earthen villages, they were in a mood to seek revenge on the whites of any company.

Ashley was suspicious of them. But he wanted horses, whether to replace those Henry had lost the previous fall to Assiniboins or to dispatch a pack train due west into Wyoming is uncertain. Anyway, he took a chance. He anchored his boats as far offshore as the river channel allowed—it was narrow and crooked at that point—and held a series of councils. The Arikaras convinced him that their hearts were pure. Trade began—ammunition for horses. By evening Ashley had secured twenty or more head and the Arikaras were well armed.

To keep the Indians from stealing the horses back, forty men camped with the new property on a sandbar near the lower village—in spite of a threatening log breastwork which the Indians had erected on the bar earlier in the spring. The attack began at dawn. The heaviest shooting came from behind the breastwork.

In a twinkling most of the horses and eleven white men were dead. After a period of paralyzing confusion, the survivors fled down the river banks or got aboard the keelboats with as many of the injured as could be picked up. Some of the latter died. All told, casualties came to fifteen killed and nine wounded.

Utterly terrified by the debacle, Ashley's boatmen refused to try a run past the villages. Some wouldn't even consent to stay anywhere on the river. These quitters and some of the wounded Ashley sent in one of the keelboats downstream to Fort Atkinson, the outpost founded by the abortive Yellowstone Expedition. By letter he asked Colonel Henry Leavenworth, the commander at Atkinson, for help. He also sent a young trapper named Jedediah Smith and one other volunteer overland on a dangerous express to Andrew Henry. He then took twenty-three effective men and those of the wounded who agreed to stay with him several miles south to the Cheyenne River and settled down to await events.

Henry and fifty men, traveling by canoe from the Yellowstone post (and ignoring the Arikaras' invitation to land and trade), reached Ashley first. In some agony they discussed their next move. They could not tell how Colonel Leavenworth would respond to Ashley's appeal. Meanwhile time was running out. Their earlier disasters had shaken their credit in St. Louis. If they could not put trapping parties into the field this fall, they would be bankrupt.

In the end they decided to avoid both the Arikaras and the Blackfeet by obtaining horses from the Sioux and sending a party overland from where they were to the country of the Crows in central Wyoming. The horse-trading went slowly, however. Before the whites had obtained sufficient pack stock, word arrived that Leavenworth was moving upstream against the Arikaras.

With him came an army of two hundred soldiers, scores of trappers, and several hundred eager Sioux auxiliaries, the latter two groups commanded by Joshua Pilcher of the Missouri Fur Company. Ashley and Henry dropped their overland idea and decided to join the punitive expedition, a move that proved a serious mistake.

The Sioux engaged the enemy first outside their villages. As the rest of the army appeared, the Arikaras fell back behind the stockades. The Sioux grew bored with the siege that developed and departed after gorging themselves and their horses in the Arikara cornfields. After being bombarded ineffectually by Leavenworth's small cannon, the Arikaras sued for peace. Leavenworth was willing to settle on lenient terms, but Pilcher and the trappers demanded stern enough punishment to awe every tribe along the river. Before any sort of firm conclusion could be reached, the Arikaras simply decamped, slipping away from their villages unnoticed during the dead of night. With no one left to hold councils with, Leavenworth started back to Fort Atkinson. In defiance of his orders men from the Missouri Fur Company thereupon burned as much of the mud-plastered towns as was inflammable.

Intertwined controversies immediately erupted. The military praised Leavenworth's conduct as judicious and declared that he had gone as far against the government's allies, the Indians, as he should have in support of private enterprise. The trappers of course thought otherwise. Pilcher condensed their attitude in an angry open letter to Leavenworth which was published in the *Missouri Republican* on October 15, 1823: ". . . You came (to use your own language) to 'open and make good this great road'; instead of which, you have by the imbecility of your conduct and operations, created and left impassable barriers."

The causes behind the trouble also stirred heated discussion. A large body of opinion, particularly in the East, insisted that Ashley's company was illegal at best and should not have been defended by any military action whatsoever. Ashley was accused of "invading" Indian land (New York *American*, October 19, 1823) with a force of hunters "destroying more game in a year than [the Indians] would make in an age;" naturally the savages fought back (Detroit *Gazette*, October 17, 1823). The frontier states denied the charges with equal vociferation. In Congress, Missouri's Senator Benton insisted that Indian unrest sprang not from American trapping but from British intrigue. "The public mind has been most scandalously abused," he cried. Someone was trying to "overwhelm American traders with public odium" so that the British could continue in "the exclusive enjoyment of the fur trade beyond the Mandan villages." And so on.

Some of this talk would embarrass Ashley a few months later during his campaign for the governorship of Missouri. His first concern now, however, was to retrieve his sinking fortunes. So far as he and Henry were concerned, Leavenworth had accomplished nothing: the Montana fur grounds remained untrappable, the Missouri River unusable. Having wasted weeks of precious time on the campaign, there was nothing left now but to revert to the horseback trip they had envisioned before the advent of the military.

Henry got first call on such horses as they could purchase in the vicinity of Fort Kiowa, a trading post in central South Dakota. With these and the majority of the men he detoured far around the Arikaras to the Yellowstone. From there he would send men south into the Big Horn Basin of Wyoming and perhaps across the Rockies to the Snake. Ashley meanwhile struggled to find more pack stock for a small party he wanted to send directly west through the Black Hills into the Big Horn country, there to meet Henry's men. Leader of the group was young Jedediah Smith. Among the dozen or so men under him were three whose names would become familiar indeed along the Oregon Trail—Thomas Fitzpatrick, William Sublette, and James Clyman.

It was a hard-luck trip from the beginning. Ashley finally had to rent horses at Fort Kiowa, promising that his party would return the animals and their hired guide as soon as they could trade for horses of their own. Late September was at hand when at last they jogged off into the valley of the White River. Trying to shorten its windings with detours, they nearly perished of thirst. Eventually they found Boise Brule Sioux, from whom they bought enough horses to enable them to return the rented ones. Some of the men probably wished they had gone back too. The country grew steadily worse: gummy clay that during a misty rain balled up in great lumps on the horses' feet; cactus so dense that there was hardly room to spread out a bed. In the spectacular Badlands of western South Dakota they were boxed briefly in canyons so narrow they could not turn the horses and some of the company had to spend the night, Clyman insisted, "without room to lie down." A grizzly bear mauled Jedediah Smith, laying open his scalp, removing one eyebrow, and all but tearing off an ear. After sewing up the other wounds, Clyman approached the ear, "put in my needle stitching it through and through and over and over laying the lacerated parts togather as nice as I could with my hands." Ever afterward Jedediah Smith wore his hair long.

In time they joined Henry's men from the Yellowstone post and another group from the Missouri Fur Company. They apparently wintered with a camp of Crow Indians in the valley of the Wind River, near present Dubois. They swapped for some more horses, trapped a little, no doubt enjoyed the ready hospitality of the Crow women, and joined a tremendous buffalo hunt—a thousand animals slaughtered in a single great chase, according to Clyman, whose reminiscences constitute almost our only record of the adventures.

By February, Smith was restless and wanted to get his men away from the others, across the mountains into virgin territory. The direct way from the Wind River to either the Snake or the Green was along Wilson Price Hunt's old route over Union Pass. But February was too early and deep snow turned the party back. Hoping to find another way, Clyman made a relief map by heaping up sand on a buffalo robe and finally gleaned from the Crows directions to a route south of them. He may already have known that a passage lay in that direction: Stephen Long, for example, had been aware of Robert Stuart's crossing of South Pass when Long started for the Colorado Rockies in 1820. And it is always possible that Andrew Henry may have said something about it while the parties had been forming at Fort Kiowa. In that event, Clyman was simply clarifying directions. Or perhaps everything sounded brand-new. It is unlikely that we shall ever know.

As the group worked south up the Popo Agie fork of Wind River, the weather turned fierce. Powdery snow lashed like needles on the shouting gales. Buffalo vanished. When Sublette and Clyman, out hunting one morning, finally sighted three bulls "in a verry open and exposed place," their first concern was not to stampede the precious brutes. Tying their horses out of sight, they crawled for nearly a mile over snow and ice and succeeded in wounding one of the animals. While Clyman stalked it down, Sublette returned for the horses. Darkness caught them. They spread their robes on ground frozen as hard as iron. Snow particles searched through every crevice of their beds. By dawn they were too numb to hold flint and steel for striking a fire. Sublette rolled up again in his robe, ready to die where he lay. In a dim, instinctive search for warmth, Clyman ran his hands through last night's ashes. "to my Joy found a small cole of fire alive not larger than a grain of Corn." He got a blaze going. They warmed up enough to saddle their horses and rode to the shelter of timber four miles away. They arrived so rigid that Sublette could not dismount without help. But they had brought in a little meat.

The entire party crossed into Sweetwater Creek not many miles east of South Pass. But the gales hammered so relentlessly that they could not proceed. Retreating eastward down the creek, they found shelter in a grove of aspens beside the bleak stone ridges which border the stream on the north. Here they stayed for two or three weeks. Then the mountain sheep on which they subsisted grew too wild to kill and they had to move on. Before departing from the pleasant grove, they dug a cache. In it they placed extra powder and lead, and agreed that if they became separated during the spring hunt they would reassemble at the cache by June 1.

It was mid-March, 1824. The wind still roared as they inched back up the Sweetwater. Where the stream bends north toward the peaks of the Wind River Mountains, they left it and angled off through rolling swales of sagebrush, suffering afresh from thirst and hunger until Sublette and Clyman produced another buffalo. Some of the party had not eaten for four days. "now you may suppose we had a happy time in butchering . . . many of the men eating large slices raw."

Their camp that night must have been close to the top of the Pass, 7550 feet above sea level. Yet the impression was not of a defile such as is commonly connoted by the word *pass* but rather of a broad plain, sagebrush rising stiffly above the crusted, windswept snow. Running off to the northwest were the spectacular, ice-sheathed crags of the Wind River Mountains. Southward were gentler hills dotted sparsely with trees. The area between was twenty or more miles wide; some later emigrants would even call the stretch a plateau. It became the key to the West not because of any intrinsic passlike features, but because of the streams that led to it through a land of bitter deserts— Sweetwater Creek from the east, Little Sandy and its tributary Pacific Creek from the west. For 150 or more miles to the south one could drift across the divide at almost any point; but those were thirsty passages. The only safe way was to follow the creeks.

Even then it was easy to grow dry. Smith's men did. As they moved down the Pacific slope through the interminable wastes that border the Green River, they missed under the snow and ice the long quagmire where Pacific Creek oozes into being. When at last they reached its parent stream, Little Sandy Creek, toward noon, they started chopping eagerly at the ice with their tomahawks. It was thick; winters are cold up there. They hewed holes as deep as they could reach. Still no water. Dismayed, they were above to give up. Then Clyman "pulled out one of my pistols and fired in to the hole up came the water plentifull for man and beast."

On March 20 they reached the Green. Here the group split. Jedediah Smith went south with some of the men. Thomas Fitzpatrick took Clyman and a few others northward, probably as far as Horse Creek, near present Daniel, Wyoming. Indians stole their horses. Small matter. Beaver were thick: back on Wind River the Crows had said the animals were so plentiful that a hunter did not need traps; he could just walk along the riverbank clubbing them. Fitzpatrick and the others did not quite do that, but they did trap afoot for six weeks.

When time came to return to the appointed meeting place on Sweetwater Creek, they cached their furs and traps in the ground, hung their useless saddles in tree branches, and started walking. Amazingly, they ran into the very Indians who had stolen their horses. They got the jump on the startled savages, recovered the animals, and retrieved their furs. Then back through South Pass they went. It was the first repeat journey. Within that context—planned repetition—argument over who may or may not have crossed the gap ahead of them becomes irrelevant. Trails form when steps follow consciously one upon another. That was what happened this time. Never again would the way be forgotten.

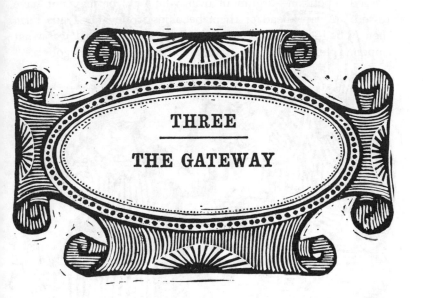

THREE

THE GATEWAY

10

STAMPEDE FOR FURS

Fitzpatrick's group reached the cache of powder and lead near Sweetwater Creek ahead of Smith's party.[1] As they waited beside the gurgling stream for the others, they wondered where it went—into the Platte or into the Arkansas? Did it grow deep enough farther downcountry that furs could be floated along it in a bullboat made of buffalo hides stretched over a willow frame? Boat travel would certainly beat packing and unpacking fractious horses every day.

Fitzpatrick and Clyman rode fifteen miles downstream to check. The creek stayed shallow. Fitzpatrick turned back, but Clyman was restless. He walked on east, planning to wait for the others wherever the stream became navigable. What happened to his horse he does not say. Probably Fitzpatrick took it back to the cache to use as a pack animal.

As Clyman trudged along, the Rattlesnake Hills curved toward him from the north. They were suited to their name: granitic, jagged, almost devoid of vegetation. The harsh, pink-brown, slabby rock was polished slick by ancient ice and wind. When

[1] Considerable speculation has been expended on the origin of the name Sweetwater. Its first known contemporary use occurs in William Ashley's diary, April 14, 1825, an offhand reference that suggests the word was already familiar to his men. If so, the creek was named at least by 1824. This all but rules out the fable that the baptism occurred when a packhorse loaded with sugar fell into the stream. Actually, the name is a natural for clear, fresh water in a country where most creeks are turbid with silt and bitter with alkali. Sweetwater quite possibly is an English translation of a name picked up from the Indians.

the sun struck it just right, its feldspar crystals glinted until the cliff faces seemed to shine with an inner heat.

Here and there the hills thrust out a blockading arm across the channel of the creek. The Sweetwater sliced abrupt gorges through these obstructions; future travelers would generally avoid these canyons by detouring around the tips of the arms. In other places the gaunt mountains pulled back to form giant coves. The Sweetwater ambled across the flats in a coiling ribbon. Paralleling its course on the south was another chain of hills, somewhat higher than the Rattlesnake Mountains, but more gently rounded and softened near their tops with tufts of trees. The broad valley and the coves between the mountain ridges contained very little timber—and little brush higher than a man's knees. Movement could be detected for miles.

Of the various short canyons the Sweetwater cut through the Rattlesnake granite the one farthest east was the most abrupt, a narrow slit only a quarter of a mile or so long but four hundred feet deep. Later emigrants named the place Devil's Gate and skirted it easily by a short swing to the south. On east the land flattened out, its sterility broken by detached round humps of granite. The most prominent of the humps, about three miles from Devil's Gate and close to the Sweetwater's northern bank, would became famous to westbound emigrants as Independence Rock, herald of the true mountains. To James Clyman, who for three days had been wandering beside more prominent bastions, it seemed less impressive. He passed it without comment and so came to a larger stream of whose identity he was not yet sure —the North Platte.

At the junction of the streams he hollowed out a sleeping place in a copse of willow brush and was about to light a fire when a war party of Indians rode by and camped on the other side of the creek. After they had quieted down, he slipped away through moonlight that seemed painfully bright, walking backward to confuse chance trackers. The next day, while he was exploring the nearby fiery-red canyons of the North Platte, the alarm was repeated with another band of savages. After that there was no movement whatsoever. For eleven days he waited beside the Sweetwater—"heard nothing of my party began to get lonesome examined my store of ammunition found I had plenty of Powder but only eleven bullets." He decided he had better use the ammunition trying to reach civilization instead of looking for his friends, whom he might not find.

Weeks later, far down the Platte, he crawled into the shade of a cottonwood tree, listened to swallows twitter overhead, and thought of home. He was sick of walking. Why not speed the trip by riding one of the wild horses that grazed nearby? Killing a buffalo with one of his precious bullets, he made a halter of the hide and crouched beside a watering place. His idea was to "crease" a horse—ticking the nerve along the neck with a bullet and stunning the animal long enough for him to seize it. Finally he dropped a fine black stallion, rushed over and put on the halter. The animal never budged. He had killed it. Perhaps he was fortunate; how a lone man could have managed a wild stallion bareback is difficult to imagine. It would have been quite a ride.

By now he was so lonesome that when he saw a camp of Pawnees, he walked over to it. The Indians would have killed him if one warrior had not taken a capricious fancy to the white man's long hair, unbarbered for more than a year and bleached by the sun—Clyman had lost his hat during the Arikara battle and had gone bareheaded ever since. Very gladly he let the buck hack off his locks with a dull butcher knife ("I bearly saved my scalp but lost my hair") and the Indian turned him loose.

With a dry horse bone he killed two badgers that were fighting each other and stumbled on, carrying their meat in a "bundle" made of grass and willow bark. Life fuzzed. Rains soaked him and he could not light fires. He had to swim several streams; mosquitoes were a plague. "A number of times I tumbled down asleep but a quick nervous gerk would bring me to my feet again." He had been walking for eighty days—600 miles. Suddenly Fort Atkinson loomed in front of him like a mirage out of his torpor. "I swoned emmediately how long I lay unconscious I do not know ... I made several attemps to raise but as often fell back for the want of strength to stand after some minnites I began to breathe easier but certainly no man ever enjoyed the sight of our flag better than I did."

Clyman had scarcely left the rendezvous on the upper Sweetwater when Jedediah Smith's party arrived. Hot weather sent a rush of snow water into the stream, and the trappers decided it could be navigated after all. Partly it was wishful thinking. Without the need of manpower to pack and unpack horses, most of the party could return to the fur grounds of the Green and stay almost indefinitely if Ashley would send in supplies.

While Fitzpatrick and two other men built a canoe-shaped leather boat for carrying the furs and the message to the settlements, Smith rode down the Sweetwater to find Clyman and bring him back to the trapping party. He located the camping place in the willows. He saw the Indian tracks. But he did not see Clyman, who was off exploring the canyons of the North Platte. Concluding that his friend had been slain, Smith rode sadly back to the rendezvous.

The groups parted. Fitzpatrick's bullboat bobbed along fairly well until it reached the cataracts in Devil's Gate. There it sank. (Clyman could hardly have been out of sight on his way east.) The three navigators lost two of their rifles, their camp gear, and all of their bullet lead. But they did manage to dive for and retrieve most of the furs. After caching these and hammering a few makeshift bullets out of the brass fittings of their one surviving rifle, they too started walking eastward. They reached Fort Atkinson ten days behind Clyman. They were, Clyman writes, "in a more pitible state if possible than myself."

Pitiable Fitzpatrick may have been. But he went to work with astounding energy. First he wrote Ashley a long letter telling about the wealth of beaver beyond the mountains and about the best route for reaching it. He asked for supplies; and since Ashley came with far more than Smith's small party required it is fair to assume that some of the men from Henry's Yellowstone post, who had wintered near Smith on Wind River, had followed the first group over South Pass (practically a highway now) and that Fitzpatrick had seen them somewhere along the Sweetwater. This essential letter written, Fitzpatrick sold the cached furs to courtly, moody Lucien Fontenelle, a trader at one of the Council Bluffs posts, rented horses, and rode back to Devil's Gate for the pelts. He had them at Fort Atkinson by the end of October 1824—and was ready to head straight back into the mountains with Ashley for more.

General Ashley needed good news. In August he had been defeated by the thinnest of margins for the governorship. Almost immediately thereafter Andrew Henry had come in from the upper Missouri with a disappointing catch and word that Minnetarees had robbed the Yellowstone post and had killed six men. Two more men had been lost to Sioux. In fact, every company on the upper river had been pummeled so severely that each was retreating. Henry too had had enough. Not even the cheering letter from Fitzpatrick about rich new country along the Green could tempt him out again.

This left it up to Ashley to take a supply caravan into the Rockies and buy his men's catch (mostly in exchange for merchandise) before the pelts could be siphoned off by some other alert trader, as Fitzpatrick's had been siphoned off by Fontenelle. He moved fast, squarely into the face of winter. First, he persuaded his longsuffering creditors to put up another $8000 worth of goods. Then he went through the usual routine of procuring a trading license.

A new wrinkle had been added to these documents. Stirred by the criticism of trapping which had surged up in the East after the Arikara battle, Congress had sought to tighten the government's control over the fur business. On May 25, 1824, an act was passed which required "Indian agents to designate from time to time Certain Convenient & Suitable places for Carrying on trade with different Indian tribes, and to require all traders to trade at the place thus designated and at no other place." The statute was anachronistic. Once, for example, the canoe Indians of the old Northwest had paddled as much as three hundred miles to bring their furs to the great fairs at Michilimackinac and Prairie du Chien. But the custom of extending liberal credit to the Indians and then following them to their hunting camps to collect the debts as fast as the pelts were acquired had long since made fixed posts obsolete for all but the trade in buffalo robes. Even the Indians disliked the extra travel which obedience to the law entailed. But neither their protests nor those of the fur companies availed. The act stayed on the books, and the western fur-gatherers learned to ignore this new stipulation in their permits as blandly as they did the strictures against trapping. After all, they weren't trading with Indians, except incidentally. They were supplying their trappers. So the licenses really didn't mean anything; they were just a form a man had to fill out in order to slip past the government's snoopers into the Indian country. Once there, he set up shop wherever he chose.

Even the geography Ashley used in obtaining his permit was a myth. His license granted him the right to trade with Snake Indians "at the junction of two large rivers supposed to be branches of the Buonaventura and Colerado of the West." The Colorado was known to flow into the Gulf of California; the Buenaventura was presumed by mapmakers of the time to flow into the Pacific. Since they were thought to be entirely different river systems, it is difficult to see how anyone could suppose that they or their branches joined.

Actually, of course, Ashley was not trying to present careful geography. He was going through the routine of putting down on a required license certain vague place names garnered from Fitzpatrick's letter and from the inaccurate charts available to him. He could not have known at the time, and neither could Fitzpatrick, that the Buenaventura did not exist. No one would know it until after fur trappers had unraveled the totally unexpected topography of the Great Basin, which is without drainage to the sea.

As Ashley prepared his supply train, a St. Louis newspaper, using information that must have come in Fitzpatrick's letter, remarked that the mountain trappers "have discovered a passage by which loaded wagons can at this time reach the navigable waters of the Columbia River. The route lies south of the one explored by Lewis and Clarke and is inhabited by Indians friendly to us." The statement did not raise as many eyebrows as it might have a few years earlier. During the preceding three summers small caravans of wagons had pushed across the plains to Santa Fe. Fitzpatrick's information, added to Ashley's knowledge of the Santa Fe adventure, may have persuaded the general to add a single vehicle to the pack mules and horses he assembled at Fort Atkinson in late October 1824. From the standpoint of beginnings that lone vehicle is of minor historic interest. It was the first wagon to aim toward Oregon, but it did not get far.

Winter is a harsh time on the high plains. The caravan, which started in November and traveled somewhat north of the Platte River, hoped to add to its food supplies at the Pawnee villages on the Loup Fork (east-central Nebraska). The Indians, however, had wandered off west toward their hunting grounds. As blizzards howled, rations in the caravan shrank. Feed for the livestock disappeared under two feet of snow; soon the men were supplementing their own diets with the stringy meat of animals that had starved to death. Drifts grew all but impenetrable and somewhere along here—Ashley's narrative of the trip neglects to say where—the wagon was abandoned.

Veering south to the Platte, the travelers overtook the Pawnees. The weather improved, but the Indians said that even so the whites were foolish to keep going west at such a season; they had better hole up until spring at the junction of the North and South Platte rivers, where the last considerable supply of firewood was available. Ashley's circumstances would not permit the delay, however. He paused at the junction only long enough to let his animals recuperate. Then, fortified by extra horses and buffalo robes which friendly Indians traded to him, he left the future Oregon Trail and pushed on up the South Platte to the foot of the Colorado Rockies. He followed that route because the Indians said more trees grew along it for fuel than along the North Platte, which Fitzpatrick and Clyman had descended during the summer.

Snow and cold again made travel dreadful. Within sight of the chill white hulk of Long's Peak, Ashley again had to let his men and animals rest, this time through most of February 1825. Then he forced the caravan to pack up again.

> Around us . . . everything was enveloped in one mass of snow and ice, but, as my business required a violent effort to accomplish its object, notwithstanding the mountains seemed to bid defiance to my further progress, things were made ready and on the 26th we commenced the doubtful undertaking. Our passage across the first

range of mountains, which was exceedingly difficult and dangerous, employed us three days.

Matters then improved. As often happens, snow was not so
deep in the high valleys. The first touches of spring softened the
air; the wayfarers were even able to trap a little as they went.

They swung north along the east base of the Medicine Bow
Mountains, then veered west again. Somewhat southeast of the
site of Rawlins, Wyoming, they reached the North Platte. Either
Clyman or Fitzpatrick, both of whom were with the caravan,
recognized the river, although they had never seen this section
of it. It flowed north, however, and Ashley wanted to go west.
So instead of following the Platte to the Sweetwater, he crossed
the Continental Divide at shallow Bridger's Pass (still south of today's U.S. Highway 30) and, sliding slightly northward, emerged
into the broad, dry Wyoming saucer now called Great Divide
Basin.[2] Fortunately, the party found snow to melt. Otherwise, as
Ashley remarked, the basin would be a most difficult area to
cross. Emigrant wagons, indeed, could never have crossed it.
Sweetwater Creek, farther north, proved their salvation.

Bewildered by the topography of the basin, on April 4 Ashley
and a few men climbed a butte, hoping to locate a creek that
flowed west into the Green. They saw nothing useful—but Crow
Indians saw them. The savages followed their tracks and a few
nights later made off with seventeen horses. Nine men pursued
the thieves as far as Sweetwater Creek, turned back empty-
handed. But at least the whites had found out where they were.

The packs of the lost animals were redistributed on the backs
of the men. On April 19 they reached the Green, far enough south
that they could see the spectacular east-west chain of the Uinta
Mountains into which the river plunges. The snowy summits suggested beaver streams. Ashley appointed a rendezvous for July
10 near the foot of the Uintas. (It turned out to be almost on
the present Wyoming–Utah border at the mouth of Henry's Fork,
which is a quite different stream from the Henry's Fork of the
Snake in Idaho.) He split his party into four trapping groups.
One of them he led down the Green himself in two buffalohide

[2] Not to be confused with the far larger Great Basin of Utah and Nevada.

boats, each approximately sixteen feet long and seven feet wide.

It was a wilder ride than he had bargained for. The Green breaches the Uinta Mountains in a thundering horseshoe canyon. The chasm's lower stretches, partly embraced by today's Dinosaur National Monument, are fantastic, bright-hued sandstone cliffs in places half a mile tall. A few later river runners in stouter boats would drown in the seething caldron, but somehow Ashley's cockleshells bobbed through.

Emerging damply at what has since been Ashley Creek (near Jensen, Utah, on Highway 40), the party met to their astonishment a pair of French trappers from a group who had come north out of Taos, New Mexico, under Etienne Provost and a man named LeClerc. After some jockeying around and a little deeper exploration of the Green, the parties joined, Provost's horses carrying the goods Ashley had floated through the canyon.

Provost knew this country from previous visits. He led the way to the western end of the Uinta Mountains, crossed the Provo River (it should be spelled Provost) swung northward, and came within thirty miles of Great Salt Lake. Veering eastward, he then brought the combined groups to the rendezvous site on Henry's Fork. General Ashley of the Missouri militia had completed a rugged loop that would be difficult to follow even today.

All told, 120 men were gathered at the wilderness depot. Twenty-three (twenty-nine by some counts) were deserters from the Hudson's Bay Company. In their persons the American and British ends of the Oregon Trail pulled briefly together.

One of Astor's Canadian partners in the Pacific Fur Company who drifted back into the employ of the North West Company after it had secured Astoria was barrel-bodied Donald McKenzie. McKenzie, it will be remembered, had made the western overland crossing with Hunt. In 1816, it became his herculean job to develop for the new owners of Astoria the fur trade of the southern Snake—that is, the lower half of Idaho, through which he had traveled so desolately in 1811.

McKenzie knew that the mountain Indians could not and would not trap. He knew that he would have to abandon the classic trading patterns of eastern Canada, whereby Indians brought furs to fixed posts for barter, and instead would have to produce the pelts with his own hunters, as Americans had begun doing east of the Rockies. With this difference: the American trappers, many of them veterans of the lonesome Kentucky woods, were content to go out in all-male parties. McKenzie, however, had to depend on a motley gang of French-Canadian *voyageurs* and Iroquois hunters who wanted their Indian wives along with them to keep house in the mobile wigwams and prepare the skins after their husbands had dragged the beaver from the streams. This meant, in effect, trapping with a regular village and its hullabaloo—dogfights, horse races, family squabbles, community sings, and crying babies. Some of the Catholic *voyageurs* and converted Iroquois even held a form of religious observance on Sundays. As fur-producers, the Snake River brigades do not sound efficient. Nevertheless, McKenzie made them work.

For a base of operations he built Fort Nez Percé in the tawny wastes where the Walla Walla River flows into the sun-dazzled, mesa-girt Columbia. From there, beginning in 1818, he pushed his brigades along Robert Stuart's old route (the future Oregon Trail) into southern Idaho. Alexander Ross, another ex-Astorian who worked with McKenzie for a time, nicknamed him Perpetual Motion. During his endless moves he discovered Bear Lake on the border between southeastern Idaho and Utah, which Stuart had missed. He reached Pierre's Hole west of the Tetons and may have crossed into Jackson Hole. His men entered the valley of the Green before Jedediah Smith did. The long horse caravans by which William Kittson brought them supplies from Fort Nez Percé and took their furs back to the navigable waters of the Columbia wore clear paths for the future into the arid soil.

The fur brigades did not hold to the route, however. In 1821, the year McKenzie's contract was up and he returned East, the North West and Hudson's Bay companies amalgamated under the name of the latter concern. New brooms whisked in every direction. The starting point for the Snake River brigade was shifted to Flathead Post on Clark's Fork of the Columbia, near the Continental Divide in western Montana. The move brought the trappers closer to good beaver country—and also to the Blackfeet. During the next few years the Indians struck so savagely at the brigades that after one furious battle Finan McDonald, who had crossed the Divide first with David Thompson in 1807, declared he would not return to the Montana area until beavers grew "Gould Skins."

In 1824, the Hudson's Bay Company's governor for all Canada, regal, pudgy little George Simpson, swept over Athabaska Pass with the new chief factor for the Pacific Northwest, Dr. John Mc-Loughlin. McLoughlin, a white-haired giant six feet four inches tall, was then forty years old and married to the half-breed widow of Alexander McKay, an Astorian who had died aboard the *Tonquin* during the massacre at Nootka. McLoughlin and Simpson abandoned Fort George, as Astoria had been renamed, and early in 1825 began building, as headquarters post for the Columbia Department, massive Fort Vancouver. The new establishment, which soon would boast an orchard, grain fields, docks for ocean-going schooners, a church and jail as well as many cabins and warehouses, stood a hundred-odd miles inland from salt water on the north bank of the broad river, a few miles above the island-studded mouth of the Willamette. During the next two decades Fort Vancouver was the most famous fur-trading post in America. Without it and its factor, John McLoughlin, the history of the Northwest becomes inconceivable.

Even before Fort Vancouver was started, Simpson and Mc-Loughlin heard that American trappers had crossed the Rockies. The move was not unexpected. The Hudson's Bay Company had watched sharply American activity on the upper Missouri. They had picked up from the newspapers stories of Floyd's proposals in Congress to found settlements on the Columbia and of the Ashley-Henry intent to cross to the headwaters of the same river. Unless those trappers were somehow checked, an invasion of the Oregon country would inevitably follow. This was bad enough. Even worse was the American trapper's historic role throughout the East and Midwest as the forerunner of settlement. The fur trade ended as soon as settlers came into an area. This suited American patterns of growth. But the Hudson's Bay Company wished to preserve the transmontane West (at least that part of it north of the Columbia) as a perpetual source of pelts.

Thus, when Alexander Ross was appointed to lead the 1824

199

brigade from Flathead Post in Montana to the Snake country of Idaho, he was specifically warned to have nothing whatsoever to do with any American trappers he chanced to meet.

Characterizing Ross, in George Simpson's words, as "a self sufficient empty headed man ... full of bombast and marvelous nonsense" is perhaps overly severe. But he could not manage his Iroquois. Although he knew it was a mistake, he let a group of them wander off to trap independently during the spring and summer of 1824. Somewhere near the Green they were robbed by Snake Indians of nearly everything they possessed—900 beaver (they said), 54 traps, 27 horses, 5 guns, even clothing, to say nothing of their courage. They did have another 105 beaver hidden in a cache, however. When the terrified Iroquois chanced across Jedediah Smith and six of his men roaming westward in October, perhaps near present Blackfoot, Idaho, they offered their 105 pelts to the Americans in exchange for safe conduct back to Ross' party, camped in Lemhi Valley 150 miles to the northwest.

This beat trapping—and also would bring the Americans in touch with an experienced group who, through its knowledge of the area, could save the interlopers months of groping. Smith agreed at once. And when Ross turned his brigade back to Flathead Post, the Americans tagged along, looking over the country as they went. "I take [them] to be spies," the leader wrote unhappily in his journal. But he did not know how to get rid of them. He even let them hang around the post during the time (November 26 to December 20, 1824) the next brigade was outfitting itself for its winter and spring hunt.

During that month Ross was replaced as brigade leader by a far abler man, squat, muscular, tempestuous Peter Skene Ogden. When Ogden started south with his heterogeneous brigade of fifty-eight men and an unspecified number of wives, Smith's Americans again tagged along. They spent several snowbound weeks with the Canadians in Lemhi Valley. Ogden did find a measure of revenge by trading them supplies, at his own prices, for the 105 beaver they had obtained from the Iroquois. Then the Americans hurried on and found their own revenge by trapping the streams ahead of Ogden as both groups moved south.

During the latter part of May 1825, in what is now northern

Utah, Peter Ogden was startled to encounter still more interlopers. The first group was Provost's party from Taos. Shortly
thereafter a second arrived with a skirl of truculence—twenty-
five or so Americans led by Johnson Gardner from Andrew Henry's
post on the distant Big Horn. A little earlier Gardner's men had
met several of Ogden's trappers working the nearby streams and
had prevailed on them to desert, bringing their pelts with them.
The easy victory sharpened Gardner's appetite. Raising an American flag that someone had been packing through the hills all
the way, presumably from St. Louis, he took his trappers belligerently into the British camp. There he lured others of the
brigade away from the Canadians by offering more for their 700
skins than the Hudson's Bay Company ever paid its men for pelts.

Although Ogden had not seen Jedediah Smith for weeks and
did not see him among the invaders, he nevertheless suspected
Smith's scheming in the background. "A sly cunning Yankey,"
Ogden's clerk William Kittson had called Jedediah in his journal.
And Ogden exploded in his own writing about "that damn'd all
cursed day that Mr. Ross consented to bring the 7 Americans
with him to the Flat heads." But there is no direct evidence that
Smith was involved in the encounter. Gardner seems to have been
the prime mover.

The wounds inflicted, he rubbed in salt. He told Ogden that
this was American land: "remain at your peril." [3]

Tension leaped; guns were cocked. But no one fired the ir-
revocable shot.

As the groups prepared to separate the next day, Gardner repeated his geopolitical errors. His misinformation probably arose
from garbled rumors trickling into the mountains about Congressman Floyd's and Senator Benton's reiterated bills to occupy
Oregon and establish forts on the Missouri. The frontier was
inclined to let suggestion stand for accomplishment. At least
Gardner seemed to have no doubts about the future. He blurted,
according to Ogden,

> ... you will see us shortly not only in the Columbia but at the Flat
> Heads & Cootanies as we are determined you Shall no longer re-

---

[3] The episode occurred south of the 42nd parallel in territory belonging to Mexico.

main in our Territory, to this I made answer when we should receive orders from our Government to leave the Columbia we would
but Not before   to this he replied our troops will make you this
Fall   we then parted.

The Americans and the Hudson's Bay Company deserters rode
triumphantly eastward to the rendezvous on Henry's Fork. There
in July Gardner gave his version of the clash to Ashley. The general was an adept politician. Yet in all likelihood he did not sense
the long-range international developments inherent in the encounter. Foresight was not the forte of the American frontiersman. On learning of Ogden's defeat, Ashley no doubt laughed
heartily with the rest of the boys and filed the event in his memory
as a rousing way to garner a few hundred extra pelts. Perhaps
more could be plucked next year from the same source.

Next year, however, was sufficient unto itself. Ashley's immediate, burning concern was with *this* year's harvest. Cheer-
fully he lashed his loads onto his packhorses and prepared to go
home to his creditors. He not only had furs enough at long last
to satisfy their most pressing demands; he also had an exciting new
idea about the old routines of the business.

Traders had always made their big money by swapping supplies
at astronomical markups to unsophisticated Indians in exchange
for pelts on which abnormally low values were placed. When
white trappers had been substituted for red hunters, variations
of the barter continued. Wages for trapping were in large part
paid in the form of merchandise. Even the so-called free trappers
(men not bound by contract to any particular employer) swapped
at least part of their take for useful articles—what good was
money in the wilderness? But once the navigable rivers were
left behind, no standard routine existed for providing those goods.
Men took with them what they needed for each trip, plus odd-
ments of fofarraw for their Indian women back in the hills. On
their return they received credits for their pelts on the company's books and drew against that credit for alcohol to celebrate
their success and then to outfit themselves for the next hunt.

Where trading posts stood relatively close to the hunting
grounds the haphazard system worked. But no American posts

existed anywhere near the country which South Pass had opened
to an inrush of eager trappers. What were the men to do? Riding clear to the Missouri to exchange pelts for merchandise would
be impossible within the short slack season of summer, when furs
were not prime enough to justify hunting. But, so Ashley reasoned from the experience of this one gathering in 1825, supplies
could be brought to the men. They should not be brought to a
fixed post, however. South Pass had thrown open the whole of
the Far West for them to roam through (if they could outwit
the Hudson's Bay Company and the Mexican government) and
a traditional fort would cramp this heady new freedom of movement. Rather, let the supplies come to an open-air gathering located afresh each year to suit the conveniences of the moment.
There, at an annual frolic a week or two long, the classic patterns
of the trade could be re-established: an exchange of supplies at
high markup to unsophisticated mountain men for pelts at depressed prices. Three dollars a pound was the mountain rate Ashley established for furs that would bring close to five dollars in
St. Louis. Getting them to St. Louis, however, was not easy.

Essentially very simple in its patterns, the rendezvous system
nevertheless controlled the operations of the great fur stampede
during the next dozen tempestuous years. Peter Skene Ogden
recognized its advantages immediately. On July 1, 1826, from
Burnt River in the eastern part of today's Oregon, while his American rivals were assembling for their second rendezvous three
hundred miles away in Cache Valley, he wrote unhappily to Governor Simpson about his handicaps:

> In all the different expeditions to the Snake Country two thirds of
> the time is lost travelling to and from headquarters, far different
> is the mode the Americans conduct their trapping expedition, their
> trappers remain . . . in their hunting ground and their equippers
> meet them annually secure their furs and give them their supplies
> and although great the expense and danger they have to encoun-
> ter to reach the Missouri, still they find it to their advantage to
> conduct their business this way.

Although trappers were abused economically by the system,
they liked some of its results. Charles Keemle, a fur trader turned

newspaper publisher, put the matter this way in his *Missouri Herald and St. Louis Advertiser* (November 8, 1826): Although many of Ashley's men had been away from the settlements since 1822, they "are too happy in the freedom of those wild regions to think of returning to the comparative thraldom of civilized life." This freedom, which they arrogated to themselves in defiance of United States law, the mountain men turned, as an incident of their craft, to the good of their country. Thanks to Ashley's rendezvous system they need worry no longer about supplies. Each summer, so they were promised (and in full faith they believed that promise) new quantities would come to them up the valley of the Platte, over South Pass—the eastern half of what a later people would call the Oregon Trail. They were free to roam wherever streams or the promise of streams took them. Roam they did. Within a single decade they mastered the entire complex geography of the Rocky Mountain area and much of the farther West. Probably no other comparable amount of topographic information was ever assimilated so thoroughly anywhere else in so brief a time.

There was one stubborn area which they did not master, however—the Oregon country. Forewarned by Johnson Gardner's blatant challenge to Ogden, the Hudson's Bay Company stiffened its determination to keep the United States away from the Northwest.

The Convention of 1818, which gave citizens of each country equal rights of trade and settlement, was due for review before 1828. A boundary treaty might emerge from that review. If so, the British government might yield to the Americans the land south of the Columbia River. In optimistic moments the directors of the Hudson's Bay Company hoped that "south of the Columbia" might be taken to mean "south of the Columbia's principal southern branch," the Snake—or, as the Americans then called it, the Lewis River. But the Bay Company's main concern was the richer area spreading north of the Columbia as far as Alaska. They were particularly anxious about New Caledonia, the old name for British Columbia, whose furs were brought by pack train to the Columbia River and down that stream in barges to ships waiting at Fort Vancouver. All that area must somehow be kept safe from penetration.

The Americans, on the other hand, wanted the fine harbors of the Puget Sound country. (Mexico controlled the only other first-class bays on the Pacific, those of California.) Accordingly, the diplomats of the United States were insisting on a boundary at least as far north as the 49th parallel. Their claim, however, would not be tenable if no Americans were established anywhere near the Columbia and Britons were. One way to keep the American out was to remove temptations that might lure trappers northward—that is, to strip the country bordering the Columbia bare of beaver. Governor Simpson summed up the point thus in a letter in July 1827 to John McLoughlin, his giant factor at Fort Vancouver:

> The greatest and best protection we can have . . . is keeping the country closely hunted as the first step the American government will take toward Colonization is through their Indian traders and if the country becomes exhausted in Fur bearing animals they can have no inducement to proceed hither.

The eastern and southern boundaries of present Idaho became, roughly speaking, the frontier where the battle of the pelts was fought. It is questionable whether American trappers, including General Ashley, ever sensed that political motives lay behind their opponents' ruthless exploitation of the beaver streams. Their own practice was to grab everything in sight without thought for the future; they probably supposed (if they considered the matter at all) that the British were acting in similar fashion.

So now the second route to the West was being barred. First, Blackfeet had closed the remote passes beyond the upper Missouri. Now the English were solidly athwart the even more vital trails along the Snake River. No shooting war developed from this second conflict—the Honorable Company had grown too adroit for that—but the semblance of peace made the barrier no easier to breach. In fact, the vaunted mountain man of the West never did succeed in pushing through.

11

THE BRITISH BARRIER

Jedediah Smith went east with Ashley from the 1825 rendezvous on Henry's Fork. Supplies were still short in the mountains. Ashley had not anticipated Provost's trappers from New Mexico or the defectors from the Hudson's Bay Company. In order to repair their welcome inroads on the stores, if possible, Smith was going to rush in another supply caravan during winter. In return for his pains, and probably for some of his furs too, Ashley was accepting him as a full partner in the enterprise.

The two men and their twenty roustabouts crossed South Pass but did not follow the Platte to Council Bluffs. Instead, they left the Sweetwater for the Popo Agie and followed that stream toward navigable water on the Big Horn River. They had several cogent reasons for abandoning what they now recognized as the best horse trail back to the settlements.

First, there was—at some unspecified location east of South Pass—a cache of forty-five packs of furs; Ashley separated briefly from Smith to pick them up. Added to the pelts he already had acquired at the rendezvous, this brought the total to approximately 9000 pounds, worth $45,000 or more in St. Louis. Packing that much fur, in addition to camp gear, required many horses and men—yet both could be better employed west of the mountains. As soon as Ashley could load his pelts into bullboats, in order to float them down the Big Horn and Yellowstone rivers to the Missouri, he could send his trappers and their animals back to the Green. (Not all the horses went, however; several were lost and one man was wounded in scuffles with Indians.) Finally, he hoped to meet along the Missouri a military expedition which he knew was in the country that summer making treaties with the savages. Its protection would enable him to dispense with still more men during the rest of his trip to St. Louis.

The soldiers were there because, in spite of the collapse of the 1819–20 Yellowstone Expedition, the frontier had kept prodding the government to establish a military post high on the Missouri.

As a compromise step in that direction, Senator Benton in 1824 had prevailed on the War Department to spend $10,000 entering into treaties with the river tribes. To do this in appropriate style, 476 soldiers supported by eight keelboats were sent along with the negotiators. Benton hoped that some of these troops would be stationed in the Mandan villages during the next winter, and that cumulative results of the show would persuade the Army to maintain a permanent garrison on the upper river.

A mounted company and two infantry battalions left Fort Atkinson in May 1825. General Henry Atkinson was in command of the soldiers; Indian Agent Benjamin O'Fallon supervised the treaty-making. All told, seventeen different tribes and subtribes were gathered in from the prairies to be awed by this exhibition of might. Skyrockets and artillery displays were particularly effective. But then the Crows found out what made the cannons fire, and lost their fear. Secretly they stuffed the touchholes of the big guns full of dirt and confidently grew insolent with Agent O'Fallon. Losing his temper, O'Fallon knocked down a Crow chief with the butt of his pistol. A melée developed. Interpreter Edward Rose leaped into it, larruping his adopted tribesmen left and right with a gunbarrel. This distraction gave Atkinson time enough to rush in some infantry, and at a subsequent feast of buffalo ribs the Crows decided that they too had better sign the papers.

The Blackfeet never did. Although Atkinson pushed many miles beyond the mouth of the Yellowstone, his scouts could find none of the confederated bands of that surly nation or any Assiniboins. He abandoned the effort and also Benton's idea of wintering some of the troops at the Mandan villages. "Vegetable food," he said, "is deemed indispensable to the health of the troops, & this could not be had at the Mandans," a curious development, since those Indians were the principal agriculturists of the Missouri. More critically, Atkinson also decided that occasional troop movements through the Indian country were a better method than forts to keep the savages in hand.[1] Home the Army went. Whatever dim

[1] The Army's preference for mobile displays of force over permanent establishments, in the Indian country, prevailed until well into the 1840s, and even then gave ground slowly. What changes might have been brought to the history of the West

hope still remained that the Missouri might become a usable way to the Pacific thereupon ended forever.

Smith and Ashley met the expedition at the mouth of the Yellowstone, transferred the furs to one of the Army's keelboats, and returned to St. Louis in comfort. On October 30, less than a month after their arrival, Smith started back for the mountains with a sizable caravan nursed along by approximately sixty men. Their mode of travel was still unusual enough for the *Missouri Republican* to mention that they were going by land and not up the Missouri by keelboat or steamer.

For winter it was a tremendous journey. The party left the river where the Oregon Trail later would, at the Kaw (Kansas). But they forded the Kaw near its mouth, as the trail would not do, and started westward along its north bank. At the site of Topeka there was another variation. The later trail would ford the Kaw here and angle northwestward over the Vermillion, the Blue, and along the valley of the Little Blue to the Platte. Smith's caravan, however, continued up the Kaw to its Republican Fork and followed that stream a few score miles before veering sharply north to rejoin the standard route. In other words, the eastern tip of the great trail, though perhaps known to random wanderers, had not yet become automatic for travel.

After crossing South Pass, Smith again left the trail. Traveling through what must have been bitter weather, he worked up the Green, crossed to the Hoback and evidently entered Jackson Hole, either to trap for himself or to supply by prearrangement trappers already there, or both. From the Snake he turned up Salt River in western Wyoming and crossed to Bear River via Thomas Fork, a stretch which duplicated in part Robert Stuart's detour during the fall of 1812. He wintered either at the mouth of the Bear or perhaps farther around the east side of the Great Salt Lake near the Weber.

When Ashley left St. Louis in March for the rendezvous of 1826, held that year in southeastern Idaho's Cache Valley, he too eschewed the eastern end of the trail, traveling instead the usual

---

by a contrary policy (by military forts along any of the routes to Oregon, for example) is of course idle guesswork.

fur-caravan route all the way up the Platte from its mouth. After crossing South Pass he continued to Cache Valley by the undulating way along Sandy Creek to the Green to Henry's Fork and then along the horseshoe curves of Bear River. Although trappers may have known of direct trails through the immense, sterile deserts that lie between Sandy Creek and the Bear, caravans did not yet deliberately risk that thirsty and dangerous stretch.[2]

The spring hunts had been vigorous. Smith perhaps trapped the complex hills and canyons between the Wasatch and Uinta mountains. Another party reached Flathead country and in August made noisy threats to the factor at the Hudson's Bay post on Clark's Fork about the American government's designs on the Columbia. David Jackson nearly starved in the grisly deserts west of Salt Lake, trying to find its nonexistent outlet, and then retreated into the mountains north of what is now Boise, Idaho. Another party, formed in part of deserters from the Hudson's Bay Company, ran directly into Ogden himself. This time there were no cheap pelts for Ashley to pick up. As Ogden reported matters in a letter of October 10, 1826, while exploring the streams "which discharge on the South side of the Snake River . . . we met with a party of Americans and some of our deserters, in all 28 . . . . the few beaver they had I obtained from them from our deserters in part payment of their debts and the remainder in trade with the Americans."

Even without those pelts enough beaver came to the Cache Valley rendezvous to content Ashley—123 packs. But dependence on furs alone was risky. Surer profits lay in freighting the pelts to civilization and bringing back goods enough to keep the trappers busy. At the conclusion of the rendezvous he transferred the merchandise that remained from the summer's trading and the service of his forty-two hunters to the new firm of Jedediah Smith, David Jackson, and William Sublette. The price was

[2] The short cut across the desert would be worked out at least by 1836 and would be named for two different mountain men: Greenwood Cutoff for Caleb Greenwood, who is said to have reached the West with the Astorians; and Sublette Cutoff for William Sublette. It involved a stretch of forty-plus miles without a drink for man or stock.

$16,000, from which was deducted $5000 owed to Smith from his and Ashley's brief partnership. In payment of this debt the general agreed to accept beaver in the mountains at $3 a pound, or to transport it to St. Louis and sell it for the new company at a charge of $1.12½ a pound. On its part, the firm of Smith, Jackson & Sublette agreed to sell its entire next year's catch to Ashley and to order from him, for delivery at Bear Lake the following July (1827), merchandise worth not less than $7000 or more than $15,000. The exact amount would be specified in a message sent to Ashley no later than March 1, 1827, in time for him to ready his caravan.

The new partners plunged hard for success. Jedediah Smith started south through Utah, found fewer beaver than he expected, pressed doggedly across the Mojave Desert and reached Southern California. Jackson and Sublette went north, competing with Ogden, trading as well as trapping. They entered the spectacular Wyoming "hole" that soon would bear Jackson's name and later discovered the geysers and rumbling subterranean phenomena of Yellowstone Park (unless, as seems unlikely, Colter had seen the displays first during his traverse of the area in 1807–8). By year's end they were back in the valley of the Great Salt Lake. Although Smith had not reappeared with word of his needs, the other two partners roughed out a list of supplies they wanted from Ashley.

On January 1, 1827, Sublette started east on snowshoes with a single companion, wiry Moses Harris—nicknamed Black because his complexion looked, an acquaintance remarked, "as if gunpowder had been burned into his face." They carried dried meat on their backs, and fifty pounds of coffee, sugar, and other supplies on a huge Indian pack dog. The trek turned into another of the West's gruesome ordeals. They seldom found game enough to stave off hunger. Until they reached the Sweetwater they had little to drink but melted snow. Along the woodless Platte they often had to keep moving half the night to escape freezing. They outwalked the dog. Time after time it limped into camp hours behind them. One starving evening they fell on it and weakly beat the feebly resisting animal to death. The meat kept them going until they killed a lone rabbit; that, and later a few wild turkeys, buoyed them along an Indian trace—in eastern Kansas now, the Big Vermillion, the Oregon Trail—to an Indian village. Sublette traded his pistol to get a horse for Harris, whose ankles had given out. They floundered into St. Louis on March 4, four days after the specified time. Ashley honored the contract nonetheless.

The general sent agents west this year to handle his interests. Sublette led the caravan, after less than a month's rest. Before starting he acquired a new license for his firm, authorizing them to trade, among other places, at Horse Prairie, a little east of the Hudson's Bay Company's Flathead post on Clark Fork, and at the junction of the Lewis (Snake) and Columbia rivers. These gestures became routine during the next few years and were legal enough: the Convention of 1818, renewed indefinitely in 1827, granted equal rights of commerce to citizens of both countries. But paper rights were one thing; asserting them was another. Though American trapping parties bothered the English somewhat in the Flathead area of western Montana, they never reached the junction of the Snake and Columbia. And no rendezvous was ever held deeper inside the Oregon country than Pierre's Hole, just west of the Tetons. Simpson's policy of ravaging the land was paying off.

The future was nevertheless incipient in the caravan of 1827. It took the first wheels across South Pass. Their rumble was faint —a two-wheeled gun carriage on which was mounted a fourpounder cannon pulled by a pair of mules. Presumably the artillery was taken along to awe the Indians, but somehow it missed a sharp skirmish near the Bear Lake rendezvous site: Blackfeet against Snakes and Utes, aided by six whites, one of whom was William Sublette. So far as records show, the gun's only shot was a salute of welcome to Jedediah Smith. At three o'clock on the afternoon of July 1 he dramatically returned from California, gaunt and empty-handed, with only two men and a Snake Indian guide he had picked up near Salt Lake.[3]

[3] The boom of that salute to Smith reached Mexico City. In the course of its transmission the rendezvous swelled to a military fort—after all, Ashley was associated with it and he was a general—the single cannon to three pieces of artillery, the gun carriage to five wagons. Smith's visit to California was called an "iruption,"

Deep snow in the Sierra Nevada Mountains had forced Smith to leave all but two of his party and $5000 worth of beaver in the San Joaquin Valley of central California. Crossing the deserts of Nevada and Utah to report his situation to his partners had been a harrowing experience, yet within nine days he was taking another party back across the Mojave to retrieve his furs and men. The previous trip had been difficult. This one was catastrophic—but it did let him see, eventually, how Hudson's Bay Company operated.

Mojave Indians slaughtered ten of his men at the crossing of the Colorado River, somewhat north of present Needles, California. Suffering fiercely from thirst, the nine survivors made the August crossing of one of America's most deadly wastes by traveling at night. He found his men, but before being allowed to proceed was harried by suspicious California officials. To avoid packing his beaver to the next rendezvous, he sold them for fifty cents less a pound than he could have obtained in the mountains. He spent about $1500 of the $3920 he received on supplies for his men and invested the balance in 250 horses and mules. The animals would be worth fifty dollars each at the rendezvous—if he got them there.

Continual rain, bottomless mud, and flooded streams held progress to a miserable crawl as the party moved northward into Oregon, trapping as much as weather and their remaining traps allowed. During May and June they slogged painfully through the tangled, fog-clammy mountains along the Oregon coast. On July 14, 1828, on the Umpqua River, Indians attacked. Fourteen men and an Indian boy who was in camp with the whites perished. One man escaped the battle. Jedediah Smith and two more survived because they were out looking for a usable trail.

Nearly four weeks later the survivors reached Fort Vancouver. Factor John McLoughlin and Governor Simpson, when he arrived a little later on one of his rare hurricane visits, showed them every

and the Mexican government told our representative that it was very unhappy about the whole affair. By contrast, the Hudson's Bay people did not mention the episode in their correspondence. Their policy was working quite smoothly without government help.

courtesy. McLoughlin dispatched a brigade with Smith to recover as much of the Americans' property as possible. In the dismal rains of fall they buried the eleven skeletons they were able to find, and slowly gathered together thirty-eight horses and a few more than 600 pelts. After loftily informing Smith that the salvage operation cost the company £1000 "independent of the loss of Profits we had reason to calculate" from the brigade's interrupted trapping, Simpson bought the furs and horses for $2369.60. Altogether, the property Smith had possessed before the Indians' attack might have grossed, at the rendezvous, five or six times that. The debit column carried, in addition, twenty-five deaths.

Still another American, Joshua Pilcher, intruded on Simpson's attention that winter. An attempt by Pilcher's decaying Missouri Fur Company to enter the mountain trade had ended disastrously and the firm had dissolved after the Bear Lake rendezvous of 1828. Pilcher and a handful of men wintered at Flathead Lake in northwestern Montana, less than a hundred miles east of the Bay Company's post on Clark's Fork. Half of the few pelts they managed to obtain they had to trade to the British for necessary supplies.

Faced with ruin, Pilcher by letter proposed to Simpson a joint, illegal venture. If Simpson would furnish him an outfit, he would lead it across the Divide onto the headwaters of the Missouri. This was Blackfoot country, rich in beaver since it had been scarcely touched by trappers; but it was also American land, where the Hudson's Bay Company had no right to be. Simpson replied, on February 18, 1829, that "although the protecting laws of your Government might be successfully evaded by the plan you suggest still I do not think it would be reputable in the Honble Hudsons Bay Co^y to make use of indirect means to acquire possession of a Trade to which it has no claim."

Thus reproved, Pilcher released his men to David Jackson, who was wintering nearby, and left the mountains through Canada with an eastbound Hudson's Bay Company express. Learning from Simpson where Jackson was, Jedediah Smith almost simultaneously left Fort Vancouver to rejoin his partner. Legend has it that in return for Simpson's generosity Smith promised that his company would no longer trap in the Snake region. More likely he and his partners withdrew because they had learned that staying was not worthwhile. In Simpson's bland words to his superiors in London, "the Flat Head trade I do not think is likely to be disturbed in the future, as the exhausted state of the Snake Country, and the great loss of life which has occurred therein, will in all probability break up their trapping parties."

Trapping parties, perhaps. But another yeast was bubbling in the United States. The 1827 renewal of the joint-occupation convention with Great Britain (either power could abrogate it on a year's notice) had been received with noisy dissatisfaction by American expansionists. Various of them wrote letters to newspapers and sent memorials to Congress. Most indefatigable of all was a half-mad schoolteacher, writer of textbooks, and able land surveyor named Hall Jackson Kelley. Empirically, Kelley was quite wrong. Yet historically, as an embodiment of what would come to be called Manifest Destiny, he was completely right.

Drearily pious and overly studious (he said he ruined his eyes reading Vergil by moonlight), Hall Kelley held a bachelor's degree from Middlebury College, Vermont, and Master of Arts degrees from both that college and Harvard. Nicholas Biddle's 1814 edition of Lewis and Clark's journals fired his interest in Oregon. As fast as travel books and congressional debates about Oregon appeared in print he read them. After moving from his New Hampshire home to the environs of Boston, he thirstily sought out mariners who had touched the Northwest coast and could tell him about it.

In 1828 he presented to Congress, through John Floyd of Virginia, a memorial urging that the United States government grant to settlers a huge block of land fronting the Pacific and extending inland a hundred miles from the mouth of "the grand river Oregon." If Congress promised these settlers adequate protection, then Kelley's memorialists "and three thousand others . . . engaged sacredly to preserve it for posterity in its brightest lustre." The figure of three thousand was pure figment, of course, but it sounded impressive in the newspapers.

Another inflated idea concerned the ease with which Oregon could be reached. This belief stemmed in part from William Ashley. Ever the publicist, Ashley granted long interviews to the newspapers after each of his ventures West. The trail he followed was represented as "level and open." "Wagons and carriages could go with ease as far as General Ashley went. . . . The elevation is exceedingly small where the passage of the mountains is effected —so small as hardly to effect the rate of going of the caravan and forming at the most, an angle of three degrees, being two degrees less than the steepest ascent on the Cumberland road." [4]

Fuzzily afloat with this idea of gentle roads was a staggering misconception about the Willamette River, which flows into the south side of the Columbia slightly below (west of) Fort Vancouver. During the homeward trip of the Lewis and Clark Expedition, Clark had filtered out of Indian talk and maps drawn on pieces of bark a notion that the Willamette rose on the western slope of the Rockies, at a lake the Spaniards called Timpanogos. Later charts increased the error by identifying semimythical Timpanogos with Great Salt Lake. Actually, of course, the Willamette rises in the Cascade Mountains of central Oregon and flows fewer than two hundred miles to the Columbia.

Would-be emigrants who pored over the mistaken charts naturally believed what they saw—we are all inclined to believe anything ennobled by print. They supposed, so George Simpson of the Hudson's Bay Company heard from Jedediah Smith, that once they had reached Salt Lake in their wagons, they could "embark on large Rafts and Batteaux and glide down current about 800 or 1000 Miles at their ease to this 'Land of Promise.' "

Mountain men knew better. Horrified at the thought of Kelley's three thousand colonists trying to cross the continent on a road he himself had represented as "better for carriages than any turnpike in the United States," Ashley wrote to Senator Benton that "it will be an act of humanity to suppress any thing of the kind at this time. They have not the least conception of the misery they would lead their families to by such an act."

Meanwhile Simpson was learning from Jedediah Smith about the Nevada and California deserts. Greenhorns, he wrote smugly to his directors in London about the same time Ashley was writ-

[4] From the *Missouri Herald and St. Louis Advertiser*, November 8, 1826, copied on December 9 in the nationally read *Niles' Weekly Register* of Baltimore.

ing to Benton, could not cross those stretches. "And the other route by Louis's River [the Snake in Idaho where the Oregon Trail eventually went] Settlers could never think of attempting. So that I am of opinion, we have little to apprehend from Settlers in this quarter, and from Indian traders nothing . . . I feel perfectly at ease. . . ." No doubt he was even more at ease when he learned that on January 9, 1829, shortly before he penned his dispatch, Congress had defeated still another bill to explore the territory west of the Rockies, erect forts between California and Alaska, and extend the jurisdiction of the United States over the entire area so far as American citizens were concerned.

Almost while Simpson was deciding to relax, the eastern end of the Oregon Trail received its final shape. Most early caravans had journeyed up the Platte from its mouth, and some would continue to do so for years (the Mormons did in 1847, for example). Circumstances, however, were gradually shifting the route southward, near the point where the Missouri ceases its western trend and turns north. The last of the Indians were moved from the area in 1825 and this allowed the log hamlet of Independence to take shape on a pretty bluff three miles inland from the beginning of the river's great bend. That same spring (1827) Fort Atkinson was replaced by Fort Leavenworth, only forty miles upstream from Independence. Immediately the little town became the jumping-off place for traders bound toward Santa Fe, and in 1829 the fur caravans began following the first leg of their path.

William Sublette pioneered the way. Although steamboats later would speed travel by maintaining regular schedules to the docks that served Independence, he led his men that March across 250 miles of cold, miry road from St. Louis, seeking shelter in scattered corncribs and sheds along the way. After a pause to test the dubious entertainment of Independence, they jogged westward well south of the Kansas River. After forty miles they left the Santa Fe trail and angled northwest. They swam their horses across the Kansas where Topeka now stands and rode cross lots, so to speak, still northwest over rolling prairies, splashing in and out of the troublesome streams until finally the trail settled more or less into the valley of the Little Blue.

Debased Kansas Indians begged and a little farther on Pawnees threatened. Vicious thunderstorms crashed, but spirits brightened. Spring was catching up. Grass rippled under the wind; new leaves touched the scattered groves with misty green; profusions of flowers blossomed everywhere.

Gradually the way led into the low, sandy hills called the Coasts of Nebraska. (*Nebraska* was an Indian name for the Platte; early French *voyageurs* once had spoken of the *coteaux de Nebraska*, the hills along the Nebraska River. This gradually was anglicized to the Coasts of Nebraska, to the utter bafflement of amateur etymologists among the emigrants.) The pull over the hills would tax wagons but probably did not bother Sublette's horses and mules. Three hundred sixteen miles out of Independence, near the upper end of ninety-mile-long Grand Island, the caravan reached the Platte. (More amateur etymology: a later emigrant, not understanding that Platte means shallow, wrote in his journal, "The name Platt is a very appropriate one for it is so broad and has such a number of islands in it that it looks like 3 or 4 rivers platted together.")

The sandy, island-studded stream, sometimes as much as three miles wide during floods, became the subject of innumerable wry jokes: a river too thick to drink, too thin to plow, too shallow to sail on, too broad to shoot a rifle across. Save on its islands, no trees and very little brush grew in its broad valley. Buffalo dung, supplemented by bits of driftwood, had to be used for fuel.

Though the eye could not discern the slope, the ground tipped steadily upward. The climate grew drier. The curly grass seemed sparse, yet supported tens of thousands of buffalo. The enormous sky oppressed some travelers; others found the vastness merely monotonous. They stared, either apathetically or in amazement according to their natures, at cactus and sagebrush and prairie-dog towns 500 to 600 acres in extent. Mirages shimmered. Antelope were magnified by heat waves into charging Indians, buffalo into groves of trees. Always, in spring, there were masses of flowers. And always, as John Charles Frémont put it later, "Indians and buffalo make the poetry and life of the prairie, and our camp was full of their exhilaration. In place of the quiet monotony of the march ... shouts and songs resounded from every part of the line, and our evening camp was always the commencement of a feast which terminated only with our departure on the following morning. At any time of night might be seen pieces of the most delicate and choicest meat, roasting *en appolas,* on sticks around the fire and the guards were never without company."

A hundred-plus miles of travel up the Platte brought Sublette's caravan to the forks of the river. During the high water of spring the union was difficult to find. The streams converged gradually; both were a thousand or more yards wide, shallow and dotted with islands. Sublette's horses may have crossed the South Platte near its mouth; later wagon drivers were inclined to avoid the myriad channels and marshy ground by continuing up the south bank of the south branch until the leader found what he considered an easy ford. Some went as far as sixty miles, toiling through the deep sand at the base of O'Fallon's Bluff, before crossing the river and climbing over the intervening ridge to the North Platte. The approach to that stream at Ash Hollow was always a surprise after so much monotony—precipitous ravines that terrified some wagon drivers of a later era into lowering their vehicles with homemade windlasses.

Gradually, in extreme western Nebraska, the ridges bordering the southern side of the North Platte's broad valley grew into high, stone-faced bluffs fantastically eroded—Court House Rock, named for its fancied resemblance to the courthouse in St. Louis; delicate, isolated Chimney Rock, which, said one unimaginative diarist, "runs up something similar to the First Presbyterian Church of old Dr. Smith's"; and massive Scott's Bluff, looking to one viewer like "the ruins of some vast city erected by a race of giants."

Sublette had reason to note Scott's Bluff. It was named for Hiram Scott, who had been with Sublette and Ashley at the Arikara battle of 1823. In 1827 Scott had gone as Ashley's representative with the caravan that took the cannon to the Bear Lake rendezvous. The next year, returning downstream with Sublette, he died at the base of the bluff.

Stories vary. Some say that Scott fell ill, others that he was wounded when Indians attacked. Two men were delegated to float him in a bullboat to where the great bluff thrusts its clay-andstandstone prow toward the shallow meanders of the stream. Help was supposed to be waiting there, but confusion of some sort occurred. For motives of self-preservation that no doubt seemed justifiable at the time, Scott's attendants abandoned him and hurried after the caravan. The next year (Sublette's 1829 caravan? No record says) his skeleton was found at the base of the bluff. Washington Irving declares in *The Adventuers of Captain Bonneville* that Scott crawled sixty miles to the spot, found no aid, and died. William Marshall Anderson, traveling in 1834, says the abandoned trader crawled two miles. Anderson goes on to rail at the desertion as "cruel and heartless inhumanity" by a "Presbyterian scoundrel," name not given, although Anderson says he knows the name. What direct connection Sublette may have had with the act and what his thoughts were as the caravan plodded by the bluff in 1829 remain unknown.

The land separating the nose of Scott's Bluff from the river was deeply gullied and sometimes boggy. To avoid the stretch, caravans often cut through the hills seven or eight miles behind (south of) the butte's bold headland. They found the blessed shade of a few pines and cedars, and as they pulled onto the top of the ridge their hearts jumped at the first sight of the Rockies, dim blue under the cloud caps in the west. These outposts of the principal chains originally were called the Black Hills from the gnarled pines cloaking them; today they are known as the Laramie Mountains.

Laramie's Fork sparkled clear and cold out of the south. The flats on the tongue between it and the Platte were a favorite campground, deep grass shaded by plum, willow, box elder, and occasional tall cottonwood trees. Beyond Laramie's Fork the trail pulled away from the Platte (its red canyons were rough) and wound along the bumpy toes of the Black Hills, now and then toiling across the steep-sided ridges that reached toward the river. Here and there the way touched the Platte, then shrank from it again to avoid deep ravines. Travelers used to the flat valleys were sometimes frightened by what seemed the dangerous pitches of this stretch.

The climate meanwhile grew increasingly arid, the ground increasingly sterile—as much, Frémont correctly recognized in

1842, from the extreme rate of evaporation as from the lack of rain and the encrustations of alkali that dotted the flats. Rattlesnakes and the tracks of grizzly bears appeared more frequently. The sun blazed, the hoof-crushed sagebrush—it grew in knotted mats now—smelled like turpentine, clouds of caustic dust stung eyes to a perpetual redness.

In the vicinity of modern Casper, the trail crossed to the north bank of the Platte. To the left rose famous landmarks, the Red Buttes. Although it was possible to go with horses through the red canyon of the Platte which lay beneath those buttes, most travelers saved a few miles by veering away from the stream directly toward the Sweetwater. Moving southwest (the Platte had turned due south), the cavalcade plodded through a bleak depression later called Emigrant Gap and crossed grisly flats whose skimpy bits of water were poisonous to stock.

After that inhospitable stretch the name Sweetwater needed no explanation. The travelers struck the creek near turtlebacked Independence Rock, an irregular half-globe of shiny brown granite that rose 193 feet about the gray plain at its highest point and stretched not quite a mile in circumference. The train splashed to the south side of the Sweetwater here, skirted the slit of Devil's Gate, and then for miles paralleled the hot, bare Rattesnake Hills. Above their jagged tops the travelers caught their first cool exciting glimpse of the snow peaks of the Wind Rivers.

South Pass lay dead ahead. In 1829, however, Sublette left the Sweetwater trail at about where Highway 287 crosses the stream today and turned north to the Popo Agie. After a pause to outfit some waiting trappers, he pushed on up the Wind River and made his way via Two-gwo-tee and Teton passes to the main rendezvous site in Pierre's Hole. The trip from St. Louis to Idaho had taken his horse caravan about four months.

His disciplines and routines had been exact. The packers were divided into messes of eight to ten men each, headed by a leader who received supplies for them, checked conduct, and enforced orders. Each man was responsible for two mules, his riding horse, and all their gear.

In Indian country camp was placed, if possible, with one side against a stream. The other three sides were protected by breastworks of saddles and baggage. The space inside was left large enough so that all the caravan's animals could graze there at the end of thirty-foot picket ropes.

Stops were made early enough to allow the animals to be hobbled, watered, and grazed outside the circle under guard. At sunset Sublette bawled, "Ketch up! Ketch up!" The horses were driven in a cloud of dust into the camp hollow. Each man caught and pegged down his own charges at the end of a rope attached to an iron-tipped, iron-bound stake two feet long and two inches in diameter. Guards, changed every three hours, paced the barricades throughout the night.

The stock was turned outside again at the first glimmer of dawn, to graze under guard while breakfast was prepared and scouts looked over the nearby hills and ravines. Then the mules were caught and packed—a daily eruption of squeals, kicks, stampedes, and bellowed oaths. An angry drover sometimes tried to control his mule by seizing its ear between his teeth while he pulled the cinch tight. Angry mules retaliated by bloating like balloons, bucking the contents of half-adjusted packs helter-skelter, and kicking their handlers into the middle of next week. The first mess to complete its matutinal uproar received the lead-off place in the line, behind Sublette. The rest ate dust, including Sublette's second-in-command, who always brought up the rear.

Wagons would have obviated this daily packing and unpacking; wagons required fewer men and animals. Wagons were familiar and had been used on the Santa Fe Trail since 1822. Frontier newspapers regularly reported that wagons could travel without difficulty to South Pass and beyond. But for a long time wagons never so much as started along the Oregon Trail. One cannot help wondering why.

For one thing, mule trains traveled more rapidly. Near the rendezvous, which sometimes was held away from the trail, mules were more flexible. And there was the matter of good politics.

One way to strengthen Congress' interest in Oregon was to show how easily American colonies could be established there. When reporters fed questions about roads to returning mountain men, the listener understood what was expected. Believe what you want to believe; an old human custom. Remembering the long flat stretches of the plains and valleys, men like Ashley said truthfully that wagons could make the trip. Remembering, as they readied their caravans, the ravines and river fords and the knotted sagebrush that could shake a wagon worse than a stream bed full of round stones, they stuck to their mules.

Until 1830. In that year William Sublette decided to make the experiment. By chance 1830 was also the year during which Andrew Jackson gathered, through his Secretary of War John H. Eaton, data for a presidential message "in answer to a resolution of the Senate relative to British establishments on the Columbia, and the state of the fur trade, &c." Ashley would testify. Pilcher would testify. Most certainly Smith, Jackson, and Sublette, the only men in America who knew more about the subject than Ashley and Pilcher—would be asked to testify. To say that the Senate's curiosity about the Columbia motivated the first wagon train on the Oregon Trail is no doubt stretching coincidence too far. But the timing without question influenced the testimony the partners sent to Eaton after the trip.

(It might be noted further that in Boston in 1829 Hall Jackson Kelley organized The American Society for Encouraging the Settlement of Oregon Territory. Again he proposed a march of 3000 colonists to Oregon from a rendezvous in St. Louis, each man to receive for his pains two hundred acres of farmland on the Columbia. To help persuade three thousand people to sign up, he presented in 1830 an exhaustive "Geographical Sketch of that Part of North America called Oregon." He drew historical, descriptive, commercial, zoological, agricultural, and anthropological data from every printed source he could find, particularly the journals of Lewis and Clark. The mass of details accumulated into a picture of Oregon, "improved and embellished" by man's enlightened arts, as "the loveliest and most envied country on earth." Although vague about routes, Kelley envisioned "land passages . . . from the Mississippi valley, and from the gulf of Mexico to the Pacific ocean, . . . *new channels* [Kelley's italics] through which the products of America and the Eastern world, will pass in mutual exchange." By 1830 land passages of that magnitude could hardly mean anything other than wagon roads.)

The fur-trade rendezvous of 1830 was scheduled to be held

east of the Divide, near Riverton, Wyoming, where Popo Agie Creek flows into Wind River. Once again William Sublette and Black Harris carried the market list to St. Louis, traveling in the dead of winter not with one but with several pack dogs. The experience was gentler than the express of 1827. By February 11, 1830, they were in St. Louis.

Eighty men rode with the revolutionary caravan which Sublette started back toward the mountains on April 10. The figure suggests that some pack mules may have gone along with the twelve wagons which were the core of the experiment. Of these twelve, two were Dearborns, light four-wheeled carriages curtained on the sides, each pulled by a single mule. These may have been used for carrying a passenger or two as well as the personal effects of the leaders. The other vehicles were more substantial— high-sided Murphy wagons whose prototypes had been soundly tested on the Santa Fe Trail; each carried 1800 pounds and was drawn by five mules. At a rough estimate, twenty-two men and fifty-two mules were able to move in these wagons, without daily packing and unpacking, as much merchandise as forty-five men could have handled in a pack caravan of ninety or more mules.

There was still another innovation. To fill out menus until buffalo were encountered along the Platte, Sublette drove with the caravan twelve beef cattle and one milk cow. As matters developed, only eight had to be devoured.

The route probably duplicated the one Subtlette's mule caravan had used the year before—the exact Oregon Trail as far as the turn-off to the Popo Agie. Speeds varied from fifteen to twenty-five miles a day. Road-builders went ahead to cut down the banks of ravines. They built at least one bridge in Kansas, over Cannonball Creek between the Vermillion and the Blue. One road worker was killed and another crippled by a collapsing bank; "easy" wagon travel had its difficulties.

On July 16 the train reached the Wind River rendezvous and was no doubt resoundingly toasted in diluted grain alcohol. For reasons not stated, the two Dearborns were left in the mountains. (There is no record of what became of them.) But the surviving beef cattle and the patient cow trudged back to the settlements with the ten large wagonloads of fur. The three partners, who had sold their business to the Rocky Mountain Fur Company, went along as well.[5] In St. Louis they learned (if they did not already know it) that the government would appreciate their views about the British establishments on the Columbia. On October 29 they complied by sending a long letter to Secretary of War Eaton. It reached Eaton in time for President Jackson to include it with Pilcher's and Ashley's testimony in the message he sent to the Senate on January 24, 1831.

The arguments in that famous presidential message followed approximately the same pattern of logic used in most of the anti-British documents of the time.

Point one: *The nature of the posts being erected in the Northwest by the Hudson's Bay Company shows that the British contemplate exclusive occupancy of the Oregon country.* The partners' letter described the big new Fort Vancouver which Jedediah Smith had seen under construction during the winter of 1828–29. The people of the United States were grimly informed ". . . every thing seemed to combine to prove that this fort was to be a permanent establishment." Pilcher, in his testimony, made the same point and urged that the British be ejected under terms of the Monroe Doctrine, which left no part of the American continents open to European colonization.

Point two: *The British are deliberately excluding Americans from an area into which Americans have every right to go.* Although Smith gratefully acknowledged the aid given him at Fort Vancouver after the Umqua massacre, the partners insisted that "The inequality of the convention with Great Britain in 1818 is most glaring and apparent, and its continuance is a great and manifest injury to the United States. The privileges granted by it have enabled the British to take possession of the Columbia river, and spread over the country south of it; while no Americans have ever gone or can venture to go on the British side." Ashley was even more blunt. Without citing instances he raised the old specter of Indian depredations incited by the English fur companies, and asked for 500 mounted troops to clear a way through the savage tribes of the Rockies.

[5] The Rocky Mountain Fur Company was composed of Milton Sublette (William's brother), Thomas Fitzpatrick, Jim Bridger, Henry Fraeb (generally written Frapp in reminiscences), and Jean-Baptiste Gervais.

Point three: *The country being appropriated by Great Britain is valuable not only for its furs but, potentially, for whaling and naval stations, commerce with China, salmon fisheries, agriculture and stock raising.* Pilcher, who had reached no farther than Fort Colvile in northwestern Washington, grew rhapsodic over the last point. Horses throve on the inland plains under "a clear sky, a serene atmosphere, and a soft and brilliant sunshine. The nights, when the moon is near full, and the hemisphere studded over with stars, are indescribably beautiful." He also described at length the enormous salmon runs, which could be a "a great article of subsistence and exportation." Prophetically, he concluded that in the area around Fort Vancouver "a great city and powerful nation will grow up."

Point four: *The Columbia was easily reached.* Said Pilcher: "The man must know but little of the American people who supposes they can be stopped by any thing in the shape of the mountains, deserts, seas, or rivers; and he can know nothing at all of the mountains in question, to suppose that they are impassable." He himself had traversed the Rockies at several points between South Pass and Athabaska Pass in Canada. "I say, then, that nothing is more easily passed than these mountains. Wagons and carriages may cross them in a state of nature without difficulty, and with little delay in the day's journey."

No matter how flatly made, however, Pilcher's statement—like Ashley's to the newspapers—was supposition. But now Smith, Jackson, and Sublette came forward to offer their wagon train as proof. True, they had gone no farther than Wind River. But "the ease and safety with which it was done prove the facility of communicating overland with the Pacific ocean."

Conclusion: *What is holding us back?* The contents of the Smith-Jackson-Sublette letter to Eaton reached the press immediately and were widely reported and commented on. The St. Louis *Beacon* declared on November 4, 1830, that the experiment with the wagons "shows the folly and nonsense of those 'scientific' characters who talk of the Rocky Mountains as the barrier which is to stop the westward march of the American people." The Philadelphia *National Gazette* added on November 30, "In a few years, a trip to the Pacific by way of the Rocky Mountains, will be no more of an undertaking than was a journey from the

Atlantic cities to Missouri twenty years ago. Well and truly may it be said that 'Westward the Star of Empire takes its way.'"

Nothing to it—yet strangly, once these political manifestos had been fired, wagons stopped running toward Oregon. They kept on rolling to Santa Fe, however. Entering that trade in 1831, Smith, Jackson, and Sublette used wagons as a matter of course. (During the trip Jedediah Smith was killed by Comanches.) But when Sublette returned to the Rocky Mountain fur trade in 1832, he did not use wagons. True, in 1832 he was bound for Pierre's Hole and the passes on that route would have been difficult for wheels. He did not use wagons in later years, however, when the rendezvous shifted back to Green River, at the end of a road he himself had declared to be practical.

One is almost tempted to believe that except on paper the Oregon Trail was not easy for wagons in those days before iron axles had been invented, in a climate so arid that desiccated spokes fell from their hubs, in a region so woodless that fires had to be built of buffalo dung and a blacksmith often could not generate enough heat for reshaping an iron tire to a shrunken wheel rim. Mules did not have to be reforged or caulked at the seams before tackling the rivers. During the heyday of the fur trade, no mountain man who had watched Sublette's experiment with wagons ever attempted to duplicate it. That ordeal was reserved for greenhorns who knew no better: for an Army captain on leave to take a fling at the pelt business and—of all unlikely people—for Christian missionaries.

THE AMATEURS

During 1830 and 1831, Hall Jackson Kelley bustled back and forth between Boston and Washington, holding meetings in the first city to explain his emigration plans to would-be colonists and in the last petitioning Congress to help his migrants. He wanted the government, first, to supply troops and arms and, second, to grant his colonizers the sovereign right of procuring land from the Indians by treaty, together "with such other powers, rights, and immunities as may be at least equal and concurrent to those given by Great Britain to the Hudson's Bay Company."

Marchers were to assemble in St. Louis on January 1, 1832—there would be sea transport for heavy freight and reluctant walkers—and, although Kelley's original proposal called for men only, he soon included families. The women and children were to be provided, at each emigrant's own expense, "with covered horse wagons, containing each a bed and two blankets." As proof that the vehicles could make the trip, Kelley cited in full the testimony of Joshua Pilcher and Smith, Jackson, and Sublette. Military rule was to prevail during the trip. But, he added, its strictness would be deprived "of much of its asperity and arbitrary discipline, by the mild reform which virtue, refinement and female presence conspire to produce."

Probably the Society's books never showed five hundred persons enrolled at any one time, and many of those who did sign were curiosity-seekers with no real intent of traveling to the Columbia. The manufacturers of the area nevertheless took fright. A large migration would tighten the labor shortage already pinching New England's bustling new factories. Besides, if people were eager to tame a wilderness, what was wrong with newly opened Maine? (Many Boston financiers had speculative interests in Maine; new communities there would also create fresh markets for Massachusetts industry.) To counteract Kelley's influence, a hack writer named William Joseph Snelling was prevailed on to prepare two scathing articles for the February and April 1832 issues of *New-England Magazine*.

Hack or no, Snelling spoke from surer ground than Kelley did. He at least knew the frontier. He was a son of Colonel Josiah Snelling, builder and for many years commander of Fort Snelling on the upper Mississippi, northern anchor of the defense scheme which once had included the abortive Yellowstone Expedition of 1819–20. After a boyhood in Minnesota, West Point had seemed tame to young Snelling. He quit, drifted to St. Louis, met a band of Dakota Sioux and, at sixteen, wintered with them on the prairie.

Returning to his father's post, he married the daughter of a French-Canadian *voyageur* (she died within a year), traded with Indians, and served as guide for Long's expedition to the Red River Valley. Out of these experiences he wrote *Tales of the North West; or Sketches of Indian Life and Character.* He took the manuscript to Boston, found a publisher, and became a minor literary lion. His head turned, he forsook what he knew and leaped headlong into the virulent personal journalism popular at the time. After composing a turgid set of heroic couplets satirizing certain Boston poets, he found a new target in Hall Jackson Kelley.

Untrained emigrants, he scoffed, would not be able to kill the numerous buffalo. The caravan would starve; owls and rattlesnakes would become dainty morsels. Horses too would perish on the prairies, which the Indians twice a year burned as barren as the "Zahara." The animals that did not starve would be stolen by the savages or driven away by wolves. Floods and snow would cause disastrous delays. Fifty predatory tribes "whose very names are abominations" lurked along the route. Fur traders talked about wagons, but "did any white man ever cross the Rocky Mountains who will say that a white woman could have followed him? . . . The best construction we can put on [Kelley's] behavior is, to suppose his hallucination so strong as totally to obnubilate his faculties. . . . We affirm that he has perverted every fact he has touched."

Before the articles actually appeared in print, the two men who conceivably might have made the migration work also had decided that Kelley's scheme was highly impractical. One was Captain Benjamin Louis Eulalie Bonneville, French-born graduate of West Point stationed at Fort Gibson in the Indian territory of eastern Oklahoma. The other was Nathaniel Wyeth, a twenty-nine-year-old minor partner in a Massachusetts ice company which cut its product on a pond near Boston, hauled it by six-horse teams to the wharves, and shipped it as far away as New Orleans and the West Indies. Wyeth's salary and his share in the company profits came to $2400 a year. A trapper's wage was about two hundred a year.

Bonneville and Wyeth, who at that point did not know each

other, were both interested in the ramifications of the fur trade. To gain information about the Northwest, each had enrolled (Bonneville only briefly) in Kelley's American Society for Encouraging the Settlement of the Oregon Territory. Had the migration suited their plans, they might have gone along for the strength a troop-protected caravan would have lent their own parties. But both were quick to cut loose from the dreamer as soon as it seemed to them wise to do so.

Bonneville moved first. In 1831 he was thirty-five years old, prematurely bald, of medium height, compact, used to command, curious and intelligent. The routines of frontier Army posts had come to bore him, yet he had felt at first hand so strong a pull from the western lands that, like Thoreau, he simply had to walk toward Oregon. But Bonneville's walking was more than philosophical. Early in 1831, presumably at Fort Gibson, he met a man who could show him the literal way West—Joe Walker, a veteran of the Santa Fe trade. To Walker's know-how Bonneville could add financing through a former member of the ill-fated Astoria venture, Alfred Seton, who since had become a New York businessman. After talking matters over, the Santa Fe trader and the Army captain decided to take a two-year flier at fur-trapping in the mountains. Since Bonneville was producing the money, he assumed over-all command of the expedition. From that moment on, Hall Kelley was forgotten.

On asking for leave from the Army Bonneville wrote, on May 21, 1831, to his commanding general Alexander Macomb that he wanted "no outfit, no presents for the indians, no command . . . no protection"—just a leave of absence so that he could map the country, "visit the American and British establishments, make myself acquainted with their manner of trade and intercourse with the Indians, finally endeavor to develop every advantage the country affords and by what means they may most readily be opened to the enterprise of our citisens."

In granting the request Macomb asked Bonneville to bring home data about geography and about the war-making capacity of the Indians within the territorial limits of the United States. He did not mention the British. And he specifically stated—shades of Vérendrye and of every other unsupported trader who ached to find the Western Sea!—"It is understood that the Government is to be at no expence, in reference to your proposed expedition, it having originated with yourself. . . ."

Like Kelley and a great many other people in the United States, Benjamin Bonneville had read of the wagons which Smith, Jackson, and Sublette had taken West. Walker of course was familiar with the wagons used in the Santa Fe trade. So when the new associates went to Missouri in the fall of 1831 to start hiring trappers and roustabouts, they included twenty heavy freight vehicles in their plans. William Sublette, the wagon pioneer who was also to be returning to the mountains in the spring of 1832, had no such notion left in his mind.

In Boston, meanwhile, Nathaniel Wyeth was maturing his own trading plans. Reading omnivorously in books borrowed from Kelley, he grasped at once the problem which had turned Alexander Mackenzie and other Nor'Westers to a search for ports on the Pacific—the high cost of transporting goods from the East. Lewis and Clark's journals convinced Wyeth, as they had Astor, that the inland trade should be fortified by ships sent around the Horn to the Columbia; goods could be taken from there to his trappers with horses available for a song in the Northwest. He added minor wrinkles of his own. He would draw additional profits by drying salmon and shipping it, with his furs, back to the United States in barrels. Perhaps he could even grow tobacco in Oregon. Two things his reading did not reveal, however, were the full power of the Hudson's Bay Company on the coast and the vicious competition he would meet from his own countrymen in the Rocky Mountains.

When Congress refused Kelley's society aid, the date of its migration was postponed. This delay and what Wyeth considered the "impractical and inhuman" decision to add women and children to the caravan persuaded the former ice merchant to cut himself away from Kelley. He began soliciting recruits of his own. He assembled traps, guns, vermilion, beads, cheap knives, buttons, nails, hammers, and whatever else he thought might appeal to the savages. He found enough money to prevail on the captain of the brig *Sultana* to sail on shares for Oregon, carrying in addition to merchandise one thousand empty barrels for bringing back salmon.

Wagon talk infected Wyeth, too. He built three freighters thirteen feet long and four feet wide, shaped like boats so that when he came to rivers he could disengage the vehicles from their wheels and float them across. Correctly surmising that the western sun would dry out ordinary caulking, he dovetailed the joints so carefully that the strange hybrids were watertight without oakum.

His men were to be uniformed in coarse woolen jackets and pants, striped cotton shirts, cowhide boots. Each was to carry a rifle, a bayonet, and a small axe. To inspire them across the dusty miles he ordered ten bugles. Each recruit promised fidelity and obedience to his leader. And each paid him, as treasurer of their joint-stock Pacific Trading Company, forty dollars to help defray expenses as far as St. Louis.

Wyeth enlisted about half as many men as he had hoped for. Twenty-one assembled in Boston, including his older brother Jacob, a doctor from New Jersey, and his nephew John Wyeth, a rambunctious youth of eighteen. Four others he had won through his voluminous correspondence promised to meet the group in Baltimore. One of these was a graduate of Dartmouth named John Ball. Ball had left a mediocre career as a lawyer to run an oilcloth factory and was equally unhappy with that. He jumped at the chance to go West, and is the only one of Wyeth's crossing who left a relatively unprejudiced picture of his fellow adventurers. He considered most of them loafers and ordinary laborers, hardy, rough, and illiterate, out for a lark and easy profit. But he liked Wyeth, chin-whiskered, lean-faced, a Yankee to the core: ". . . an active business man and in his way, a great philosopher— all learned by observation . . . a good hunter, fertile in expedients, and will mend a gun, or a wagon, or any other implement, with no other instrument than his jack knife."

During the early months of 1832 the Boston contingent met each night in Wyeth's home to discuss needs and routines. Just before they left, Snelling's first attack on Kelley appeared in *New-England Magazine*. Partly as a result of its unfavorable publicity, a jeering crowd lined the streets of Cambridge to watch Wyeth's hangdog gang march by with their amphibian freight wagons, which some wag christened Nat-wye-thums.

After camping for a few raw March days on an island in Boston harbor to inure themselves to hardship, the group sailed to Baltimore. There they picked up the other four members and loaded their paraphernalia onto the new Baltimore and Ohio Railroad for a sixty-mile ride to the end of the line. They hiked across the Alleghenies and caught a steamer down the Ohio. Some were surprised and offended when Wyeth put them to work loading wood onto the boat to help pay for their fare.

Wyeth had a talent for friendship. St. Louis' hardened traders might well have let other rivals as green as these Bostonians flounder off to destruction. But Kenneth McKenzie of the American Fur Company (who recently had done the impossible by establishing posts in the upper Missouri country and opening trade with the Blackfeet) was enough taken by Wyeth to advise him to sell his Nat-wye-thums, although he received only half what they cost; the country was too rough and the streams too swift for wheeled vehicles like those. McKenzie also suggested that the party take a steamboat to Independence and attach themselves to William Sublette, who was preparing a mule caravan for the rendezvous.

Sublette might have refused. He was behind schedule. Grass had started slowly in the unusually cold, wet spring of 1832, and his livestock were in poor shape. He knew that the supply caravan which reached the rendezvous first would capture the cream of the pelts from the thirsty trappers. (Sublette was taking with him 450 gallons of undiluted alcohol in tin containers curved to fit a mule's packsaddle. Transporting spirits into Indian country was illegal, but sometimes special permits were issued so that boatmen laboring with the towropes on the Missouri could have a dram at night. Sublette had applied for a permit for "boatmen" and had received one. Getting that illicit cargo to the rendezvous first would be quite a coup.) Bonneville was two weeks ahead, with twenty wagons. Furthermore, as Sublette probably knew, the powerful American Fur Company was planning to muscle into the mountain trade that year by sending a caravan to the rendezvous from its new post, Fort Union, near the mouth of the Yellowstone.

The thought may even have touched his mind that perhaps Mc-Kenzie of the American Fur Company had sent these greenhorns to him so that they might slow Sublette still more in his race to the rendezvous.

It is difficult to relish a man who is a potential handicap. Moreover, if Wyeth ever did reach the mountains, he might grow into still another competitor—although from the looks of his crew this development hardly seemed likely. Yet in spite of these objections, Sublette agreed to shepherd the tyros westward. His only requirement was that the newcomers give absolute obedience to his orders about daily travel. Surely Wyeth's rough-and-ready charm had something to do with all this.

In what must have been a panting hurry the greenhorns discarded that part of their equipment which the grinning old-timers told them was useless, and replaced it with items better adapted to the trail. They obtained the now-standard mobile larder—two oxen and sixteen sheep to eat until buffalo were available. They purchased thirty-four horses. Nineteen of these carried their traps and a dab of trade goods. (The rest of the merchandise had been sent to the Columbia by ship.) Fifteen horses carried provisions to supplement the walking beef and mutton. As soon as the packs were consumed, the animals could be used by the men for riding in turn. Until then the tyros would have to hike, as would many of Sublette's crew. As two of Wyeth's men looked over the hubbub of the gathering caravan and envisioned the footsore miles to the Pacific, they had second thoughts and deserted.

All told, some eighty men marshaling nearly three hundred animals walked and rode out of Independence on May 13, 1832. The same day, not quite a hundred miles farther west, Captain Benjamin Bonneville was building rafts under the amazed scrutiny of throngs of Indians, so that he could float his twenty wagons across the flooded Kansas River.

Bonneville had hoped that wagons would save him the delay of daily packing, but somewhere short of the Platte the saddle caravan and its walkers passed him. No record of the meeting survives. But surely Wyeth examined with great curiosity the lumbering vehicles, some pulled by mules and some by oxen. He probably exchanged words with Bonneville—the two amateurs possibly knew that once they had belonged to the same colonizing society —and it would be strange indeed if Wyeth did not ask Sublette what had turned the trader against wagons. Sublette's answer may well have been a Socratic question about which of their parties was making the better time.

Along the Platte the neophytes fell ill with one of the most persistent and uncomfortable complaints of western travel, one often ignored in travel books. "Our men troubled with relax," Wyeth wrote in his journal. Many sufferers would later blame these sudden, devastating attacks of diarrhea (which they spelled in an almost infinite number of ways) on the warm, turbid waters of the Platte. Others pointed to boiled buffalo meat from winter-poor animals. (John Ball of Wyeth's party recalled that health improved when diet changed to fat, roasted meat.) A few thought it one more phase of "mountain sickness"; and possibly the thin, dry air of the higher altitudes did add "relaxes" to the violent headaches, nausea, and dizziness that wracked some susceptible travelers as far as South Pass and beyond.

Whatever its cause, the affliction was painfully embarrassing in a flat valley that offered neither shelter nor convenient leaves. At best the spasmodic gripings were inconvenient; at worst they were so debilitating that the victim could not travel without help. Unfortunately for the peace of mind of Wyeth's party, the chief sufferer among them was Nathaniel's brother Jacob, the group's doctor.

Other discomforts mounted. Wyeth's journal indicates frost nearly every night from western Nebraska to eastern Oregon. The days were hot and dusty and the insects fierce. (June 7, near Chimney Rock: "my face so swelled from the musquitoes and ghnats that I can scarce see out of my eyes and aches like the tooth ache.") Chapped lips puffed and split. Nothing dramatic— just plain misery. Under such circumstances, others of the party found Oregon less and less glamorous. Three of them, wanting to quit but ashamed to back out publicly, tried (in Wyeth's words) "to ruin the expedition by ruining the horses." Deliberately they injured the animals' backs by putting sharp objects under the packsaddles. Finally the trio decamped during the dark of one night, taking three sound, precious horses with them.

Wyeth crippled another animal trying fruitlessly to overhaul the deserters. No one could now ride but the sick and those out hunting game.

Laramie's Fork in southeastern Wyoming was too deep to ford. Sublette put his men to making bullboats. They thrust the butt ends of willow branches into the ground along the outline desired, gathered the tops, and laced withes transversely through the framework. Buffalo hides were cut to fit, stiched together, and stretched across the skeleton. A slow fire was built underneath to dry and warm the skins. Melted buffalo tallow mixed with ashes was rubbed into every seam and allowed to harden. The light boats were then turned right side up and launched. To Wyeth they looked flimsy. In spite of Sublette's warning about the boisterous current, he built a solid raft of cottonwood logs, affixed a long rope, and had his best swimmer carry the cord across in his teeth. But when the men tried to haul the raft across, it caught on a snag and dumped some of their powder and most of their blacksmithing equipment irretrievably into the stream.

Through cold rain and hail they stumbled along the rough base of the Black Hills (today's Laramie Mountains). When Bonneville came along two weeks behind them (he had crossed the South Platte and Laramie rivers by sewing hides over his wagon-beds and turning them into boats) he found the route hair-raising. "Then began," he wrote General Macomb later, "one of the most broken countries I ever beheld, frequently letting my wagons down the bluffs with long ropes 80 men to each wagon." After talking to the captain three or four years later, Washington Irving gave the episode a more literary polish:

> Rugged steeps and deep ravines incessantly obstructed their progress, so that a great part of the day was spent in the painful toil of digging through banks, filling up ravines, forcing the wagons up the most forbidding ascents, or swinging them with ropes down the face of dangerous precipices—

which is not quite the way in which Smith, Jackson, and Sublette had described wagon travel along this stretch.

Meanwhile the dry air was at work on the hard-used vehicles. Irving again: "The wood-work of the wagons also shrank so much that it was with difficulty the wheels were kept from falling to pieces." Finally, along the Sweetwater Bonneville had to resort to an expedient many a later emigrant would employ with curses and dismay. He took the tire off each wheel, whittled out flexible arcs of wood, and nailed these around the exterior of the felloe, or rim. (If a man lacked nails he had to use rawhide cords, let them shrink, and hope for the best.) Firewood was laboriously gathered and the tires heated red-hot in the flames. They were then quickly slipped into place and shrunk onto the enlarged rim by a sudden application of cold water. Sometimes, if a man was handy and understood what he was about, the repair jobs worked pretty well.

After the tepid Platte, the Sweetwater tasted good to Wyeth's men. They also had good fat meat to eat. But the horses lacked fodder. As the caravan started through the barrens on the far side of South Pass, Wyeth wrote in his journal, "Many of my horses have given out and the rest are failing fast and unless we soon come to better grass they will all die and leave me on foot." One midnight Indians compounded the problem by roaring up close, pouring bullets and arrows into the camp, wounding a few animals, and making off with ten more, including four of Wyeth's. However, he had reached such a state that he could be philosophic about it: "mine were all poor and sore backed and useless."

Rendezvous that year was in Pierre's Hole. To reach it Sublette left what would become the road to Oregon and turned up the Green, crossing from its headwaters to the Hoback. The Hoback flowed into the Snake (or Lewis) and hence could be considered part of the Columbia. Wyeth felt a ceremony was in order: "... drank to my friends with mingled feelings from the waters of the Columbia mixed with alcohol and eat of a Buffaloe cow made this day 30 miles and 25 yesterday   The grass much better." But, in spite of that improvement, he had to admit "Three of my men are sick and I have no spare animals for them."

The invalids dragged far behind. Impatiently Sublette ordered Wyeth to mount them. To comply he had to unpack some of his horses and bury the goods in a cache. Even then it was a rough go. Animals slipped and fell; a summer snowstorm lashed them one night; the sick still could not keep up. But finally they all reached the rendezvous. Better yet from Sublette's point of view, no other caravan was ahead of them.

Two hundred trappers and two or three times that many Nez Percé and Flathead Indians waited eagerly. The savages put on a stirring show, sweeping forward on horseback in a thunderous, mile-wide line to fire three volleys of welcome with their muskets. Strange details sometimes catch an observer's eye; Nathaniel's nephew, young John Wyeth, saw that lost, blood-quickening sight this way: "As there was a pleasant breeze of wind, their hair blew out straight all in one direction, which had the appearance of so many black streamers."

Sublette unpacked his 450 gallons of straight alcohol. Prices varied according to the competition; in general a diluted pint went for a pound of beaver—three dollars. A large beaver might weigh a pound and a half. A man who caught two hundred in a year was doing well. Proportionate to income, then, the alcohol was expensive. But perhaps the men did not look at it that way. Most of them had just survived a year marked by frequent onslaughts of hunger and acute physical discomfort, of long stretches of monotony punctuated by flashes of mortal danger. Memories of this one spree at the rendezvous, some ammunition, fofarraw for their squaws, and perhaps a new pair of wool pants to replace their black, baggy, greasy buckskins were all they could carry with them into next year's harshness. Few of them saw any reason for laying up treasures in heaven. They played hard while they could. For example, at this rendezvous a few of the boys poured a kettle of alcohol (they slurped it out of kettles, not cups) over a friend and set him afire. Somehow he lived through it, and fun's fun.

Wyeth's malcontents, however, found less to cheer about. They demanded a meeting to discuss the future. When he refused to reveal his plans (probably he was not sure himself at this point), nine of them—including his brother and nephew—resigned. Eleven others agreed to continue with him to the mouth of the Columbia. The equipment and horses they still possessed were divided as equably as possible, and no doubt fresh animals were purchased from the Indians.

Eleven greenhorns (though they were passing beyond that stage by then) were too few to risk the Indian-infested region.

Wyeth made arrangements to go into southern Idaho, where he could pick up the normal trail west, with trapping brigades led by Milton Sublette and Henry Fraeb of the Rocky Mountain Fur Company. The combined parties had traveled only six or eight miles when they spotted a moving village of Gros Ventres Indians. The Gros Ventres were allies of the Blackfeet and hence, so far as the trappers were concerned, the same as Blackfeet—three grades lower than the Old Nick himself. At this moment, however, neither party was quite sure it wanted a fight. Emissaries tentatively approached each other. The white ambassador was a half-breed whose father had been killed by Blackfeet. He used his semblance of peace merely to get close enough to the approaching Gros Ventre chief to slay the Indian in revenge. He managed to lift the dead man's scalp, and the battle was on.

The whites rushed messengers back to the main camp for reinforcements. The Indians forted up in a swampy thicket of willows. For a time the opponents amused themselves by exchanging long-range shots. But after William Sublette galloped up with a swarm of whites, Flatheads, and Nez Percés, the trappers decided to attack. One measure of Wyeth is the fact that the veterans put him in charge of a detachment that led a flanking movement against the Gros Ventre rear. The charge failed—during the maneuvers some of the whites and their Flathead allies caught each other in a crossfire—and then a rumor flashed through the ranks that another band of Indians was attacking the main camp and its treasures in Pierre's Hole. Everyone except a few guards rushed back. There was no enemy about. By then it was too dark to return to the besieged, who in spite of the guards managed to slip away through the shadows.

Despite the rather ludicrous ending, it had been a bloody to-do. How many whites and their Flathead allies were slain varies with the accounts left by several eyewitnesses. It was probably close to a dozen. Several more were severely wounded, including William Sublette. The Gros Ventres later said they had lost twenty-six killed, including women and children. It was hard to be sure; the Indians had carried off most of their casualties. But enough corpses and dead horses remained in the willows, Wyeth wrote a week later, that "the stench was extreme . . . I soon retired from this scene of disgusting butchery."

Patched up after the battle, Wyeth's men and the others moved south across the bleak Snake Plains. After crossing the river in bullboats—Wyeth was becoming an expert—they encountered buffalo and decided to make meat against starving times. The trappers ran the fat cows down on horseback, "a dangerous method," said Wyeth, "expensive in horses and Requiring much skill in Riding." He had no horses fit for such a chase and had to hire his meat killed. When one of his greenhorns tried hunting mountain style a few days later, "we lost one Horse . . . by throwing his Rider and Running among the Buffaloe and going off with them." They found butchering, cutting the meat into thin strips, and drying it to be tedious. One small distraction did ripple the monotony. Many of the trappers had their Indian wives along. During a brief rainstorm one "was delivered of a Boy in the bushes whither she had retired for the purpose." In less than an hour she was back, ready to go. There were other acquisitions from the savages who trooped along: "Our party have taken lice from the Indians they are a great trouble as well as the Musquitoes."

Still moving south, they crossed the Blackfoot River and moved over broad, dreary plains—tangles of wild rosebushes, currants, rushes, willows, and glaring sand flats. Something about the location or its great, light-struck vistas must have touched Nathaniel Wyeth; two years later when he wanted to build a trading fort in the area he came straight to this spot. Many a later emigrant who had never heard his name would bless the pinpoint of semi-civilization that he created here in the intolerable emptiness. At this point he had returned to the main course of the Oregon Trail.

The trappers, however, did not actually follow the trail-to-be as they moved on past the spot where the city of Pocatello now stands. They zigzagged up and down the streams to catch what beaver they could, even though the pelts were not prime. Off to the north the Snake shut itself into a cliff-walled chasm of basalt. The plains south of it, which the trappers crossed to get from stream to stream, were choked with dense sage, punctured with outcrops of black lava, sliced by narrow, perpendicular gorges. "A melancholy and strange-looking country," Frémont called it a decade later, "—one of fracture, and violence, and fire."

When they reached the Raft River, they turned southwest up it toward the mountains on the Idaho–Utah border.[1] Wolves serenaded them, "making more noise," Wyeth wrote, "than 50 village dogs and better music for they keep in chord." The air was so crisp and dry "that percussion caps explode without striking and I am obliged to put caps on and fire immediately except in the night when we consider it safe to keep the caps on the guns." On August 22, somewhere beyond the Raft's tributary, Cassia Creek, Wyeth became a true mountain man: he caught his first beaver, "a large one." In general, however, pickings were lean. The Hudson's Bay Company had seen to that.

On the twenty-ninth Fraeb's and Sublette's trappers dropped south to the Humboldt River of Nevada. On their own now, Wyeth's men, greenhorns no longer, trapped westward through the desolate mountains just north of the Idaho–Utah border—"an indescribable chaos," Wyeth said, its canyons "of the most difficult character to follow." Fat black crickets two inches or more long crawled on the ground and roosted in the sage. The Indians ate them with relish. So, in starving times, did white trappers. Although Wyeth's men were not quite reduced to that, food was often short. They subsisted on the few beaver they caught and on cakes of pulverized berries and odorous salmon traded from shy Digger Indians.

In mid-September they regained the Snake where it turns north, followed it a way, and turned into western Oregon. After a month of discouraging trapping they separated into two groups and straggled off to the Hudson's Bay post located at the junction of the Walla Walla and Columbia rivers—a post christened in 1818 Fort Nez Percé by its builder, Donald McKenzie, but by 1832 more generally known as Fort Walla Walla. It stood in sun-smitten

---

[1] This Raft River route would be used in later years by many of the wagon trains bound for California. See George R. Stewart, *The California Trail* (McGraw-Hill, 1962) pp. 48, 136. The area was well known, having been trapped first by Donald McKenzie's Nor'Westers, then by competing Americans and brigades of the Hudson's Bay Company.

desolation, a sand flat bordered on the south by crisp tawny hills rolling down to treeless bottomlands. But westward was a stupendous sight—vast Wallula Gap where the broad, sky-bright Columbia bursts through flat-topped, cliff-girt mesas of lava on its way to the sea.

At Fort Walla Walla, Wyeth wrote, "we saw a bull and cow & calf, hen & cocks, punkins, potatoes, corn, all of which looked strange and unnatural and like a dream. They [the trader in charge of the post, Pierre Pambrun, and his clerk] gave me a decent change of clothes which was very acceptable." Pambrun also lent the wayfarers a barge and a guide for the trip down the river to Fort Vancouver, and agreed to look after the Americans' horses until they returned.

Floating along the great river was luxury at first, but soon they reached the first rapids—low, thunderous Celilo Falls, a favorite fishing point at which Indians from hundreds of miles around gathered during the salmon runs. Flood waters of spring swallowed the falls completely and experts even took barges over them without excessive trouble. But in the fall they were unnavigable. Wyeth had to hire fifty Indians to carry the barge around them while he and his men portaged such furs and goods as they possessed on their own backs.

Below the falls came the Short Dalles, a narrow rock trough with perpendicular walls scarcely twenty feet high "through which the whole waters of the mighty Columbia are forced with much noise and uproar." Wyeth and a few Indians shot through the uproar in the barge; his men, "frightened withall," walked around.

So it went, more dickering with the thieving savages, more portaging, heavy gray skies, dense forests replacing the bare hills of the interior, and Mt. Hood's towering white cone immediately to the south, "a more stupendous pile," in Wyeth's eyes, "than any of the Rocky Mountains." Fort Vancouver, when they reached it on October 29, looked splendid.

The *Sultana,* scheduled to be riding there with the Pacific Trading Company's merchandise and fishing equipment, was not in evidence. To fill his time while waiting, Wyeth took four men in a canoe more than a hundred miles to the mouth of the river to study the entire salmon operation. At Fort George (as Astoria had been renamed) he learned from an incoming brig belonging to the Hudson's Bay Company that the *Sultana* had been wrecked. The Pacific Trading Company faced the winter with absolutely nothing on which to operate.

Farther east Wyeth's fellow amateur, Captain Benjamin Bonneville, was not having much better luck. Bonneville never did reach the rendezvous in Pierre's Hole—and may not have wanted to. As he was bouncing through the sage on his way down to the Green River from South Pass, farther west than wagons had ever gone before, the American Fur Company's mule caravan under Lucien Fontenelle overtook him. Fontenelle paused just long enough to hire away some of Bonneville's best Delaware Indian trappers and then hurried on to Pierre's Hole. Perhaps a company would have a better chance of staying intact if it kept to itself. Bonneville turned up the Green only as far as Horse Creek, near present Daniel, Wyoming. There, to protect his livestock and men while they replenished strength after their "easy" wagon trip from the settlements, he built a small square stockade in the traditional pattern—a solid fence of upright cottonwood logs fifteen feet high, defended by blockhouses of unhewn timber at opposite corners.[2]

His scouts lured in a few free trappers. Bonneville liquored them up on a wild debauch and signed them on to replace the Delawares. They told him that winters in the area were severe and that he would have better luck up north on the upper Salmon. So he left his wagons parked beside the stockade and led a mule caravan into Idaho, passing on the way the dismal battlefield of Pierre's Hole. During the winter his brigades scattered out in standard fashion but did not fare well. Some of the men were

[2] The mountain men sometimes called the stockade Fort Nonsense or Bonneville's Folly, evidently because the captain planned to winter there where wind and cold were notorious. The epithet delighted later writers on the fur trade, who have perpetuated the appellation on the grounds that Bonneville intended the establishment as a trading post. I can find no evidence that he did so plan or ever use it as such, except incidentally during the rendezvous of 1833. Washington Irving's offhand reference is probably closer to the fact; Irving gives the stockade no name and characterizes it as a temporary defensive "breastwork."

robbed by Indians; a few were killed. Twenty trappers who went east across the mountains into Big Horn country were seduced by Crow Indians into deserting to the savages with their horses, traps, and pelts—an unusual wrinkle even in the feverish competition that was rapidly killing off the mountain beaver trade.

News of Bonneville's presence in the Snake Country undoubtedly reached McLoughlin at Fort Vancouver but probably did not worry him any more than Wyeth's presence did. His brigades had held off experts. Neophytes were not likely to bring trouble.

Wyeth's collapse, indeed, was so complete that his men asked for their release. (One had died at Vancouver of "colic" during Wyeth's trip to the mouth of the river.) Two of his erstwhile partners in the defunct company he hired back on wages to help him as *engagés*. The others found such work as the Hudson's Bay Company could give them. The former lawyer, John Ball, opened the first school in the Northwest for the half-breed children of the traders. In the spring a few men joined the nine retired Hudson's Bay *voyageurs* who were building farms in the fertile Willamette Valley somewhat northeast of modern Salem. One way or another, however, most of them eventually returned to the States. Only two, Solomon Smith and Calvin Tibbetts, stayed on, to achieve in time a fame of sorts as the first permanent American settlers in Oregon.

All told, and even granting the Bay Company's nervousness about American pretensions to the Northwest, Wyeth's dissolving expedition could hardly have struck Factor John McLoughlin as a forecast of the future.

SALVATION BOUND

Seeing no threat in Wyeth—and liking him besides—McLoughlin was his usual generous, sociable self with the American. He granted him the full hospitality of the extensive fort, let him see what he wished of its grain fields and nearby sawmill, its orchards, shipping dock, warehouses, and living quarters, and during the winter lent him a canoe and equipment for exploring the Willamette Valley.

Wyeth was impressed with the Willamette. In his journal he wrote "I have never seen a country of equal beauty except the Kanzas country.... If [Oregon] is ever to be colonized this is the point to commence."

The evaluation was accurate. The Willamette Valley was the point where settlement did begin. Yet Wyeth jotted the words absently, a random allusion to the old settlement schemes which had originally put him in motion. He was no colonizer. That was Hall Kelley's dream, from which Wyeth had disassociated himself a year since. Yet in that year he had learned enough of this wild, free land to know that he wanted to stay as a fur trader—a business which would be ruined by settlement. Ironically enough, in his efforts to salvage his affairs he would become the unconscious, almost accidental agent of colonizers.

He began his search for new ways and means by joining, with his two *engagés*, a Hudson's Bay Company brigade under Francis Ermatinger bound for the Flathead post in northwestern Montana. Through the cold, wet month of February 1833 they toiled up against the current of the Columbia. They had a long way to go—Fort Colvile in northeastern Washington, Clark's Fork, and finally the western fingers of the Rockies.

As the canoes inched slowly along, Wyeth and Ermatinger had time to gossip about every aspect of the trade. None of their talk changed the Bostonian's mind. More than ever he was convinced that his original idea of supplying trappers from the Pacific was sound—with one refinement. When he left Boston he had intended to put trappers into the field himself. Since then he had learned that a ruthless opposition was too firmly anchored along the streams for him to crowd in as a hunter.

Competing with their suppliers, however, might be something else. As he had surmised in Boston, the Columbia route, relatively untroubled by hostile Indians and bordered east of the Cascades by a wealth of cheap horses, was far more economical than the longer trail from St. Louis. Why hadn't it been tried before?

Perhaps because the trade had been started by men drifting west out of St. Louis, landlocked men without the feel of ships in them. Perhaps because the English hold on the Columbia seemed unbreakable. Indeed, as Wyeth now realized more clearly than he had in Boston, the Hudson's Bay Company could present formidable barriers if Governor Simpson and the directors in London so ordered. On the other hand, Wyeth's welcome at Fort Vancouver had made him believe that the giant monopoly might be amenable to a good Yankee suggestion about profits.

He put his ideas into a letter to George Simpson from Fort Colvile on March 12, 1833. If the Hudson's Bay Company would furnish him with trade goods at a specified markup, he would transport the merchandise to the annual rendezvous of the American trappers, buck his own countrymen for the pelts being bartered there, and resell whatever he got to the Hudson's Bay Company at an agreed price.

Since an answer would take a long time reaching him, he needed other strings to his bow. Searching for these, he left Flathead Post with Ermatinger's brigade and trapped south through the Montana Rockies. Band after band of Flathead and Nez Percé Indians fell in with them until more than a thousand Indians were wandering along, herding close to two thousand horses. A few white trappers appeared. Groups formed, split away, reassembled. Ermatinger swung back into Flathead country; Wyeth, who had made contact with some of Bonneville's men, continued south. On the Snake he joined Bonneville himself. As they rode toward the rendezvous together, the Bostonian proposed that his fellow amateur outfit him for a trapping venture in California. It was a novel and exciting idea, but it evaporated when Wyeth reached the teeming rendezvous and saw again how much potential wealth awaited the man daring enough to break through the traditional patterns.[1]

The gathering that year was held in the wide sage valley with the white-capped peaks of the Wind River Mountains cool to the

---

[1] Bonneville remembered the California suggestion, however. In the fall of 1833 he sent a large party into the Mexican province under Joe Walker. It proved a difficult and profitless but historic, expedition. Among other things, Walker discovered Yosemite Valley.

east, where Horse Creek flows into the Green. Bonneville's stockade was within sight. So were Bonneville's wagons, hard-weathered by the long winter and the dry spring. But no one paid them much attention.

This was perhaps the biggest, most exuberant of all the mountain carnivals. The usual gangs of Indians were there, showing off their expert horsemanship with a dazzle of color. Bonneville's scattered brigades assembled, none with very many furs. Dozens of free trappers rode in. The American Fur Company camped cheek by jowl with the Rocky Mountain Fur Company, the cocky rivals the first-named was preparing to break. Watching the goings-on with relish were some of the mountains' first tourists and health-seekers, among them the son of President-to-be William Henry Harrison and an English sportsman, Sir William Drummond Stewart. (Actually, Stewart was a Scot, but the mountain men considered him a full-blown Englishman.)

Each camp of mountain men had an iron-handed bully whom it matched vociferously against the bullies of other camps. Each had a champion racehorse with which it challenged all comers. During and after these somewhat formal contests, the general populace raised informal hell—gambling, brawling, treating each other in raw alcohol at exorbitant prices, and decking their Indian sweethearts in gaudy finery (connections, incidentally, that often proved more enduring than the reference may suggest).

As Wyeth watched bale after bale of furs pile up in exchange for liquor, ammunition, knives, cloth, and shoddy trinkets, he swung from the California scheme back to his plan of a supply base on the Columbia. But the base would not be just a transshipping point. He would model it after Fort Vancouver, self-sustaining with its own farms and domestic animals. He would enrich it further by salmon fisheries. Never mind George Simpson. If possible, Wyeth would work out spheres of influence with the Hudson's Bay Company. If not, he would challenge them. This idea was big—big enough that he decided suddenly to go East with it and lay it before some of his business friends in Boston in the hope that they would finance him.

So that he could approach his backers with something solid in hand, he obtained from Thomas Fitzpatrick and Milton Sublette

246

a contract to bring in their 1834 supplies from St. Louis, replacing their usual equippers, William Sublette and Robert Campbell. (Sublette and Campbell would not like that when they learned it and, he guessed, would do their best to defeat him.) As a bit of showmanship to titillate moneyed Boston folk, Wyeth also decided to take two Indians east with him. One was a sulky Nez Percé warrior, aged about twenty, who wanted to see the sights. The other was a thirteen-year-old half-breed, son of a Flathead squaw and a French-Canadian *voyageur*, whom he intended to train as his personal retainer and interpreter.

For reasons irrelevant to this narrative, the returning fur caravans forsook the Oregon Trail and took their pelts to navigable water on the Big Horn. There they built bullboats for floating the furs and buffalo robes to the Missouri. Wyeth was the first to finish his craft. In a hurry to reach Boston, he did not wait for the protection of the full flotilla, but shoved off recklessly ahead. His crew consisted of Milton Sublette, his two *engagés*, and his two Indian boys.

Behind him, Bonneville loaded his furs into three bullboats and entrusted the cargo to Michel Cerré. With four men and forty-six horses (other trappers had been detached to hunt the Big Horn country) the captain returned to the mountains. It was a flagrant bit of arrogation, for his Army leave was due to expire in the fall. But he had spent a great deal of money for negligible returns and wanted to recoup. Besides, like Wyeth, he had fallen in love with the wilderness. (One reason, suggests historian Hubert Howe Bancroft with a shrill of outrage, was an obliging sequence of toothsome squaws.) Although he had made sketches for valuable maps and had gathered information for General Macomb about natural conditions and Indian tribes, he had not yet surveyed the British establishments of the Northwest. This he proposed to do the following winter.

To justify himself, he had somehow found time between the rendezvous and the Big Horn to write General Macomb a long letter. In it he included data about the Hudson's Bay Company which almost certainly he had picked up from Nathaniel Wyeth. He gave the information a peculiar and belligerent twist. If the United States government intended to seize Oregon, "the sooner it shall be done, the better." Although Fort Vancouver was potentially strong, most of its men were generally away trapping. The interior posts were "feeble" and "too much exposed . . . to offer the least violence to the smallest force." Fort Walla Walla, "handsomely built but garrisoned by only 3 to 5 men, may be easily reduced by fire, or want of wood, which they obtained from the drift." The Indians were peaceful. The whole Northwest, Bonneville thought, might be subjugated by a subaltern's command; yet, to be safe, "I would recommend a full company." He intended to investigate the country still further during the ensuing winter and under the cirmumstances, so he implied, the general surely would not mind his staying AWOL another year or two.

The Hudson's Bay Company of course did not yet know of this double-barreled threat against them by two self-appointed apostles of Manifest Destiny—a Yankee trader spreading grandiose commercial ideas and a strayed Army captain proposing even more inflated military projects. (And by Hall Jackson Kelley, who simultaneously was making a lone, incredible odyssey toward Oregon by way of Mexico and California, still dreaming of an American colony on the Columbia.) Even if the company had known, the extent of its alarm would be questionable. The entire business was too green, too impossible, to have been taken very seriously.

After hard labor—the bullboat kept grounding on sandbars—and tense encounters with Indians, Wyeth's small group reached the junction of the Yellowstone and the Missouri, where William Sublette and Robert Campbell were building a post to buck the American Fur Company. Milton Sublette decided to stay. Wyeth pressed on. He traded his sodden bullboat for a twenty-two-foot sailing canoe and launched it onto the Missouri with men who had never before seen the river. Before he was out of sight, William Sublette in all probability began reproving brother Milton: wasn't it too bad, really, to let a rank outsider from Boston shave away some of the profits of their trade?

By November Wyeth was in Cambridge. Criticism rattled around his ears. The father of one of the men who had deserted early on the westward march spread public letters of censure about Wyeth's conduct of the expedition. More annoying was Professor Waterhouse of Harvard. Ghost-writing under the name of Nathaniel's young nephew John B. Wyeth, Waterhouse published a book satirizing the entire endeavor.[2] The attacks might have discouraged cautious investors. But the Messrs Henry Hall, Tucker, and Williams agreed to support Wyeth, partly on the basis of his contract with the Rocky Mountain Fur Company.

Exuberantly he plunged into the time-consuming job of dispatching a shipload of supplies to the Columbia by the *May Dacre*. On the way she was to procure plants and domestic livestock from the Hawaiian Islands; Wyeth was totally earnest about building a post self-reliant enough to ignore Fort Vancouver. He wrote detailed instructions to an agent in St. Louis about buying horses, mules, and equipment for an overland expedition of sixty or seventy men. He spent more precious time corresponding with two naturalists who wished to go West with him, John Townsend and Thomas Nuttall. Nuttall, who had gone partway up the Missouri with Hunt's Astorians in 1811, was a friend of Wyeth's; during his first trip West, Nathaniel had collected seeds and skins for the naturalist. Townsend, a protégé of Nuttall's, was a twenty-five-year-old surgeon and ornithologist from Philadelphia.

On top of all that came a party of missionaries, bound for the mountains to redeem the Flatheads. Could they ship their heavy equipment to Vancouver on the *May Dacre?* Could they travel overland with his party? Would he help stimulate interest in their project by speaking to church groups about the benighted savages? Above all, could they exhibit his Indians in their drive to raise funds? To each of these bothersome requests Wyeth amiably assented.

The missionaries' zeal was the flowering of a strange and now-

[2] John B. Wyeth, *Oregon; or a Short History of a Long Journey.* The *New-England Magazine* used a review of the book (April 1833) to sneer again at people who would colonize Oregon: "Nothing since the time of the Crusades has equalled the Oregon expedition in absurdity; and what makes the matter worse, is, that the adventurers acted on the suggestion of a madman [Hall Kelley], and against all warning and advice.... He who, after reading this work, shall start for the Northwest coast, by way of the Rocky Mountains, is an idiot or a lunatic, and the country will be happily rid of him. "

famous concatenation of events. In 1831, three Nez Percés and one Flathead had arrived in St. Louis with a fur caravan from the upper Missouri. They wanted to see the sights (think how many white men were curious about Indians) and to visit William Clark, a legend among the Nez Percés since the Lewis and Clark Expedition. They may or may not have been interested also in finding religious teachers, but William Walker, a Christianized half-breed trader, got the notion that this was what they wanted most. He did not actually see the four visitors (two died in St. Louis), but he wrote letters to the East in which he implied that he had. He spoke of their poor deformed skulls (their heads were normal) and of their hunger for the Word of God. His letter, which created considerable stir in evangelical religious circles, eventually blossomed in the Methodist *Christian Advocate*, along with an editorial cry: "Let the Church awake from her slumbers and go forth in her strength to the salvation of these wandering sons of our native forests."

The man chosen to lead the mission was Jason Lee, a black-bearded, powerful backwoods farmer six feet three inches tall. Lee had been converted during a revival at the age of twenty-three. Three years later he entered the Methodist Academy at Wilbraham, Massachusetts, to brush up on his education, but had money enough to last only a few months. He was thirty when his missionary call came. As companion he chose a twenty-seven-year-old nephew, Daniel Lee. To teach at their mission school the Lees engaged Cyrus Shepard, a thirty-five-year-old bachelor schoolmaster from a village near Boston. Shepard was almost unbalanced in his ardor, yet in Oregon, partly because of his unswerving sincerity, he became the most respected of the lot.

Wyeth explained Indian tribal names to the missionaries. Although the Nez Percés may once have pierced their noses, they had long since abandoned the custom. The word *Flathead* derived from a sign-language symbol for the tribe. They did not deform the skulls of their infants by pressing the bones into a peak between two boards; that practice was confined to the tribes along the Northwest coast. Like all Indians, the Flatheads and Nez Percés were religious in the sense that they had a strong interest in learning how to propitiate the forces which ruled their overwhelming environment. To this primitive pantheism the mountain Indians added a surprising amount of information (and misinformation) about Christianity.

The lore, mostly bits of Catholic ritual, had come to them through Hudson's Bay Company traders and, more powerfully, through converted Iroquois hunters who had married mountain squaws and settled in their villages. Bits of Episcopalian formalism had come through Spokane Gerry, an Indian boy Simpson had taken to a missionary school in the Red River area and who in 1830 or so had built a shack on the site of what is now Spokane, where he proposed to educate his fellow tribesmen. Wyeth had made several entries in his journal about the Indians' long, devout Sunday ceremonies. Bonneville too had noticed their zeal and later told Washington Irving that the Flatheads and Nez Percés would not travel on Sunday lest they offend the Great Spirit. He added ". . . they even had a rude calendar of the fasts and festivals of the Romish Church and some traces of its ceremonials. These have become blended with their old wild rites, and present a strange medley." Both amateurs further agreed that the moral standards of the Nez Percés and Flatheads were much finer (from an Occidental point of view at least) than those of the other tribes they had encountered.

The data excited the Lees. Even more exciting was Wyeth's flat statement, made at a church meeting to which he agreed to go, that "any white man gaining their confidence, therefore, will be able to mold and fashion them to any reasonable measures and principles."

With success thus beckoning, the missionaries made their ways independently to the Missouri frontier. Following Wyeth's advice, they bought cattle for sustenance and hired two helpers, Philip Edwards and Courtney Walker, who would be useful not only on the trail but later in rowing their heavy equipment from the *May Dacre* up the Columbia to whatever site they selected for their station. Unlike the Flatheads, the whites then overcame their objections to Sunday travel and hurried after Wyeth's caravan—for by now the Bostonian was an old enough hand to be leading the train himself.

They ran straightway into the standard miseries of the trail.

A furious rainstorm filled even their boots with water; a horse bucked off its pack and vanished; they slept in wet clothes. Indian dogs ate fifty pounds of their bacon and they lost one of their beef cows. In shocked amazement Shepard watched a Kanzas chief hunt lice through his wife's hair: "...when any game is taken it is immediately secured in the mouth as though it were a precious morsel." Diarrhea arrived on schedule, but frail Cyrus Shepard learned to stand guard with it in the rain. One night the horse herd stampeded. "Being unwell, I was out at the time...and barely escaped being trampled." In spite of all this, he enjoyed the first part of the trail, "a most romantic country, beautifully diversified with hill and dale, prairie and woodland—the prairie clothed in a robe of lively green interspersed with elegant flowers in rich profusion and variety."

Jason Lee did most of the hunting for the party; Daniel Lee and Shepard preferred to stay in camp tending the stock and singing hymns. On one searingly hot day, Jason, the naturalist Townsend, and a hunter named Richardson killed some badly needed buffalo twelve or so miles from the Platte. Parched by thirst after the dry chase, the missionary and the naturalist started for the distant river for a drink. Richardson stopped them, "plunged his knife into the distended paunch, from which gushed the green and gelatinous juices, and then insinuated his tin pan into the opening," straining off some water. The popeyed tyros declined the drink. But when the hunter held forth the beast's heart, says Townsend, "my thirst and hunger got the better of my abhorrence; I plunged my head into the reeking ventricles and drank until forced to stop for breath." Ashamed, he glanced toward Lee. The missionary looked at his wry, blood-smeared face and laughed until tears ran down his cheeks. That earthy acceptance of mountain ways may be the reason why the trappers of the caravan, while disliking Lee's errand, liked the man himself. Not that he accepted their morals. He regularly reproved their incessant profanity, for example, but always, said Townsend, with "the mildness and affectionate manner peculiar to the man."

The miles dropped slowly behind. A hunter brought to camp a baby antelope hardly bigger than a kitten. The men named it Zip Coon; the missionaries fed it milk from their cows, and the packers transported it by mule in a pannier woven of willow twigs. Zip Coon liked to ride. When camp was broken in the morning, he ran over beside the mule and waited to be lifted into his basket. Cyrus Shepard, who filled pages of his journal discussing the state of his soul, never mentioned the tiny mascot to which he gave milk.

The spring of 1834 had been dry. The South Platte and Laramie rivers, whose fords had troubled Wyeth in 1832, were crossed without difficulty. On the shady flats near the bank of the latter they saw a group of William Sublette's men preparing to build a fort of cottonwood logs. Though christened Fort William, the post was generally called Fort Laramie. After it had passed into the hands of the American Fur Company (they rebuilt it of adobe) and then to the United States Army, who enlarged it as a permanent military cantonment, it became the most important caravansary on the Oregon and California trails.

The Black Hills west of Laramie frightened the tenderfeet into dismounting at times and walking. "Rock jutted over rock," Townsend wrote, "and precipice frowned over precipice in frightful and apparently endless succession." After they had forded the North Platte and had turned toward Sweetwater, a hot wind hurled sand into their faces, coated their food, and one night toppled their tents. For a time the entire caravan was on short rations. It was Jason Lee who killed the elk that tided them over until they found buffalo again.

South Pass, Shepard wrote, was "barren in the highest degree." Crossing the desert from the pass to the Sandy, the missionaries' sore-hooved cattle dragged far behind the main caravan. Fearful of Indians, they made camp in a dry stream bed, milked the cows, "drank the pleasant beverage [Shepard writing] and committing ourselves to the care of Him that neither slumbereth nor sleepeth, spread out blankets laid down and sank sweetly into the arms of soft repose." Rising by starlight the next morning, they managed to catch the caravan and plod on to the difficult ford over the Green.

Wyeth was pushing hard. As far back as Independence he had sensed that he was likely to be double-crossed if he did not get the Rocky Mountain Fur Company's goods to the rendezvous first. The meeting was held that year on Ham's Fork of the Green, in southwestern Wyoming, and by July 20 he was there—a creditable fifty-one-day trip for a relative newcomer at the business. But William Sublette had traveled faster. Arriving well ahead of the Bostonian, he persuaded the Rocky Mountain Fur Company to repudiate its contract with Wyeth. Opening his bales and kegs, he then harvested the cream of the business. Wyeth was left to glean crumbs and cast about once again for means to shore up his tottering affairs.

The rendezvous was as wild as ever: indiscriminate shooting, howling, fighting, fornicating, and gambling at the Indian game of hand—to which the unwary were attracted (said tourist William Marshall Anderson in his diary) by a rich bank of fofarraw, drums, songs, and a handsome Flathead female shill, in person a Circe, who seduced victims into "hells of corruption." The missionaries mention relatively little of this, or of the grizzly bear and buffalo which were slain on separate occasions within one of the camps to the tune of frantic uproar. They may not have seen much. Because of shortage of grass, camps were scattered and frequently moved, and the men of God seem to have done little visiting, save for a formal call on William Sublette and Thomas Fitzpatrick.

On Sunday, June 22, several Flathead and Nez Percé Indians came to their tent to see their magic Bible. Impressed, the savages promised to trap beaver with which to pay the whites for introducing civilization to their villages. In spite of this naïve misunderstanding of motives, Shepard felt encouraged. Lee, however, was beginning to worry. The party still had to reach Fort Vancouver, transfer their heavy goods from the *May Dacre,* and row several hundred miles back upstream before jumping off to a site not yet chosen. Reaching the Lord's vineyard and building cabins before the mountain winter closed in was looking more and more difficult. Anyway, this was a barren, inhospitable country, unfit, so far as he could see, for the farming which he felt should be taught the Indians along with the doctrines of salvation. Might there not be better places closer to the Columbia? Surely he asked Wyeth, and surely Wyeth told him of the Willamette Valley.

The Bostonian meanwhile had decided to open a trading post in the Snake River area. There he could trade his rejected goods for furs brought to him by free trappers; for buffalo robes, dried meat, moccasins, and similar articles made by Snake, Flathead, and Nez Percé Indians. The decision made, he left the rendezvous abruptly, before it was finished. The scientists, missionaries, and the Scottish sportsman Sir William Drummond Stewart, who had wintered with Jim Bridger, tagged along. So did more Indians than Wyeth liked, for they mixed their horses with his until it was impossible for him properly to guard his own precious animals.

They worked up the winding Ham, through lovely meadows bordered by the perpetual gray of the sage. They passed the site of Kemmerer, Wyoming, and cut sharply west up what appeared to be the highest mountains they had yet tackled. On July 4 they crossed the divide through shimmering aspen groves and slanted down a steep hill into a tributary of the Bear. At the conclusion of the day's twenty-one-mile ride, on a meadow where they met some of Bonneville's men bound for St. Louis with the captain's furs, Wyeth decided to let the men celebrate the holiday. "I gave them," he admitted wryly to his journal, "too much alcohol for peace took a pretty hearty spree myself."

"Independence . . . ," mourned Jason Lee in *his* diary. "They were as abject, degraded slaves as ever groaned under oppression's yoke . . . slaves to Satan and spirituous liquors." To escape the tumult, some of the sober ones went fishing with willow poles and hooks on the end of common string. They quickly caught thirty pounds of trout averaging fifteen inches in length.

After the deserts that had stretched almost without interruption from western Nebraska to beyond the Green River, the north-trending valley of the Bear looked like a foretaste of heaven. Grass was knee-deep; rustling trees provided easy firewood; trout leaped at the hook from crystal water. If this haven for recruiting livestock had not existed (the deserts ahead were even bleaker than those beside the Green), one wonders how many of the later emigrant trains would have survived to reach Oregon. But there were troubles also. Mosquitoes swarmed. Impetuous tributaries pouring out of the mountains to the east had to be crossed. Ridges protruding from the forested highlands forced travelers either to splash back and forth several times through the deepening stream or climb up and down the rocky humps in the way, one of them a thousand feet above the valley floor. On such a stretch the mule carrying Zip Coon fell and broke one of the antelope's legs. It had to be killed.

On another grassy meadow they fell in with a Hudson's Bay Company brigade under Thomas McKay, half-breed son of Alexander McKay who had perished on the *Tonquin*, and stepson of John McLoughlin. McKay led a motley gang: thirteen Indians from various tribes, several squaws, and seventeen French-Canadians. He and Wyeth greeted each other cordially, but McKay was surprised to see, after the rendezvous was over, so many heavily laden pack mules in the Americans' caravan. What was Wyeth up to? McKay decided to follow along and see.

North of today's Montpelier, Idaho, amid gnarled piñon pines and junipers, they reached a stretch of intermittent mineral springs, most of them now lost under the waters of a reservoir. Many of the springs had accreted for themselves tall cone-shaped mounds of spongy yellow rock; the orifices of others were flush with ground that echoed hollowly under the impact of a man's boots. Only one, named Steamboat Springs for the way it puffed, was hot; but several were effervescent and named Beer Springs by wistful trappers, who professed to find them tasty. Cyrus Shepard did not like them at all.

Two miles farther on rose a rocky promontory called Sheep Point, from the numbers of mountain sheep on it. The Bear River made a hairpin curve around this soaring headland and then drifted south to the Great Salt Lake. Wyeth left the river at Sheep Point and led the caravan three miles northwest across sun-crisped, curly grass and through a saddle in the low hills to the crooked Portneuf. Later emigrants would generally follow the Portneuf's watershed to the Snake, but Wyeth moved farther north to a parallel stream, the miry Blackfoot. During the day's twenty-mile ride his men killed three grizzly bears. The last one, big as a steer, charged into the middle of the caravan. Horses snorted and reared—and kicked the bear severely. The trappers poured more than thirty bullets into the roaring monster. At last he died in the shallows of the stream and four men strained to drag him onto the bank. Jason Lee's sole comment on the episode: the animal "was to [*sic*] poor for food."

That night the trappers probably would not have stooped to bear steak anyway. Buffalo abounded again. Bonneville and ten or twelve men were camped nearby, drying meat for a trip to Oregon. As soon as Wyeth's camp was in order, he and Sir William Stewart rode over for a call. Since the standard mountain drink, grain alcohol laced with creek water, was raw, Bonneville smoothed out the concoction on special occasions by adding honey; "a happy compound," he reminisced later to Washington Irving, "of strength and sweetness, enough to soothe the most ruffled temper, and unsettle the most solid understanding."

Over the mead Bonneville told them something of his bad luck since parting from Wyeth on the Big Horn a year before. Leaving the bulk of his men at a winter camp in the Portneuf country, he had started with three companions to look over the Hudson's Bay Company's posts on the Columbia. At times he cut far south from the Snake toward the mountains on the Idaho–Utah border, as Wyeth had done while trapping the region two years before. Like Wyeth, he did not cross the Snake but followed its broad arc through southwestern Idaho. He crossed the lower Owyhee (named for natives of Owyhee [Hawaii] who had been killed there while trapping with Nor'Westers many years before), but somehow missed the standard trail up Burnt River into Oregon. Rather, he continued straight down the Snake and tangled himself in the mountains which had caused Ramsey Crooks and Wilson Hunt such despair during the winter of 1811–12. Bonneville had somewhat better luck—although the term is relative. Washington Irving reconstructed a single morning of the trip:

> The snow was from two to three feet deep, but soft and yielding, so that the horses had no foothold, but kept plunging forward, straining themselves by perpetual efforts. Sometimes the crags and promontories forced them upon the narrow riband of ice that bordered the shore; sometimes they had to scramble over vast masses of rock which had tumbled from the impending precipices; sometimes they had to cross the stream upon hazardous bridges of ice and snow, sinking to the knee at every step; sometimes they had to

scale slippery acclivities, and to pass along narrow cornices, glazed with ice and sleet, a shouldering wall of rock on one side, a yawning precipice on the other, where a single false step would have been fatal.

Unable to continue down the river, the quartet scrambled desperately up the mountains. For three days they lived on a mule that had collapsed. For three more days they ate nothing whatsoever. Finally they broke through into the lower valley of the Imnaha River in extreme northeastern Oregon. Nez Percé Indians, fascinated by the captain's bald head, at last agreed to sell him salmon and deers' hearts in exchange for an old plaid jacket which he cut into strips to make it go farther.

An Indian guide led them back into the Snake's wild canyon and around the Wallowa Mountains, later the beloved home of famed Chief Joseph. Prevailed on to help the pain-wracked sixteen-year-old daughter of a chief—"uncommonly beautiful in form and feature," naturally—Bonneville steamed her semi-conscious in a vapor bath, dosed her on gunpowder dissolved in cold water, put her to bed under a load of furs, and the next morning prescribed a diet of colt's-head broth. She recovered (naturally).

This was an area of British influence. Trying to counteract it, the tattered Americans told the Nez Percés that if all the people in the United States were to camp on the banks of the Snake, they would drink the river dry. The destitute representatives of this great power then departed for the nearest Hudson's Bay Company outpost to seek help. On their way down the Walla Walla River they must have jogged close to—perhaps even across —the site on which Marcus Whitman less than three years later established his famous mission.

They reached Fort Walla Walla on March 4, 1834. As travelers they were received by Pierre Pambrun, the agent in charge, with urbane courtesy and provided with everything they needed for their immediate comfort. As traders, however, they were clearly unwelcome. Pambrun declined to furnish them additional supplies that might be used for barter. Vastly irritated, Bonneville lingered for only two days and then returned, more or less along his original route, to Idaho.

During the summer he held his own rendezvous in the valley of the Bear, fearing to lose both his men and his furs if he brought them within reach of his cutthroat competitors at the general gathering on Ham's Fork. Actually he would not have lost much. Walker's California expedition had produced nothing but information. His other brigades had garnered only four thousand dollars' worth of furs, and he owed in wages alone more than twice that sum. But, he told Wyeth fiercely over the honeyed mead, he was not licked yet. Oregon promised much, and no Britishers could keep him out. He was going back that very summer and spend the winter there.

The keg empty, Wyeth and Stewart tottered back to their own camp. The next day they left Bonneville to his meat-drying and moved down the Blackfoot. On July 14, on the southeast bank of the Snake, between the Blackfoot and Portneuf rivers, Nathaniel Wyeth reached the bottomlands he had seen two years before —a desolate flat (Lee complained in his diary about the blowing sand), a bright green band of cottonwoods on the far margin of the stream, and dim above the treetops the outlines of distant buttes. He decided to build his post there and name it Fort Hall in honor of one of his backers.

McKay's Hudson's Bay brigade joined the Americans and for two weeks the motley groups camped side by side. On Sunday, July 27, at McKay's request, Lee delivered an exhortation to trappers and Indians assembled under the rustling cottonwoods. Afterward there was horse racing. A collision mortally injured one of McKay's French-Canadians. The next morning his friends wrapped him in a buffalo robe, buried him outside the half-built fort, erected a cross for a marker, and built an "empalement" (Shepard's word) around the grave. "... service for him," wrote Wyeth, "was performed by the Canadians in the Catholic form by Mr Lee in the Protestant form by the Indians in their form as he had an Indian family. he at least was well buried."

Time was wasting. When McKay resumed his westward march on July 30, the missionaries and Captain Stewart went with him. Chasms slashing across the hot sage plain occasionally forced the travelers far back from the river canyon. After a fruitless two-day hunt for mountain sheep, they regained the Snake near spectacular Thousand Springs, where white foams of water burst from the middle of the canyon's north wall and, wrote Lee, "rush with impetuous fury and astonishing splendor down the rugged bank. . . . How astonishing are the works of God."

The Indians they met were agog over the white men's handful of cattle; once fear had been overcome, chiefs vied for the privilege of driving the beasts. These were an impoverished people called Diggers, who went almost naked and lived in huts of willows covered with long dry grass, dwellings that appeared to Lee like haycocks. "Having so long been accustomed to dwell in tents, to me they seemed quite comfortable."

The canyon banks fell away and they camped near present Glenn's Ferry. Two flat islands broke the broad river into three channels. Future travelers would cross here, work northwest to the blessed cottonwoods which gave the Boise River its name, and rattle down that stream to its mouth, where they again forded the Snake before striking inland. McKay used the island crossing. He told the missionaries and Captain Stewart that he was going north to the Salmon River country to trap and trade. What he actually did, a few weeks later, was swing to within five miles of the mouth of the Boise and there build Fort Boise, an even cruder post than Wyeth's Fort Hall.[3] His intent, of course, was to intercept Indians who might otherwise be tempted to trade with the American. And so, out of the dog-eat-dog rivalries of the fur trade, the three chief recuperating and supply points of the inchoate Oregon Trail—Forts Laramie, Hall, and Boise— were erected during the summer of 1834.

Completely on their own now, the missionaries and the British sportsman crept westward through the dreary desolation bordering the south bank of the Snake. One evening Cyrus Shepard had convulsions; another day he and the Lees quarreled bitterly for reasons not stated. Turning north, they crossed the mouth of the Owyhee, as Bonneville had done. From the Owyhee they slogged over an interminable hill, crossed bleak Malheur Valley,

---

[3] McKay's post was christened Snake Fort, but to save confusion this account will use the name Fort Boise, by which it became more commonly known a few years later, after it had been relocated near the mouth of the Boise River. Both forts stood many miles west of the modern city of Boise.

circled a gaunt volcanic butte, and struck the Snake again. But only for a moment. Following either Indian advice or a map of McKay's, they veered away from the mountains to the north up narrow Burnt Canyon and over drab sage deserts to the welcome grass of Powder River Valley.

The cattle lagged appallingly. The men whose turn it was to drive them had to start well ahead of the others each morning and continue long afterward in the evening. Fortunately the Indians helped, putting the travelers back on the trail when they strayed and once giving the Lees two fine horses. Jason felt that God's hand was with them. Why else would the savages "be taking so much more interest in us than in others?"

Ahead of them the sky was smeared with smoke. Thousands of square miles of prairie and forest were ablaze. The wayfarers floundered uncertainly into the haze, detouring to avoid islands of fire or to locate grass for their animals. After crossing mountains where fallen treetrunks smoldered on either hand, they reached Grande Ronde River and there overtook Bonneville.

The captain had marched directly into Oregon from the Blackfoot without visiting Fort Hall and was now waiting for his scattered trappers to reassemble. He had sent scouts due westward to find a direct way across the Cascade Mountains into the upper Willamette Valley, hoping thus to avoid both the difficult rapids of the Columbia and the unfriendliness of the Hudson's Bay Company.[4] His explorers did not find a way, however; roaring fires in the defiles and on the ridge tops turned them back.

Captain Stewart and the missionaries did not wait for the report. Doggedly they pushed along the regular trail over the Blue Mountains, the way so steep and the air so choked with smoke that the gaunt cattle could scarcely be forced ahead. On top, the cow-drivers—Philip Edwards and Cyrus Shepard that day—were given what little food remained while the others hurried ahead to Fort Walla Walla. To their dismay they found that Pambrun had nothing to eat but fish and bread. With this the missionaries made do (the drovers arrived in due time, after being lost one night), but Stewart killed a horse in his disgruntlement. They were still

---

[4] The hope of such a direct short cut into the Willamette would also allure later parties, sometimes fatally.

camped at the post, making arrangements for Pambrun to take care of the cows and rent them a barge, when Wyeth reappeared.

A week after they had separated from him, the Bostonian had christened Fort Hall with "a bale of liquor." Leaving twelve of his party to man it, he crossed the Snake by a trapper trail, the naturalists still with him, and turned westward along the base of the Sawtooth Mountains to the Boise River. He descended this without seeing McKay. Crossing the Snake again, he picked up the missionaries' tracks. Although he trapped as he went, he made better time than they had and was only two days behind when he met Bonneville in the Grande Ronde Valley. They discussed the possibility of Wyeth's bringing the captain supplies from the *May Dacre*. As for the few furs they were both taking in Oregon, said Wyeth, they had been "seized from the common enemy ... so far so good." On he hurried to carry the attack to the enemy's doorstep. The country was "burned black as my hat," the horses suffered dreadfully, and one torturing night the party had to camp without water.

After the brief regrouping at Fort Walla Walla, the parties split again and went down the Columbia in scattered canoes and a barge. It was a wet, hard trip. Gales roared through the gorge and threatened to swamp them—Wyeth lost one canoe entirely and severely damaged another. At one portage Townsend's group found the missionaries breast-deep in water, rain pouring overhead as they struggled to pull their barge ashore. "They were most abundantly soaked and bedraggled."

They needed help when they reached Fort Vancouver, and McLoughlin gave it generously. But, according to a later missionary, William H. Gray, he also seduced them. He did not want missionaries educating the Flathead and Nez Percé Indians to the true value of their furs, settling them on farms, and spoiling the trade. He would rather have them keeping peace and promoting temperance among the retired *voyageurs* and degraded Indians of the Willamette. Therefore, in Gray's view, McLoughlin overemphasized the difficulties of maintaining a station among the nomadic Flatheads, where Blackfeet were accustomed to raid. At the same time he played up the lushness of the Willamette and the possibilities of service among sedentary Indians who

truly did deform their heads. To prove his point he furnished
Jason and Daniel Lee guides and let them spend a week exploring the fertile valley. They returned convinced.

Other historians, particularly Bernard DeVoto, believe that by
the time Lee had reached the rendezvous far back on Ham's Fork
of the Green he had realized that neolithic savages could not be
turned into practicing Methodists by prayer and good works. To
avoid failing at what he had come so far to do, the would-be missionary abandoned his original goal and turned to a valley where
farms and rudimentary but familiar forms of civilization already
existed. There, according to the unfriendly estimate of his activities, he fell prey to worldly riches and became the chief real-
estate agent for the developing migrations.

Moving westward behind Lee and Wyeth, Bonneville followed
the Umatilla River on its diagonal course to the Columbia. That
way he missed Fort Walla Walla. But the Indians declined to
trade with him—on orders from the common enemy, the captain
believed—and again Pambrun refused necessary supplies to a
deputation of Bonneville's hungry men. Fearing to winter in so
inhospitable a region, the captain returned to the Rockies.

Wyeth's vine withered more slowly but just as surely. His ship,
badly damaged by lightning off South America, did not reach
Fort Vancouver until the day after he did, too late for that year's
salmon run. He nevertheless went vigorously to work. Anchoring
the May Dacre bow and stern to a rock on Wapato (now Sauvies')
Island at the mouth of the Willamette, he unloaded pigs, sheep,
goats, poultry, cuttings of grapes and figs, sugar cane, and sweet
potatoes. While his men began building a fort, he located a farm
in the Willamette. During the dead of winter he went back up
the Columbia with a large group of trappers, including several
Kanakas recruited in Hawaii. Just beyond the Cascades he split
the group, sending half to Fort Hall. The twelve Kanakas in the
Fort Hall party deserted, each taking a horse. With the other
half, Wyeth traded unsuccessfully with the Indians and later
made a cold, hard-luck trip into the interior of Oregon.

On his return to Fort Vancouver in February 1835, he was astounded to find Hall Jackson Kelley recuperating in one of the

post's abandoned cabins. The wild-eyed colonizer, traveling much of the way alone, had managed to cross Mexico, reach Baja California, and ride north to San Francisco. There he persuaded a former trapper named Ewing Young to settle with him in Oregon. Young added a few followers; then a gang of horse thieves fell in with them, and after an appalling journey during which Kelley was afflicted with a raging fever, they reached the Columbia.

McLoughlin received them coldly. He thought, incorrectly, that Young was one of the horse thieves and ordered him away from the fort. He knew, through newspapers reaching him from the United States, that Kelley was an advocate of driving the Hudson's Bay Company out of the Northwest. Even so, he gave the sick man food and shelter in a rickety cabin.

Bridling at what he considered inadequate treatment and trumpeting about his rights as an American, Kelley borrowed seven pounds from McLoughlin and took passage home on a Hudson's Bay Company ship. Bonneville also left the country in 1835 and embarked on a successful struggle for reinstatement in the Army. Wyeth moved from disaster to disaster. After seventeen of his men had died from disease or violence he too gave up in 1836, sold Fort Hall to the Hudson's Bay Company a year later, and returned to his ice business.

McLoughlin no doubt felt justified in congratulating himself. Competitors had been repelled without violence. Noncompetitors were isolated in the Willamette. There were only two dozen of them—the handful that had accompanied Ewing Young from California and nineteen men, including the missionaries, who had been associated with Wyeth. Surely no threat lay there.

But one of the things that turns a trail into a road is familiarity. Glowing letters which the missionaries wrote home about the country were printed in the religious press. Hall Kelley fed statistics to Congress. Townsend wrote a widely read account of his experiences. America's most celebrated man of letters, Washington Irving, published best-selling books about Astoria and the adventures of Captain Bonneville. Back in the United States Oregon was becoming more than a name.

More important, perhaps, was the slow diffusion of the knowledge that for the first time in history the Oregon Trail had been traveled in a single trip from end to end. (Fur-trade ventures, even Wyeth's, had been interrupted and filled with detours.) The men who had made the monumental journey were not wild trappers but humble missionaries, driving with them that most homely of domestic adjuncts, milk cows with calves. No trail over which a cow has once trudged can ever again seem wholly awesome. Furthermore, during that year three establishments with all that they implied about help for the desperate had taken shape beside the way. And at the end of the road there stood not simply the unfriendly fort of a foreign power, but the nucleus of an American settlement.

Looking backward analytically, if he ever did, John McLoughlin might well have revised his congratulations and concluded that 1834 had turned into a fruitful year for the United States after all.

FOUR

SUNBONNETS

14

CIVILIZATION'S ADVANCE GUARD

Samuel Parker was fifty-four years old when he felt the stirrings of adventure. After graduating from Williams College in 1806, he had gone as a home missionary to the raw frontier of western New York state. As the country settled, Parker settled with it. He held Presbyterian and Congregationalist pulpits in various hamlets of the Finger Lake area. By his second wife he fathered three children whose ages in 1833 ran between ten and sixteen. He was handsome, fussy, stingy, shrewdly observant, soundly analytical, and enormously sure of himself. At the time of his middle-aged excitement he was teaching at a girls' academy in Ithaca. One would hardly expect him to chuck job and home and take off for the Northwest on impulse. But that is what he did.

As in the case of Jason Lee, the impulse came from William Walker's letter in the *Christian Advocate* about the Flathead and Nez Percé Indians who had journeyed to St. Louis in quest, perhaps, of religious salvation. On reading the appeal, Samuel Parker dashed off a letter offering his services to the American Board of Commissioners for Foreign Missions, a cooperative organization supported by Presbyterian, Congregational, and Dutch Reform churches.

The commissioners had already contemplated a mission in Oregon. In 1820 they had established a station in the Hawaiian Islands and since then had discussed, somewhat desultorily, using the establishment as a starting point for the Northwest. Nothing had happened, however. Funds were short and demands for support world-wide. Moreover, laborers in the vineyard preferred peaceful regions that supported dense, if heathenish, populations —China, for instance—where opportunities for numerous conversions seemed bright. A handful of nomads, many of them addicted to indiscriminate slayings of white men, suffered by comparison. Unbalanced zealots transported by sudden enthusiasms did volunteer from time to time. But educated, patient missionaries able to teach primitive minds in an intelligible and interesting way were hard to find.

A family man of Parker's age and inexperience in wilderness living scarcely seemed the answer. The Board turned down his offer. But Samuel Parker was not inclined by nature to brook denial. He secured as potential companions two youngish bachelors, Samuel Allis, twenty-nine, and John Dunbar, thirty. He then toured the churches around Lake Cayuga, exciting missionary societies with his handsome face and fervent eloquence. After receiving from the First Presbyterian and Dutch Reform congregations of Ithaca a pledge to finance an exploratory trip beyond the Rockies, he again bombarded the American Board, asking only that it provide $450 a year for the support of his family during his absence.

Thus beset, the commissioners authorized the journey. They did suggest an alternative: if, on reaching the Missouri frontier, the three explorers found a trip to the Oregon country inexpedient, they should content themselves with establishing a mission among the Pawnees along the lower Platte.

The trio reached St. Louis six weeks after the fur caravans and Lee's Methodists had departed. Envious of Lee, Parker wished to go on with only a single guide for protection. Horrified churchmen in the city told him he was mad; so tiny a party could not possibly survive. "If these statements," Parker sniffed by letter to the Board, "came from Roman Catholicks or Fur Traders who disregarded religion, we should not have regarded them, but they are from intelligent, experienced, Christian men."

Feeling that the Board's alternative suggestion now became operative, Allis and Dunbar departed for the Pawnees. Not Parker.

He returned home, hitched up his buggy, and in the dank cold of November and December 1834 toured the little churches of western New York, searching out recruits and funds for another effort.

In Steuben County he was approached by a chunky, round-headed doctor named Marcus Whitman. Whitman was just the sort Parker wanted. The son of impoverished pioneers, he had trained himself in medicine by "riding" for two years through the lumber camps of western New York as an apprentice to a doctor named Ira Bryant. He had taught Sunday School and had urged temperance in roughneck communities. Later he had studied for two sixteen-week terms at a medical college in Fairfield, Ohio, winning his degree in 1831 at the age of twenty-nine. If in today's view the training seems skimpy, it was better than that possessed by most country practitioners of his time. For reasons now unknown, however, medicine in the tiny town of Wheeler left him dissatisfied. Seeking fulfillment, he had offered himself to the American Board as a medical missionary but had been rejected on his admission of severe recurrent pains in his side. Since then, however, his health had improved and he told Parker that he was eager and fit for Oregon.

Traveling still farther west, to Amity in Allegany County, Parker met a tall blond woman, "symetrically formed" and buxom —136 pounds. She was Narcissa Prentiss, eldest daughter of a master builder called Judge in deference to his single term on the county bench. Narcissa was an exotic name for a potential missionary, but it suited her. Comely, possessed of a lovely voice and bubbling good humor, she had many admirers. Although twenty-six, she had not married. She was very devout. As her most recent biographer, Nard Jones, points out, she had absorbed in full the misty, romantic notion that the Indians of the western United States were the true natural man of the Philosophers, ready for fruitful development as soon as their spirits were properly touched. Parker's zeal brought her vague yearnings to focus and she offered herself as a missionary—providing, of course, that it was proper for unmarried females to go to Oregon.

This time the American Board accepted Whitman's appeal and authorized his joining Parker on an exploratory trip into the land of the Flatheads. Logically enough, Parker thereupon put the thirty-three-year-old bachelor doctor in touch with the spinster. The two had already heard of each other through their church work and possibly had met. But in January 1835 there was no time to use the mutualities as the starting point for a normal courtship. Parker was determined not to miss the fur caravan again this year. He granted Whitman time enough to visit Narcissa's home only over a single week end. The stay was sufficient, however, for them to reach an understanding: If a mission station among the wild Indians of the West was a suitable spot for a woman, he would return for her and they would be married.

The two men traveled separately to St. Louis, arriving early in April. Whitman rode horseback, put his horse and saddle in a livery stable and lost both when the barns were consumed by fire. Journeying more easily and expensively by stagecoach and steamboat, Parker appeared immediately thereafter, unrumpled in the same garb that he wore for teaching in the girls' academy at Ithaca—a white stock tied neatly under his chin and a tall plug hat atop his head. He would wear the costume most of the rest of the way across the continent. It was symbolic enough. The bulk of the United States, like Samuel Parker, was dreadfully short of realistic information about the dusty way West.

The American Fur Company's caravan would be led that year as far as Fort Laramie in southeastern Wyoming by moody Lucien Fontenelle.[1] Parker sought him out in St. Louis, probably after talking to his employers. None of them really wanted any Bible-packers along, but they didn't quite dare risk popular condemnation by saying so. Grudgingly Fontenelle told the missionary-explorers that they could go with his caravan if they got themselves to the company's new Bellevue fort near Council Bluffs on

---

[1] In 1834 Astor sold the Western Department of the American Fur Company to Pratte, Chouteau and Company of St. Louis. In 1834–35, Pratte, Chouteau and Company absorbed the Rocky Mountain Fur Company. In 1838 Pratte, Chouteau and Company became Pierre Chouteau, Jr., and Company. The mountain men ignored all those name changes and continued to call the successors of the Western Department by the old, ingrained title—the American Fur Company. Most narratives that touch on the period (including this one) avoid confusion by following their lead.

time. He was going to move up the north bank of the Platte this year, as Ashley had done a decade before and as the Mormons would do a decade later; and he had no intention of waiting for anybody.

His peremptoriness startled the missionaries into catching a steamboat the very next day. But the Missouri was not ready for haste. Low water and snags caused one delay after another. On April nineteenth Parker noted in his journal, ". . . one of the main shafts-large, made of iron was broken, by too much *steam* being raised, common steam and the fumes of whiskey." Halted thus, the travelers took a wagon as far as Liberty, a small town opposite Independence, inland a few miles from the river and nearly two hundred miles short of their destination. In Liberty they learned there was no hurry after all. The steamboat on which Fontenelle was traveling had gone aground on a sandbar far downstream.

Liberty was as far as any of the boats were going to run. The rest of the trip would have to be made overland with horses. Here Parker's frugality came into full bloom. He had had a hard time squeezing money for this trip out of impoverished church missionary societies and he was already vexed that Whitman had lost a perfectly good animal and saddle in a barn fire—as if it had been Whitman's fault. Now he declared that they should limit themselves to one horse each for riding and a single mule for packing their tent, camp gear, personal goods, ammunition, medical instruments, hymnbooks, and whatever trade goods they might need for bartering in the wilderness. Whitman could not pry another animal out of him even by suggesting that they might need a spare in case anything happened to one of the others.

Nearly four weeks passed before Fontenelle arrived and was ready to go. For a time he carted some of the missionaries' excess baggage in one of his wagons. Then a series of rainstorms struck, the vehicles mired, and Fontenelle ordered the goods out. Along came a wagon driven by one Moses Merrill, a Baptist who had attached himself to the caravan for its protection as he returned to his mission near the company's fort at Bellevue. Merrill had just jettisoned some of his own baggage to ease his horses. But one simply did not say no to Samuel Parker, serene above the mud in his white tie and tall plug hat. Into Merrill's wagon went the explorers' impedimenta.

Marcus Whitman did not say no to him, either. Parker told him flatly that although they ate crosslegged on the ground in a tent possessing limited conveniences, all must nevertheless be "conducted on good style; for I would not dispense with attention to decencies, because beyond the boundaries of civilization." That was fine—if someone else packed the mules, pried the wagon out of the mud, chopped the wood, cooked the dinner, washed the tin dishes, and cared for the stock. Whitman did, while Parker dilated his nostrils to savor the evening breeze and later relaxed to the soothing patter of raindrops on their tent. Now and then he pursed his mouth disapprovingly when the doctor came in exhausted and smelling of mule sweat, and forgot to wash before eating.

It was a hard two-week trip. Streams were flooded. They had to raft goods across rivers that normally were fordable. At several swamps the men had to unload the bogged horses, shoulder the loads, and wade out of the muck with the equipment on their own backs. Fontenelle's roustabouts sought to drive away the resultant chills with large libations of whiskey. Legend has it that once they endeavored to make Whitman drink with them. He refused, declaring he would not touch the bottle though they held him under water until he drowned. On another occasion, so the tale runs, they pelted him and perhaps Parker too with rotten eggs.

Whitman reached Bellevue worn out and tortured by the old pains in his side. He hoped he might rest a bit while the caravan prepared for the long jump to the mountains, but almost immediately he was called on for help. The missionaries and most of the trappers were camped on a farm which Fontenelle owned, a mile or so below the fort. It was bottomland and the rains had turned it into a quagmire. As the men slopped listlessly about their work, several of them fell ill. Symptoms were violent— diarrhea, vomiting, agonizing cramps, fever, thirst, and convulsive shivering. The skin shrank. First the fingernails and then the face turned blue.

In 1835 no one could miss the signs—Asiatic cholera. It had first struck the United States three years before and had roared terribly across the country, perhaps the worst killer the United States has known. The summer of 1832 was the worst time—in New York City alone 3000 people died—but it continued sporadically afterward and would break out violently again on the emigrant trails during the Gold Rush of 1849. Written accounts did little to allay the terror it created. For example, a professor of Natural Philosophy at Miami University, Oxford, Ohio, was moved by a resurgence of the disease in 1833 to deliver himself of a discourse entitled "The Cholera, God's Scourge for the Chastisement of Nations." To people who might soon catch the disease he said:

> And the excruciating—the awful agony of the sufferer is such as to render him an object of amazement and terror to all around him. The sight is sufficient to shock and appal humanity. . . . Physicians, men of the stoutest nerve and inured to scenes of suffering, confess themselves completely unmanned, and thrilled with horror.

The author then assigned seven reasons for the plague: slavery, mistreatment of the Indians, intemperance, politics (which led men "to compromise everything like honesty, integrity or dignity of character for the sake of carrying a point . . ."), national infidelity, division among churches, and individual sins. Not all amateur analysts covered quite so much territory, but they generally agreed that the disease struck hardest among persons addicted to vice and spirituous liquors.

No one really knew a cure, but many remedies were suggested, especially through *The Cholera Gazette,* which published sixteen issues between July 11 and November 21, 1832, to disseminate information about the epidemic. A patient must be kept warm. Suggestions: steam him with vinegar poured on hot bricks placed under his bedclothes. Or raise the bedclothes on hoops and burn a cupful of alcohol between his legs. Bleeding, particularly by cupping the epigastric arteries supplying the abdomen wall, was considered useful; in fact, bleeding was employed for all ailments. Purges were popular: "Puke with tepid salt and water" or with ipecacuanha.

Marcus Whitman was ill in his tent with his usual side pains on June 10 when Fontenelle sent him an urgent message. He dragged himself out to do what he could. No doubt he bled the sufferers, as he bled himself and Parker whenever they felt rocky. He also recommended that Fontenelle move his men out of the bottomlands to a drier, fresher location on the bluffs. This may have done the trick; or perhaps the disease just burned itself out as quickly as it had come—it often did. Although three men died and several, including Fontenelle, were violently ill, the enfeebled caravan was ready to move on June 21.

June 21 was a Sunday. The missionaries refused to budge. Fontenelle, far behind schedule already, left without them. The majority of the men were too weak to ride many miles those first days, however. By starting early on Monday and pressing hard, the missionaries, equipped now with an extra pack mule, were able to overtake them by dark. This time there was no mockery of Marcus Whitman.

Fontenelle was using the journey to conduct another experiment with wagons. The emphasis of the fur trade was shifting toward buffalo robes—in 1835 they brought more on the market than beaver did—and transportation problems were shifting correspondingly. Robes were unwieldly to pack on mules. Though persistent attempts were made to float the bulky cargo in shallow-draft boats down the spring flood of the Platte, the river's erratic sandbars nearly always frustrated the efforts. Wagons would be better—if wagons could be taken readily as far as Fort Laramie, the outpost of the robe trade. To learn, Fontenelle took with him six light wagons in addition to the usual long line of pack stock, handled on this occasion by sixty men.

Although the cholera had delayed them long beyond the normal travel dates, events went as usual—crashing thunderstorms; rivers forded by covering the wagon boxes with skins; Indian scares; dysentery. Whitman was so afflicted with the last that he could not keep up with the caravan, let alone cook supper or pitch the tent. Parker, traveling earnestly westward to save the heathen, thereupon jogged ahead to dine with the brigade leader while the doctor, who reached the campground late at night, crept into bed without supper. The next day Fontenelle, the disbeliever, sent a man back to look after the packs and help Whitman on and off his horse until the doctor could navigate on his own again.

More than a thousand tall, clean, handsome, colorfully clad Oglala Sioux fell in with the caravan just short of Laramie and continued with it to the fort. The Indians were curious about the missionaries. Several came into the tent one evening while Parker was reading his Bible. Calling on such rudiments of sign language as he possessed, he endeavored to teach them the purport of the book and the proper methods of worshiping God. Bogging down, he stood and sang a hymn instead. The fascinated Sioux politely shook his hand as a way of expressing appreciation, "and," he assured himself in his journal, "the expression of their countenances seemed to say, we want to know what all this means."

The Word, he felt, was needed. When the caravan and its tins of alcohol reached Fort Laramie, whites and Indians staged a thunderous drunk. One trapper shot at another. "I'm a dead man!" cried the wounded (in Parker's account). Then he reconsidered. "No, I'm not." The assailant thereupon reloaded to finish the job but was disarmed by bystanders. Even more distressing was a buffalo dance by the Sioux, who donned shaggy masks and horns and cavorted in imitation of the animals. The applauding trappers rewarded the performance with generous slugs of alcohol. Parker was not amused: white men debauching red men for acting like beasts! "What will become of their immortal spirits?"

But these were not Flatheads. His and Whitman's duty lay beyond the mountains. After six days at Laramie, the caravan moved on toward the rendezvous, led now by Thomas Fitzpatrick. The wagons, however, stayed behind: taking them farther was deemed impractical.

On South Pass they noticed the surprising chill of the high-altitude nights even in August. By forced marches they crossed the deserts bordering the Green and turned upstream to the appointed site under the morning shadows of the Wind River Mountains, where the creek draining New Fork Lake ran into the main stream, near modern Big Piney. Fort Bonneville stood twenty-five miles to the north.[2] Bonneville's twenty decaying wagons probably still sagged outside the crude stockade—no diarist ever bothered to mention what ultimately became of the historic vehicles. But Whitman heard of them and later used them as part of his proof to the American Board that women could cross to the Oregon country.

The rendezvous was standard—scores of trappers and, by Whitman's estimate, two thousand Indians. Most of them packed a burning thirst, aggravated by the unusually long wait for the delayed caravan. Parker, though, was at last beginning to sense why a trapper acted as he did; even after seeing young Kit Carson fight a pistol duel on horseback with another man over an Arapaho squaw, his concern for immortal souls was not so toplofty as it had been at Fort Laramie. Whitman, perhaps the only doctor ever to reach an early rendezvous, was meanwhile called on to ply his trade again. Jim Bridger had been packing a three-inch arrowhead in the flesh of his back for three years; its barbed point had stuck in a bone and cartilage had grown around it. Another trapper had borne a similar arrowhead for more than a year. Whitman stretched both of them out and went to work without anesthetic in front of a ring of staring mountain men and Indians.

Great medicine: the next day the Flatheads and Nez Percés (who disappointed Parker by having neither flat heads nor pierced nostrils) came around to talk about spiritual healing. The missionaries also talked with William Stewart, the Briton who had gone to Fort Vancouver with Jason Lee the previous fall and who in the spring had returned to the rendezvous with Francis Ermatinger of the Hudson's Bay Company. From Stewart the newcomers learned that the Methodists had marched straight past the original red seekers for truth and had set up shop in the Willamette. So Parker was not too late after all; the Flathead field was wide open.

---

[2] Bonneville himself had left a little earlier that summer with his pelts by way of the Big Horn Basin, where he detached Joe Walker and a brigade to trap. The captain planned to return with supplies in 1836, but his difficulty with the Army and the discouragement of his backers kept the plan from materializing. As a fur trader Bonneville was finished.

Unfortunately the two men had been sent to explore, not to establish a station. If they spent the rest of the summer pinpointing a site and later returned East to report and engage workers, no building could be started for at least two years. To their enthusiasm, fired by the wistful insistence of the Indians that they did want to learn about God (a concept the savages related vaguely both to their own mythology and to the white man's wonderful power of making cloth, guns, and whiskey), two years seemed unbearably long. Besides, Whitman had Narcissa in the back of his mind. After prayers in their tent that evening, he remarked that if only their party had consisted of three men, they could save a year by having one member go East while the other two continued searching for an appropriate site.

Parker replied that an extra man was unnecessary. He would explore alone. Whitman was aghast. Four months on the trail had left the elderly preacher as innocent of campcraft as he had been at the beginning. He simply could not make such a trip unattended.

God would attend him, Parker said. With such assistance he could not fail.

The next morning he asked the Nez Percé chiefs if they would escort him on an exploratory tour through their country and then deliver him at Walla Walla, so that he could go down the Columbia and winter at Fort Vancouver. The Indians agreed with a shout of excitement and promised him one of their best young men as a personal retainer. Captain Stewart further assured the dubious Whitman that the Nez Percés were the most reliable and peaceful Indians in the mountains and would do as they promised. If an interpreter could be hired—he turned out to be Charles Compo, a French-Canadian with a Nez Percé wife—then what seemed at first blush an insane idea might very well succeed.

Thus it was agreed: Parker would find a site and the next summer would meet Whitman's reinforcements at the rendezvous with full details. Of course, he said, he would need both pack mules for the trip. He gave Whitman $5 for purchasing a replacement. Since good horses sold at the rendezvous for $75 to $100, one can imagine the scrawny, sorebacked discard the doctor was finally able to buy. Whitman would not be traveling alone. Having discovered a Nez Percé boy named Tackitooits (Whitman rechristened him Richard), he enlisted the lad to go East with him so that they could learn more of each other's language. The envious father of another boy named Ais (he became John) then asked if his son could go too. Anticipating the Board's disapproval on the grounds of needless expense, Whitman demurred. Parker, eager to please his new hosts, overrode the objections; and the doctor, like Wyeth, found himself with two young savages to shepherd through the shocks of civilization.

On August 22 the fifty-six-year-old schoolteacher settled his plug hat firmly on his head, said farewell to his companion, and began his incredible trek. He jogged north with Bridger's trapping brigade as far as Pierre's Hole, then on over the hair-raising trails of the Salmon River Mountains of central Idaho with his swarming, ecstatic Indians. He taught them to say the Lord's Prayer and the Ten Commandments by rote, demanded and received special foods from them, and took copious notes, often while so sick he could scarcely ride, of everything he saw. Recast later in an enormously popular book and also incorporated into hundreds of lectures which Parker made throughout New England, these data gave the United States its first thorough look at a large part of the Northwest.

After he had departed, Whitman waited another five days beside the Green for the fur caravan to start for Bellevue. The trip was uneventful, though no doubt arduous. But at least his health had improved in the mountains. When he reached western New York state early in December 1835, he was bursting with energy.

He needed it. In order to be sure of catching the American Fur Company's 1836 caravan to the rendezvous, where Parker supposedly would be waiting, he wanted to start back to St. Louis by early February. This gave him two months in which to complete his arrangements with the American Board of Commissioners for Foreign Missions—arrangements not only for himself but also, he hoped, for the bride he would take West with him.

He put one of his Indian boys with Parker's family in Ithaca. He took the other to his old home town of Rushville, where he made his headquarters in the home of a friend. He wrote letters to the Board justifying their expense, and adapted his laconic journal to serve as a report of his trip. He wrote a long reply in answer to a question propounded by David Greene, secretary of the American Board: "Have you carefully ascertained & weighed the difficulties in the way of conducting females to those remote & desolate regions and comfortably sustaining families there?"

Yes, Whitman said. Fontenelle of the American Fur Company had promised assistance. The missionaries would use wagons for the first part of the trip—although twenty vehicles had already crossed South Pass, he admitted that he probably would drive them no farther than Fort Laramie. By then the females would be well enough adapted to rigorous living to take to saddles— sidesaddles, of course; no white woman of the time would have considered putting on pants and riding astride. Some male tourists at the rendezvous professed shock at seeing even squaws ride that way.

They would drive cattle with them, Whitman continued. He expatiated on the wild game available for food. Not knowing of Wyeth's impending bankruptcy, he said that heavy equipment could be sent to the Columbia as Lee's party had sent theirs— by Wyeth's trading ship. He was sure that flour and other staples could be purchased from the Hudson's Bay Company.

Having been West, he was convinced that none of the problems of travel or living was insuperable. The big block lay closer to home—the question of associates. The mission would urgently need what was then called a mechanic, a jack-of-all-trades capable of handling the manual chores that would beset even the humblest construction work. An even more pressing need, at least in the eyes of the church, was for an ordained minister to be in charge of the station. Whitman was a doctor only and could not elevate heathen souls to salvation. Unless a minister was found, the Board would not authorize the mission. Without the mission, there would be no marriage. That was Whitman's agreement with Narcissa Prentiss.

As soon as he reached New York state, he went to see her at Angelica, Allegany County, where her family was then living. The outlook was not promising. Apparently the Board had kept Narcissa informed about prospective candidates for the mission, and there were precious few of them. Even these few were hedged about by contingencies. As the worried couple discussed the situation, Narcissa brought up, out of desperation, the names of Henry Harmon Spalding and his wife Eliza.

It is strange that she should have done so. Her experiences with Henry Spalding had been painful. He had a warped, brooding, vindictive nature—as well he might. He was an illegitimate child. When he was fourteen or so months old, his mother had bound him out to foster parents who, in return for raising him, could command his services until he was twenty-one, a not uncommon arrangement in those days. He seems never to have seen her again. He hated the shadow of her passionately.

He grew up near Wheeler, where Marcus Whitman later practiced medicine for almost two years. He was educated only to the extent that he could scratch out his signature and read printing with difficulty. When he was seventeen, his foster father became enraged over something, got liquored up, took a whip first to his wife and then to Spalding, howled "Bastard!" at the boy, and threw him out of the house. Towns of equal size lay to the south and to the north of him. For no particular reason, the weeping boy stumbled north to Prattsburg, where Judge Prentiss and his family then lived.

For the next four years he lived with a schoolteacher, working for board and room and attending class when he could. In 1825, the people of Prattsburg opened an academy, a then-popular halfway step between common school and college; Judge Prentiss was one of its trustees. Spalding meanwhile had experienced conversion and had determined to become an ordained minister and missionary. The training for a theological degree was a long haul for a poor man twenty-two years old (a longer road than Whitman had been able to face when wavering between theology and medicine), but Spalding resolutely entered the academy as the oldest member of his group. He was awkward, lonely, and agonizingly bashful. In 1828, when he was twenty-five, Narcissa also enrolled. She was nineteen, beautiful, popular, gay. She smiled on him out of natural kindliness, and Henry Spalding fell hopelessly in love.

He learned, perhaps through their church work together, that she too wanted to be a missionary. That was enough to convince Spalding that he was just the man for her. He blurted out a proposal and was completely embittered when, to his astonishment, she refused him. In his hurt he proclaimed throughout Prattsburg that he would never go to a mission that housed Narcissa Prentiss; "I question her judgment"—a remark that Narcissa's hot-tempered father took more amiss than she did.

A little later Spalding began a courtship by correspondence with Eliza Hart, who lived off east toward Utica. She was frail, scrawny, dark, and coarse-featured, the antithesis of Narcissa, although Spalding did not know that when he began writing. Eliza was also alert and kind, and the possessor of an appeal which does not emerge in print but which strongly attracted those who penetrated her shy and rather forbidding exterior.

She fell in love with him, or at least with his missionary dreams. When he went to Western Reserve College in Ohio, where he supported himself with part-time jobs, she followed him and waited patiently until he earned his bachelor's degree. After his graduation, they were married and shifted to Lane Theological Seminary in Cincinnati. As Spalding put matters in his inimitable way to the American Board, he "married for the express purpose of giving my wife the opportunity of pursuing the same Theological studies with myself." While she studied, she took in boarders— and Spalding kept on with part-time jobs.

When they left Lane in the spring of 1835, Eliza was pregnant. They went to her home near Utica while they waited for the baby—and for an appointment. During the summer, Spalding visited old friends in Prattsburg (by this time the Prentiss family had moved to the next county) and there he was ordained a Presbyterian minister. He was thirty-two. Whatever else might be said of the poor bastard, he at least had been persistent.

Others things might be remarked. When their baby was still-born in October 1835, the father wrote, "The Lord most righteously chastised us for our sins." In recommending the Spaldings to the American Board, one of their references stated that Eliza, well loved by a large circle of friends, was "one of the best women

for a missionaries [*sic*] wife with whom I am acquainted." As for
Spalding, he was pious, industrious, and willing to make sacrifices.
"He can turn his hand to almost any kind of handy work, is not
remarkable for judgment and common sense . . . is sometimes too
much inclined to denounce or censure those who are not as zeal-
ous and ardent as himself . . . jealous."

During the fall the Board appointed him, with some reserva-
tions, to the Osage Indian mission in western Missouri. As a going-
away present, Eliza's father gave the couple a horse, harness,
and a light wagon especially constructed to withstand the rigors
of western roads.

At about the same time a letter arrived from Marcus Whitman,
asking if Spalding would consider an appointment among the
Indians beyond the Rocky Mountains. How much the doctor
knew of the minister's early love for Narcissa is uncertain. Her
nature is such that one assumes she told him. In the face of these
larger urgencies, the matter may not have seemed important to
Whitman.

As Spalding read the letter, he must have thought sourly that
the woman who had rejected him was now asking him, in effect, to
make her marriage to another man possible. It may have crossed
his mind also that the Board would hardly approve of a last-minute switch in assignment. Under the circumstances generosity
did not cost anything. He told Whitman he would go if the Board
permitted.

The Board did not authorize the change. Its representatives
and Whitman continued to work feverishly to find another candidate. One by one each prospect withdrew. Completely desperate, Whitman again urged Spalding on the commissioners.

The date on which Whitman had hoped to leave for the West
arrived and passed. At last an ambiguous letter arrived from the
Board's secretary. Whitman interpreted it to mean that if Spalding
himself expressed a wish to go to Oregon, the Board would authorize the switch.

Whitman immediately rode from Rushville through deep snow
to Prattsburg, hoping to catch Henry and Eliza there. But they
had already attached sleigh runners to the light wagon and were

driving to Cincinnati, where they planned to board a steamboat for St. Louis and western Missouri. The doctor nevertheless pressed on, reasoning that the pair would not have traveled on the Sunday which had intervened. They hadn't, and he managed to overtake them.

No one can possibly know what thoughts went through Spalding's mind. Undoubtedly he mentioned Eliza's poor health, perhaps sincerely, perhaps as an escape. Legend has it that she retired alone to their inn room and prayed for an answer. It came out ambiguous, too. Christ had instructed his ministers to preach to all the world—mountain Indians as well as Osages. In other words, she would go wherever her husband led.

Did it occur to Henry Spalding that as an ordained minister he would outrank Whitman at the mission? Did he reflect that forever after Narcissa Prentiss would owe her marriage to him? Or was he being truly Christian when he resigned his own ambitions among the Osages and said his original promise still held: he would go with Whitman if the Board sent him a clear-cut authorization. The letter could catch him either at Cincinnati or St. Louis. No time would be lost. Whatever his destination proved to be, he had to go through both cities.

As far as Whitman was concerned, this was tantamount to settlement. Of course the station still needed a mechanic, but that was the Board's problem. He'd found the minister, hadn't he?

By chance the Board received, at almost the same time it received Whitman's letter, an application for Oregon from William H. Gray, a devout twenty-six-year-old cabinetmaker of Utica, who had learned of the opening through a minister with whom Whitman had corresponded. (Gray did not know Eliza Spalding; their coming from the same area is just another of the coincidences of the entire strange situation.) The man Gray cited as a reference searched hard for good points, said he was a skilled worker, healthy, and abstinent. He then said that William Gray was not good missionary material; the carpenter evinced "a confidence in his own abilities *to a fault* . . . is a *slow scholar.*" In fact, Gray's teachers at school called him a complete dullard. His monumental ego nevertheless had led him in the fall of 1835 to start studying medicine. The physician who tried to teach him soon threw up his hands in defeat.[3] Now Gray wanted to be a missionary. With no further search into his qualifications, the harassed Board told him to overtake the party in Missouri. The secretary also wrote Spalding, addressing the letter to Cincinnati, and directed him to change his destination to Oregon.

The road to Cincinnati took the Spaldings through Angelica, where the Prentiss family lived. Spalding stopped long enough to apologize to Judge Prentiss and to Narcissa for the derogatory remarks he had once made about her. He did it on February 16 or 17. On the eighteenth Marcus Whitman and Narcissa Prentiss (she dressed herself in black) were married. The Spaldings did not stay for the wedding of the couple with whom they had said they were willing to associate themselves, but plodded on through miserable winter weather toward their still-unknown destination.

If these four oddly suited people had stayed at home, they probably would have remained undistinguished, even in the narrow little towns of western New York. But they listened to the first faint whispers that were beginning to stir through the country about the land beyond the mountains, and as a result more words have been written about them than about any other pioneers in our history.

Eliza Spalding and Narcissa Whitman were the first women to cross the North American continent—that in itself would be piquant enough for a volume or two. In addition, for Narcissa this was a honeymoon trip, and she was beautiful to boot. During her wedding journey she and her husband would sleep in the same tent with the brooding, jealous, rejected suitor whose generosity, if that is the word, had made her marriage feasible. Imagination could hardly have invented such a situation. But the ordinary wrenchings of life did. And as long as these four were fated to be the precursors of civilization in the Northwest, it seems fitting enough that they should take a few of civilization's grubbier complications along the trail with them.

[3] Thirty-five years later, dullard Gray wrote A *History of Oregon*. Acidly prejudiced and enlivened with sour, nonacademic humor, the book is nonetheless full of telling observations and is essential source material for the period of which it treats.

15

SKY OF BRASS, EARTH OF IRON

On the way to Pittsburgh to catch a steamboat down the Ohio, the Whitmans and their two Indian boys joined forces with Dr. Benjamin Satterlee and his ailing, twenty-three-year-old bride, Martha. Neither Dr. Satterlee nor Dr. Whitman could diagnose the young woman's complaint (it sounds like tuberculosis), but she refused to turn back. Her husband had just been assigned to the Pawnee mission which had been founded by John Dunbar and Samuel Allis, Parker's companions on his short-lived 1834 trip; and his wife was not going to interrupt his budding career now. Besides, she had responsibilities. She was chaperoning Miss Emaline Palmer, who was traveling to the same mission to marry Samuel Allis.

In Pittsburgh the travelers learned that the Spaldings were two weeks ahead of them. Henry had sold his horse but had shipped the wagon to St. Louis. For Eliza's sake Spalding very much hoped that wagon travel would prove as feasible as Whitman insisted, for the trip was beginning to look formidable. Ominous advice had just come to him from George Catlin, an artist who had considered himself an authority on the West ever since his 1832 trip up the Missouri to paint pictures of the Indians who hung around the trading posts. Flatly Catlin told Spalding that the fatigues of a journey across the plains would "destroy" white women. The details Spalding summarized somewhat incoherently in a letter to the Board: "1400 miles from the mouth of the Platt, on pack horses, rivers to swim, and every night to spend in the open air, hot sun and storms, the buffalo meat we can live on doubtless." Furthermore, "the enthusiastic desire to see a white woman prevailing among the distant tribes, may terminate in unrestrained passion consequently in her ruin."

Like ailing Martha Satterlee, however, Eliza refused to be the cause of a turning back. Calmly she told her husband that she would trust in God and go forward without fear.

In Cincinnati they tarried to visit old friends from Lane Theological Seminary, and there the Whitmans overtook them, as did the Board's official permission to switch to Oregon. Though Narcissa may have felt restraint on meeting Spalding again, there was none with Eliza. By the time the united party had reached St. Louis, she was writing, "I like her very much. She wears well upon acquaintance. She is a very suitable person for Mr. Spalding—has the right temperament to match him. I think we shall get on very well together."

In St. Louis they picked up a letter from the War Department (addressed to Spalding alone; that showed who was in charge, didn't it?), authorizing the two men to establish a station in the Indian country. And it was Spalding who arranged special steamboat rates to Liberty, where the party would make connections with an American Fur Company vessel bound to Bellevue, the departure point for the supply caravan. Spalding's long struggle for an education had inured him to charity. He confronted the captain of their boat with a pompous statement of their cause and demanded, rather than requested, preferential treatment. The embarrassed man, retreating like other captains Spalding had faced down along the Ohio, reduced the party's costs from $180 to $100. And when the newly married Whitmans indulged themselves one evening on the upper deck to watch by moonlight the majestic confluence of the Missouri and the Mississippi, Spalding recalled them to their place, striding up from below. "I could have dwelt upon the scene still longer with pleasure," Narcissa wrote plaintively. "But Brother Spalding called us to prayers and we left."

They outfitted themselves in Liberty while waiting for the fur company's steamboat, Diana. They bought tin dishes, hunting knives to wear strapped to belts about their waists, staple foods, and extra clothing. They purchased fourteen horses, six mules, four milk cows, and thirteen beef cattle. They acquired a heavy farm wagon to supplement Spalding's light vehicle, and that meant buying more harness. (It does not appear whether the wagons were canvas-topped, like those revered in our folklore. The big freighters used on the Santa Fe Trail and the carts being introduced by the fur company were roofed with canvas; probably these were too. It was the logical way to combat weather.)

To help drive the cattle and attend to the chores they hired a white youth named Dulin and another Nez Percé boy, who happened to be in town looking for a way home. (Curious Indians every now and then went to the settlements with the caravans.) They bought saddles for everyone, including sidesaddles for the ladies, and enough heavy, oiled, striped cotton cloth called bed ticking to make a conical tent large enough for sheltering the entire party. Expenses came to a horrifying twenty-eight hundred dollars.

During the bustle William H. Gray arrived. About the same time Samuel Allis appeared from the Pawnee mission to marry Emaline Palmer—Spalding conducted the services. But there was worry amid the rejoicing. Martha Satterlee was dying.

To save freight expenses, the missionaries loaded their baggage into the two wagons and sent the vehicles overland to Bellevue with the cattle. Because the distraught Satterlee wanted Whitman to stay with him and his wife, it became the lot of Gray and Spalding to make the trip. The others planned to follow by steamer.

Five days after the advance caravan had left, Martha Satterlee died. A grave was dug beside the river and on Sunday, May 1, the little group gathered for the final rites. In the midst of the services the American Fur Company's steamboat chugged around the bend. To Whitman's and Allis' consternation it did not put into the dock serving Liberty, as it was supposed to do, but sailed on. To stop it the dismayed missionaries stampeded from the open grave to the water's edge, waving and shouting. The captain tooted his whistle, waved back—and went on. His action, in view of the company's promise that the boat would stop in Liberty, has never been adequately explained.

The missionaries had to catch the supply caravan at Bellevue; in no other way could they cross the plains. If they could not travel the two hundred miles to Bellevue by boat, then they must go the slower, harder way by land. Rushing back to the grave, they hurried through the services. Then, although it was Sunday, they began frantic preparations for the unequal race.

Save for such personal items as the travelers had planned to take on the steamer, their entire complement of baggage had been sent ahead with Gray and Spalding. Buying duplicate items wrenched Whitman's conscience; expenditures had already exceeded the Board's anticipation. But there was no help for it. He bought what was necessary and rented oxen and a wagon to carry the load. But he did not include a tent. Thus the carefully reared females—Narcissa, Eliza, and Emaline Allis—abruptly found themselves sleeping on the ground with no covering other than their blankets. It was the beginning of a long struggle to dress and undress and meet sanitary needs in modesty. Naturally their journals do not mention it. Neither do the diaries of the pioneer women who followed them. But it must have been a very real problem, especially along the Platte, where dysentery created its invariable havoc and not so much as a willow bush grew to afford privacy.

They crawled up the Missouri to a ferry that crossed to Fort Leavenworth. The six of them and their gear were too much for the rented oxen. After they had crossed the river, Whitman sent Allis ahead on a horse to bring Spalding back with the light wagon.

Spalding appeared in miserable shape. During the uproar of driving the livestock onto the ferryboat he had been kicked in the chest by a mule. On the boat itself a fractious cow whose halter he was holding had leaped overboard and pulled him into the river. That evening a storm leveled their tent and he had shivered out the rest of the night shelterless in a cold spring downpour. The next day he had been almost too sick to navigate.

Fortunately he and Gray had acquired another helper just before the accidents, Miles Goodyear. Miles was thin, tow-headed, and ragged. He looked to the missionaries to be sixteen. Actually he was nineteen. Orphaned at five and bound out at ten as an apprentice to a Connecticut farmer, he had started West as soon as his service was finished. "He was determined," Gray wrote later, "to be his own man," and the mountains seemed the place for that. When the missionaries found him trudging alone over the prairie he had not eaten for two days and possessed no powder for his ancient rifle. But he was not discouraged. Yes, he told them, he'd lend a hand in return for his vittles as he moved toward the freedom he wanted. With infinite relief, Spalding turned his share of the chores over to the boy.

Whitman bled the aching Spalding and gave him a gigantic dose of calomel. Spalding grew sicker. Then a message arrived from the Otoe Indian Agency at Bellevue, eighteen miles to the north. A man was desperately sick there and could the doctor please come? Whitman rode ahead and so learned that the caravan, this year in the charge of Thomas Fitzpatrick, had left the day before without them. Once again it was traveling up the north side of the Platte.

After treating the invalid and sending a guide back to his own party, Whitman raced after the fur traders. Fitzpatrick proved to be ruthlessly blunt. No, he would not wait. He had four hundred horses and mules to keep in check. He carried tens of thousands of dollars' worth of goods on his pack animals and in seven big freight wagons, each drawn by six mules. His partner Milton Sublette, who recently had lost a diseased leg by amputation, was jouncing along with them in a little cart pulled by two mules hitched in tandem. The ubiquitous Scot, Sir William Stewart, and a friend named Sillem were on hand with two more carts. The whole was shepherded by seventy men. They were due at the rendezvous on the Green River, Fitzpatrick said, by July 4 (it was now May 16 or 17) and he could not spare a day. The missionaries were welcome to travel with the caravan if they caught up. But he would not disrupt his timing to suit their convenience.

At least Whitman had learned what he was up against. Back to the Otoe Agency he galloped. The first problem was to get his party to the north side of the Platte. Strangely enough, no aid appeared from the Agency, and the all-but-helpless missionaries, their three young Indians, and two hired hands (Dulin and Goodyear) were left to their own resources.[1] The wagons had to be

---

[1] The Otoe Indians were away on a hunt; but John Dunbar of the Pawnee mission was there. So was the Otoe agent, John Dougherty, and, presumably, so were various Agency workers. Other establishments near Bellevue must have contained able-bodied men. But evidently no one was impressed by the group's historic nature, and they all ignored the struggles of the desperate greenhorns.

unloaded before they could be dragged through the sandy river bottom. For ferrying the baggage and passengers Whitman obtained a boat of buffalo skins, but during the night Indian dogs reduced its capacity by eating part of it. Satterlee was still grief-stricken, Spalding was sick, the hired hands had enough to do with the wagons and livestock. Back and forth among a mile of sandbars and potholes Gray and Whitman dragged the skin canoe, transporting a single passenger and two or three boxes per trip. Much of the time it rained. By Thursday evening Whitman was so chilled and exhausted that he could scarcely crawl up the bank after the day's last crossing. On Friday they finished. But the big farm wagon had been damaged as it lurched over the riffles and they had to spend Saturday morning repairing it. All this while the caravan was getting farther ahead.

Should they break a commandment by traveling on Sunday? Sterner members said no; the Lord might punish them by putting the caravan entirely out of reach. After anxious prayers, however, the majority decided that it was a chance they would just have to take. At the Elkhorn River, which they forded on Monday, the group bound for the Pawnee mission left them and the Oregonians pressed on by forced marches that sometimes lasted until midnight. At Loup Fork, a hundred miles or so from the fording of the Platte, they overtook the caravan, which had been having shakedown problems of its own.

Routine now established itself, fur-caravan routine. At the first pallor of dawn the shout to arise rang through the camp. This stirred the picketed, hungry mules to a hideous braying to be turned loose for breakfast. On every hand figures bustled about, packing up. By six Fitzpatrick was shouting for men and wagons to fall into line—the missionaries were seldom able to gather themselves together that soon—and the caravan lurched off on its serpentine course. Fitzpatrick rode in the lead. Behind him came the long single file of pack mules, then the fur company's wagons and Sublette's mule cart. Eating the dust in the rear plodded the missionaries. Miles Goodyear rode first as pilot for the teams. Behind him Gray drove the four horses that pulled the baggage-laden farm wagon. The Spaldings and Whitmans followed in the lighter two-horse vehicle—though sometimes, to escape Spalding's growing irritability, the doctor and his bride changed to horseback and accompanied the Indians and Dulin, who brought up the rear with the cattle. The Spaldings never took to saddles; Eliza's health did not allow.

The caravan traveled until about eleven, nooned under the blazing sky in a huge sprawl until about two, and continued until six or so. Streams were the biggest trouble, both their steep banks and the water itself. Diaries of the party do not mention the expedient, used wherever possible by later travelers, of raising the wagon boxes above water level by driving chocks of wood between the beds and the frames. Probably the device was employed, however; loading and unloading at each creek was hard not only on the goods but on time and tempers. But raising the beds would not suffice at major rivers. Out the packages came, to be heaved onto the tallest horses or loaded into bullboats. Women crossed like the baggage, on horses or in bullboats. The empty wagons were taken over in one of two ways. Sometimes they were turned into precarious boats by covering the boxes with waterproofed skins. Or sometimes a dugout canoe was worried under the wheels of each side, the canoes were lashed together by sticks, and the vehicle was teetered across by men hauling on long ropes. The Indian cattle drovers sometimes splashed after their herd on horseback. Or sometimes they stripped naked, tied their shirts around their heads, waded in afoot, and swam. "Such a snorting & hallowing you never heard," Narcissa wrote, "at the same time you can see nothing save so many heads floating upon the water."

The cow herd could seldom keep up and generally reached camp at dark or later. They found wagons and packs arranged against a stream in the usual large hollow square. What section of the square the missionaries occupied is not apparent in their reminiscences. They might have liked privacy, away from the hair-curling, automatic profanity and the show-off prancing of the men; but greenhorns were generally placed in the safest spot, beside the stream. The barricade of wagons and baggage, it should be noted, was not tested by armed Indians that year or for many years thereafter. But the savages of the plains had other ways of being pestiferous. They haunted the camps to beg and to steal whatever object was left momentarily unwatched. They occasionally raided horses or mules that strayed a little distance from the camp, but seldom bothered oxen or cattle. They frequently robbed and occasionally murdered stragglers. It behooved trains to keep together, and in general the fur caravans did. The only part of the missionary group that was ever in danger of physical violence—fortunately it did not materialize—were the drovers bringing up the sore-footed cattle in the rear.

Within the bounds of the caravan's routine, Narcissa and Eliza worked out their own housekeeping habits. Variety in menus was no problem: there was none. Though Narcissa does not mention the staples of the later migrations—bacon, beans, and rice—the missionaries doubtless ate them during the first part of their journey. They had tea, coffee, and sugar. They carried ample flour. They may have had pickles and vinegar. Thanks to their cows they had the luxury of milk and cream and probably made butter.

They had trouble learning the awkward art of baking outdoors enough bread every day to satisfy ten hungry people. In theory it was simple. One mixed flour, warm water, soda, and salt in a large tin basin, meanwhile keeping out blowing sand and mosquitoes, which sometimes got stuck in the mass in such numbers as to turn it black. The kneaded dough was then flattened until it was an inch thick and put into a liberally greased Dutch oven or an iron skillet with a heavy lid. Coals were then heaped on the lid. The trick was to cook the inside of the bread through without turning the top and bottom crusts to charcoal.

Before buffalo were sighted, the missionaries butchered two of their beef cattle, sharing some of the meat with Fitzpatrick. The usual frantic excitement attended the appearance of the first herd. Whitman indulged the women by stopping the wagon long enough to let them run onto the bluffs for a closer look at the stirring sight. Male travelers meanwhile seized rifles and galloped in frenzied pursuit, to discover (as Cornelius Rogers put it in 1838) that "on account of the peculiarity of their shape, few, except those who know at what part to aim, succeed in killing them." Mountain men who did know made wanton slaughter among trailside herds, shooting just for practice. Many a carcass was left untouched; from most only the tongue and choice hump ribs were taken for food.

The meat could be prepared in various ways: boiled for ten minutes (longer cooking toughened it), cut into thin strips and dried into jerky, fried, or roasted on the ends of sticks. Having mastered the different methods the year before, Whitman appointed himself cook. Thereafter their flour was used only for thickening broth. At first Narcissa delighted in meat three times a day, rounding out the meals only with tea. "I relish it well and it agrees with me.... So long as I have buffalo meat I do not wish anything else." This on June 27. But by July 22 she was wearying: "I fancy pork & potatoes would relish extremely well. Have been living on fresh meat for two months exclusively. Am cloyed with it"—a satiation that seems never to have afflicted mountain men. They could eat buffalo endlessly, as much as eight pounds per man at a sitting.

As every schoolchild now knows, cookfires were built of buffalo dung. ("I suppose now Harriet will make a face at this," Narcissa wrote home, "but if she was here she would be glad to have her supper cooked at any rate, in this scarce timber country.") While the men of the later migrations unpacked, pitched tents, and tended to the stock, the women and children wandered around the nearby plains with sacks or pieces of canvas, picking up enough round dry chips to last through supper and breakfast. The missionary women probably had to glean the dung also; it was part of housekeeping.

The usual method of burning it was to dig a shallow trench in the direction of the prevailing wind and heap the trough full of fuel. The coals glowed with very little flame—adequate for cooking but small comfort on a cold night. If a hard rain fell during the afternoon, supper was served cold—unless someone had found driftwood along a stream bank. Wood was eagerly sought and often carried many miles. After sagebrush had been reached, its knotty stems furnished a quick, hot fire. Finicky eaters, however, thought that sage ash in their food spoiled its taste. They claimed, indeed, that sage chickens, a game bird which inhabited sage country, were quite inedible (something that this writer, who grew up among the aromatic plants, never noticed) and that any fresh meat which happened to brush against the pungent, gray-green leaves might as well be thrown away.

Like hundreds of wistful women who followed them, Narcissa and Eliza (to the extent of her health) tried to preserve the amenities. Like the trappers, they ate off the ground from tin dishes with hunting knives. Unlike the trappers, they spread out an India-rubber cloth in lieu of table covering, whittled forks from sticks, and either folded blankets for seats or drew up boxes. For a time Marcus made a ceremony of conducting Narcissa to her place—"in a way that would make you laugh to see us," she wrote proudly. But Eliza was too sick to laugh, Spalding too high-minded for vanities, and Gray too resentful of this starchy blonde who disdained his self-important ways. Still, she enjoyed the expanding freedom and adventure of those early days. "I was never so content and happy before." She even invited the Englishmen, Fitzpatrick, and Black Harris to tea one afternoon. They were gracious and merry, and everyone had a marvelous time. Except Gray. He had a bilious prejudice toward all things English; anyway he did not believe in truckling to people who claimed superior rank.

A week's rest at Fort Laramie gave the women an opportunity to do their first laundry since leaving Missouri. "It is very pleasant," Eliza wrote, "to fix my eyes, once more, upon a building." Narcissa exclaimed over real chairs with seats of buffalo hide. They savored their first Sunday of quiet in more than a month, and were pleased that several mountain men congregated under the nearby cottonwood trees to listen to Spalding's sermon on the prodigal son.

The fur company and Stewart left their vehicles at the fort. The missionaries were persuaded to abandon their large wagon also. But not the little wagon, the Dearborn. Although it was Spalding's property, accounts agree that Whitman was the one who determined to take it as far as Oregon if possible, and so became its slave.

Since its carrying capacity was limited, baggage from the big wagon was repacked for mule travel. Much had to be discarded. But what? Animosities that had been smoldering along the Platte flared openly. Tired tongues began recriminations, then caught themselves just short of eruption and painfully stitched the ragged edges back together. In stiff politeness the packs were readjusted more or less to suit everyone.

Whitman's determination led one-legged Milton Sublette to continue in his mule cart. Sublette's presence in turn led the fur company to dispatch a pair of men to help work out a road through the Laramie Mountains that had caused Bonneville so much trouble. They chopped cottonwood logs out of the way in the bottomlands, dug through gully banks, leveled side hills. In spite of them the wagon upset once, the cart twice. Wheels jolted agonizingly over stones, sage stumps, and transverse buffalo trails. Still, Eliza preferred the wagon to her sidesaddle. Growing faint under the broiling sun, she fell off her horse twice and once blacked out completely.

As caravans usually did before crossing the Sweetwater, this one camped near bowl-shaped Independence Rock. The rock's brittle granite was already accumulating the crudely lettered names which a few years later led Catholic missionary Pierre-Jean De Smet to call it the great record of the desert. Names daubed on with paint or axle grease weathered better than did those chiseled into the exfoliating rock. Gray says this group added more lettering. Surely someone included the names of the first white women to look on the massive, oval, swaybacked hummock —and perhaps the writing was the first in axle grease, unless Bonneville or Smith, Jackson, and Sublette had felt a similar urge a few years earlier. Or was weariness in the missionaries' camp too great for vanities? No record tells.

From Independence Rock, Fitzpatrick sent an express ahead to let the waiting trappers know when he could be expected at the rendezvous. Inevitably the messenger also relayed the astonishing information that two white women were approaching. The sensation was tremendous. In addition, a group of Nez Percés, puffed with importance, were bearers of a letter from Samuel Parker to the newcomers. Under the leadership of Joe Meek, a burly, black-haired Virginian twenty-six years old and already famous as a slayer of grizzly bears, these Indians and several trappers decided to make the delivery of the letter and the welcome of the women a momentous occasion.

They met the caravan after it had crossed South Pass and while it was toiling through the sagebrush toward the Little Sandy. Riding like demons, they swept along its full length, howling and firing their rifles as fast as they could reload. The men in the caravan howled and fired in return. Horses plunged; dust billowed; the train jolted to a stop. Everyone gathered around as Whitman stepped forward to accept the letter. There were quick glances of appraisal at pallid Eliza, longer ones at Narcissa. Then the expression of the doctor's face showed that the news was bad, and the missionaries forgot their reception committee.

Parker was not coming to the rendezvous. He had meant to. After a pleasant winter at Fort Vancouver, with time out to visit Jason Lee in the Willamette, he had boated with a Hudson's Bay brigade up the Columbia to Fort Walla Walla. On horseback he had examined the Spokane country and the area around forts Okanogan and Colvile in northern Washington. But he was fifty-seven years old, and when he faced the prospect of riding several hundred miles across the snowy mountains of Idaho to the Green River, his energy ran out. So he had substituted this letter instead, a vague, rambling account of general areas that might do for missions. Entrusting the missive to some Indians, he had then returned to the comforts of Fort Vancouver.

Whitman and Spalding looked at each other in consternation. The letter gave them none of the specific information they needed. Exactly where were they supposed to go? Should they entrust themselves and their wives to no more escort than these red savages whose language they did not understand? What preparations, if any, was Parker making to help them erect and furnish their buildings before winter gripped the land?

At the moment they had no choice but to continue to the rendezvous and there adjust their thinking to this catastrophic development. They forded the Green and worked up its far bank to the triangle between Horse Creek and the river, the limit to which Bonneville had taken his wagons. The views of the two men about what they had accomplished was perhaps affected by the way their wives had taken the trip this far. Spalding wrote to the Board from the rendezvous, "Never send another mission over these mountains if you value life and money." But Whitman wrote, "I see no reason to regret our choice of a journey by land." By now, the two colleagues were not seeing eye to eye on anything.

Before leaving New York, Narcissa had made several dresses of a bright calico print that she had hoped would impress the Indians. Perhaps she put one of them on in preparation for this occasion. Fifteen hundred Indians had assembled at the rendezvous and most of them turned out to stare at her and Eliza. As the ladies stepped to the ground, no doubt feeling self-conscious, a line of Nez Percé squaws formed to welcome them. The Indians' experience with trappers had led them to believe that whites always greeted women with a kiss. One by one they filed by, planting a resounding buss on the lips of the newcomers.

Later the massed warriors of four tribes—Flatheads, Nez Percés, Shoshones, and Bannocks—staged a thunderous horseback show in full regalia: war paint slashing their naked ribs, feathers, leather shields, streamers of bright cloth and animal tails fluttering from their lances. After things quieted down, the leaders of the mountain men paid court to their visitors. Shaggy workaday trappers walked back and forth in front of the conical tent, hoping for a smile. The nervier ones bobbed in to ask for Bibles or tracts. Sensing what she thought was a spiritual void, Narcissa wrote home that they could have passed out two mule loads of literature for the boys to read when they came in tired from their hunting.

Both women started compiling Nez Percé vocabularies. Eliza, who had an aptitude for language and to whom the Indians would always be instinctively drawn, made good progress. Narcissa didn't. According to Gray, she spent too much time flirting with men like Meek and Fitzpatrick and that Englishman Stewart. "In consequence of these attentions or interruptions, she did not acquire the native language as fast as Mrs. Spalding."

The reminiscenes of both the trappers and the missionaries make scant reference to the standard sinfulness of the rendezvous. Perhaps the presence of white women elevated the tone of the gathering—unlikely. Or the boys were considerate enough to slip out of earshot—possibly. Or they were so overwhelmed by the event that they wrote about it rather than about the familiar carousals—probably.

Six days after the missionaries arrived, Nathaniel Wyeth appeared on his way to the States. (He would never return to the mountains; a few months later he sold Fort Hall to the Hudson's Bay Company.) He had ridden over from the Columbia with a brigade commanded by John McLeod and Tom McKay of the English concern. They brought with them verbal and written intelligence from Samuel Parker, who suggested that his colleagues continue to Walla Walla under protection of the Bay Company. The brigade leaders added their own invitation, and in relief Spalding and Whitman accepted. They hoped now to join Parker at Vancouver and there obtain from him the information they needed.

On July 18 they swung southwestward through blistering heat to what would become Sublette's Cutoff. Though the English were pessimistic about taking a wagon very far, Whitman was insistent. He had lost one hired hand at the rendezvous—Dulin—but had replaced him after a fashion by a Negro named Hinds, who was ill and wished to stick close to the only doctor in reach. A vociferous gang of Indians went along, lodgepoles rattling as the squaws trotted by, their babies' black heads jiggling in papoose-carriers strapped to the mothers' backs, the wolfish dogs baying away after jackrabbits and antelope.

After the triumph at the rendezvous—as tremendous a reception, perhaps, as any women anywhere ever experienced—the return to routine was an anticlimax. It was also uncomfortable. The Indians refused to halt for the noon rest to which Narcissa and Eliza had grown used, and the brigade toiled dustily along with the savages. The women found the omission hard to bear. Indeed, the earlier lilting sense of adventure had vanished from the trip for Narcissa (it had never existed for Eliza) and she could not recover it. She tried, castigating herself severely. The struggle she waged with herself appears in the vacillating, disjointed entries she made each evening in the journal she was keeping to send back to her family.

The account of July 27, while they were making their way down the Bear River, is a fair sample. It starts matter-of-factly. The caravan is shrinking in size: McKay has detached thirty trappers, and several lodges of Indians have departed on their own business. Some of the cattle have had to be shod because of sore feet. And then the outburst comes, so different from the sort of thing she had written on the way up the Platte. The trigger is the dried buffalo meat which is now their principal food.

> I can scarce eat it, it appears so filthy, but it will keep us alive & we ought to be thankful for it.... (Girls do not waste bread, if you know how well I should relish even the dryest morsel you would save every piece carefully.) Do not think I regret coming. No, far from it. I would not go back for a world. I am contented and happy notwithstanding I get very hungry & weary. Have six weeks steady journeying before us. Will the Lord give me patience to endure it. Feel sometimes as if it were a long time to be traveling. Long for rest, but must not murmur. We are told we shall find the heat greater as we go on....

That appalling heat! Day after day it pressed down with the dust, until on August 2 she cried, "Truly I thought 'the Heavens over us were brass, & the earth iron under our feet.'" In addition to heat there were nervous tensions. The fester of discord between Spalding and her had long since bred a similar animosity between Spalding and her husband. Gray, too, was a trial with his egotistical, holier-than-thou attitude. There was no escape from any of the problems except through her faith. July 24: "...the privation has been made good to me by a rich supply from the fountain head God, the Father, Son & Holy Ghost. O blessed blessed privaledge, that such a sinner *as I* may have access to a mercy seat through such a Saviour as Jesus Christ."

She worried over her husband's bullheaded struggles with the wagon. As they were crossing the mountains to Smith's Fork, the maddening vehicle stuck fast in a creek and he spent hours up to his waist in water, trying to pry it loose. Then they encountered side hills so steep that it upset twice. "It is not very greatful to my feelings to see him wear out with such excessive fatigue as I am obliged too." Three days later an axle broke. She rejoiced, thinking he would have to abandon the wagon. But no: "They are making a cart of the hind wheels this afternoon and lashing the forward wheels to it, intending to take it through in some shape or another."

Even the smell of sagebrush had become offensive to her. She complained about it for the first time on August 2, although she had been riding through it for weeks. Perhaps a clue lies in that new distress. Perhaps Narcissa was experiencing for the first time the miseries of morning sickness. Naturally her journal never breathes so delicate a matter. Still, realization of her pregnancy must have come to her at about this time. The child, a girl, would be born on March 14, 1837. Presumably conception had been accomplished during the pause at Fort Laramie in mid-June; one has difficulty imagining it as occurring in the big communal tent with the Spaldings perhaps awake on one side, William Gray humped sourly on the other, and the hired hands snoring across the way.

The distress the forming embryo brought her must have been more than physical. Despair was chipping at her, too. Where was she taking this new life? Samuel Parker, the man they had counted on to find a site for their home, had failed them. After another site had been found and a cabin erected, would sharing it indefinitely with the Spaldings prove endurable? More to the point, to what end would the effort lead? By the time the caravan had reached the brief, blessed relief of Fort Hall—its fried bread and turnips were a luxury—Narcissa had been surrounded by Indians for nearly four weeks. Was she beginning even then to glimpse the red face of reality and sense the truth that later would overwhelm her—that she was following a romantic dream through desolation into failure?

At Fort Hall, Miles Goodyear said that either the wagon left or he did. The missionaries chose the wagon. Miles wandered off with the trappers to follow his own dream of becoming a mountain man; marrying an Indian, he eventually became Utah's first white settler; he was growing corn near the Great Salt Lake when Brigham Young's Mormons arrived. Missing his help more than Narcissa's journal admits, the missionaries labored with a Hudson's Bay brigade on down the south bank of the Snake. At the crossing of the Portneuf, "it seemed as if the cows would ran mad for the Musquetoes." Sagebrush was "so stif and hard as to be much in the way of our animals & waggon." Heat continued to oppress. A meal of elk meat and another of fresh salmon were delightful changes. But "the hills are so steep rocky that Husband thought it best to lighten the wagon as much as possible & take nothing but the wheels, leaving the box with my trunk." That accursed cart! At the island ford over the Snake, where the trail struck northwest toward the Boise River, both the wagon and the mules turned topsy-turvy. Tangled in the harness, the animals nearly drowned. But "after putting two of the strongest horses before the cart & two men swimming behind to steady it, they succeeded in getting it over."

At Fort Boise, five miles above the junction of the Boise River with the Snake, Narcissa was able to do her third laundry since leaving Liberty. Circumstances were disagreeable: "no shelter to protect me from the suns schorching rays." But at least the Hudson's Bay people at the post persuaded Whitman to give up his struggle with the cart. They also left at Fort Boise five sore-footed cattle, to be traded for others at Fort Walla Walla.

Like the first ford of the Snake (near today's Glenn's Ferry), the one at the mouth of the Boise was also broken into three parts by islands. The women crossed the first two channels on horse-back, but the third was too deep. Gingerly they switched to a raft made of rushes and willows; a pair of mounted Indians towed them across with ropes. Blessedly unburdened by the wagon, they worked up Burnt River, always a fearful spot for wheels, and across the endless sagebrush to Powder River Valley, memorable for a tall, lone pine that long served as a landmark.

By then horses and cattle were playing out. Worried lest Parker leave Fort Vancouver by sea before they could talk to him, the group decided that the Whitmans and Gray should hurry ahead with the Hudson's Bay people to catch him. The Spaldings would follow with the cattle, the Indian boys, and the tent. At least speed is the excuse the journals give for the separation, but one wonders if deeper frictions were not at work. As soon as Narcissa was free of the Spaldings, her journal began to sing again. Once again she and Marcus took a noon rest: "my Husband who is one of the best the world ever knew is always ready to provide a comfortable shade with one of our saddle blankets spread open upon some willows or sticks placed in the ground." Coming into Grande Ronde they lingered behind the others to pick berries.

Beyond Grande Ronde, at sunset, they had from the cool, fir-covered summits of the Blue Mountains their first glimpse of the Columbia River Valley, the white cones of Mount Hood and Mount St. Helens glittering in the distance. "Enchanting," Narcissa wrote of the view, a word she had not used before. The next morning she felt "remarkably well & strong . . . but could not see any reason why I should." Just freedom, that was all.

Pressing themselves hard and riding well east of the route by which the trail would later descend from the Blue Mountains (the so-called Oregon Trail approximately followed U.S. Highway 30 through today's Meachem toward Pendleton) they encountered the Walla Walla River a little above the fort. The post itself they reached on September 1, in time for breakfast. A cock crowed and Narcissa nearly wept. "No one knows the feelings occasioned by seeing objects once familiar after long privation." Nathaniel Wyeth had made a comparable remark at the same spot four years earlier.

No particular gain resulted from their having hurried so. The Whitmans were still at Fort Walla Walla when the Spaldings arrived two days later. Though once they had planned that Spalding would investigate sites while the others were at Fort Vancouver, the separation had evidently smoothed out ruffled tempers and now they decided to go together to the Hudson's Bay Company's great bastion on the lower river.

They left livestock and Indian boys at Walla Walla. The post's factor, Pierre Pambrun, himself escorted them down the glass-clear water in a huge batteau, thirty or more feet long, the *voyageurs* singing at the oars. The change was exhilarating, but had its own discomforts. One day the wind blew so hard that the impatient travelers had to lay to. At an Indian camp at the portage around the Dalles, Narcissa picked up fleas, her dress "black with these creatures, making all possible speed to lay siege to my neck and ears." Every plait was full. She ran screaming after her husband, who brushed away as many as he could, but she found no real relief until she could get into her baggage for "a change in my appeal."

She saw the "flathead" Indians who had started all this—actually Chinooks who by an arrangement of boards pressed their infants' skulls not flat but into a high peak. On September 12, 1836, they breakfasted at the Bay Company's busy sawmill and there, in accordance with custom, spruced themselves for their entry into Vancouver, "the New York," Narcissa said, "of the Pacific Ocean."

Parker was gone, having caught a ship that had offered. To soften the shock, the gentlemen of the fort showed the ladies every gallantry. McLoughlin urged them to winter at his post while their husbands explored, for by now Narcissa's condition was apparent. But she would rather have her baby in the wilderness with her husband than surrounded by strangers. Eliza too was opposed to a separation.

What to do? By now the rupture among the colleagues was open and they had agreed that they would have to find two sites, not one. Officially the separation was explained on the ground that by dividing they could spread their message farther, not only among the Nez Percés (by letter Parker had recommended a station at the junction of the Clearwater and the Snake, site of modern Lewiston, Idaho) but also among the Cayuses in the vicinity of Fort Walla Walla. After earnest discussion they decided to look over these places and, if the spots seemed satisfactory, to return for building materials—and for their wives. The men, accompanied by Gray, left on September 21. They would be back within a month, they said.

HATE YE ONE ANOTHER

The explorers made their decisions quickly. They went up the Walla Walla River twenty-two miles from Pambrun's post and on the north bank, framed by a bend of the stream and by Mill Creek, found a meadow called Waiilatpu, The Place of Rye Grass.

Waiilatpu, which lies about five miles west of today's city of Walla Walla, Washington, was allotted to Whitman on considerations no longer known.

While Gray remained behind to bring up supplies and start a cabin, Whitman and Spalding, guided by several Indians, rode another hundred miles eastward across dry brown hills to the vast, timberless trough where the Clearwater River breaks into the Snake. Parker had recommended a station at the confluence. His judgment was sound; the twin cities of Lewiston and Clarkson later took form there. But the Nez Percés who met the whites at the river junction wanted the station ten miles farther east, on Lapwai Creek. Touched by their importunities, the reluctant Spalding finally agreed.

By then it was October 12. The two missionaries nevertheless hoped still to winter with their wives at their respective stations, the first homes ever to shelter American white women west of the Rocky Mountains—or west of the lower Platte and Kansas rivers, for that matter.

They would have to hurry. While Gray and Whitman labored on the cabin at Waiilatpu, Spalding went down the Columbia for the women and for more supplies. He arrived at Fort Vancouver on October 18. On November 3, he, his wife, and Narcissa Whitman, speaking to each other no more than necessary and escorted by a Hudson's Bay Company brigade, started with several boatloads of supplies on an uncomfortable journey up the rain-drenched river. Narcissa remained at Fort Walla Walla until her cabin could be roofed. Eliza and Henry Spalding, helped by a hundred excited Indians, loaded five thousand pounds of goods on twenty horses and rode directly to Lapwai, planning to start housekeeping in a skin tent. Gray, who had been devoting his energies to the Whitmans' station, was now directed to help the Spaldings.

He stayed with them for three weeks and three days, working with logs that the Indians brought on their backs out of the mountains for a cabin destined to be forty-eight feet long and eighteen feet wide—schoolroom in one half, living quarters in the other. Long before the chore was completed Gray began sulking. Why couldn't he have a station of his own?

The cry of the Flatheads for religious instruction was what had started the missionary movement into the Northwest, but as yet no one had gone to the Flatheads. William Gray might be the very man for them. But he must not be too headlong. With more prudence than he characteristically showed, he decided that before making up his mind he should spend a year learning the Flathead language and looking over the country. To do this as easily as possible, he would make his headquarters at the Bay Company's Flathead post in western Montana, where Wyeth's friend Francis Ermatinger was in charge. Ermatinger would be starting upstream from Fort Vancouver shortly with supplies, and Gray could travel with him.

About Christmas he left Lapwai, hoping to intercept Ermatinger at Fort Walla Walla. By Gray's own account it was a rough trip. He started in a canoe with two Indians. Ice forced them onto horses. Deep snow and slippery trails led them back to river travel. When he reached Walla Walla, he learned that Ermatinger might not be along for several more days. Too restless to wait (or to help the Whitmans at nearby Waiilatpu), he went on down the Columbia, dragging his boat over the ice here and there and recklessly running the Dalles—"the waters are truly in a coiling, curling, scalling, rolling, foaming condition."

On February 21, 1837, he reached Fort Vancouver. There he almost surely learned that reinforcements for Lee's Methodist mission, southward in the Willamette Valley, had sailed from Boston with stirring fanfare the previous July and on December 23 had landed in Honolulu. Because of difficulties in arranging adequate ship passage from the islands to the Columbia, the group would not actually arrive until May; but Jason Lee was already full of plans for them. Gray may even have learned something about the group's personnel. In one respect it was unique: it contained five women and only three men. The males included a carpenter, a blacksmith, and a fussy little self-important physician named Elijah White, of whom more in a later chapter. White and the blacksmith were married; their wives and children (one for White, three for the blacksmith) were with them. The other three females were spinsters, a state soon to end. One was Cyrus Shepard's fiancée from Lynn, Massachusetts; another would marry Jason Lee; the third would find a husband in a later missionary group.

There were still other exciting developments for Gray to contemplate at Fort Vancouver. A spy named William Slacum had spent most of January prowling around the huge post and the Willamette Valley, openly collecting information for the United States government about British strongholds and policy in the Northwest, and suggesting to the handful of American settlers there that they send a petition to Congress asking for United States jurisdiction over Oregon. These same Willamette settlers, strongly supported by Lee's Methodist mission, had also dispatched a party aboard Slacum's brig to California, there to buy and drive back a herd of several hundred cattle. The animals, they thought, would help make them independent of McLoughlin, who loaned the Americans milk cows from Fort Vancouver's small herd but refused to sell the creatures outright and compounded the irritation by demanding that all calves be turned back to him. To the Americans this looked like economic bondage. They resented it. They fully intended to become as independent as their own efforts, abetted by the distant Congress of the United States, would allow them.

In other words, as Gray perhaps recognized, an American colony was slowly coalescing around the Methodist mission. If the missionaries east of the Cascade Mountains hoped to match it, now was the time to start. Gray too began to think of bringing in more Christian Americans—literally bringing, with himself marching grandly in the lead.

Within a week he was on his way back up the river with Francis Ermatinger, generally called Frank. Frank Ermatinger would become a familiar figure to the migrants of the early 1840s. Journal after journal sings his praise, and from the accounts one envisions a debonair and contented man. But his own intermittent correspondence with a brother in the East shows a different view—discouragement, frustration, and bursts of violent passion.

When Gray met him, Ermatinger was thirty-nine or forty years old and his hair was beginning to whiten. After a fair education in England, he had joined the Hudson's Bay Company as a clerk in 1818. His transfer in 1826 to Fort Okanogan on the Columbia

River in north-central Washington had delighted him. "Being appointed to this side of the mountains," he wrote his brother Edward, "is reckoned by the Sanguine as a sure step to their promotion." But the goal he desired, respect and rank as a chief trader, eluded him, even though in 1832 he was put in charge of the dangerous Flathead post on Clark Fork, with particular instructions to resist, by superior trapping and trading, threatened encroachments by the Americans.

His love life had been equally discouraging. The squaw he married somewhere west of the mountains proved faithless. He cut off the ears of her Indian paramour and for this "injudicious" act was censured by the company. This did not prevent him from starting to pay court, about 1835, to his boss' daughter, Maria McLoughlin—"a quite interesting young lady," Narcissa Whitman had written after meeting Maria in September 1836. Since McLoughlin's wife was half Cree and half Swiss, Maria was only one-quarter Indian. This, together with her father's powerful status, made her much sought after by the leading men of the company. Ermatinger never had a chance. Maria was in her teens; Ermatinger was crowding forty. During the winter of 1837–38, McLoughlin told him that his attentions were not welcome. But Frank stayed devoted to the old gentleman: "I never had more respect for any man in my life . . . am allways improved while in his company."

Ermatinger had fathered a half-breed son by his faithless squaw—who, incidentally, hanged herself in the spring of 1837. The father did not want the boy, whose name was Lawrence, to learn of the tragedy, "nor do I wish he should ever know who his mother was." For a time Lawrence stayed at Vancouver. McLoughlin was nominally his guardian. The people at the fort fed him well, but they had so many little half-breeds about "of all tribes, that they cannot pay the attention to them that the children require; the consequences are that their morals are not good nor their habits of cleanliness charming." Lawrence, the father feared, was actually becoming vicious. So when the supply barges started slowly back up the river on March 1, 1837, Ermatinger took the lad with him to see what he could do about training him.

Hearing at Fort Walla Walla of the birth of the Whitmans'

daughter, Ermatinger, Gray, and Pambrun rode to Waiilatpu to see the wonder. Back at the Fort, Ermatinger switched his brigade to horseback and headed northwest through the rolling Palouse country, traveling slowly because of deep, soft snow. Where the city of Spokane now stands, they came on a camp of Spokane Indians. The brigade halted to let their famished horses rest and were amazed, two days later, to see Spalding appear with several pack horses and five Nez Percé Indians. They were bound north from Lapwai to Fort Colvile to obtain garden seed and other supplies from the trader there, Archibald McDonald.

The advent of white medicine men, or missionaries, invariably excited the Indians of the interior Northwest. The Spokanes were no exception. They already had a teacher of their own blood, Spokane Garry, who had received his education back east at Red River. Garry welcomed Gray and Spalding warmly, and translated when Spalding delivered a sermon summarizing the story of the creation, original sin, the coming of a Saviour and His crucifixion. The Indians shouted in amazement and said that yes, they wanted to learn more.

Carried away by the fervor of the reception, Spalding and Gray decided that the latter should not wait a year as originally planned, but should immediately hurry East for associates. He should take with him, as exhibits, three natives of each of the different tribes to be served by the reinforcements. The party, furthermore, should drive along cheap Indian horses to exchange in the settlements for cattle and sheep, which the returning party would drive back with them across the mountains. The horses used in the bartering and the livestock so obtained, it should be noted, were to remain the property of the Indians. Horses and red emissaries for the trip East were to join Gray at the rendezvous on Green River that summer.

Whatever else may be said of the agricultural phase of the hastily conceived plan, it at least showed a sounder grasp of reality than the American Board sometimes evinced. They were primarily interested in counting souls, and so were most of the workers they sent forth. But Spalding and that "dull scholar" Gray already realized, even more clearly than Whitman yet did, that before the Indians could be truly converted they would have to be divorced from their nomadic ways, settled down, and civilized.

The decision made, Spalding borrowed fifteen bushels of seed potatoes from Spokane Garry and returned to Eliza at Lapwai, intending to resume his interrupted journey to Fort Colvile during the summer. Gray and Ermatinger continued eastward. After a pause at Flathead Post, they pushed deeper into the Rockies. Presently they fell in with a traveling village of Flatheads. With the Indians they crossed the Continental Divide to the headwaters of the Missouri. There Blackfeet stole several Flathead horses. A war party sent after the thieves failed to recover the animals, but did kill five enemy men and capture a woman.

Back at the Flathead camp, the victors put the captive squaw in the center of a ring and began a war dance around her. As drums beat and rattles jingled, five Flathead women, laughing hideously, fastened the bleeding scalps of the slain enemy on the ends of willow sticks and bobbed them in the squaw's face. One scalp was her husband's, another her brother's. This gave the show real zest—and William Gray an opportunity to make his pitch. In the diary he was keeping for the eyes of the American Board, he wrote, "I can imagine nothing except contrasting the horrors of the damned with the joys of Heaven, that seems to give any idea of the disgusting scene before me. When will these savages learn their real situation and want?" As soon, obviously, as the American Board sent William Gray back at the head of a devoted party to teach them; that was when.

On June 15, back west of the Divide in the Salmon River country of Idaho, the time at last came for him to leave for the States. In his diary he says that he started for the rendezvous with six Flathead men, four women, and three boys. One of the boys was Ermatinger's son Lawrence. Somewhere in the savage mountains the despairing father had concluded that the only way to tame the lad was to send him East to his Uncle Edward in St. Thomas, Ontario. Gray, whose ultimate destination was western New York state, promised to see Lawrence as far as Buffalo.

On June 1, the day the five Blackfeet were slain and the scalp dance racketed outside his tent, Frank Ermatinger wrote his brother not about the excitement of Indian life but about the sadly funny troubles of a spouseless father trying to raise a half-breed son toward whom he felt some tugs of responsibility:

> Lawrence has inbibed the vile practice of piddling his bed and he must absolutely be broken off it before you can recommend him a decent one. I have since he has been with me succeeded tolerably well, by making him get up before going to bed myself. His ears too have been neglected. They are equal to those of my mule, and I doubt now whether, even with care they can be brought to a reasonable compass. Give them a trial and let him wear hats for with caps we can never succeed. . . . You know my means and the object is to obtain the most good for him at the least possible expense, bearing in mind, however that I do not wish him to be neglected to save expense.

Gray, Lawrence, and the Flatheads had a cold, waterless ride across the barren Snake Plains to Fort Hall, which the Hudson's Bay Company had bought from Wyeth and was rebuilding out of adobe bricks. Along the Bear River, they fell in with John McLeod's brigade bound from Fort Walla Walla to the rendezvous to undersell the Americans, exactly as Wyeth had proposed doing years earlier. With McLeod, Spalding had sent several horses for Gray to trade for cattle on behalf of the Indians, and four Nez Percés to include among his exhibits in the States. Of the four, however, Gray considered only an old man called Isaac to be adequate. The others he found lazy and undependable, and dismissed them. The horses he kept.

The rendezvous was held beside Horse Creek again. However genteel the gathering of 1836 may have been out of deference to Narcissa and Eliza, this one returned to normal patterns. "From the noise and yelling of persons about," Gray surmised in his diary on July 11, "I should think they were mad or intoxicated with liquors. I have also heard in a loud voice the dying words of the Saviour on the Cross repeated, followed by a loud laugh. No tongue can tell the blasphemy that is carried on." He discovered further, that mountain men actually trafficked in red female flesh.

Fitzpatrick brought in the supply caravan on July 18. He had learned from Whitman's struggles that wagons could go through the Laramie Mountains, and this year he brought twenty carts with him to Horse Creek. As usual Sir William Drummond Stewart was along, attended on this jaunt by his hired Baltimore artist, Alfred Jacob Miller, whose paintings of trapper and Indian life are now standard adornments in books dealing with the early West. Stewart's junkets were growing fancier and fancier. In 1837, so trapper David Brown would recall, he set up a huge tent of the sort used by army field staffs on campaign and invited fifty leading mountain men to a banquet of buffalo tongue washed down by uncounted bottles of "choice old liquors of his own importation." Presumably Gray was not among the feasters, but he did have supper one evening with artist Miller.

When he learned, amid the carousing, that Fitzpatrick would not start East until August 10 or so, Gray determined impulsively to go ahead on his own. Because of a Blackfoot scare, most of his would-be exhibits for the American Board dropped out. White men were equally unwilling to risk the trail in small numbers, but after considerable urging he gathered together a mixed party of sorts. Its exact make-up is uncertain. His diary entry of July 24 indicates two whites, young Lawrence Ermatinger, and five Indians—an Iroquois he calls Big Eneas, three Flatheads, and a Cree who had been adopted by the Flatheads. Later diary entries give slightly different numbers and change the Cree to the Nez Percé sent by Spalding, old Isaac. Gray's *History of Oregon*, written a third of a century afterward, muddies the matter still more. And Catholic accounts, which Protestant histories overlook (just as Catholics overlook the Protestant stories of the trip) increase the perplexity yet again. The confusion is not without a bloody sort of significance.

The Nez Percés and Flatheads, it will be recalled, had received instruction in Catholic ritual from converted Iroquois who had settled among them. Catholic stories say that the delegation of Indians who sought teachers in St. Louis in 1831 really wanted priests. Funds for a Catholic mission were unavailable, however, and so the Protestants—Lee, then Whitman and Parker—reached the scene first. According to Parker, he and Whitman were enthusiastically received by the Flathead chief, Insula. Catholic sources say, however, that Insula was very puzzled that these supposed men of God had no black robes, no rosaries, no crucifixes. Why?

He asked a wise Iroquois, old Ignace La Mousse. Ignace said that Insula had been right to worry: Whitman and Parker were not bearers of the true religion. He himself, old Ignace, would go east immediately in another attempt to produce genuine Black Robes.

He and his two sons, ages twelve and fourteen, traveled to St. Louis that same summer (1835). He saw Bishop Rosati, had his boys baptized, and asked for priests. Then back to the mountains they rode by unrecorded routes and waited. Rosati, however, still lacked funds. The teachers who appeared in 1836 were Whitman again and Spalding—married, which made them look to the Flatheads like mountain men and not like the amazing celibate priests of whom the Iroquois told.

The 1837 caravan failed Ignace also. But here came Gray, bound on some kind of religious errand and looking for Indians to go with him. Ignace decided to travel East with the white man and see Bishop Rosati again. He took with him three Flatheads and one Nez Percé (old Isaac?). This Catholic list of five Indians, derived from the Jesuit missionary, Pierre-Jean De Smet, is comparable to the list given by Gray, who calls his Iroquois guide Big Eneas. Eneas, of course, may well have been a phonetic mistake for Ignace.

These similarities are strange indeed—assuming the reliability of De Smet's hearsay account, which at least is not open to charges of self-justification, as are Gray's diary and *History of Oregon*, the only extant eyewitness reports of the 1837 trip. It is incredible that William Gray, eager to use Indian exhibits for impressing a Protestant board with his skill and devotion as a potential missionary, would knowingly have enlisted Indians who desired Catholic instruction. It is almost as incredible that old Ignace, after all his work to produce Catholic teachers, would guide a man intent on establishing the Protestants. The 1830s were not an era of denominational generosities; bigotry burned red-hot and was accounted a virtue. All I can make of the muddle is that in his impatience and impenetrable egotism Gray assumed that the Indians were Protestant—after all, Spalding had sent Isaac to him. He wanted them to be Protestants. Therefore they were Protestant—period. Isaac perhaps was. As for the three Flatheads (who may or may not have been part of the group which came with Gray out of Idaho), perhaps they did not understand yet how bitter white men's religious differences could be. God was God, wasn't He, purveyor of magic powers to His initiates? Learning that old Isaac was bound for the great Medicine Lodge, perhaps they and Old Ignace may have decided, on typical Indian impulse, to take advantage of the trip that offered. All we really know is that five (possibly six) Indians told Gray they would go along. Perhaps they went, after all, just to trade horses.

When mountain men heard of the proposal, they told Gray he was mad. Gray retorted loftily that he would put his trust in God. According to David Brown's memory, Jim Bridger thereupon slapped the butt of his rifle and roared in exasperation, "Sir, the grace of God won't carry a man through these prairies. It takes powder and ball!"

The party went ahead regardless, riding fifty to sixty miles at a clip. Repeated signs of hostile savages shook them into doing much of the traveling at night—or so Gray wrote, perhaps preparing his readers for the attack that eventually came. At Fort Laramie, where they lay over for two days while their horses were shod, they were again warned and again paid no heed. Inevitably then, near Ash Hollow in western Nebraska, the Sioux appeared.

For some reason not apparent (except for dramatics), the fight swirled off into the waters of the Platte. Gray's horse was shot damply from underneath him. (It grew to two horses in his *History of Oregon*). He waded ashore, laid down his rifle like a true Christian, and walked ahead to arrange a parley. The Sioux let loose a fusillade. "One ball passed through my hat, slightly wounding me on the back part of my head." The jar brought light even to William Gray. "I concluded that blood and murder was [*sic*] the determination of our enemies."

Finally the whites arranged a conference through the mediation of one "Joseph Papair" (never identified) who was traveling with the Sioux. During the talk, the enemy rushed treacherously past the negotiators, fell on Gray's Indians, and "butchered them in a most horrible manner." Or so Gray wrote the story in his diary. But a report leaked back to the mountains that William

Gray, missionary, made a deliberate deal with the Sioux: If they would spare the white men and Lawrence, they could have without further resistance the scalps of the mountain Indians, who were at the time sitting peacefully off to one side waiting for the conference to end.

The truth? Well, the mountain men believed the story. Spalding feared reprisals. Without indicating whether or not he had heard the full accusation, he wrote the Board, "It is said that [the Nez Percés] will demand my head or all my property" in return for the old Isaac and the horses—the Sioux took fourteen out of twenty-three animals. Gray's shrunken party ate two more between Ash Hollow and the Missouri.

One is tempted to add a further speculation. Suppose that somewhere west of Ash Hollow, Gray, the self-appointed founder of a new Protestant station in the West, had discovered to his horror that his Indian exhibits were actually looking for Catholics. Might not an arrangement with the Sioux, after they appeared so providentially, have spared him painful and perhaps disastrous mortification in front of the American Board? [1]

On reaching St. Louis, Gray paused for five days. He prepared his diary for submission as a report to the American Board, a filtering process which vitiates it as a historical document. He also sent the United States government a bill of $2096.45 for the horses and packs the Sioux had taken from him. The charge was not allowed. Spalding later had to solicit funds from friends in the East to buy cattle to give to the Nez Percés who had lost horses on this deal that was going to help civilize them.

From St. Louis, Gray went to western New York. He visited Parker in Ithaca and audited a few lectures at Whitman's old alma mater, Fairfield Medical College. Ever afterward he tried, with limited success, to have people address him as Doctor. Somehow he persuaded the very reluctant American Board to assign him three couples and a bachelor helper for service in the Northwest. The bachelor, twenty-three-year-old Cornelius Rogers,

---

[1] Perhaps I should say that I venture the suggestion on my own responsibility. Catholic sources certainly breathe no suspicion of foul play. They say only that the western Indians, traveling with Gray but searching for priests, were slain in a battle with the Sioux.

hailed from Cincinnati. The others were New Englanders: Elkanah and Mary Walker of Maine; Cushing and Myra Eells of Connecticut (Cushing Eells took a bottle of Connecticut water West with him), and Asa and Sarah Smith of Massachusetts. Every one of them married especially for this trip; only the Walkers seem to have gone through a prior engagement period. Not to be outdone, Gray met through Parker a Miss Mary Dix, courted her one evening, became engaged the next morning, waited four more days, married her after supper on February 24, 1838, and the next morning departed with her for Independence, where he had ordered his flock to assemble.

His charges wanted to go by water, as had the two reinforcement parties which had reached Jason Lee during 1837. Gray refused: on shipboard he would have no one to domineer. Parker rescued him, writing the Board that, after trying both methods, "I had rather go across the continent three times than around the Cape once." The Board thereupon told the three couples they would have to go to Independence and join Gray.

The wayfarers landed at the Independence docks at 7 P.M., April 15. To their dismay they learned that the town was three or four miles distant from the river. While the husbands unloaded the baggage, bachelor Rogers hurried off to find Gray. Eventually he appeared with horses for the women. They had done little riding before and mounted gingerly under the thick darkness of a cloudy sky. Fearfully they rode up what seemed to them a precipitous hill, their husbands walking beside, holding the bridle reins and wading above their shoetops in mud. Swarms of baying dogs advertised their belated arrival to the village. There they learned that for housing nine people Gray had rented two rooms, each containing one bed. The four women doubled up in the beds; the men slept on the floor. Instantly William Gray and Asa Smith took a profound dislike to each other.

They spent the following week sorting their baggage and buying livestock—twenty-five horses and mules, twelve cattle, a light one-horse wagon. Gray allowed each member a single suitcase, 24 × 20 × 10 inches (Cushing Eells managed to crowd his bottle of Connecticut water into his). For provisions Gray bought, Myra Eells said in her journal, "one hundred and sixty pounds of flour, fifty-seven pounds of rice, twenty or twenty-five pounds of sugar, a little pepper and salt." It was not enough to feed eleven people—the party added to its numbers by hiring a mountain man named Stevens to be guide and roustabout and another, Paul Richardson, to be their hunter. Richardson had been hunter in 1834 for Jason Lee's party and was used to missionaries, but he could not make buffalo appear where there were none. Gray drove the wagon; each of the other males struggled with pack horses.

The fur caravan, consisting of two hundred animals and seventeen carts and wagons (plus, as usual, Sir William Stewart), was led in 1838 by Andrew Drips. It left Westport, twelve miles beyond Independence, on Sunday. The missionaries declined to travel on that day and on Monday had to push hard to catch up. When they did, it was obvious to Myra Eells, who reported the meeting in her diary, that Drips did not want Gray along. She thought it was because Drips feared the missionaries would be unwilling to stand guard at night. Gray promised that the men would take their turns, and Myra thought the assurance won the mountain man over. More probably Drips looked at the females and gave up. How could you make them pay for what Gray had done? All right, he said, come ahead. As the caravan stretched out for half a mile ahead of Myra Eells, she thought it had "much the appearance of a large funeral procession in the states."

These four women were the first to travel the eastern end of the Oregon Trail, up the Kansas River to its ford near present Topeka, northwestward via the Blue to the south bank of the Platte near Grand Island. (The Whitmans and Spaldings had come up the Platte's north bank from Council Bluffs.) They also forecast the attritions that would sandpaper the nerves of the pioneer families who followed them. Evening after evening Myra Eells and Mary Walker wrote their bone-weariness into their diaries. Dust. Dirty food. Cramped quarters: two couples had to share each of the party's two eight-by-twelve tents, with only a curtain between them for privacy.

Lacerating quarrels over petty events became inevitable. Gray fell into a temper because Smith and Walker killed an injured calf without consulting him. Mr. and Mrs. Eells sided with Gray;

the tempest divided the party for two days, until prayers in Gray's tent brought temporary peace. Personal idiosyncrasies became grating monstrosities. Mary Walker found Smith "a hog at the table"; his and his wife's continual whispering behind the dividing sheet of their tent drove her almost frantic. Even Mary's own husband was a problem: "Should feel much better if Mr. W. would only treat me with some cordiality.... If I stir it is forwardness, if I am still it is inactivity.... More is expected of me than can be had of any one woman." On May 27, just beyond Chimney Rock, she summed up the general feeling in two irritable sentences: "We have a strange company of missionaries. Scarcely one who is not intolerable on some account."

The routine physical discomforts afflicted them. They slept in storm-soaked bedding, endured diarrhea, ached, and vomited. After missing several meals, Cushing Eells at last was able to down a little gingerbread with the aid of the water he had carried from East Windsor, Connecticut. But no matter how sick they were, they had to crawl out of their blankets at three-thirty in the morning and drag through as many chores as strength allowed.

Although the fur company continued with its carts beyond Fort Laramie, Gray did not wish to manhandle a wagon through the rough hills. He surrendered the vehicle and the little comforts it had provided. At the rainswept crossing of the North Platte, blue with cold, cramped by dysentery and pregnancy pangs, Mary Walker sat down and "cried to think how comfortable my father's hogs were." As for Sarah Smith, Mary sniffed, *she* wept practically the entire distance to Oregon.

Rendezvous that year was held east of the Divide near modern Riverton, Wyoming, where Popo Agie Creek runs into Wind River. The Hudson's Bay Company had so undersold the American that Drips declined to compete with the English on the Green. Instead he sent out a messenger to tell the wandering trappers of the new location. The messenger did it by fastening a scrawl to the side of an abandoned log storehouse on Horse Creek: "Come on to Popoasia: plenty of whiskey and white women." The trappers found the note, and so did Frank Ermatinger of Hudson's Bay Company.

To escape the carousing, the missionaries crossed Popo Agie

Creek and pitched their tents under cottonwood trees on a tongue of land between the streams. In a pet the Smiths left the Walkers and set up their own lodge of buffalo skins. "Husband seems to like to stay in the tent *now*," Mary exulted acidly. When Sunday arrived, she and the other ladies put on their best dresses to listen to Elkanah preach. The sight of them inspired some of the Indian wives to emulation. Several embarrassed mountain husbands bought sleazy calico at outrageous prices from the traders and asked the missionary women to sew it into modish dresses for their squaws.

On the night of July 4, Mr. and Mrs. Eells were awakened in the tent they shared with the Grays by the furious barking of their dog. Several drunks reeled up to the tent door, where Eells stepped in front of them. They had come to settle accounts with Gray, they said, and for good measure were going to rough up the rest of the hymn-singers. Myra Eells, trembling beside her bristling hound, declared hopefully to her journal, "Had they attempted it, the dog would have torn them to pieces." Gray was less confident. Crouched in a dark rear corner of the tent, he fumbled shells into a rifle. He did not have to use it. Eells' resolute stand in front of the men diverted them. They tried to make him sing a few bawdy songs with them, asked sarcastically whether they were disturbing him, lost interest, and reeled away. Mrs. Eells gives no indication in her account that anything other than alcohol might have motivated the episode.

Bridger's brigade came in from the Blackfoot country on July 5, whooping with joy because a recent epidemic of smallpox had all but wiped out that once implacable tribe. Hearing that Gray was on hand, fifteen or twenty mountain men (not including Bridger), rushed over the creek and put on a scalp dance for him. The uproar so unsettled Myra's valiant dog that it fled across the Popo Agie and she and her husband had to spend the rest of the day luring it back.

On July 8 Ermatinger's crew appeared. With them rode Jason Lee and Philip Edwards of the Willamette mission. Edwards had recently completed a hellish drive up the coast with the California cattle and had had enough of the Wild West; he was going home to Missouri to live. But Lee was intent on bringing white homes to Oregon. Although two parties of reinforcements had reached him during 1837, he wanted scores more families, together with tens of thousands of dollars' worth of agricultural implements, carpentry tools, and domestic appliances which no doubt would be useful at an Indian mission but which might prove even more handy in helping a white colony to take form. Lee also carried with him for presentation to Congress the petition which William Slacum had recommended to the Willamette settlers, urging the United States "to take formal and speedy possession" of Oregon. "The country must populate," the petition said. (There were fifty-one settlers in the Willamette then. About half were Americans, including the Methodist missionaries. The others were retired French-Canadian *voyageurs*. Of the fifty-one residents, thirty-six signed the petition urging occupation.) "The natural resources of the country, with a well-judged civil code, will invite a good community. But a good community will hardly emigrate to a country which promises no protection to life or property." Therefore let the government of the United States make that promise to the world by asserting sovereignty.

Lee, in short, was now seeing himself as minister to future Americans, not to degraded Indians.[2] Nevertheless, the appeal inherent in benighted savages was too potent to overlook. So he was taking with him, as advertising gimmicks, a pair of dramatically peak-headed teen-age Chinook boys whom he had christened Thomas Adams and William Brooks, after popular Methodist divines of the day. He also had with him the three half-breed sons of Thomas McKay of the Hudson's Bay Company whom he was taking to an eastern school.

On his way to the rendezvous, Lee had visited Whitman and Spalding, and had told them his plans. Surely the Presbyterians deserved as much as the Methodists. Enviously, Spalding wrote

[2] James Douglas, in charge of Fort Vancouver during McLoughlin's furlough, also saw Lee in that light. After the arrival by ship of the second group of Methodist reinforcements, he wrote the directors of the Hudson's Bay Company (Nov. 15, 1837), "Were we satisfied that the sole objects of these Missionaries, were the civilization of the Natives and the diffusion of moral and religious instruction, we should be happy to render them our most cordial support and assistance, but we have all along foreseen ... that the formation of a Colony of United States Citizens on the banks of the Columbia was the main or fundamental part of their plan."

a letter, which Whitman also signed, asking their Board for 220 helpers—teachers, preachers, mechanics, and their wives, plus a flour mill, iron, steel, hardware, and trade goods. All they ever received, however, was what Gray was bringing them: nine people, counting himself, and no equipment whatsoever. When the final score is added, include the fact that the men and women of the interior missions endured not only every normal toil of pioneer homemaking but found time also to hold reading and singing classes for Indian children, teach Sunday School, deliver sermons, counsel cleanliness, and nurse the sick. They did it with pathetically inadequate supplies and in the face of a growing awareness that they were certain to fail: the Stone-Age savages of the Northwest could not be turned into either farmers or Protestants before the iron march of settlement, which the missionaries were helping channel, trampled down the very people they had come to save.

Gray read the letter to the Board and was annoyed that Spalding and Whitman had not waited to consult with him before sending it. Besides, its inflated demands made his efforts look picayune, and he might not be properly appreciated. Certainly his traveling companions did not appreciate him. At that moment Asa Smith was composing a letter to the American Board for delivery by Lee:

> What I am now to write I whisper in your ear, but would not say it to the world. We have not found Mr. Gray such a man as we hoped to find.... He is rash & inconsiderate ... has assumed a great deal of authority over us & talked to us in a very harsh & unbecoming & may I say abusive manner.... This has rendered our situation very unpleasant.

As events will show, there were times Asa Smith needed harsh and abusive talk.

On July 12 Ermatinger started back toward Fort Hall. In addition to the mission party, he accepted from the fur caravan a Swiss emigrant who would do more than every preacher in the land to guarantee American civilization on the Pacific. The fellow was thirty-five years old. He had good manners and was attentive to the missionary ladies. He wanted a new life, just what he wasn't sure. But somewhere in the West he would find it. His name was Johann Augustus Sutter. After looking over Oregon, he wandered south into California, obtained a Mexican land grant, and built Sutter's Fort on the Sacramento River. Ten years after his trip with the bickering missionaries, gold was discovered in one of his millraces. It ruined him—but that is another story.

Riding uncomfortably with Ermatinger's unsympathetic fur brigade, Gray and his missionaries toiled over South Pass. In the waterless desert between the pass and the Green River, on Sublette's Cutoff, Asa Smith decided he could endure no more and lay thirstily down to die. His wife stood beside him, wringing her hands, and the caravan, not wanting to die with them, left them behind. Along came an American trapper, Joe Meek, hurrying to overtake the English brigade and go with it to Fort Hall. Joe was nursing a mountain-sized hangover by sipping now and then from a container filled with the hair of the dog which had so grievously bitten him. It was the only liquid he had. He offered some to Smith, who moaned and turned away. Joe grew angry at that and gave Smith a brief lesson in what harsh, unbecoming, and abusive language really can be. He then forced Sarah Smith up into her saddle and dragged her willy-nilly after the caravan. Presently he glanced back. The strategy had succeeded. Deciding not to die after all, Smith was climbing back aboard his horse. He followed the caravan into camp and a little later wrote the Board reflectively that sea travel was better. "The more I think of our journey, the more satisfied I am that it is improper for missionaries, especially females, thus to travel."

Neither Meek nor the Hudson's Bay brigade was traveling farther than Fort Hall, at least for the time being. During the rest of the way to Waiilatpu, the missionaries would have to depend on themselves, on their hired help, and on an unrecorded number of greenhorns, including John Sutter, who were continuing to Oregon. To relieve this sobering prospect, however, the missionaries found at the fort supplies and fresh horses which Marcus Whitman had sent out from Waiilatpu to meet them. It may be that whoever brought the supplies, perhaps a trustworthy Indian or two, also returned with the travelers without receiving the dignity of a notice in their journals.

While the missionaries were at Fort Hall, Indian messengers from the Willamette Valley appeared, hurrying after Jason Lee with word that Anna Maria Lee, his wife of a year, had died in childbirth. So had Lee's baby. The Indians who had come so far with the news declined to go deeper into lands of enemy tribes. With uncharacteristic charity, Gray released Paul Richardson, the missionaries' patient buffalo-hunter, to ride back east in an effort to overtake Lee. To fill Richardson's place Gray hired a roustabout named Conner. To obtain Conner he also had to' take on Conner's pregnant Indian wife.

For Mary Walker, all this had particular impact. She herself was five months pregnant, and a fear that would beset many another pioneer wife leaped through her: What if her baby, like Anna Maria Lee's, came when there was no help? The sight of Conner's bulging, cheerful squaw offered scant reassurance. Did coming into the wilderness to help the savages mean that one must live like a savage?

On the party crept. For the first time they had no experienced companions to help smooth their way. But luck and such skills as they had acquired so far on the trail held. They got through— with great discomfort, to be sure, but with singularly little real trouble. Their bickering intensified. Along the Snake, where fortunately the Indians were not hostile, Gray grew so exasperated with the people he had hoped to lead West in triumph that he deserted them entirely and forged ahead with only his wife. Incredibly, the couple reached Waiilatpu without accident.

Behind them, in Grande Ronde or thereabouts, Conner's squaw paused to give birth. The next day she was traveling again, but helping her along impaired Conner's efficiency and annoyed the people he had been hired to serve. Nor could Mary Walker keep from visualizing herself in the squaw's position. "Feel anxious to reach the end of this journey," she told her diary.

The party's bachelor, Cornelius Rogers, next complicated matters by suffering a bad fall from his horse. Movement was so painful that he could not hold to the caravan's pace. When he dropped behind, the Smiths lingered with him (willingly, one surmises, remembering the incurable antipathy between the Smiths and the Walkers) and this gave Conner and the new mother a chance to slow down also. Thus the travelers came into Waiilatpu in three segments, Mr. and Mrs. Gray first; the Eellses and Walkers next, on August 29; and the Smiths, Conners, and Rogers, on August 30, 1838.

On the thirty-first, after the new arrivals had crowded Narcissa Whitman's kitchen almost beyond her endurance, the men tried to make plans for the future. Arguments were instantaneous. "None of them," Mary Walker wrote, "love one another well enough to live in peace together." Certainly no one was willing to share the same station with William Gray. Vehemently they proclaimed as much. In the end the Spokane (Tshimakain) mission, which Gray had gone East to secure for himself, went to Eells and Walker. After an antagonistic stay with the Whitmans, Asa Smith and his wife were shunted off to a new post at Kamiah, above Spalding's Lapwai, where Lewis and Clark's old Lolo Trail came down to the Clearwater River from the Bitterroot Mountains. The Grays and Cornelius Rogers were assigned to the Spaldings.

The Flatheads got no one.

17

THE FEVER CATCHES

For some people—crackpots, if you will—the here-and-now always wears a dull gray face. Life's shine lies out beyond. Take Lewis A. Tarascon, of Shippingport, Kentucky.

Fired by the proposals of Congressman John Floyd for the occupation of Oregon, Tarascon during the 1820s had circulated at his own expense broadsides proposing that the United States obtain from the Indians beyond the Missouri a strip of land one hundred miles wide reaching westward all the way to the Multnomah (Willamette) River and on that strip establish a wagon road. At first Tarascon's arguments followed Floyd's—the United States could thus get the fur trade from the English, open commerce with Asia, forestall European colonies on the Pacific, provide a market for goods manufactured in the East, and so on. Soon, however, these considerations grew pallid. By 1836 Lewis Tarascon had caught a truly dazzling vision of the great Northwest.

As he explained his plan to the world in a series of pamphlets, his first step would be to set up a nonprofit colonizing company. He would capitalize the company at $20,000 by selling shares for $100 each; if a poor but deserving mechanic or farmer could not afford a whole share he could have a fraction of one. With the money thus obtained Tarascon, as the company's agent, would buy land on the west bank of the upper Mississippi. (The Missouri was too muddy and full of snags for a dream so crystal.) On this land he would build a communal village. At the peep of day the citizens would sing a hymn, eat breakfast together, and march off to their work to the strains of band music. The name of the community, in capital letters, would be STARTSPOINT.

As soon as Startspoint was flourishing, "I, the said Tarascon," would locate other sites for other communities, each one a little farther west, until the orderly, guided migration arrived "at the natural gap of the Rocky Mountains, in the forty-second degree of northern latitude"—presumably South Pass. Astride the Continental Divide, of whose sterile sage wastes in the vicinity of forty-two degrees north Tarascon obviously had not the foggiest conception, his colonists would erect "the CITY OF UNION of the two hemispheres—a city where reason, having so far traveled, will attract all mankind and where all will fly to enjoy her blessings." But even this was not the ultimate. From Union the colonists would move on to the Columbia, to

> the city of PERFECTION, a true model city, of enlightened and virtuous men, doing each other all the good they can . . . making themselves their laws by majorities' loud votes, settling all their discrepancies by quick, friendly arbitrations, preventing misconduct by good education . . . by their admirable example, inducing all mankind to come to their city.

Obviously these standard aims of democracy could not be achieved in dull Kentucky, but only out beyond, in Oregon. If Tarascon sold a single share of stock, records do not show it. But here and there other societies were beginning to form which did attract members and which did disseminate information about the Northwest. One of the earliest, a spiritual heir of Hall Jackson Kelley's American Society for Encouraging Settlement of the Oregon Territory, was the Oregon Provisional Emigration Society of Lynn, Massachusetts.[1] Organized in 1838 and charging its members annual dues of $3, the Oregon Provisional Emigration Society proposed to secure the Northwest for the United States by dispatching two hundred Christian families to Oregon in 1840, there to prepare for a wave of future settlers. Each adult member of the proposed trip was to contribute $400 to the general coffers, plus $200 for each child, and in return the Society would furnish all items needful for the journey.

To further its aims the group published, for about 800 subscribers, eleven issues of a paper called *The Oregonian and Indian's Advocate*. (The Indians crept in because Society officials believed that although the red men east of the Rockies had become too degraded for redemption, those in Oregon might still be saved by a fresh, high-minded approach.) The Society even sent an agent into the Midwest to drum up recruits, but a depression lay heavily on the land; the $400 fee and the communal-religious cast of the organization made prospects hold back. The 1840 migration and the Society died for lack of interest; but during its lifetime the newspaper did distribute considerable information (and misinformation) about the Oregon country and did serve as a clearing house for other potential migrants who were beginning to gather together and discuss ways and means of getting West.

Most of these societies were located in recently opened sections of the Midwest—Illinois, Iowa, western and southern Missouri. Population pressures were building high heads of steam. To the nation as a whole, the primary economic factor was probably the swift growth of cities, but rural and frontier areas shared the headlong expansion. In the decade from 1830 to 1840, for example, Missouri's population almost tripled—140,000 to 383,000.

[1] Lynn, it will be remembered, was the home of both Cyrus Shepard, who had gone to the Willamette with Jason Lee in 1834, and Shepard's fiancée, who had sailed around the Horn to him with the first group of Methodist reinforcements.

Between 1835 and 1840 Iowa jumped from a few hundred to 43,000. Under such circumstances land speculation became a mania. A family moved into a newly opened area, purchased government land at one or two dollars an acre, cleared away the trees and made other improvements, possibly sold the holding at breathless profits, and either moved on or invested the increase in some growing community nearby.

Where the Missouri River bends northward, this flood of land-hungry pioneers came to a sudden dam. Beyond the river lay Indian country—in which, during the early 1830s, many eastern tribes had been resettled side by side with older residents. This new home the United States guaranteed to the natives, as usual, "for as long as the grass shall grow and the rivers shall run." At first, settlers did not resent being excluded. Although the eastern edges of the Indian country were recognized as fertile, most of it was considered part of the Great American Desert, fit only for nomadic savages; no more soil adaptable to white ways was deemed to exist until after one had crossed the mountains and entered the magic land of Oregon.

The development of the frontier was further slowed between 1837 and 1840 by an acute depression. Prices of farm produce skidded, dragging land values downward with them. As always happens when the here-and-now turns gray, the shine of distance grew correspondingly brighter. Restless farmers caught at a notion that unfailing markets existed in the Northwest—at the Hudson's Bay Company forts (which in the next breath they spoke of driving out of the country), among the Russian settlements of Alaska, and across the ocean in the starving Orient. Furthermore, so they dreamed, these places could be reached easily and cheaply by water transport, whereas in the Midwest most farms were plagued by backwoods roads of bottomless mud. And, finally, there was the old American instinct which urged that when things went wrong at home, you simply loaded up the wagon and moved on farther west—to perfection. Lewis Tarascon had sensed at least that much of history's truth: "Is it not the inclination of many members of the American family to move westwardly? and is it not sound policy to open a passage for them, that they may not be impeded in their progress . . . ?"

Frontier newspapers by 1839 were saying the same thing. In the fall of that year, taking note of the growing numbers of emigrating societies, the *Missouri Republican* commented on

a strong disposition on the part of numerous persons in the west to remove to the Columbia. This inclination has been steadily growing for years and frequently manifests itself in attempts to raise colonies for the purpose of migrating; and although these attempts, thus far, have proved fruitless, still the failure of one appears not to check the spirit of others.... Our Government has already too long neglected this subject, and the day is not far distant when the restless spirit of the people alone will compel attention to it.

It was into such yearnings that Jason Lee moved in September 1838, hunting reinforcements for his Willamette missions. Personal tragedy increased the drama of his arrival. At one o'clock in the morning, September 8, Paul Richardson and a fellow courier reached Lee at the Shawnee mission, five miles west of Westport, with word of his wife's and baby's deaths. There was no point then in turning back. By canoe Lee went on down the Missouri, tinged by a melancholy that would pull at the sympathies of many a matron. With him he took his two Chinook boys, Thomas Adams and William Brooks, and Tom McKay's three half-breed sons.

Learning that a church conference was meeting in Alston, Illinois, he put ashore there on September 22. Unannounced, in buckskins, he and his five youngsters strode into the meeting hall. It was the beginning of a series of dramatic lectures on Oregon. People in Illinois were eager to hear about the West, and Lee gave them a stirring show. One of the highlights of his program was hymn-singing by his five charges. After the three half-breeds had dropped out to attend school (one at Whitman's alma mater, Fairfield Medical College), one of the true Indians, peak-headed William Brooks, offered, as a substitute for the hymns, an appealing little speech about the need of Oregon Indians for teachers.

The depression notwithstanding, the Board of Managers of the Missionary Society of the Methodist Church was so dedazzled that in November 1838 it voted Jason Lee $40,000 for taking fifty helpers and a shipload of equipment around the Horn to the Willamette. To assist in raising the sum, Lee spent six months stumping the East. He even asked permission to address Congress. The request was denied, but through Senator Linn of Missouri and Representative Caleb Cushing of Massachusetts, the petition he had brought from the Willamette settlers asking United States jurisdiction was presented to both houses. Accompanying the presentation were bills to establish military posts and authorize other forms of occupation. Since some of the proposals would violate the joint-occupation treaty with Great Britain, the majority of Congress frowned and the bills were tabled. Congress, however, did authorize the Secretaries of War and State to gather more information on the subject. Their findings, together with lengthy reports by Linn and Cushing, were printed and widely distributed at government expense.

Cushing went farther. Using a review of two recent books on the West, Samuel Parker's *Journal of an Exploring Tour Beyond the Rocky Mountains* and John Townsend's *A Narrative of a Journey Across the Rocky Mountains,* he launched in the influential *North American Review* (January 1840) a double-column, twenty-seven-page history of the United States' claim to Oregon. He said little about the books he supposedly was discussing. His thesis, rather, was what he considered the folly of the government in letting the British stay in the Northwest.

> The Hudson's Bay Company ... availing itself of the blindness and supineness of the Federal Government, has thrust itself within our limits, and intrusively acquired, as [Alexander] Mackenzie foresaw it might, a monopoly of the commerce of that wide-spread and noble domain of the United States situated on the Pacific Ocean. We trust, however, that this foul blot on our national honor will ere long be wiped out, if there is one spark of true patriotic feeling left in the breasts of Congress or of the Federal Administration. ... We have but to say peremptorily, that the thing shall stop, and it will stop. ... [The Government must] be impelled forward by the irresistible voice of the people.

Before Cushing's article appeared but probably while it was being prepared, the ship *Lausanne* sailed from New York on

October 9, 1839, with fifty-one men, women, and children bound for Oregon—Jason Lee and his new wife, six other ministers, a doctor, farmers, carpenters, blacksmiths, and teachers, four of the latter being unwed females. The New York *Journal of Commerce,* while remarking that the group's "primary object, we believe, is to carry the gospel to the Indians," could not refrain from adding that "among other things, it will expedite the settlement of the Territory."

Unknown to the *Journal* and to the *Lausanne*'s passengers, fifteen male overland emigrants long since had started West to expedite settlement and wrest Oregon from economic thralldom to the Hudson's Bay Company.

They too had caught fire from Jason Lee. The kindling was a speech Lee made on September 30, 1838, in the Main Street Presbyterian Church of Peoria, Illinois. But the ignition had come from one of Lee's peak-headed Indians, Thomas Adams. Falling ill in Peoria, Indian Tom had been left behind in the charge of charitable Christians. During his convalescence he hung around Joe Holman's wagon and cooper shop. One of the yarns he spun there in his clumsy English to the other loafers was of the unbelievable numbers of salmon in the Columbia; of the ease with which they were caught, dried, and stored; of the year-round sustenance they furnished to the Indians of the Northwest. Joe Holman, who was only twenty-two and itchy-footed, thought he would like to see so extraordinary a sight. Being a cooper, he also thought (as Nathaniel Wyeth had thought before him) that money might be made stowing pickled salmon into barrels and shipping the fish throughout the world.

As young men will, Joe and his friends enlarged on the idea until in imagination they became proprietors of a "city at the mouth of the Columbia that should be the New York of the Pacific"—the same term by which Narcissa Whitman had described Fort Vancouver in her diary. Perhaps the dream would have stayed just a young men's fancy if it had not been wrenched into tangible shape by Thomas Jefferson Farnham, an ambitious lawyer, thirty-five or so years old, who recently had arrived in Peoria from Vermont.

On March 28, 1839, Farnham called a meeting in the rooms

of Mr. Justice Butler to discuss a venture into Oregon. Records do not indicate whether or not Indian Tom Adams attended.[2] Anyway, this was now white man's business. Stirred by Farnham's eloquence, fifteen men formed themselves into the "Oregon Dragoons" to march into the Northwest, establish American sovereignty, resist the Hudson's Bay Company, take up land, pickle fish, and make their fortunes. Mrs. Farnham designed a flag for them on which she stitched *Oregon or the Grave* and rode with them for three days as they aimed a single wagon and several horses toward their equivocal goal.

They reached Independence after the annual fur caravan had departed. Compared to the cavalcades of the trade's heyday, the one of 1839 was such a shrunken affair that the Peorians would have increased its size by more than half. The fur trade was perishing. Overtrapping, the competition of the Hudson's Bay Company west of the Rockies, and a shift in fashion from beaver hats to silk ones had left only a handful of men in the mountains. In 1839 Moses (Black) Harris and nine roustabouts took to the Green River rendezvous no more than four two-wheeled carts, each drawn by two mules and each carrying 800 to 900 pounds. A considerable amount of the weight consisted of tins of alcohol; that demand, at least, was imperishable.

The rest of the caravan, as the Peorians may have learned, was heterogeneous. It included two hunters, one of them Paul Richardson, who had pursued Lee east with word of his first wife's death. Also along was a twenty-nine-year-old German-born doctor, Frederick Wislizenus, out on his own from his new home in Illinois to see the sights. There were two missionary couples. One, a friend of Spalding's, was named John S. Griffin. After the American Board had declined to finance him on a trip West to join Spalding, Griffin raised contributions from the Congregational Church of Litchfield, Connecticut, hired a skilled mechanic, Asahel Munger, to help him, and started out. Munger was mar-

[2] Tom left Peoria in the spring of 1839 and on May 2 caught up with Jason Lee in Schenectady to become part of the missionary's lecture entourage. The other peak-headed Indian, William Brooks, was ailing. On May 29 he died, and only Tom remained as Lee's chief exhibit from the Northwest. He returned home with the reinforcements aboard the *Lausanne*.

ried. Perhaps this inspired Griffin. On the way through St. Louis he tarried a day or two to woo a maiden possessed of missionary ambitions and the somewhat incongruous name of Desire. The list given above accounts for seventeen persons. Wislizenus says twenty-seven rode west with the caravan. Who the other ten were and what became of them is not known. Just possibly one or more of them were flotsam from the new emigrant societies springing up in the Midwest, and as such deserve a footnote in our histories as the first avowed settlers to travel the Oregon Trail.

In lieu of other evidence, however, Farnham's fish picklers become the first avowed settlers of record. They numbered eighteen by now. One of their new recruits, added in Independence, was a farmer named Robert Shortess. In the strange linkages of the migration, Shortess, like Jason Lee, would draw more settlers toward Oregon than he ever fully realized.

Robert Shortess himself, however, and his new friends—many of them would soon be his enemies—did not reach Oregon by way of the normal route. In Independence, where they learned they had missed the supply caravan by more than a week, they encountered two veteran mountain men, Philip Thompson and Andrew Sublette. Thompson and Sublette suggested that the emigrants go down the Santa Fe trail to Bent's Fort in Colorado and then turn north to a post which Andrew Sublette, in partnership with Louis Vasquez, had built on the South Platte River about forty-five miles north of present Denver. From this post traders would be going across the mountains later in the summer to a ragtag fort named Davy Crockett, recently built by Philip Thompson and two partners in Brown's Hole on the Green River, in extreme northwestern Colorado. At Fort Davy Crockett the wayfarers might make connections with a party bound for Fort Hall and from Hall journey the rest of the way to Oregon with a Hudson's Bay Company brigade. Furthermore, the Oregon Dragoons could obtain protection on the first leg of the roundabout route if they hurried after a Santa Fe wagon train which had just started west from Independence.

Hastily the dragoons sold their wagon and purchased in common a mule to carry their powder and a circular tent big enough to house them all. (They owned their riding horses and some pack stock individually.) They bought 200 pounds of flour, 150 pounds of bacon, and smaller amounts of sugar, tea, and coffee. They repaired their arms and molded bullets. As others would do after them, they overorganized, dividing themselves into platoons so that at the sound of appropriate trumpet calls they could quickly fall into line each morning as stentorian orders from Captain Farnham directed. On May 30 off they rode. Farnham carried strapped to his back a large notebook in which each evening he jotted observations he later ballooned into a popular and profitable travel book.

Three soon turned homeward, but the others found one fifty-six-year-old replacement named Blair in the wagon train. The farther they went, the more they bickered. One morning near present-day Larned, Kansas, while they were simultaneously wrangling and striking the big tent, someone bumped a loaded gun. It went off—the sort of accident that became routine during later migrations—and severely wounded Sidney Smith. A doctor who happened to be traveling with the wagon train, which was then a few miles ahead of them, patched up the invalid and the caravan further provided Smith with a carriage. But at the Cimarron Crossing of the Arkansas River, the wagon train turned south through the edge of the Oklahoma Panhandle. The Dragoons' route lay on up the river. For the rest of the way they would have to care for Smith themselves and, until he was mobile again, drag him from camp to camp in a litter.

Altercations increased. Three more men went home. Led by Shortess, several of the others suggested that Smith be abandoned on the prairie—according to a story told later by Farnham and his supporters. A dastardly lie, cried Shortess and his friends when they heard the charge. Farnham says that because of the horrifying proposal he resigned his captaincy. Shortess says that Farnham resigned because he knew he was about to be thrown out for incapacity and a "low, intriguing disposition."

One way or another they got Smith to the Bent brothers' huge adobe fort on the Arkansas River in southeastern Colorado. By then the wounded man had knit enough to ride, but the split in the party had become irreconcilable. Farnham and four others hired a mountain man to guide them directly across the mountains to Fort Davy Crockett in Brown's Hole. Shortess and the remaining seven went north to Fort St. Vrain (near Sublette's and Vasquez' post on the South Platte) to wait for the party which Philip Thompson had said would cross later that summer to Brown's Hole. During the delay three more dragoons lost interest, but when the mountain men finally started over the Rockies in September, Shortess and his remaining companions trudged resolutely along with them on a hungry trip.

By that time Farnham was well on his way to Oregon. At Fort Davy Crockett he and his companions met hunter Paul Richardson, Dr. Wislizenus, and two others of the 1839 caravan. From them they learned something of the caravan trip along the regular trail.

As far as the forks of the Platte in western Nebraska the journey had been standard enough. The South Platte, though, had been higher than usual. As the diminutive caravan toiled up its sandy south side, looking for a ford, 380 lodges of Sioux Indians appeared on the opposite bank and set up a mile-long village of skin tents—between two thousand and three thousand Indians, Asahel Munger estimated in his diary. Immediately two dozen or so of the Indians crossed the river to ask for whiskey. Black Harris, the caravan leader, told them he had none and stalled them off until dark. Frantically he then buried his tins of alcohol before the Indians could find them, take over, and soar out of hand. The outnumbered travelers spent the next day scared stiff as throngs of Indians swam across the river or paddled over in bullboats to trade and to stare at the two white women. At night their thousands of dogs chorused, wrote Wislizenus, "such music as I never yet have heard." At last the savages decamped and Harris dug up his alcohol. The unearthing took place on Sunday and gave the missionaries an unexpected day of rest. Then on they went.

The Oregon Dragoons were not the only ones to quarrel. Beyond Fort Laramie, Eliza Munger grew "almost sick for want of light bread." But flour was short and Griffin, the boss of the small missionary group, would not let her bake. The altercation grew too thick for Eliza's husband to handle. Unhappily he wrote in his diary, "I look to God in this case, my soul is troubled. Oh how good [to] trust in Jesus."

Once again the rendezvous was near Horse Creek, site of some of the most roistering carnivals of the past. But in 1839 an era was guttering out. The company drove such hard bargains that the remaining trappers were infuriated and vowed to quit. But live how? Most, said Munger, were too poor to go to the States. "What to do they know not." They were so discouraged, in fact, that (according to Wislizenus) there was almost no carousing at the rendezvous.

Frank Ermatinger, who was now in charge of Fort Hall, attended the gathering with a small brigade of twelve men, plus the usual hundreds of Indians. When Harris and his roustabouts started back east to Missouri with such furs as they had obtained, the Englishman once again succored helpless pilgrims and took the missionaries, the German doctor, and their anonymous companions as far as Soda Springs. There fourteen men and two women left his brigade and turned aside to the Blackfoot River to dry buffalo meat to last them to the Columbia. Few actually arrived there, however. At Fort Hall, dissensions split the group. Some, so it is said, suddenly spoke up for going to California.

While the arguments crackled, Munger borrowed a mule on which to search for some strayed horses. "She rared up, jumped, and kicked until she threw me off and broke my shoulder." Dr. Wislizenus put him back together. While Munger was healing, all but the missionaries left Fort Hall. Eight vanish from the records; perhaps they went to California, perhaps to Oregon; perhaps—who knows? The hunter Paul Richardson, Dr. Wislizenus, and two others started back to Missouri, routing themselves through Brown's Hole and New Mexico in order to avoid the unpredictable Sioux along the Platte.

Only the missionaries clung certainly to Oregon. After eight days' recuperation, Munger labored on westward with his wife and the Griffins. They fell out with each other, too. Munger found shelter for more than a year at Whitman's mission; Griffin and his wife moved in on friend Spalding at Lapwai. In time both new couples drifted on to the Willamette. There Munger committed suicide by throwing himself, during a religious ecstasy, into his own forge.

Brown's Hole, Dr. Wislizenus thought, was lovely, a valley perhaps thirty miles long and five or six wide—a widening, actually, of the awesome canyon by which the Green River thunders around the Uinta Mountains. Tremendous, colorful cliffs sheltered the bottomlands. Grass always grew, and trappers liked to winter there. Fort Davy Crockett, however, did not match its surroundings. The post was a hollow square of wretched log cabins, "the worst thing of its kind," Wislizenus wrote, "we have seen on our journey." The place's common nickname was Fort Misery. When the doctor's group and Farnham's group rode into the hole from opposite directions late in the summer of 1839, the inhabitants were subsisting principally on dog meat.

Oregon was little better than Davy Crockett, hunter Richardson told the emigrants. The Willamette farms were unproductive, soggy by winter and parched by summer; at all seasons settlers were plagued by fevers and fleas. The report so discouraged two of the Oregon Dragoons that they turned back with Richardson.

Farnham and his two remaining supporters went on with an Indian guide whom they hired for fifty loads of ammunition and three bunches of beads. Eventually they gained the Willamette. As Farnham looked over the primitive community, he found himself agreeing with Richardson's estimate. Though he helped the settlers prepare still another petition asking for United States jurisdiction, he decided against waiting for the blessing to be achieved. One story is that he got lost during a rainy night and had to stand up to his knees in a swamp until dawn, a contretemps that he permitted to sour his whole viewpoint. Whatever the cause, he packed up the petition intended for Congress and left Oregon by ship on December 3. From the Sandwich (Hawaiian) Islands and later from New York City he wrote to American newspapers letters entitled "Oregon Bubble Burst," in which he decried the entire Northwest. As will appear, these outpourings turned back several would-be settlers.

Farnham's hot-tempered opponent, Robert Shortess, came into

Brown's Hole with his companions a month or so after Farnham had left. By that time the season was late for a trip to Oregon. Shortess' friends decided to build a cabin and spend the winter. Two of the local mountain men, however—Robert (Doc) Newell and Joe Meek—decided to go to Fort Hall for supplies and Shortess traveled with them. At Fort Hall, Ermatinger gave the former Missourian a job helping two Indians and a French-Canadian *voyageur* shepherd fourteen horses laden with furs to Fort Walla Walla. The Indians deserted during a snowstorm. The two whites, neither of whom spoke the other's language—perhaps it helped prevent the usual bickering—finished the job alone.

After wintering at the Whitman mission, where Munger and his wife were also staying, Shortess continued down the river not by boat but by riding horseback, as Farnham had done, along hair-raising Indian trails through the heavily timbered Cascade Mountains, well back from the Columbia's tremendous gorge. He liked the Willamette and wrote letters to Missouri, especially to his friends the Applegates, singing the country's praises. Though such influences really cannot be gauged, it is likely that his literary efforts attracted as many emigrants as Farnham's dissuaded. And so, even unwittingly and at a distance, the two enemies managed to fight each other to a stand-off.

Back at Brown's Hole, Shortess' four erstwhile companions (including the cooper Joseph Holman) finished their log cabins and settled down for the winter. All were in their early twenties and carefree. They dried buffalo meat, shot jackrabbits, and perhaps found red bedmates their reminiscences neglect to mention. It was not a bad winter—for them. For the mountain men the outlook was gloomier. Would there even be a rendezvous in 1840? If not, where could a trapper sell his pelts and buy his necessaries?

Cheyenne Indians depressed the outlook still further by stealing a hundred head of horses from the herd in Brown's Hole. In an Indian-reasoned kind of retaliation (you get even with the next fellow, no matter what his responsibility), some of the Brown's Hole trappers, led by Philip Thompson, stole fourteen animals from the Hudson's Bay Company at Fort Hall and lifted another thirty from Snake Indians they encountered on their way back to Fort Misery. The easy success inspired Thompson to head with a larger group toward California to rob the Mexicans. But if a man did not wish to become a bandit or, equally distasteful, go East to the confines of the settlements, then what?

As well as they could, some of the boys—Doc Newell, Joe Meek, William Doughty, Jack Larison—kept trapping during the winter. By February 1840 they had collected, and their squaws had prepared, some three hundred pelts. But game was scarce and they were too short of supplies to wait for whatever caravan might be coming from St. Louis during the summer. Winter or not, someone had to break through to Fort Hall and swap the furs for goods.

Newell volunteered to try; reminiscences do not indicate if other mountain men went with him. But the four dudes did. The ordeal turned out to be worse than even Newell had bargained for—weeks of zero cold and needles of snow driven by shrieking gales. At times they had to spread their blankets on the deep snow for the horses to walk across. The buffalo on which Newell had counted did not appear.[3] Once he staved off starvation for the party by butchering his pet dog; another day they survived by eating a wildcat. Their horses fared better; the animals could graze where wind had blown snow off exposed hillsides or on cottonwood shoots beside the frozen streams.

The trip to Fort Hall took forty-five days according to Newell, sixty days according to emigrant Amos Cook. The Peorians continued to the Columbia with a Hudson's Bay brigade. Newell returned to Brown's Hole with his supplies. He may have arrived in time for the birth of his third half-breed son on April 17, 1840. The oldest boy, born in 1835, had been named Francis; the next, born in 1838, was William. For some reason the father did not get around to picking out an English name for this last arrival, born into such troubled times. Whatever the Indian mother called him presumably was enough.

[3] The shortage resulted from a mystery of mountain ecology that has never been explained. When white men first saw the Green River Valley in Wyoming, it teemed with buffalo. During the 1830s, however, the animals began to disappear. Presumably they drew back east of the mountains to the plains. By the time the big emigrations to Oregon began, buffalo were rare west of Independence Rock and practically nonexistent west of South Pass.

When summer came, the handful of men remaining at Fort Misery gathered their families together and started north up the Green to see who, if anyone, would appear at the rendezvous. It must have been a somber little caravan. Five-year-old Francis Newell was probably riding alone by now, and William, two years and three months, could manage by being tied Indian-style to a saddle. The unnamed baby traveled in a papoose-carrier strapped to his mother's back or hung to the saddle horn. The sore-backed pack horses squealed and bit each other; the trailing poles for the buffalo-skin lodges raised faint tendrils of dust against a limitless backdrop of gray-green sage.

Andrew Drips, Henry Fraeb, and Jim Bridger arrived with a picayune train. This was the last, they said. The American Fur Company was leaving the mountains for the plains and transforming itself into an odorous purveyor of buffalo robes—strictly an Indian job, the bucks hunting and the squaws laboriously scraping and tanning the bulky pelts. Not until after the Civil War would white men join in and complete the slaughter of the once uncountable herds.

Drips had brought with him to Green River the usual mixture of wayfarers. One was a short, fat (five feet six, 210 pounds), red-faced, Belgian-born Catholic priest named Pierre-Jean De Smet. The Flatheads had finally succeeded. In 1839, two of them had crossed the Continental Divide to the Yellowstone River, built dugouts, and paddled downstream to the new St. Joseph's Mission at Council Bluffs. There they had met De Smet. Later Bishop Rosati had authorized the Belgian to look over the mountain field. One of the overjoyed Flatheads made an unbelievable winter trip to Montana to prepare the tribe for the arrival. The other Indian accompanied De Smet with the caravan, leaving Westport in April 1840. A week out of the village the priest was felled by the malaria which would afflict him intermittently during the next five months. He would ride horseback as long as he could hold himself in the saddle, then lie in one of the traders' carts, "where I was jolted about like a malefactor . . . into the most singular positions . . . cold as an icicle or covered with sweat and burning like a stove."

Also bouncing along with the 1840 caravan in two wagons of their own were three self-supporting Protestant missionary couples—Mr. and Mrs. Harvey Clark, Mr. and Mrs. Alvin Smith, Mr. and Mrs. P. B. Littlejohn. Riding in two other wagons were Joel Walker (a brother of mountain man Joseph Reddeford Walker, discoverer of Yosemite), Joel's wife, and their five children. This was another "first"—the first nonmissionary wife and the first white children to travel the Oregon Trail.[4]

The Shoshone Indians at the rendezvous staged an old-style show. Firing their guns, they raced headlong toward the wagons, garish in paint, feathers, wolf tails, and necklaces of bear and eagle claws. The smaller contingent of Flatheads knelt more sedately under the vast sky to receive De Smet's blessing. *Voyageurs* from Ermatinger's brigade who had not seen a priest for years wept openly. One of them, also a Belgian, left the brigade and became the priest's personal retainer on a staggering trip up the Green River, across Jackson Hole, and into the Bitterroot Valley. There De Smet determined to establish a mission the following year, 1841. The decision made, he and his *voyageur* crossed with an escort of seventeen Flathead warriors through the still-dangerous land of the Blackfeet to the Yellowstone and returned by river to St. Louis.

It is not clear why the Joel Walkers and the Protestant missionaries did not abandon their wagons at the rendezvous and, like their predecessors, continue west on horseback with the Hudson's Bay people. Perhaps not enough horses were available. Perhaps, like Whitman, they were stubbornly determined to take the vehicles as far as possible. Anyway, they stuck to their wheels. That kind of travel was too slow for Ermatinger. He went ahead and the missionaries asked Black Harris how much he would charge to pilot them as far as Fort Hall.

The figure Harris named would have taken every bit of cash they possessed. In dismay they turned to Newell. Doc said he would pilot them if the wagon owners would also employ at day wages, as road-builders for the trip, Joe Meek, Caleb Wilkins,

---

[4] The next year the Walkers continued south from the Willamette to California and so were not true Oregon settlers.

William Craig, John Larison, and possibly one or two other destitute mountain men. The cost came to less than Harris' figure and would result in easier traveling. The wagon-owners agreed.

The undercutting annoyed Harris. As Newell dryly recorded the incident in the memorandum he kept sporadically to sum up the main events of each preceding several months, "I think he intended murder he Shot at me about 70 or 80 yards but done no damage only to him self." In another recollection, Newell adds that he quirted his horse straight for Harris, who dived into a thicket. Drips then announced loudly that if any more antics like that occurred, he would hang the first man to shoot. Peace of sorts returned.

The trip through the mountains to Bear River and on to Fort Hall took sixteen days and exhausted the draft stock. Only Whitman's cart had gone farther, to Fort Boise, and beyond Boise the route was said to be impossible. At last the travelers abandoned their vehicles. Newell bought the two which had belonged to the missionaries—or perhaps accepted them in lieu of cash payment. Caleb Wilkins obtained one of Walker's; and it seems, though records are unclear, that the Hudson's Bay Company accepted the other in exchange for supplies.

Glumly the mountain men watched the missionaries jog out of sight. That job was done. Now what?

How about settling in the Willamette? someone asked. There were few reluctant nods.

And drive the wagons with us, Newell added.

Wilkins agreed. Ermatinger, who wanted a road opened to Fort Walla Walla, offered to send along the company's wagon and a driver for it. Newell, who was to act as leader, pilot, and road-builder, hired Joe Meek to handle one of his vehicles. Newell's other wagon seems to have been taken apart and its parts used to repair the others.

Hitching up mules and horses which almost certainly had never seen harness before, the pioneers started out on September 27, 1840. Wilkins and Newell had their families and children with them. Meek, whose squaw had deserted him, took along his sullen little half-breed daughter, Helen Mar, named for the heroine of a book he had read in a winter camp. Craig, Larison, and

342

some other trappers fell in with their Indian families. Like Whitman, they found the lava boulders and the sagebrush, some of it as tall as the mules, a maddening ordeal. The stock began to play out. They shifted their goods to pack horses, discarded the wagon boxes, and went on with just the running gears. Somehow they got up Burnt Canyon and through the timber of the Blue Mountains. Finally, late in fall, they reached Whitman's mission at Waiilatpu.

Helen Mar, infested with vermin, and Newell's infant son were too sick to travel farther. The mountain men left the children for Narcissa to care for, as later she would care for other waifs cast at her door by the accidents of the trail. (The year before, 1839, Narcissa's own two-year-old daughter and only child had fallen into Mill Creek and drowned.) The fathers drove on to Fort Walla Walla, left the wagons, and on horseback finished the journey to the Willamette to stake out their claims.[5]

Meek, now wifeless, never returned for his daughter. But early in the spring of 1841 Doc Newell came back to fetch his son. At last he had a name for his boy—Marcus Whitman Newell. At Walla Walla he picked up his wagon and two American cows that had been left at the fort by one of the missionaries.[6] Loading them onto a barge, he floated and portaged them to the Willamette. He was proud of what he had achieved. On April 19, 1841, he wrote in his memorandum, "this is to be remembered that I Robert Newell was the first who brought waggons across the rocky mountains."

From the beginning it had been so: fur men were always the ones who cast ahead and made possible the long way West.

Whitman, too, was impressed. What he himself had tried so hard to do had at last been accomplished. Now that the way had been opened, he told Newell, others would follow. Two years later, indeed, remembering Newell's wagons, Marcus Whitman would be the one to persuade doubters that the entire crossing really could be made on wheels.

[5] Craig and Larison, who were married to Nez Percés, went to Lapwai Creek to be near their wives' people.
[6] What happened to the other two wagons does not appear. The trail west was dotted with vehicles that made small history by reaching such-and-such a point and then were cast off and forgotten.

18

GOD'S GADFLY

The contentious missionaries of the Northwest did not achieve brotherly love after their arrival in the vineyard. Their antagonisms, rooted deep in personality quirks, grew so dismaying that at times Elkanah Walker and occasionally even Marcus Whitman vaguely contemplated giving up the effort and selling their stations to the better-financed Methodists of the Willamette.[1]

The acrimonies spilled over into letters they wrote to Boston to the American Board of Commissioners for Foreign Missions. Wearied at last of recriminations, the Board early in 1842 decided on radical surgery. William Gray, Asa Smith, and Henry Spalding were to return home. The stations at Kamiah, Lapwai, and Waiilatpu were to be closed. The Whitmans and Cornelius Rogers were to move in with the Eellses and Walkers at Tshimakain, the remote Spokane mission, which henceforth would be the sole operating Presbyterian-Congregationalist unit in the Northwest. Even at their most captious, the missionaries had not anticipated so crushing an adjustment, and the orders obviously were going to cause consternation when they arrived.

Delivery of the sealed letter was entrusted by the Board to a pompous little busybody who had been associated with the Methodist mission in the Willamette for three years, Dr. Elijah White. White had arrived on the Columbia by ship in 1837 with the first reinforcements sent to Jason Lee's original station. After three years as the group's physician, he quarreled with Lee and in 1840 returned home aboard the *Lausanne,* Captain Josiah Spaulding commanding—the vessel on which Jason Lee had sailed to Oregon with his fifty cohorts after his dramatic ride East in 1838.

[1] By this time the Methodists had established a branch station under Daniel Lee at the Dalles. It stood a little back from the Columbia at the foot of a tier of brown basaltic bluffs, amid a scattering of yellow pines, just downstream from the first of the roaring rapids that tortured the river's thrust through the Cascade Mountains—Celilo Falls and then the gut of the Dalles itself. The station stood 150 river miles closer to the Willamette than did Whitman's Waiilatpu station, 125 miles closer than the Hudson's Bay Company's Fort Walla Walla. As a result, the Dalles mission soon became a key point on the Oregon Trail.

Any United States citizen who came near Oregon in those days seemed to feel an overpowering compulsion to pass on to his government his views about the disputed territory. Captain Josiah Spaulding was no exception. White helped him compose for transmission to Congress a lengthy document in which observation and hearsay were indiscriminately mixed. Among other things, the Spaulding report charged that the Hudson's Bay Company deliberately incited Indians to attack American citizens on the coast.

Such atrocity stories were not unique; the British had been accused of similar bloodthirstiness since the days of the American Revolution. By the end of 1841 the charges would hardly have been heeded if Senator Linn of Missouri had not just then tossed into the congressional hopper still another bill for the occupation of Oregon—a document produced this time with an eye on the pending arrival of Lord Ashburton to discuss with Secretary of State Daniel Webster certain adjustments in the boundary between Canada and the United States from Maine westward to ... Oregon perhaps?

As a blunt reminder that Oregon existed, Linn proposed thrusting United States sovereignty into the jointly occupied Northwest by three devices. First, he wanted the courts of Iowa to extend their jurisdiction over Americans in Oregon. Second, he proposed appointing an Indian agent for keeping an eye on the Hudson's Bay Company and the savages it supposedly excited. Finally, and most importantly, his bill authorized the United States government to give to every male settler in the Northwest over eighteen years old 640 acres of land, plus 160 acres for his wife and 160 more for each child. The key word is *give*. In 1841, government land elsewhere was sold to settlers at an average price of $1.25 an acre.

Linn's opponents at once pointed out that the United States probably could not appoint Indian agents or convey sound title to lands in a country whose ownership was still a moot point. But of course that was part of Linn's purpose—to settle at last the question of sovereignty.

Very few people in the East possessed firsthand information about Oregon. One who did was Dr. Elijah White. He was summoned to Washington and offered the ambiguous position of sub-agent for the Oregon Indians at half a subagent's usual salary, but with a promise of a full agency and full salary if the bill should pass. There is evidence that he was also authorized to draw on the government's secret service fund to help start emigrants west with him by running advertisements in newspapers and hiring an experienced guide to pilot whatever wagon train assembled.

By no mere coincidence, Lieutenant John Charles Frémont, the new son-in-law of Missouri's other senator, Thomas Hart Benton, was at about this same time directed to "explore" the Oregon Trail as far as South Pass and from his examination prepare a report on travel conditions and on suitable locations for military forts. Though exact manipulations cannot be reconstructed, a faint odor of "deal" clings to these arrangements. The administration naturally did not wish the Ashburton-Webster negotiations embarrassed by outbursts of jingoistic talk in Congress and the press—outbursts sure to be generated by debate on Linn's Oregon bill. On the other hand, the frontier states were certain to raise an uproar if the federal government appeared too supine in the face of Ashburton's approach. White's appointment to a minor post and Frémont's explorations toward but not into Oregon may have been offered to Linn as sops for his constituents. In return, Linn may have agreed to let his explosive occupation bill lie quiet while Webster's discussions with Ashburton were under way. In any event, the bill did lie quiet.

All that White saw in the arrangements was White. The job of subagent to, say, the Iowa Indians would have been mediocre. In Oregon, however, Dr. Elijah White would be the only authorized representative of the United States government. Every person there, from McLoughlin on down, would have to heed him. By the time the doctor reached the Willamette, indeed, he would consider himself vested with as many powers as a full-fledged territorial governor.

Westward toward Independence he bustled, quite unconscious of the purport of the letter he carried to Whitman. As one companion he signed up, in central New York, a young neighbor named Medorem Crawford, who kept the best surviving diary of the trip. (The other accounts are reminiscences, colored by the modifications of reflection.) He also picked up, for return to their homes, two of Tom McKay's half-breed sons who had come East to school with Jason Lee in 1838.

The nearer White came to the frontier, the more he expanded; and with his ballooning sense of importance a type familiar to every new settlement at last pushes into the annals of the Trail. This is the promoter. The gentlest of the kind spread their gospel in order to justify themselves by persuading others to believe as they believed. The more ambitious hoped for various sorts of aggrandizement, including political power which they thought might be seized in the new territories by a man with foresight enough to build a core of personal followers. Elijah White was of this kind, and at the outset circumstances seemed disposed to gratify him.

Everywhere he spoke, he was heeded by attentive audiences— Linn's pending bill with its promise of free land to settlers guaranteed that. "Last night," he reported concerning a typical appearance, "the noble church was filled . . . and I talked an hour and a half with all my might."

His speeches have not survived, but the contents are easy to guess. He talked of climate, of course, of land and markets. His peroration probably echoed a keynote sounded by Caleb Cushing in his 1839 Report on the Territory of Oregon: "This movement [the western advance of the frontier] goes on with predestined certainty, and the unerring precision of the great works of Providence." Other speeches made throughout the land during the early 1840s expatiated on this theme of the happy linkage of Providence with the expanding United States. In the summer of 1845, in the *Democratic Review*, editorial writer John L. O'Sullivan stumbled onto the words "Manifest Destiny" to sum up the feeling. Repeating himself in December in the New York *Morning News*, O'Sullivan cried that America's claim to Oregon "is by the right our manifest destiny to overspread and possess the whole of the continent which Providence has given us for the great experiment of liberty and federated self-government."

Private motives of many colors intertwined with these public and patriotic drives. Many of the frontiersmen who listened to the eagle-soaring speeches were the children and grandchildren of

347

volunteers who had fought Great Britain during the Revolution and the War of 1812; in the excitement of the oratory they saw themselves marching down the same pulse-quickening path, once again to humble the ancient enemy. Others among them felt the allure of new, wild places that needed taming. Many spoke longingly of freedom from strange social pressures crowding in upon them, including the growing industrialization of the country. Those from ague-ridden bottomlands along the Midwestern rivers believed wistfully that western climates were milder and more healthful. Nonslaveholding farmers who had to compete with neighbors using Negro field hands yearned for a region where slavery would not be permitted. The prospect of romantic new careers charmed many, especially young bachelors. And always in the background, giving solidity to each dream, was the hope of economic self-betterment as held out by Linn's bill—free virgin land of deep black soil for farmers; townsites, millsites, and business opportunities for the promoters of new cities.

Whatever a man's motives, he could not simply pick up and leave. Tents, guns, food, clothing, wagons, tools, and livestock for the long trip cost more than a good farm in newly opened Iowa or Wisconsin would have. The depression of the late 1830s was receding at last; many men had money to spend. And here we come hard against an unanswerable question. Why did the pioneers do it? Why did they spend so prodigiously of effort, cash, and comfort to obtain material things they could have found nearer home? Free land alone does not explain the fever; for one thing, the land was not free by the time a man had paid the price of reaching it. Part of its magnetism, rather, was as old as the things that pulled at Vérendrye and Robert Rogers, Thomas Jefferson and Meriwether Lewis, Jedediah Smith, Nathaniel Wyeth, and a hundred other toilers along the trail—a vision not of dollars alone but of something they could scarcely fashion into words, something which their nerve ends assured them existed somewhere out toward the Western Sea.

The stir of that belief filled the Mississippi Valley during the 1830s and 1840s. Young Sam Clemens was born into it in Missouri in 1835, grew up with it, laughed at its manifestations in a character he called Colonel Sellers, but eventually, in the 1860s, himself followed it West. Contemplating the intoxication, Bernard DeVoto wrote in *Mark Twain's America,*

> The immigration was under way. Its great days were just around the turn of spring—and an April restlessness, a stirring in the blood, a wind from beyond the oak's openings, spoke of the prairies, the great desert, and the Western Sea. The common man fled westward. A thirsty land swallowed him insatiably. There is no comprehending the frenzy of the American folk-migration. God's gadfly had stung us mad.

The torment that drove Io on and on and on to a fulfillment she did not understand—God's gadfly. Probably it is as good an explanation as any. What matters is not whether fulfillment was attainable in reality, but rather that at long last in the world's sad, torn history an appreciable part of mankind thought it might be. That was both the torment and the freedom—to go and look.

In order to raise an outfit for the trip, many a family had to translate the property it already owned into cash and mobile goods. Those without possessions could make the journey only by hiring out to someone who had the requisite stability. As a result mere malcontents, fugitives, and riffraff seldom accompanied the early migrations. These were substantial people, thorny individualists who were prepared to fortify their decisions with sizable investments of cash and hard labor.

At the conclusion of each of Elijah White's talks, man after man came to him and said that although he did not have time enough to prepare for the venture that spring, he would be along the next year. Even so, when White reached the rendezvous point at Elm Grove west of Independence (in spite of the name only a few elms were still standing there), he found eighteen wagons and more than 107 persons assembled. Exact numbers are hard to determine; accounts vary, and also it is difficult to be sure how many turned back after the start and how many more joined along the way. About half the emigrants were adult males, many of them single. The rest were women and children. Compared even to the fur caravans of the preceding decade, this was a small turnout, and most had probably made up their minds to take the long jump before they had so much as heard of Elijah White.

But the yeast was bubbling and he knew he was part of it—that next year, 1843, a much larger train would follow him and in that group would be many who would remember his name.

These adventurers of 1842 were not the first true emigrants to cross the plains—true migrants being definable as family groups who traveled on their own resources, unescorted by heavily armed fur caravans. The first ones had crossed the plains a year earlier, in 1841—the Bidwell-Bartleson party. They are generally classed as California pioneers. But because nearly half of them changed their minds at Soda Springs and went to Oregon, and, more important, because they first wrestled the same problems that later faced every group, they warrant a brief digression here.

The Bidwell-Bartleson party were the ragtag survivors of the Western Emigration Society. During the winter of 1840–41, the Society had enrolled five hundred members. Then letters from Thomas Jefferson Farnham decrying the entire Pacific coast and derogatory rumors spread by Missouri storekeepers fearful of losing so many customers in a single mass exodus had caused a cooling of ardors. Only sixty-nine people showed up at the rendezvous. Of these, only five were women. Two were marriageable. One was the daughter of the migrating Williams family; the other, a widow with one son, was related to the migrating Kelseys, said to be the toughest backwoods Kentuckians ever to cuss a mule. Or at least the woman said she was a widow; gossips whispered that she was in fact running away from her husband.

The emigrants possessed almost no information about the trails they would have to follow to reach California. They were saved from probable disaster when Thomas Fitzpatrick appeared at the rendezvous guiding a Catholic missionary party which Father De Smet was taking to the Bitterroot Valley of Montana for founding his Flathead mission. The emigrants joined the church group and were able to draw on Fitzpatrick's knowledge as far as southern Idaho, where the California contingent plunged off into the ghastly deserts beyond the Great Salt Lake. This dependence on Fitzpatrick was the beginning of a routine followed by all later parties—the hiring of an experienced mountain man as pilot.

Other of their experiences were also prototypes. Near Fort

Laramie a young man ironically named James Shotwell was killed by the accidental discharge of a loaded gun; nearly every later caravan experienced that happening also. The two unattached women were duly married, the first of many such ceremonies on the trail. The Williams girl took her husband near the Blue River in a ceremony presided over by an eccentric, lone-riding, sixty-three-year-old Protestant preacher who overhauled the caravan in the middle of Kansas; the widow was married by Father De Smet out in the sun-blasted sage wastes beside Green River. Both brides—in fact, all but one of the five women—chose to go with the Oregon group. Perhaps they were the ones who made up their husbands' minds. Oregon by 1841 had the sound of homes and of familiar Anglo-Saxon institutions to it; Mexican California as yet had not.

More significant than those "firsts" was the struggle of the Bidwell-Bartleson group with the perennial problem of leadership and discipline. Most earlier adventurers on the western trails had submitted to authority emanating from the outside. The Spanish colonists of New Mexico and California had marched north to their destinations under the absolute discipline of their military commanders and priests. The placid French-Canadian *voyageurs* submitted without question to an all-powerful bourgeois whose dignity was such that his hirelings often had to carry him ashore from his canoe on their backs. When American fur traders first took to the trails beyond the Missouri, practical economics enforced a comparable social organization. Laborers in the caravans obeyed directions issued them by the appointed representatives of the company—or lost their jobs in the middle of nowhere.

The Santa Fe wagon trains made the first steps toward democratic organization. No single company owned all the vehicles in a caravan, as was generally the case in the fur brigades. Rather, the train was made up of a union of several proprietors; but because their aims were homogeneous they were able to elect an experienced trail captain and follow him with relatively little discord. The emigrants were not so amenable. The bulk of them, at least in the trains before the Gold Rush, were frontier farmers—notorious individualists. Rationally, they understood that in cooperation lay strength and that cooperative efforts were best channeled through some sort of commander. Drawing on the example of the Santa Fe traders, they did try to produce from among their own numbers an acceptable sort of supervision through the hotly cherished practice of voting for leaders. But they were seldom able to make the custom work.

The failure was largely the result of their trying to impose a rigid, arbitrary social organization onto units unknown to the Santa Fe caravans—units that were fundamentally emotional and disruptive. These were the family groups. Under the rasping vexations of the trail, families (often including several married brothers and sisters, fathers and children) might fight internally; against other families they generally maintained a united front. These private cohesions gave every crotchety patriarch the nucleus of a sizable backing—a backing already predisposed to egg him on in his protests. As a result, the larger grouping of the train always had a tendency to fly apart into its more elemental pieces. After all, Cyrus, if you can vote a captain in, you can vote him back out, *caint* you?

As in any democracy, the men who courted election were not always the ones best qualified for the office. In the case of the 1841 caravan, the leading candidate was John Bartleson. His platform was simple. If he could not be captain, none of his eight husky followers would go with the caravan. Bartleson was thereupon elected.

It was not a procedure likely to generate the sort of efficient obedience that had held the earlier, more autocratic trail cavalcades together. Bartleson's electorate wrangled with him most of the way West. Resentment of him probably contributed to the departure of part of his group for Oregon, and under the hideous pressures of the Nevada deserts an almost paralyzing dissension became inevitable—but that, too, is another story.[2] In short, the voting that was supposed to provide strength for a party often was a source of its weakness. And yet one phase of a man's fulfillment has always been his right to a voice in the conduct of his own affairs. Migrations moving westward in hope of still more fulfill-

[2] See George R. Stewart, *The California Trail*, pp. 7–28. (McGraw-Hill, 1962)

ment could hardly have avoided this form of government. Democracy always has been embossed with ironies.

Elijah White wanted and expected to be captain of the 1842 caravan. To his annoyance he found himself opposed by a promoter even more glib than he was—Lansford Hastings, whose almost psychotic need to control others would contribute, in 1846, to the ghastly Donner tragedy in the Sierra Nevada Mountains.[3] At an organizational meeting held to discuss procedures, the wily electorate decided not to commit itself irrevocably to either man but to hold new elections each month, with incumbents eligible to succeed themselves.

White's familiarity with Oregon and the prestige of his position as government subagent carried the day for him, and during the voting of May 15, 1842, he nosed out Lansford Hastings for the office of leader. Jim Coates, of whom little is known, landed the job as guide. This is a bit surprising, since the caravan already possessed as one of its own members trapper Stephen H. Meek, Joe Meek's brother. Stephen had gone West with Bonneville ten years before and claimed (probably with exaggeration) to have trapped across the Cascade Mountains into the Willamette. Later he would guide several caravans—not always successfully, as we shall see. But for some reason he was, at the outset of 1842, ignored by his neighbors.

On May 16, Hastings wrote later in a guidebook he published, the start was made in "high glee, jocular hilarity, and happy anticipation, as we darted forward into the wild expanse of the untrodden regions of 'the western world' "—the white-topped wagons first and then the herd of loose livestock, their drivers (White now reminiscing) "merrily singing or whistling to beguile their way." No doubt Hastings whistled too. He knew how to be suave and charming when the occasion required, and he was already plotting how to overthrow Captain White—at least, in White's view Hastings' actions constituted a plot.

Elijah White, who was given to arbitrary rulings, almost immediately handed his rival an issue out of which to breed subversiveness. Even before the caravan reached the ford over the

[3] Again see Stewart's *The California Trail*, pp. 142–84.

Kansas River, the new captain decided that there were too many dogs in his train. The animals might go mad out on the plains; their barking might reveal the caravan's presence to the Indians. Dog-owners retorted that the hounds might warn the wayfarers of any stealthy approach which Indians might attempt. White brushed the argument aside and rammed through a motion requiring that every dog be slain. According to journalist Medorem Crawford, twenty-two animals were summarily executed. Whether or not this was the caravan's total complement of dogs is unclear, but it was enough to engender sizzling animosity among the owners.

Three days later the sixteen-month-old daughter of the Lancasters died—the first white child to perish on the trail. Dr. White diagnosed the trouble as "symptomatick fever accompanied with worms." They buried the little girl, forded the Kansas, and rolled on through dreary rains that tightened already short tempers. Finally the distraught mother could no longer bear the thought of the lonely grave and demanded that her husband take her back. Struggling for time in which to calm her, he told the caravan that she was sick and begged them to wait until she could go on again. Some refused and pulled on. For three days disintegration threatened, until on May 30 Lancaster gave in and turned his team back toward home. The others regrouped after a fashion and pushed on, finding loud fault with everything their captain did.

By the time the train had reached the Platte, necessity had forced onto it traveling methods somewhat different from those employed by the fur caravans. At night the emigrants generally parked their wagons in a rough circle rather than in a stream-bordered square. Outside the wagons they pitched their tents and outside the ring of tents they built their fires. Horses and mules were picketed as usual within the corral of wagons. But the circle did not afford enough room to accommodate the many oxen and cows that every emigrant train took with it. Since cattle rarely tempted Indians to theft, the herds were let graze loose on the nearby prairie and were rounded up each morning. Occasionally a lightning storm or passing buffalo herd scattered the animals and delayed the next morning's start. One night one of White's guards thought he heard buffalo approaching, blazed away into the shadows, and wounded two oxen. That sort of slaphappy firing also became familiar to later emigrant trains.

The fur caravans had not been finicky about cleanliness. Narcissa Whitman, it will be recalled, had been able to do laundry only three times between late April and the middle of September —at Fort Laramie, the rendezvous, and Fort Boise. The women of the emigrant caravans were more demanding about wash stops whenever good water and dry weather coincided.

In 1842 one of these laundry pauses coincided with election day, when White's first month-long term was up. The new balloting cast the dog-slaying doctor aside in favor of Lansford Hastings. Completely mortified, Uncle Sam's sole representative for all Oregon refused to continue with so shortsighted a group and pushed ahead with a few of his followers.

At Fort Laramie (handsomely rebuilt the preceding year of whitewashed adobe bricks to meet the competition of Fort Platte a little farther downstream) White was told that the Sioux were in an ugly mood. Their truculence was a year old. The preceding August (1841), beyond the Continental Divide, where the Little Snake River courses sinuously west near the present Wyoming–Colorado border, the Indians had jumped a party of trappers under Henry Fraeb. They had killed Fraeb and three or four others, but during the battle they had lost several times that many warriors. Ever since they reputedly had been spoiling for revenge against whatever white men happened along next.

The hurrying doctor and his party decided that for mutual protection they should wait for the rest of the caravan. When it came, everyone was querulous from the routine annoyances of all wagon trains—wheels shrunken until iron tires fell off, broken axletrees, sore-footed cattle, and the personal discomforts caused by sunburn, alkali water, and monotonous food cooked under difficult circumstances. But at least 1842 was a drought year and the stream fords caused no trouble.

On reaching Fort Laramie, the emigrants cut down the worst of their wagons into carts. The lamest of their gaunt cattle, for whom the drought-shriveled forage was growing scarce, they traded off at the fort, at outrageous terms, for supplies and fresh horses. They added two or three unemployed trappers to their number; then, still disliking each other intensely but held together by fear, they pushed ahead among the scrubby junipers and across the steep ravines that lay between the foothills of the Laramie Mountains and the canyon of the North Platte. Soon they met more trappers riding east toward the fort with a few packloads of furs. From this group they hired Tom Fitzpatrick to be their guide. Why they so consistently overlooked their own mountain-man companion, Stephen Meek, or what happened to the original pilot, Jim Coates, are unexplained.

On July 13, Adam Horn discharged his rifle by accident and killed a young man named Bailey. Bailey's friends wrapped him in a buffalo robe and buried him near the oval, swayback hump of Independence Rock. The train then decided to stay on where they were long enough to dry some buffalo meat and hold another election.

Hastings was re-elected captain for another month, and A. L. Lovejoy was again chosen as second-in-command. By this time the train had been in the vicinity of the rock for two or three days. Not until the wagons started on up the Sweetwater toward the gash of Devil's Gate, however, did the two leaders, Hastings and Lovejoy, feel the old American urge toward self-advertisement. Suddenly they decided to stay behind the others and paint their names on the brown granite. While they were about it, a party of Sioux Indians slipped up and seized them. The amount of danger involved varies according to whose account you read. No doubt Hastings and Lovejoy had moments of apprehension before the vacillating Indians concluded to trade their prizes back to the caravan for a few ropes of tobacco.

After the swap and for most of the rest of the way to South Pass, savages hung on the flanks of the train until, on July 22, diarist Medorem Crawford estimated that four or five thousand Sioux were camped within sight. Frémont, who was about three weeks and two hundred miles behind, says that only Fitzpatrick's skill in dealing with Indians saved the party from attack. But Medorem Crawford, who was on the spot, mentions no particular hostility. In fact, he says that several of the emigrants managed to trade good horses out of the Indians.

Probably there was more danger than Crawford realized. But

it may also be that Frémont embroidered the story to lend substance to his own dramatics. On the strength of what he heard at Fort Laramie about the Sioux, the young lieutenant decided not to risk taking two boys who were adventuring with his party any farther into the wilderness. He also made a histrionic speech to his men, stating that anyone "disposed to cowardice" would be allowed to leave. Only one man was brave enough to face that kind of contumely. After being held up to the ridicule of the rest of the expedition the fellow was discharged. The others marched boldly ahead, on tracks where women and children had gone before—but not, wrote Frémont later, until after so seasoned a hand as Kit Carson had made his will. Oh well, it made good reading when future emigrants thumbed his report in preparation for their own adventuring through lands where almost dreadful savages lurked—enough to make you shiver but not, in the 1840s, enough to endanger your scalp. The melancholy truth is that most of the caravans of the decade had far more trouble among their own members than with the Indians.

At Green River, the caravan of 1842 broke apart again. White proposed abandoning the troublesome wagons for packhorses. Hastings and most of the family men objected; they wished to keep wheels rolling clear to Oregon. Agreement proving impossible, they separated. White, who had employed Fitzpatrick, insisted that the mountain man stay with him. At last Stephen Meek came into his own; Hastings hired him as pilot. The wagon men destroyed their poorest vehicles to repair the best. With eight reconstructed vehicles, one of which soon collapsed, they pushed sullenly ahead of the others. The packhorse group meanwhile was busy chopping up their wagons to obtain wood for constructing packsaddles. Once the animals were outfitted, they traveled fast, passed the others along the Bear, and reached Fort Hall a day or two ahead of the wagons.

Richard Grant, a new man unfamiliar with the country, had just taken charge of Fort Hall. He had ridden into Idaho from Fort Walla Walla by a rough, short-cut horse trail; he said flatly, believing it, that wheels could not go the rest of the way to Oregon. Though he did not need wagons at Fort Hall, he agreed to accept Hastings' vehicles in exchange for supplies and horses.

Probably the trader meant to be helpful and was not endeavoring to stop wagon travel to Oregon, but the episode was the genesis of later rumors about the Hudson's Bay Company's deep-dyed plots to keep Americans out of Oregon.

Common modes of travel brought no amalgamation. The horse-mounted emigrants pushed separately along the Snake—White's party hurrying in front without a guide, Hastings' people traveling now with Hudson's Bay men. Medorem Crawford and eight more dragged in the rear with the exhausted cattle. At the island ford of the Snake, Adam Horn drowned, an accident that would be repeated at the same spot nearly every year thereafter. It was Horn whose gun had killed young Bailey near Independence Rock; the apparent retribution drew somber reflections from diarist Crawford. So did the laborious climb up Burnt Canyon out of the Snake; he could not believe wagons would ever negotiate the stretch: ". . . frightful precipices & in many places if our animals make one mis-step it would be certain death." Probably he was riding along the canyon's side in order to avoid the narrow, brush-choked bottom, but Newell's wagons had fought, and those of later emigrants would fight, their way right up the stream bed. Also, weariness helped make this last section look even more foreboding than it was. The first glimpse of the Blue Mountains, said Crawford, "struck us with terror . . . their lofty peaks seemed a resting place for clouds." Reality was less dramatic—"very sidling and uncomfortable rocky."

By the time Crawford reached Whitman's mission, Elijah White had delivered his shattering letter and had gone on down the Columbia by boat. Most of the others rode horseback along the south bank, heads bent against a sand-laden wind that whipped through the upper gorge full into their faces. Beyond the Dalles mission, where the riders rested and procured Indian guides, the deepening gorge forced them back into the Cascade Mountains— "horid road, logs & mud holes," rocks, precipices, foaming side streams, very little grass and dripping trees. The animals grew "hollow and weak." But they made it through to the falls of the Willamette River, beside which McLoughlin was just about to plant a new townsite called Oregon City, the first noncompany village in the Northwest. Stephen Meek, it is said, bought the first lot. If so, it was appropriate; all the way, mountain men had been in the van.

The settlers of Oregon City paid little attention to Elijah White's pretensions of authority. Finally, save for an interlude when he endeavored to be appointed territorial governor, he settled down to being a reasonably useful Indian agent in almost hopeless circumstances. His old rival, Lansford Hastings, also found Oregon less rewarding than he had expected and drifted down into California, out of this story.

Behind them, meanwhile, Marcus Whitman was reacting with consternation to the letter White had brought from the American Board. Ashamed of their own clashes, he and his colleagues had tried to resolve some of their difficulties. Thorny Asa Smith had already resigned; William Gray was about to, and go to work for the Methodists. Promised relief from those stormy petrels, the others had held an emotional love feast and were prepared to turn back to their work with renewed vitality—only to have the Board order the abandonment of every mission but one!

Whitman sent out Indian runners to summon his fellows to an emergency council. He himself already knew what he hoped they would agree to. He wanted to ride East during the winter, present the claims of the mission to the Board, and return West with the emigration of 1843, of whose probable formation he had been assured by Elijah White.

19

DESTINY'S MEN

The agitated missionaries who gathered at Waiilatpu on September 26, 1842, at first objected strenuously to Whitman's plan of riding East. Jealousy contributed to the trouble, as did suspicions of what he might say to the Board behind their backs. They said that the only available doctor should not desert his post. In addition, they felt genuine concern: Whitman's health was poor and much of the ride would have to be made during winter.

He won them by promising that he would not leave unless he found a way to keep Waiilatpu functioning during his absence and that if he did go he would carry with him letters from each of them, presenting their individual views. Why they returned on September 29 to their own stations to write these letters is not clear, but they did and during the time lag Whitman found occasion for breaking his word.

Staying at the mission during the conferences was Asa L. Lovejoy, who had been second-in-command, under Hastings, of the 1842 emigration. Before Spalding, Eells, and Walker were well out of Waiilatpu, Lovejoy offered to ride East with the doctor, an astounding gesture. Presumably Lovejoy had paused at Waiilatpu because he had not felt up to continuing to the Willamette. Yet after only two weeks' rest he was willing to make an infinitely more difficult ride back over the trail he had just crossed. It seems he must have tasted the elixir that was intoxicating White and Hastings and hoped he might promote himself into similar power by meeting the emigrants of 1843.

Whitman waited for no letters from his colleagues. On October 3, with a saddle horse each and two or three pack animals, the two men started for Fort Hall. Gray, who was leaving for the Willamette, promised to send back someone to run the station. It turned out to be a man named William Geiger.

Before Geiger arrived, a Cayuse Indian tried to break into Narcissa's room. In terror she fled the next morning to Fort Walla Walla with the three half-breed children for whom she was caring—Helen Mar Meek, Mary Ann Bridger (Old Gabe's daughter), and little David Malin, an anonymous waif for whom she had invented a name after he had been abandoned by his Mexican father and Indian mother. The rest of the winter and the next summer, her own health in wretched condition, she spent either at the Methodist mission at the Dalles or visiting the McLoughlins at Fort Vancouver. Behind her, the sullen Cayuses burned down the flour mill at Waiilatpu. Indian Agent White thereupon bustled in to set matters right, and William Geiger was able to pass the time until Whitman's return without any more undue trouble.

The doctor's own winter was far more taxing. At Fort Hall, he and Lovejoy were warned that the Sioux were still on the warpath along the Sweetwater and North Platte. To avoid the savages, the travelers decided on a thousand-mile detour through New Mexico. According to reminiscences which Lovejoy wrote in 1876, they went up the Bear River, somehow got around to the south side of the chill Uinta Mountains, and found brief refuge at Fort Wintey (Uinta) on the Duchesne River of eastern Utah.

Fort Wintey, as dreary a place as Fort Davy Crockett in Brown's Hole, was run by a Taos trader named Antoine Robidoux. Between Wintey and Taos, about where the western Colorado town of Delta now stands, Robidoux maintained another miserable post called Fort Uncompahgre. Using one of Robidoux's men as a guide, Whitman and Lovejoy managed to work a way to Uncompahgre through the rugged mesas that straddle today's Colorado–Utah border. There they obtained another guide, a Mexican, and turned east up the vast sagebrush valley of the Gunnison River. Evidently they were seeking to cross Cochetopa Pass into the San Luis Valley.

Crenellated buttes feathered with forests of pine and aspen embraced the wide valley on either side; down the middle twisted the incredible granitic canyons of the Gunnison. Somewhere in those gray wastes a blizzard engulfed the wayfarers. The guide panicked. Leaving Lovejoy alone in camp for an entire week, Whitman took the man back to Fort Uncompahgre and got another guide. Somehow, after eating a pet dog and a mule, they broke through into the San Luis Valley, turned south, and followed well-worn trails along the Rio Grande to the settlements in New Mexico, arriving in mid-December. For the short remainder of Whitman's life, his face and hands bore the scars of the journey's frostbite.

Trader Charles Bent reoutfitted the two men and gave them a guide for crossing the final range of mountains northeastward to Bent's Fort on the Arkansas River, near present La Junta, Colorado. Bent had survived an ordeal or two in his own life, and was amazed at what the doctor had accomplished. To a correspondent he wrote, "Dr. Whitman left heare [December 22] well prepared; and I think that I am not mistaken when I tell you I believe him to be a man not to be stoped by trifles."

Shortly before reaching the Arkansas, they encountered Charles' brother, George Bent. He told them that a party of mountain men was about to leave the fort for Missouri. In order to overtake them Whitman broke his hitherto inflexible rule against Sunday travel. Lovejoy and the guide dragged behind. When they reached the huge adobe post they were dumfounded to learn that Whitman had not appeared. A great scurry began. An express raced forty miles down the river to tell the Missouri party to wait. Searchers took to the back trails. They soon found the doctor, "despondent [Lovejoy remembered] and fatigued, convinced he had gotten lost because he had traveled on Sunday."

Lovejoy was in worse shape. He collapsed at Bent's Fort and stayed until summer. Whitman caught the Missouri party and rode with them to Independence, arriving in mid-February 1843. As he hurried through the state toward Washington, he talked to enough prospective emigrants to sense something of the Oregon excitement which was building on the frontier. This knowledge he carried with him to the nation's capital. There, still dressed in trail-stained buckskins and a ragged buffalo-hide overcoat, he possibly saw President Tyler and certainly saw some of Tyler's cabinet. To them he proposed not military forts along the Oregon Trail, but a series of government ranches to help future migrations with supplies and livestock, and to serve as stations for mail carriers.[1]

When Whitman arrived in Boston, his appearance offended the American Board. They gave him money for new clothes and clearly let him know that he should not have abandoned his post. Cleaned up, he doggedly told them what he had come so far to say: Closure of the missions would amount to surrendering the Indians of the interior to the Roman Catholics, firmly established both in the Bitterroot Valley to the east and at all

---

[1] Congress preferred military installations, and on May 19, 1846, passed an act authorizing them. The war with Mexico delayed their development until 1848, when Fort Kearney was completed on the lower Platte. In 1849 the War Department purchased Fort Laramie from the successors of the American Fur Company and rebuilt the establishment as an Army post.

the Hudson's Bay Company's posts to the west. Even Fort Vancouver's powerful factor, John McLoughlin, had been converted by the Papists. Whitman further assured the Board that Spalding and he were overcoming their differences. And almost certainly he added that Waiilatpu would be called on to afford Christian succor to increasing numbers of white emigrants.

His stubbornness prevailed. The missions stayed open and the Spaldings were retained on trial. Wearily then, Whitman went home to Rushville, New York, for a brief visit. There he adopted one more waif for Narcissa to take care of—his motherless twelve-year-old nephew, Perrin Whitman. With the boy he returned to Independence to join the wagon train.

The fever had swelled incredibly since his passage only three months before. The failure of the Ashburton-Webster treaty to settle the Oregon question had led Senator Linn to reopen debate on his bill, and on February 3, 1843, it had squeaked through the Senate by a 24–22 vote. Though it died without vote in the House a month later during the confusion of adjournment, the frontier was now convinced that passage of a comparable bill was only a matter of time and that those persons first on the scene in Oregon would have the pick of the free lands when the country was declared open for settlement.

Emigrant societies mushroomed in Missouri, Iowa, Arkansas, Illinois, Ohio. Some of them financed an agent in Washington to keep them informed about legislation and to lobby (unsuccessfully) for an escort of troops—J. M. Shively, who soon went to Oregon himself and in 1846 published a guidebook based on his experiences. Typical of the widely scattered groups was the Oregon Emigration Society of Bloomington, Iowa. Proposing on April 1, 1843, to societies in Independence and Columbia, Missouri, that they rendezvous together, the Bloomington group declared that its members already had engaged a physician and expected a chaplain to accompany the enterprise. It outlined plans to elect captains, lieutenants, and sergeants who would take charge of funds, accept or reject candidates at discretion, and make monthly reports to the company. "No negroes or mulattoes shall be allowed to accompany the expedition under any pretense whatsoever. . . . Every man ought to carry with him a Bible and other religious books, as we hope not to degenerate into a state of barbarism."

Those who had made up their minds to go wrote enthusiastic letters to newspapers and addressed town meetings in an effort to persuade others to join them. Among these was Peter H. Burnett, a future governor of California. Burnett kept a store in Weston, Missouri, across the river and north of Fort Leavenworth. He was deeply in debt, his wife was sick, he had six children. In healthful Oregon a family as large as his might be worth 1760 acres. On the strength of that he persuaded his creditors to let him try to remedy his fortunes in the Northwest.

By energetically stumping the area throughout the winter, he secured promises of association from several neighbors. They agreed to gather at a rendezvous point twelve miles west of Independence. On May 8, Peter Burnett started West with everything he owned stowed in two wagons, each pulled by four oxen. His family took turns walking or riding in a lighter vehicle drawn by a pair of mules. Hollywood to the contrary, these vehicles, like those used by practically all the early migrants, were ordinary canvas-covered farm wagons, not the big Conestoga freighters employed in the Santa Fe trade.

Throughout May similar groups straggled into Independence, creating a monstrous hubbub as they competed with each other and with the Santa Fe traders for extra mules, riding horses, work oxen, harness, saddles, flour, rice, coffee, guns, bullwhips, hardware, tools, rough clothing, and scores of other items needed for the long trip. Although traveling communally, the emigrants soon learned the wisdom of self-sufficiency. As J. M. Shively would put it in his guidebook, "When you start over these wide plains, let no one leave dependent on his best friend for anything; if you do you will certainly have a blow-out before you get far."

Word had spread through Missouri that livestock throve in Oregon. One source of the information was Robert Shortess, who, it will be remembered, had started West with Thomas Jefferson Farnham's party from Peoria. After reaching the Willamette on his own in the spring of 1840, Shortess had written glowing letters back to his friends, the Applegate family, urging them to follow him to land's end.

There were three Applegate brothers, Charles, Lindsay, and Jesse. Jesse was the dominant one—a spare, loose-jointed, indefatigable six-footer who had been known to walk as much as sixty miles a day about his business of surveying. Although he had graduated from a small college in Illinois and had read law in St. Louis, the outdoors pulled Jesse Applegate more powerfully than did courtrooms. While still in his teens he had tried to sign on with William Sublette's mountain men. Sublette advised him to stick to his books. Instead, Jesse turned to surveying in the recently vacated Indian lands of western Missouri. Marrying, he settled in the Osage Valley.

His brothers Charles and Lindsay took farms nearby. So did several slave-owners. Objecting to slavery and stirred by the letters from their friend Shortess, Lindsay ran an advertisement in a local newspaper announcing their intention to migrate and inviting other families to join them. Proceeds from the sale of their farms they invested in a herd of several hundred cattle, contemplating with serene confidence a far longer drive than the more famous ones made years later by Texas trail herds seeking the railroad towns of Kansas. Though the Applegate herd was the largest of the 1843 migration, many other migrants also appeared with scores of horned beasts. Added to the mules, horses, and draft oxen, these resulted in a shifting, bawling, hungry mass of animals estimated at close to 5000 head.

The people were as unsettled and confused as the animals. Estimates of their numbers vary between 875 and 1000. One pat census reported exactly twice as many men as women, 260 to 130, and 610 children, an average of nearly five offspring for each adult female. As their guide as far as Fort Hall this bewildered congregation hired a former mountain man named John Gantt. At least one small group, alarmed by the numbers, broke away from the main body and went off ahead; two of their number, Overton Johnson and William H. Winter, later wrote books about their experiences.

Sir William Drummond Stewart was back in the United States. He and his old friend William Sublette were taking several "companionable adventurers" on a paid excursion to the headwaters of the Green River. In the heterogeneous party were a few European hunters, several hot young sports from St. Louis, two German botanists, two Army officers, an ailing journalist from New Orleans, assorted wide-eyed boys, and various hired help. A little beyond the Kansas the group increased its variety by overtaking and absorbing two Jesuit missionaries and their helpers bound, with a Flathead Indian guide, for the Bitterroot Valley. All told, the excursionists numbered ninety-three persons and forty-three carts and light wagons.

As if emigrants, sportsmen, and Santa Fe traders weren't already burden enough on the neighborhood, Lieutenant John Charles Frémont disembarked at Kaw Landing with forty men, several carts, and a handsome twelve-pound cannon. He had been dispatched by the War Department on a second trail examination which this time would take him, after detours into Colorado and Utah, as far as Fort Vancouver. His guide was far-ranging Thomas Fitzpatrick.

Rawboned migrants, worried suddenly about what they had undertaken, milled everywhere, asking unanswerable questions about the trail and about Oregon. The government had done what it could to help by rushing to press Frémont's report of his first expedition. Entertaining and useful though the document proved to be, it reached no farther than South Pass. To provide something about the western end of the trail, Federal hacks prepared a short abstract from a voluminous report being written by Lieutenant Charles Wilkes, who during the spring and summer of 1841 had led a United States naval expedition to Puget Sound and the Columbia. Small exploring parties from his four ships had dipped as far into the interior as Tshimakain and Waiilatpu, and their findings, not yet carefully digested, added a few more crumbs to the available total of knowledge.

More data, not all of it reassuring, came from Philip Edwards, who lived in Liberty, across the river from Independence. Edwards had gone West with Jason Lee in 1834 and had returned home in 1838. On September 15, 1842, he wrote a long letter, later issued as a pamphlet by the Liberty *Herald*, in which he answered questions that had been propounded to him about Oregon. He liked the "Wal-Lam-Ette," as he spelled it—the rich yield of the soil, the healthfulness of the climate, the magnificent scenery. But he was discouraging about the road to this earthly paradise.

He said flatly that wagons could not go more than two-thirds of the way. He advised that "implements of agriculture and mechanics"—that is, plows, forges, and the like—be shipped around the Horn, since they could not be transported overland or purchased from the Hudson's Bay Company. He warned that "a company composed of men, women, and children promiscuously" would have to allow five or six months for the trip. And because of difficulties involved in finding sufficient buffalo meat and forage, no party should consist of more than 100 or 150 persons.

This made glum reading to a group of nearly a thousand persons needing feed for five thousand animals. Furthermore, they *had* to take their heavy equipment with them in wagons; it was far too late that year to arrange transportation by ship. On May 18 those emigrants already assembled in the neighborhood of Independence gathered in a meeting and faced the problems by the old American expedient of appointing committees—one to draw up a set of rules and regulations that would impose some sort of order on the mass exodus; another to inspect equipment and make sure all was sound; a third to call on Dr. Whitman for his advice about wagon travel.

Whitman's response lifted everyone's spirits. Certainly wagons could get through. This caravan possessed what Edwards and all other prior travelers had lacked—ample manpower. Scouts could travel well ahead of the train to locate the easiest routes through rough country; corps of shovel-and-axe men could dig down ravine banks and remove obstructions.

Thus reassured, the emigrants decided to depart on May 22 in one huge body—a dangerously late date, but a cold spring had delayed the sprouting of the grass. Assembly point was set for Elm Grove, a few miles farther west—a grove which, to their profane amusement, the wayfarers found to consist of one large and one small tree. As yet no pattern existed, for the committee had decided not to offer its constitution or hold elections until after the crossing of the Kansas River. By then the caravan would have had an opportunity to discover its organizational needs and to size up the leading candidates for office. (Whitman, incidentally, was never a candidate. He and his nephew stopped off at the Shawnee mission near Westport and did not overtake the caravan again until it was nearing the Platte River.)

Horace Greeley, editor of the New York *Tribune,* had not yet coined his famous "Go West, young man." When word of the massive upheaval reached him, he wrote testily in his paper (July 22, 1843) "This emigration of more than a thousand persons in one body to Oregon wears the aspect of insanity."

Jesse Applegate found different words for it. Years later he wrote proudly that the emigrants,

> with no previous preparation, relying only on the fertility of their invention ... have undertaken to perform, with slow-moving oxen, a journey of two thousand miles. The way lies over trackless wastes, wide and deep rivers, rugged and lofty mountains, and is beset with hostile savages. Yet, whether it were a deep river with no tree upon its bank, a rugged defile where even a loose horse could not pass, a hill too steep for him to climb, or a threatened attack of an enemy, they are always found ready and equal to the occasion, and always conquerors. May we not call them men of destiny?

The start was romantic enough. Throughout the day and far into the night of May 21 wagons and bawling cattle poured into Elm Grove. A full moon gleamed on the canvas tops; campfires twinkled. Horsemen galloped back and forth; violins and banjos played. "Our long journey," Peter Burnett remembered, "thus began in sunshine and in song, in anecdote and laughter; but these all vanished before we reached its termination."

Lacking at the outset the least semblance of discipline, Applegate's men of destiny seemed likely to bear out Horace Greeley's estimate. As the line began its slow march westward, drivers injured their stock and wagons racing each other for preferred positions. At night they indulged in clamorous fist fights over campsites and woodpiles. Somehow or other, though, they followed the Santa Fe Trail southwest across Bull Creek, just beyond present Gardner, Kansas. There they veered northwest to their route's first sharp obstacle, the Wakarusa River, flowing northwest to join the Kansas. They had to let their wagons down its steep banks by ropes. Two days later they creaked up to the Kansas River. There they built two large canoes, fastened them side by side, and bridged the intervening space with a platform of poles. Onto this shaky ferry they rolled each of their 120 wagons by hand and towed them across by ropes. The livestock were forced to swim; humans were rowed in boats. The laborious crossing took five days.

On June 1, when most of the people were across, the wagons assembled in a haphazard group for the election of a captain, orderly sergeant, and a council of nine to hear and settle whatever disputes might arise. Peter Burnett was voted captain; James Nesmith, a vigorous, strutting bachelor of twenty-two or -three became sergeant. Election to the council then began. During it, Sublette's and Stewart's excursionists rode by; one of their number, ailing journalist Matt Field of the New Orleans *Picayune,* later (November 21, 1843) wrote an account of the procedure for his readers.

According to Field, the candidates stood in a row behind the all-male electorate. At a given signal the vote-seekers marched away across the prairie. "The general mass broke after them 'lick-a-ty split,' each man forming in behind his favorite, so that every candidate flourished a sort of tail of his own, and the man with the longest tail was elected." This really was running for office. The shouting lines began to prance and serpentine. Matt Field chuckled and then grew reflective:

> They were going with stout and determined hearts to traverse a wild and desolate region, and take possession of a far corner of their country, destined to prove a new and strong arm of a mighty nation—and here they were running around in strings like boys playing snap the whip, to confuse the judges.

Almost immediately Captain Burnett found that he had accepted a thornier office than he could handle. The contention arose over the cattle. Although the savages farther west seldom troubled the animals, the thievish propensities of the semi-civilized Kansas Indians made night guarding necessary. Men without cattle or with only a family cow along for milk objected to spending part of the inclement nights watching someone else's livestock. Furthermore, the unwieldy herd held everyone back. Bad cess to 'em; we're going on ahead.

(Drenching rains added to the ill humor. Farther on toward the Platte, water ran two inches deep through the tents of Stewart's sports. Unable to build fires, they supped on cracker crumbs and whiskey. "Is this what you call a pleasure expedition?" one growled at his host. The Johnson-Winter party, traveling just ahead of the main body of emigrants, ran into such wind-whipped deluges that the mules refused to proceed and "we were therefore . . . compelled to wait on the pleasure of our long-eared masters.")

Burnett struggled for a compromise and thought he had found one when the cattle-owners agreed that if the caravan held together they would supply everyone with beef until buffalo became plentiful. The others rejected the offer. Unable to find a solution and hoping to save face, Burnett resigned on the grounds of ill health.

The caravan split in half. Sixty-one wagons belonging to families possessing no more than three cows each went ahead, with William Martin as their captain. Approximately the same number of cattle-owners elected Jesse Applegate as captain and dropped in behind. Thanks to better organization and discipline, the cow column, as it was called, soon discovered that it could match the pace of the advance group.

(Sublette's and Stewart's excursionists were also having troubles with unity. On June 7 and again on June 14 several disgruntled members turned back. They did not like the rain, the wet nights of guard duty, the daily chores. They called Sublette "His Omnipotence" and growled at his "blind and bad management." Some did not relish Sir William any better and threatened to shoot him for "overbearing rudeness." Amity was never a characteristic of travelers on the Oregon Trail. Yet perhaps a more docile people would not have tried to make the crossing. And at least they were free to do as they chose.)

So that no one would eat dust perpetually, the wagons were divided into platoons of four. Each platoon moved ahead one notch in line each day until it had its turn at the lead. Then it dropped to the rear to begin the process over again. If one wagon of the platoon was late at the moment of starting, all four lost their place. This encouraged cooperation within the groups in hurrying along their own laggards.

Each morning the guide, John Gantt, struck out ahead with a handful of road-builders. With a flag he marked ravine crossings or the easiest way around bogs. If necessary, some of the workers halted to smooth the path. Gantt also picked each nooning spot and each night's stopping place, a choice determined both by the speed of the caravan in respect to that day's terrain and by the availability of grass, fuel, and water. Because the Platte was turbid, camp was often made where clearer liquid could be obtained by digging shallow wells at the river's edge. Naturally no spot ever pleased everyone.

Later caravans sometimes traveled in double lines or even four abreast; this allowed the wagons to swing more quickly into defensive circles in case of Indian attack. Always, of course, there were individuals who slid out of line to avoid dust and rough spots or to indulge personal whim. But in general the early caravans traveled single file. The teamsters, often youths working for their board, rode in the wagon or walked beside the oxen. The father of a family was often on horseback with the hunters or the road workers or the cattle. The women and children often left the wagons to walk for long stretches, romping or picking flowers according to their ages. Hordes of dogs roamed everywhere. Many seem to have been greyhounds or Irish wolfhounds that furnished brief amusement by futilely trying to run down the antelope that occasionally came near.

Loose horses and mules trooped behind the wagons. Behind them came the huge, square, variegated herd of horned cattle. It was a phlegmatic, resistant mass, always wanting to stop and eat and always having to be forced ahead by whips wielded from horseback and by what Applegate called "loud objurgations."

Irritations were constant. Buffalo trails, sometimes worn a foot deep, jarred loose carelessly packed loads and on occasion broke axletrees. Draft oxen grew lame from cactus spines or the charred stubble of grass which Indians had burned. Hooves cracked and bled; dirt and more stubble entered; the foot festered and swelled. As soon as the caravan paused, noon or night, the owner of the ox washed the hoof with strong soap, scraped away the diseased flesh, and poured on boiling pitch or tar. The treatment was said to work.

At noon the platoons halted abreast, an arrangement that allowed friends and families to be together during rest stops. Teams were unhitched from the wagons but not unyoked, taken to water, and let graze. At one o'clock bugles sounded and the march resumed. Early rising hours had seldom allowed sufficient sleep during the preceding night, and the afternoon's oppressive heat increased drowsiness until the caravan crawled on like a great somnolent snake.

Toward sunset the lead wagons saw John Gantt motioning. On horseback he led the drivers into a circle he had marked out, exactly the right size to hold the vehicles in his care. They halted with tongues angling toward the inside, close enough to each other for a defensive ox chain to reach from one vehicle to the next and so accurately placed that the last wagon to enter closed the ring.

While the men cared for the stock and pitched the tents, the women of each platoon or mess gathered the cooking gear together and the children ranged the prairie to pick up buffalo chips. They pelted each other, of course, stole from each other's piles, and fell into noisy squabbles. Finally the meal was cooked and eaten, the dishes scoured. As the first stars appeared in the apple-green evening sky, a violin here and there struck up a tune. The men told yarns; the women gossiped; the young people flirted. At eight o'clock the first watch went out to its positions; and soon the camp was quiet save for the chomping of the horses and mules within the corral and the occasional racketing of the dogs.

At four in the morning the sentinels fired their rifles to waken the sleepers. The migrants poured groggily from their tents and began again the endless routine of cooking, packing, moving. Half the men caught horses from the herd inside the corral and jogged out to round up the cattle, some of which had grazed off as far as two miles during the night. A careful examination of the ground for tracks revealed whether any had strayed beyond sight. As the draft oxen were driven close, a furious confusion began. No one wanted to lose his place in line. The tents were hastily struck, the wagons loaded, the teams caught and hitched. The guide raised his hand, a trumpet sounded, the circle broke into a line. Another fifteen or twenty miles, one day's average travel, stretched ahead.

Stragglers were still laboring across the Kansas ford when Whitman and his nephew arrived there. Nearby was Frémont's camp. (The explorer intended to leave the usual trail at the ford, strike due west into Colorado, and find—if possible—an easier approach to the Rockies than the Platte Valley. He did not; if one had existed, the mountain men would long since have located it.) Whitman stayed a night with him, talked Oregon, and the next morning began urging the stragglers to increased efforts. Thanks partly to the doctor's insistence, the laggards caught the cow column about the time it reached the Platte. For the next several days Whitman stayed with the rear group, doctoring its sick and giving advice about travel and camping. Since he had almost no equipment of his own, he and Perrin ate unabashedly at the different messes. Some of their unwilling hosts grumbled for years about the sponging.

When the advance column reached the South Platte, they found the stream flooded by the melting of heavy snows in the distant mountains. Goods, women, and children had to be ferried in boats improvised from wagon boxes covered with buffalo hides. The oxen pulling the empty vehicles were then belabored into the flood. Chains running from wagon to wagon helped prevent the current from sweeping the vehicles away, and shouting riders on the downstream side of the draft animals kept them from turning back. The only casualty was a mule accidentally killed by rifle fire. The men were careless with their shooting. "If serious accidents do not occur," Sergeant Nesmith complained to his diary, "they will be avoided by great good luck, not precaution." (Up ahead, between the North Platte and the Sweetwater, a fifteen-year-old boy traveling with Sublette and Stewart shot himself fatally through the chest.)

Crossing the South Platte, sorting out the ferried goods, and reloading the wagons took several days. During the turmoil, Whitman and Jesse Applegate rode in from the cow camp, waiting eight miles to the rear. They went directly to the wagon of a family named Stewart, which had pulled away from the cursing workers and bawling livestock. A little later word sped through the camp that Mrs. Stewart had been successfully delivered of a baby. Until then most of the advance column had been unaware of Whitman's presence. Now their spirits lifted and the crossing was finished in high humor.

From that point on Whitman traveled mostly with the advance party, helping Gantt work out the easiest paths. Continual worries assailed them. Hunters became lost. It was no country for greenhorns. As soon as a man had pushed behind the bluffs bordering the North Platte, he found himself in a featureless immensity. "No place in the world," mountain man Jim Clyman wrote during the emigration of 1844, "looks more lonesome and discourageing than the wide Prairies of this region   neither tree bush shrub rock nor water to cherish or shelter him and such a perfect sameness. . . ."

In this vastness the normal herds of buffalo did not appear as often as anticipated. Angrily the migrants blamed the excursionists ahead of them for frightening the animals away. To an extent the charge was true. But their own trigger-happy members contributed. Nearly everyone in every caravan wanted to shoot a buffalo. Whenever a herd was sighted a frenzied group raced pell-mell after it, shooting indiscriminately and driving away far more meat than they ever secured.

They crossed the Laramie River on improvised rafts. (Legend says that only Whitman was willing to plunge first into the stream aboard his mule and carry a tow line across.) Like locusts they fell on the storerooms at Forts Laramie and Platte, driving prices up with their own competition and then complaining of high costs. The garishly dressed Sioux were amazed at their numbers. Journalist Matt Field wrote that the Indians thought all the whites were moving West and seriously discussed going East to occupy the vacated lands—the initial appearance of a *bon mot* that would be repeated regularly during the larger migrations of later years.

For two days the tired wayfarers camped on the meadows between the streams, refreshing themselves and their stock. There was even a dance at Fort Platte. Many would have liked to have rested longer. But Whitman kept goading them ahead, harping endlessly, as Applegate remembered his words, on one ruthless theme: " 'Travel, travel, travel—nothing else will take you to the end of your journey; nothing is wise that does not help you along.' " Groaning, they fell once more into their dusty line. That was the heroics of the migration: not Indian scares or thrilling buffalo hunts or flooded stream crossings but rather this remorseless, unending, weather-scoured, nerve-rasping plod on and on and on and on, foot by aching foot.

They banged off across the toes of the Laramie Mountains, crushing out a way through the knotted sagebrush, so that when Frémont came up out of Colorado a few weeks later he found a "broad, smooth highway . . . and we moved up the valley rapidly and pleasantly." So far the emigrants had been lucky, but now sudden accidents reminded them of their mortality. Bored children, fooling around, fell under the wagon wheels. One was crushed to death near the ford of the North Platte; a similar happening sorely hurt Jesse Applegate's nephew and namesake. This was another accident nearly every later caravan would meet in turn.

They left the river at the Red Buttes, where the Pathfinder Reservoir now glimmers, and creaked past Poison Creek, over the gaunt deserts to the Sweetwater. On Independence Rock someone painted proudly:

THE OREGON CO.
arrived
July 26, 1843

Showing off for two girls, Sergeant Nesmith climbed even higher up the brown, wind-glazed sides and painted their names and his own above the legend.

Nerves were fraying. Arguments erupted about hunting procedures and rates of travel. Forage was increasingly scarce. To expedite the finding of food for both men and beasts, the company split into smaller segments and toiled in ragged bunches past the naked Rattlesnake Hills. Indian alarms resulted in emergency meetings but did not succeed in reuniting the caravan. A man sickened and died, just as men do everywhere, and the travelers grew still more nervous. The clean white thrust of the Wind River peaks, bearing a summer snow few of them had ever seen before, gave their spirits only the briefest of lifts. Would this trip never end?

One comes slowly onto South Pass. Even using instruments the year before, Frémont had experienced difficulty in deciding exactly where the separation between Atlantic and Pacific drainages lay. In lieu of other markings, there in the wide gray swales, with the startling Wind River peaks rising to the north and the broken buttes of Table Mountain flat-topped against the sky to the south —in that wide gray depression later travelers took as their beacon a pair of small, almost identical cone-shaped hillocks nippled with crumbly white rock. They stand just short of the top on the Atlantic side. But it became customary to regard the cleavage between them as the gateway to the Pacific and to pass through (though it was equally practical to go to either side) with rifle fire and huzzahs. No indication exists, however, that the early caravans held any such ceremony. They labored over the dry, dusty Divide without knowing they had crossed until they saw the unfathomable immensities beyond. Most divides, for individuals or for nations, are equally imperceptible. Like the migrants of '43, the United States was far over the line into Oregon before the bulk of its people truly apprehended the fact.

The fur caravans of the 1830s, bound for rendezvous points high on the Green—at the mouth of New Fork near today's Big Piney or Horse Creek, near present Daniel—followed more or less the dry eastern leg of what later emigrants, principally the stampeders of gold-rush days, would call Greenwood's or Sublette's Cutoff. From South Pass they went down Pacific Creek to the Little Sandy and then to Big Sandy, sinuous streams on whose banks only a little runty willow brush grew. From either the Little or the Big Sandy they made a long, waterless jump to the Green—how long depended on how far down the Sandy they went before striking due west across the alkali flats: the thirsty hop might be as much as fifty miles and take an entire day and night.

Whitman and his party had made such a jump in 1836. Sublette's and Stewart's excursionists of 1843 made it also, then turned north to the icy, trout-filled lakes the Scot loved so well. The Catholic missionaries and the two German botanists did not. With their Flathead Indian guide they left the excursionists at the beginning of the cutoff and continued southwest, keeping cautiously near the Sandy's life-giving waters. Their only short cuts were direct little hops through the sagebrush in their carts from one of the stream's innumerable bends to the next. Reaching the Green, they forded it and, still traveling southwest, cut overland to Black's Fork, a lovely river coiling cold and blue between low bushes. They worked up this, crossed the future course of U.S. Highway 30S, and in what became the southwestern corner of Wyoming they found, against the magnificent backdrop of the Uinta Mountains, a grubby handful of mud-daubed log cabins surrounded by a stockade of upright pickets. This was Fort Bridger.

Jim Bridger, Old Gabe, seems to have hit on the idea of a post in the summer of 1841. He did not intend it for emigrants, but as a supply center so that the few trappers remaining in the mountains could hang on and rattle a little longer. He began one stockade beside the Green, decided against the location, and moved over to Black's Fork. It would prove a handy location to Mormons bound for Utah, but not for emigrants traveling to Oregon. Still, that is where the Catholics went, probably because they needed supplies. How they knew the post was there does not appear.

At this point Whitman and a group of scouts were riding in advance of the emigrant train, looking for a way to the Green that would not kill half the livestock with thirst; the route he remembered from 1836 would not do at all. They saw the tracks of the Catholics' carts, wondered at the continued southwestern cast, and then met someone who gave them a strange piece of information. At least Whitman sent a letter back to the train saying, as Burnett recalled the episode, that the missionaries' Flathead pilot had discovered a shorter route to the mountains by way of Bridger's post. "We, therefore, determined to go by the fort." Not quite everyone, though—somewhere along the Sandy another man sickened and died.

This long southern dip to Fort Bridger was much smoother than the mountainous western end of Sublette's Cutoff, but it was by no means shorter either in miles or in traveling time. Someone at the fort may have been spreading tales to lure customers. Anyway, the migrants stripped the shelves of the post as bare as they had stripped Fort Laramie. Whitman, still agitating for government trading houses along the trail, would estimate later that the travelers spent $2000 at the posts, wording the statement in such a way that it is not clear whether each fort collected that much or whether the sum is a total. In any event, it was enough to give Bridger a new concept of the future. All he needed was credit for laying in a stock of goods against next year's migration. In December he wrote Pierre Chouteau, Jr., in St. Louis (or rather, being illiterate, he hired someone to write for him) that the wagon trains arrived "in need of all kinds of supplies, horses, provisions, smithwork, etc. They bring ready cash from the states, and should I receive the goods ordered will have considerable business in that way with them." But he wasn't forgetting the old days either. Wistfully he added, "and establish trade with the Indians in the neighborhood, who have a good number of beaver among them."

With the Catholics and the German botanists accompanying them now, the caravan turned northwest across a sage ridge to the Little Muddy and inched up its valley through aspen groves and among islands of evergreens to a higher, more scenic divide than South Pass—Frémont, traveling just behind them, calculated that it was 8200 feet above sea level. A steep pitch then dropped them into Bear River Valley. Strung out for miles through its grassy swales, they paused to let their stock recuperate.

There Frémont came upon them. In him and his semi-military cavalcade the United States government suddenly became visible west of the Continental Divide. The different camps cheered his group lustily as the men jogged briskly by. Whenever he paused, wide-eyed boys clambered eagerly over his howitzer, here where General Ashley had brought a smaller cannon only sixteen years before, the first wheels ever to reach Oregon territory.

One Applegate youngster recalled later that he and his friends also tried unsuccessfully to plug up hot Steamboat Springs, a small geyser that puffed away on the riverbank, in the cedar-shaded area embracing Soda Springs. It was all very homelike—"an air of quiet security and civilized comfort that made a rare sight . . . in such a remote wilderness," Frémont wrote in the report that soon would be devoured by thousands of people in the East. Such reassurances swayed many a later emigrant hesitating over whether or not to risk the terrible uprooting.

At Fort Hall a third man died. At Fort Hall also Whitman received several hundred pounds of flour sent by pack train from Lapwai and Waiilatpu for distribution to the neediest travelers. Good wheat flour here in the West—that was reassuring too. But then the trader in charge, Richard Grant, told the wayfarers that wagons could not be taken to the Columbia. The emigrants stared at each other in dismay. There were not enough horses at Fort Hall to carry their women, children, food, and household goods.[2] What were they to do?

Cheerily Whitman told them. They would take their wagons. Robert Newell had done it a few years earlier. With the amount of manpower the caravan had for building roads and chopping trees in the Blue Mountains, they could manage equally well, could they not?

They believed him because they had to. They took up a collection of four hundred dollars and offered it to him if he would serve as guide. (John Gantt, his contract fulfilled, had left the Oregonians to join a small party bound for California with a load of machinery for a sawmill.) Whitman agreed. With renewed courage the train forded the broad Portneuf and moved into desolation.

The first part of their journey from the settlements had offered at least the charms of fresh grass, myriad flowers, a sense of novelty. Now there was only the need for endurance—lava boulders to bang across, steep-rimmed streams to pitch into, sagebrush to crash through, a desiccated crumbly soil that ground to power under the wheels and puffed up in choking clouds of dust. The groan of wagons in their ears; dry eyes stung by alkali; stench of

---

[2] The available supply of animals was reduced each year by restless migrants, mostly young bachelors, who, as soon as danger from Indians was deemed past, pushed ahead of the main groups, bought horses at Fort Hall, and finished the journey by pack train, reaching the Willamette sometimes weeks ahead of the slow-moving wagons.

bruised sage and overheated oxen; taste of warm dust and cow hairs—"Travel! Nothing is good for you that causes a moment's delay." Whitman ranged ahead with the advance scouts to find places that could be turned into a road, then hurried back to pull the straggling wagons together. An early snow catching them in the Blue Mountains might be fatal. *Travel!* "... the greatest and most painful anxiety to us," Peter Burnett recalled years later, "was the suffering of our poor animals. We could see our faithful oxen dying inch by inch."

At the ford of the Snake a man named Miles Eyres drowned while helping push the cow herd across the river. Whitman promised his distraught wife and children as long a refuge at Waiilatpu as they needed. They crawled down the Boise, fought a way across the river again, struggled up the nightmare of Burnt Canyon. Out on the flats leading to Powder River some weary emigrant, tired of cooking over sagebrush and long since past caring about noble landmarks, felled for fuel the great lone pine that had been a beacon for travelers since the days of the fur brigades that fat Donald McKenzie had first led into the country for the North West Company.

An Indian messenger reached Whitman with word that both Henry and Eliza Spalding were dying of scarlet fever. He turned the guiding of the train over to Stickus, a semi-educated Cayuse Indian whom he trusted, and hurried ahead to Lapwai. He found the Spaldings out of danger but then had to ride far north to Tshimakain to deliver Myra Eells of a baby. So he missed the passage of the train through Waiilatpu. Some of the men broke into the mission storehouse and helped themselves; others paid for what they got but complained bitterly over the high prices which William Geiger, acting on Whitman's instructions, charged for such supplies as he possessed. And when the doctor brought Narcissa home, sick and distraught, from the Dalles mission, he had to show her thirty-eight shattered people (including their own mission "family" of forsaken half-breeds) crowded into her rooms and demanding a winter-long succor she could not refuse. With reason she dreaded the passing of the caravans each fall (1844 would bring her seven orphaned Sager children to adopt).

In spite of the train's ingratitude and the worry and hard work it bequeathed him, Marcus Whitman always remained proud of what he had done. The Indians, he realized, were doomed. They could not be civilized, he wrote the Board the next spring, "before the white settlers will demand the soil and seek the removal of both the Indians and the Mission. . . . It is equally useless to oppose or desire it otherwise." Manifest Destiny had caught up with him and changed his function from serving the Indians to serving his own race. "As I hold the settlement of this country by Americans rather than by an English colony to be most important, I am happy to have been the means of landing so large an emigration on the shores of the Columbia." Let it be remembered, he said, that he and Spalding had brought the first white women across the mountains. He had established the first wagon road "contrary to all the sinister assertions of all those who pretended it to be impossible." His arrogation of credit is perhaps too extensive. Still, there was now meaning in a life which previously had been drifting toward futility. On the threshold of a truly new world he could write at last, "I am satisfied."

From Waiilatpu the caravan rolled on down the Walla Walla River to the Columbia. What little cohesion yet remained to it ended there. Several families traded wagons for saddle horses and rode through the gorge and mountains, fighting their cattle ahead of them. Some forced their vehicles on along the river's hellish south bank, often on bluffs high above the stream, until they had passed Celilo Falls and the Dalles. Near the Dalles mission they built rafts, pushed the wagons aboard, and floated dangerously against high headwinds to the Cascades. There they hired swarms of Indians to help line the rafts through the rapids and portage the goods around.

Still others left their cattle at Fort Walla Walla or traded them for lean Mexican stock to be picked up at Fort Vancouver. Then they whipsawed driftwood into planks and built awkward craft. The Applegate family chose this method. Just above Celilo Falls their lead boat crashed into a rock. The Indian steersman and three passengers reached shore. But a seventy-year-old family retainer and two ten-year-old boys, one Jesse's son and one Lindsay's, were drowned.

It was November. The gray drizzles of fall were seeping up the tremendous gorge. Here and there little clots of people huddled on the bleak shingle or under the dripping trees. Guessing what their desperation must be like, a few of the first men through returned with supplies for the others. The settlers of the Willamette volunteered more and sent up a rescue party under Robert Shortess, who was eager to welcome his old friends to this fine new land. At Fort Vancouver, McLoughlin opened his storerooms and sent up batteaux for bringing down the people who were going to drive his company from the Northwest. After the families had gathered themselves together and dared look forward again he loaned them tools and seed. For if this immigration did not grow crops for next year's horde, then everyone might starve. All told, he extended credit that fall and winter amounting to £6600—upwards of $31,000.

Group by group they rowed across the Columbia toward the mouth of the Willamette, the last step toward whatever place it was that henceforth would cup their lives. The Applegates in their turn passed under the stern of an ocean-going Hudson's Bay Company schooner moored to the fort's dock. English sailors leaning against the railing looked down and saw the oldest girl, Lucy, sister of one of the drowned youngsters. They called to her, as sailors will, and one of them tossed her some apples from the fort's orchard. She never saw the men again. But she never forgot. No reminiscence says she smiled that night in the wet camp under the evergreens where the city of Portland now stands. Yet she must have. The human heart, no matter how niggardly or hurt it may have been on the back trails, always finds ways to pick itself up again.

TRAIL'S END

During most of the 1840s only a few settlers passed Fort Vancouver's hundreds of acres of orchards, pastures, and grain fields, and continued on toward the sites of Tacoma and Seattle. For one thing (and in spite of the operations of the Puget Sound Agricultural Company, a subsidiary of the Hudson's Bay Company), the country north of the Columbia was deemed too swampy and heavily wooded for anything save fur-trapping. For another (and in spite of the growing chant of warhawks in the United States who wanted to plant the Stars and Stripes at Fifty-Four Forty—southern Alaska—or fight), it was generally believed by emigrant politicians, as well as by men of the Hudson's Bay Company, that the land north of the river—roughly two-thirds of the present state of Washington—would eventually be awarded to Great Britain. Accordingly, the first migrants to reach the Northwest turned south from Fort Vancouver into the broad valley of the Willamette River.

The first few of the Willamette's hundred-odd miles were gloomy. To be sure, the river's spreading mouth was navigable to ocean-going vessels. By 1843 a Yankee trading ship or two had tiptoed in to try their luck bucking the Hudson's Bay Company; and in 1844 Asa Lovejoy (who had traveled as far east as Bent's Fort with Whitman on the tremendous winter ride of 1842–43) and a friend named Francis Pettygrove hopefully platted on the lower Willamette a townsite they named Portland. But the banks of the river near their imagined city were too rough and heavily wooded to permit farming; nor was there any easy way to break through the shaggy wilderness to the fertile Tualatin Plains on the west. As a result, most of the firstcomers ignored future Portland, and in small boats which they either purchased or built they pressed on upstream in quest of more manageable lands.

They soon ran into boisterous rapids formed where the Clackamas River poured into the main stream from the east. Above the rapids, the Willamette was broken even more severely by a slanting line of ragged basalt ledges. In places these ledges reared up to form islands. Split into triple channels by the islands, the Williamette shot over the ledges in a three-pronged, hoarsely bellowing, mist-shrouded waterfall.

In the season of the salmon runs, unbelievable numbers of silvery fish fought a way up the cataract—the spot once had been a favorite Indian fishing ground—and as early as 1829 McLoughlin had foreseen the water-power potentials of the site.

Whether he intended to claim the falls for himself as an individual or for the Hudson's Bay Company as its agent is not clear, but long before any permanent American settlers arrived he had started his men building shacks nearby. The exigencies of the fur trade had kept him from developing the holdings, however; and in 1840 the enlarged Methodist mission, with McLoughlin's permission, established a branch station at the strategic locale.

The next year, 1841, two of the mission members laid personal claim to the millsites. McLoughlin protested in vain, then in December 1842 countered by platting a townsite beside the falls and naming it Oregon City. His long quarrel with his rivals —it thrust waspily into the first stirrings of local government and even gave a pinprick to international politics—is beyond the scope of this work; but at least the embryo town that sprang from it provided the arriving homeseekers from the States a center from which to spread.

Spread they did, eager for farmlands, on the most part, rather than for town lots. (After its first year and a half of existence, Oregon City could boast only sixty-two buildings.) They portaged their canoes around the falls, or they acquired horses and hurried on up the valley. Just above Oregon City they found that the stream bed bent sharply to the west, ran in that direction for a dozen-plus miles, and then resumed its southward cast, a vast trough cupped between the coastal range on the west and the densely timbered, peak-punctuated Cascade Mountains on the east.

To the north of the Willamette's brief east-west bend lay the Tualatin River and the easiest approach to the rolling hills and open meadowlands called the Tualatin Plains. Unemployed trappers had congregated there. The first to settle was Ewing Young, a mountain man who had ridden up out of California with Hall Jackson Kelley in 1834, bringing with him nearly a hundred horses and mules. In 1837 Young had returned to the Golden State for more livestock (cattle this time) and had succeeded, after an epic drive, in reaching Oregon with nearly six hundred head. After he had died in 1841, one of his neighbors, Joseph Gale, led a second party to California and brought back 600 horses and mules, 1250 cattle, and 3000 sheep. By this time the Tualatin Plains were pretty well dotted with the cabins holding the Indian wives and half-breed children of several mountain men. The emigrants of 1843, including the Applegates, decided against a neighborhood so populous and continued south up the river valley, hunting lands no one had yet claimed.

Across the bend of the Willamette from the Tualatin Plains and extending for two score or more miles along the river's eastern bank was another stretch of fertile grass-and-timber land called French Prairie. The name derived from a handful of French-Canadian *voyageurs* who, on retiring from the Hudson's Bay Company in the late 1820s, had drifted up here with their squaws and Indian children and had broken out primitive farms on which to end their days. For several years they had lived in idyllic anarchy, untaxed and ungoverned save for such benevolent paternalism as McLoughlin chose to exert from Fort Vancouver. They had no fear of Indians. Game and fish abounded. Crops grew easily, and the Hudson's Bay Company bought whatever furs and surplus wheat they offered for sale. The climate was mild, the scenery magnificent; Nathaniel Wyeth rhapsodized over the locale as early as 1833. The next year, Jason Lee was easily diverted from his proposed mission among the Flatheads to a particularly lovely spot some ten miles northeast of modern Salem (and sixty miles or so north of the Willamette's confluence with the Columbia). Inevitably, a few drifters arrived from the mountains and the remnants of the fragmented 1839 party from Peoria also moved in.

Unfortunately, French Prairie's happy lack of law could not endure. Without courts, for instance, could a dead man's estate be probated? Without some central authority, how could arrangements be made to pay a bounty for killing the wolves that preyed on the settlers' flocks? More important, so long as national sovereignty remained undecided, how could a man be certain that his land titles were secure? For several years the Anglo-Saxon settlers of the Willamette fired off almost annual petitions to Washington, D.C., asking for American jurisdiction. When action did not materialize, they finally got together in a series of tumultuous meetings at Champoeg, in a grain warehouse on the north side of the Willamette's brief east-west bend, and set up a provisional government of their own.

Under the new government's involved constitution, which was adopted at a mass meeting on July 5, 1843, every settler was allowed 640 acres of land (one square mile) in either square or oblong shape. Claimants already on their plots were allowed a year in which to file their holdings with a designated recorder. Newcomers by contrast had to report their claim boundaries within twenty days of entering on the land. To hold their acreage, both groups had to erect buildings or fences within a designated time.

This was acquisition by appropriation—a sort of squatter's law, in one sense—and ran counter to what until then had been the official policy of the United States government concerning its public lands. To say that the Oregon pioneers initiated a new trend in land matters would be oversimplifying a highly complex issue. Still, there was inherent in their makeshift constitution of 1843 the seeds of the same radical idea which back East in 1850 flowered briefly as the Oregon Donation laws (free land from the government to anyone who wanted to take up a claim in the Northwest) and reached full harvest with the national Homestead Act of 1862. It was the inevitable end of the urge that had brought Anglo-Saxon freeholders to Jamestown and Plymouth Rock more than two centuries earlier—not the gold of the Spaniards or the furs of the French, but a piece of plowable soil at which a man could point and say, "That is my mine!" Anyone could obtain it, not for dollars or through inheritance but simply by having courage enough to go to the rainbow's end, find it and tame it.[1]

The Applegates and the other migrants of '43 now had official sanction of sorts for taking what they wanted. In quest of just the right piece, they fanned out over French Prairie and west across the Willamette to the empty plains lapping the coastal range. The Applegates, who in losing two children had paid a higher price to

[1] Although the land provisions of the 1843 constitution suited the migrants who arrived that same fall, little else about the document did. They disliked the privileges accorded the Methodist mission. They were astounded by the failure to provide for taxes in the starry hope that voluntary contributions would suffice for running the government. They opposed dividing the executive powers among a committee of three rather than vesting them in a single governor. Since the newcomers had arrived in such numbers that *they* now constituted a majority, they soon revamped the document, the first of a continuing series of revisions that lasted until the United States finally extended its jurisdiction over the Northwest.

the Trail than had most of the others, found shelter from the gray
November drizzles in the abandoned buildings of the original
Methodist mission.

Outside, the leaves had fallen from deciduous shrubs and trees.
That much was familiar. Totally unfamiliar, however, was the
thought of planting wheat and having it sprout and grow throughout the winter, under the nurture of the soft rains. Fresh grass was
already pushing up everywhere; cattle and sheep would need no
hay at all! (But the nights were too cold for corn, they heard, even
in summer.) And such trees! As they rode west toward the toes of
the coastal hills, where no axe had yet rung, they eyed the magnificent groves of fir—at least a hundred feet of clear lumber in a
single trunk. One acre of such trees, it was said, would produce
30,000 fence rails, so easily split out that a single man could make
300 a day. At that rate, families sharing labor could have a cabin
up, soil turned, a crop in, and fences built by the time spring had
come back again.

Meanwhile, during that spring of 1844, three new groups were
forming on the Missouri frontier to take to the trail as soon as the
late, wet spring allowed.[2] Although Congress had declined to pass
either a land bill or one extending U.S. sovereignty to the Northwest, the emigrants remained convinced that both laws were a
matter of time. Many of them were also sure that trouble with
England would develop from the expansionism, and that too was
just fine. A St. Louis newspaper reported on May 15, 1844, a song
current among the emigrants the chorus of which went:

> Then hip-hurrah for the prairie life!
> Hip-hurrah for the mountain strife!
> And if rifles must crack, if swords we must draw,
> Our country forever, hurrah, hurrah!

[2] A fourth group, guided by mountain man Elisha Stephens (perhaps the same
Stephens who was a roustabout for the Eells-Walker-Gray missionary party of
1838) split at Fort Hall, some going to California, some to Oregon. A fifth group
were health-seekers and adventurers led by Andrew Sublette, brother of William
Sublette, who had guided Sir William Drummond Stewart's excursionists across
South Pass the year before. The execrable weather of the spring of 1844 was too
severe for three or four of Andrew's invalids; they died before the supposedly
magical air of the plains could do its work. The disgruntled party eventually dis-
banded somewhere in present Wyoming.

(Not everyone admired this contentious rush to the rim of the world. Shortly after the 1844 trains had started westward, a letter-writer grumbled in the *Missouri Republican* for June 11 that as soon as the real truth about Oregon filtered back home, "the mania will run out. . . . No man of information or in his right mind, would think of leaving such a country as this, to wander over a thousand miles of desert and five hundred of mountains to reach such as that. It is wrong in the people of St. Louis to encourage this spirit of emigration.")

How many Oregon emigrants were involved in the three caravans is conjectural. Lists in contemporary newspapers suggest 700 or 800 men, women, and children shepherding 150 or so wagons, and 1500 or more head of livestock. Reminiscences by travelers (and there are surprisingly few accounts for 1844) suggest a maximum of 1500 persons, with a corresponding increase in the number of vehicles and animals.

The smallest of the three trains was captained by John Thorp. Thorp's band, which fell in with the others out toward Fort Laramie, followed the trail favored in the mid-1830s by American Fur Company caravans and by the Whitman-Spalding party; it wound up the north bank of the Platte, along the route that in 1847 and 1848 would be deep-rutted by Mormons fleeing from burning Nauvoo to sanctuary in Utah.

A second group, much larger than Thorp's and led by General Cornelius Gilliam, ferried the Missouri at various spots from St. Joseph southward and assembled at Fort Leavenworth, Kansas. Meanwhile a third party assembled at Independence. Though it started behind Gilliam's group, the Independence caravan, which elected Nathaniel Ford its captain, planned to overtake its predecessor and continue westward with them. After the amalgamation both trains would be able to share the same guide, Moses (Black) Harris, the mountain man who nearly twenty winters earlier had come East over this same route with Bill Sublette and a single pack dog which they had finally killed in order to survive.

Another famous mountain man returned West with Ford's group—James Clyman. Early in the gale-blasted spring of 1824 Clyman, along with Jedediah Smith, Bill Sublette, Thomas Fitzpatrick, and a handful of other trappers, had rediscovered South

Pass. On leaving the mountains a few years later, Clyman had invested his savings in a store in Illinois. It was too tame. Drifting into frontier Wisconsin, he had taken up a farm and had gotten himself shot by an Indian. In 1844 he felt the old pull again and impulsively decided to ride back to the mountains. At Independence he fell in with the Ford caravan.

Most of the migrants of 1844 were equally fiddle-footed. The great majority of them had settled in Missouri only a few years earlier, and now they were pulling up stakes once again, hoping for something better at the end of the sunset trail. Though ill inclined to heed authority of any sort, they recognized ability when they saw it and put Clyman in charge of one of the messes into which they divided themselves shortly after their start.

Unprecedented rains deluged them. Stream crossings were next to impossible; so was cooking, unless a family had been foresighted enough to have tossed dry wood into its wagon. Two weeks of the most laborious slogging took the Ford party fewer than a hundred miles. During the ordeal the women in particular caught the eye of the old mountaineer and he transferred his admiration to his journal:

> *May 24.* we let down our wagons by cords over a steep rock bluff through mud knee deep an in the rain pouring in torrents me[n] women and children dripping in mud and water over Shoe mouth deep and I Thought I never saw more determined resolution even amongst the men than most of the female part of our company exhibited.

> *May 26.* The Ladies gave us a few hymns in the afternoon which had a pleasant meloncholly affect.

> *May 28.* . . . after a verry tidious & toilsome dys drive I arived at my mess wet as water could make me . . . & now commenced the tug of war for the rain again renued its strength & fell in perfect sluces . . . intermingled with vived flashes of Lightning and deep growling thunder . . . and here let me say there was one young Lady which showed herself worthy of the bravest undaunted poieneer of west for after having kneaded her dough she watched and nursed the fire and held an umblella over the fire and her skillit with the greatest composure and baked bread enough to give us a verry plentifull supper. . . . Billitts of wood ox yokes Saddles and

all kinds of matter now Became in requisition to raise our bodies
above the water and we spent a verry uncomfortable night in all
forms of moisture short of swimming.

Indians stole some stock. Clyman and two friends started
through the rain after the thieves, swam two creeks, waded
three more breast-deep and ran down their quarry among twenty
drunk Indians reeling around in a dirt lodge flooded ankle-deep.
Knives flashed. "My situation was far from being envious . . . a
rapid hail Storm out a hog wallow within all in unison the Thunder Lightning & hail the Schreems an yells." They did not recover
the stock that day, but later friendly Kaws, hoping for a reward,
returned some of the missing animals.

When they reached the Kansas River it was flooded eight or
ten miles wide, but it fell rapidly and they were able to raft across
—to camp in a sea of mud. For the next month or more the
downpours continued—"June 13. . . . A great Dijection in camp."
On July 10, far behind schedule, they reached the Platte. Heat
thickened; mosquitoes swarmed; flowers appeared "Beautiful Beyond discription." They overtook Gilliam's company at last and
the combined trains stretched out to "more than two miles of
tolerable close collumn."

Occasional violent rains still plagued them. Beyond Fort Laramie still another squall flattened every tent, "not even sparing the
delicate Ladies & small children which ran helter skelter in all
directions seeking for shelter." The next evening they overtook a
party of California emigrants "and encamped in a Jumbled mass
of Stock tents people &c &c." Overeagerness on the part of too
many self-appointed hunters kept them from benefiting as much
as they should have from the numerous buffalo they saw. But at
least they were making good time along this rough stretch of
trail through the Laramie Mountains—fourteen miles a day on
the average.

On the Sweetwater, where the Rattlesnake Hills looked to Clyman like "the refuses of the world thrown up in the utmost confusion," an emigrant named Joseph Barnett started dying of
what was called typhus fever. Clyman swung off to one side to sit
up with him until the end. A passing wagon tossed out a spade,

"which looked rather ominous." But at least Jim did not have to face the long night alone. Black Harris, the guide, with whom Clyman had ridden many of these trails in the old days, returned to stay with him. Later Clyman wrote of his old comrade, "He . . . was a free and easy soul Especially with a belly full."

Their patient was a long time dying. Sunday dragged by, and Monday. Ladies from passing wagons—the train was no longer traveling in a compact column—paused to see what they could do. There was not much. Spasms seized Barnett and he writhed in agony until death came about ten o'clock in the evening. Two or three men stopped by and helped lay the shrunken body out on a bed of fresh willows. Then, while the graying skin caught ruddy glints from the campfire, they sat around and, Clyman said in his journal, listened to Harris spin yarns of his "hair breath escapes." If Jim chose, he could have added a few tales of his own, including one of the time when he had started from near this very spot on a lonesome six-hundred-mile walk through hostile wilderness to the Missouri River, with only eleven bullets in his gun. Very exciting to hear. But, as increasing numbers of emigrants were learning, the unromantic diseases of ordinary life were sometimes harder to avoid than were Indians or grizzly bears.

The next morning they buried Barnett. Clyman scratched the dead man's name and the date, August 26, 1844, on a boulder and set it up as a tombstone. Then on they hurried, crossing South Pass and rejoining the main part of the train on the Little Sandy, a tributary of the Green. Most of the emigrants, including Clyman, went on down the Green and followed the Trail's southern dip to fresh supplies at Fort Bridger. Some of the Californians, however, and some of Gilliam's group, traveling separately, crushed through the sagebrush as due west to Bear River in Utah as the thirsty terrain would allow. Marcus Whitman had probably gone somewhere in the same vicinity with his cart; but this was the first time any considerable number of wagons had used what eventually became known as Sublette's or Greenwood's Cutoff. A man who used the route went more than forty miles without a drink and missed the refreshments of Fort Bridger; but he saved fifty-three miles on his way West. During the hurry-up days of the Gold Rush, the short cut became popular.

Beyond Fort Bridger, danger from Indians was deemed past and the caravans of 1844, like those of every other year, broke into fragments. Clyman and three others who were unencumbered with families pushed ahead with pack horses. More than once they thought longingly of the deluges of spring. For almost a thousand miles not a raindrop touched them. Along the Snake volcanic dust fogged up from the horses' feet; in eastern Oregon the smoke of forest fires oppressed them. But by traveling light they averaged twenty-five to thirty miles a day, double the rate of the increasingly weary wagon drivers behind them.

On October 13 they reached Oregon City. Already parties with boats and supplies were hurrying up the Columbia gorge to meet the half-starved families in the rear. The first of the migrants straggled into Oregon City nearly a month later. One would suppose that the first thought of every hard-taxed soul would be to settle on a farm from which he never again would have to move. But it did not work that way. As Clyman wrote shortly after his arrival to a friend back home:

> Notwithstanding the ease with which the necessaries of life are acquired, I never saw a more discontented community, owing principally to natural disposition. Nearly all, like myself, having been of a roving discontented character before leaving their eastern homes. The long tiresome trip from the States, has taught them what they are capable of performing and enduring. They talk of removing to the Islands, California, Chili, and other parts of South America with as much composure as you in Wisconsin talk of removing to Indiana or Michigan.

Fiddle-footed. In the spring of '45 Clyman led a large group of malcontents south to California. In '46 he rode back to the States, turned around in '48, and eventually settled near Napa, north of San Francisco. Fortunately for the Northwest, not all his companions of 1844 were quite so hard to suit. Nathaniel Ford, who located west of the Willamette, near the Applegates' original filings, wrote a letter home of quite a different cast:

> We had a tedious and tiring trip; but I think we are well paid for our trouble; we are in the best country I have ever seen for farming and stock raising. . . . My family are healthier than they ever

were before. My wife has fine health, and weighs heavier than she has for some fifteen years. Mary Ann, who, you know, never had any health, has now very fine health. I have got entirely clear of the dyspepsy, and can do more hard labor than I have for fifteen years.... There was raised in this neighborhood, last season, 55 bushels [of wheat] per acre ... no rust or blasted wheat ... as fine flour as I ever saw.... The prairies are easily broken with two yoke of oxen, and harrows up fine for seeding.... All the springs and streams are cool and fine flavored ... fine view ... the finest fish ....

Paradise, in short. And so far, reaching heaven's gates had brought the emigrants no real disasters. That sort of trouble was reserved for 1845.

The caravan of 1844 had eschewed the route through Marcus Whitman's mission and had found a shorter way to the Columbia by slanting along one of its tributaries, the Umatilla. But no one had yet discovered how to avoid the Dalles or, beyond the Dalles, the thundering gorge and its dismaying rapids. The people reached these desperate stretches almost completely exhausted by their long journey. Abandoning the wagons they had struggled so hard to bring with them was a wrench; floating the vehicles down the river on rafts was dangerous. Although cattle could be driven along the rough mountain trails, numbers of them were always lost during the ordeal. That few human lives had also been lost was largely due to the last-minute help rushed upstream in 1843 and again in 1844 by John McLoughlin and the residents of Oregon City.

Somehow an easier way had to be found. The settlers of the Willamette raised $2000 and with it hired Elijah White, Moses Harris, and a few others to explore the Cascade chain for a direct way between Fort Boise and the valley. The searchers failed; but the knowledge that they were looking for an easy way may have contributed to the disaster that struck a section of the 1845 caravan.

The guide of the 1845 train was Stephen H. L. Meek, a mountaineer who had seen part of Oregon with Bonneville in the 1830s and who had journeyed along the trail with Elijah White and Lansford Hastings in 1842. Dependent on him in 1845 was the largest train yet to take to the plains—3000 persons by some estimates.

The caravan was so unwieldly that its leaders split it into segments. Supposedly the three units, each of which took its turn leading the way, were to stay a day's journey apart. Such exact scheduling of course proved impossible. At one point on the Platte, Joel Palmer, chief chronicler of that year's migration, saw not three but four units of 52, 13, 43, and 37 wagons camped within three miles of each other. Stephen Watts Kearny, marching by with 250 dragoons to awe the Indians, counted 460 wagons almost nose to tail in a line three miles long.

As part of his mission to protect the emigrants, Kearny called the Sioux into council on the meadows between the competing posts of Fort Laramie and Fort Platte. His officers and the leading chiefs of the Indians sat in chairs built for the occasion by the traders at Fort Platte. Lesser warriors sat on a carpet of elkskins. Beyond them, watching intently, was a huge semicircle of curious men, women, and children. The peace pipe passed among the chair-occupiers. Kearny made a speech saying that the Indians must not interfere with the emigrants and emphasized the point by firing his two howitzers. The Indians jumped and said they'd be good. That evening a dazzling display of rockets bloomed in the dark sky. Great medicine—Kearny announced that the rockets bore messages to the Great Spirit, saying that the Indians had listened to wisdom and would let the road stay open. But when the emigrants arrived a little later, the Indians expressed dissatisfaction about the way in which the white men were frightening off the buffalo. To placate the savages, the travelers chipped in together to buy enough bread, meat, and sugar for feasting a horde of Indians under the cottonwood trees. No trouble developed; indeed, the Sioux and their relatives made no serious attacks along this section of trail until the 1850s.

Once the Indian threat was behind them, the emigrants straggled out in the usual disorganized mass. They refreshed themselves at Fort Bridger, crunched through wriggling carpets of black crickets on the Bear River, and at Fort Hall found Caleb Greenwood trying to divert travel to California. Greenwood picked up perhaps fifty wagons. Possibly he would have prevailed on even more if Stephen Meek had not spoken up and said he knew a short cut through the deserts of eastern Oregon into the southern end of the Willamette Valley that would save the Oregon travelers 150 miles. Heartened by this, several wagon drivers decided to follow Meek. Others, seeing the tracks and hearing of the experiment, swung after them, until more than a hundred vehicles were pushing up the Malheur River beyond Fort Boise.

Meek may have thought he would meet Elijah White somewhere in the desert and from him learn of the supposed pass across the Cascades. Acrimonious historians go so far as to charge that White put Meek up to the venture before it was known whether or not a pass existed. (It didn't.) Be that as it may, the wagons soon found themselves wandering blindly in grassless, waterless wastes. Abandoning all idea of crossing the Cascades, the frightened company sent ten men to the Dalles for help.

Behind them, oxen began dropping dead in the blistering heat. Thirst and starvation frenzied the humans. According to one account, some of the choking men faced three wagons toward each other and raised a tripod of their tongues on which to hang Stephen Meek. Samual Hancock and a few calmer heads hid the guide in a wagon. They said he had escaped. Too dispirited to organize a pursuit, the lost souls cursed him wanly and crept north toward the Columbia. During the night Meek slipped free, rode ahead, and found water. Amazingly, he returned to his would-be executioners and guided them to life—or part of them. Death was closing in now. The wanderers had entrapped themselves among the granite chasms breaking into the Deschutes River.

Meek got through and went to the Dalles, where succor was already being marshaled by the volunteers who had ridden for help several days earlier. (Moses Harris was one of the saviors.) Ingeniously the rescue party rigged ropes across the Deschutes Canyon, suspended a wagon box from the spidery bridge, and during two weeks of gruelling effort managed to swing people, goods, and even vehicles to safety. For some it was too late. Twenty or more people had perished in the desert. An indeterminate number of others—some estimates run as high as fifty—later died from the effects of the travail. It was by far the worst disaster of the Oregon Road—and it has an almost inevitable postscript. Out in the desert, it is said, a portion of the dazed emigrants stumbled onto a fabulously rich gold mine. Later they could not recall the exact site, and to this day no one has again seen the lost Blue Bucket diggings of Oregon mythology.

The situation at the Dalles during the fall of 1845 was almost as frightful as that in the wastelands. Neither boats nor food were available for the clamoring hundreds. In desperation Samuel Barlow determined to find a land route south of Mount Hood. Off he went with nine wagons. More vehicles under William Rector and Joel Palmer followed him. Scouts climbed the great snow cone of Mount Hood for a panoramic view of the dense forests and tangled hills. They thought they saw a way through. Slowly they chopped and burned down the mammoth trees to open a passage for their wagons. Snow struck before they could finish. They made a cache of their goods; lacking horses, they packed their women and a minimum of camp equipment on a few cows, and fought downward through a nightmare of fallen timber, clinging bogs, and roaring streams. They barely won through; had volunteers not gone ahead for still another rescue party they might not have survived. But the route was workable. The next summer Barlow commenced a toll road which, though difficult, spared thousands of later emigrants the terrors of the Columbia's gorge.[3]

By staying on the regular trail through eastern Oregon in 1845, Joel Palmer had missed the sufferings of the wagon train that had followed Stephen Meek up the Malheur. But Palmer could guess their miseries; he had been in the Dalles when the survivors were brought in. He had also seen the despair of the migrants who were stranded beside the surging Columbia; and he had gone with Barlow's party through the fearsome country behind Mount Hood. In short, he knew how arduous travel to Oregon could be.

[3] While Barlow was building his road during the spring and summer of 1846, fifteen men under Levi Scott formed the South Road Company. Among them were Lindsay and Jesse Applegate and the ubiquitous Black Harris. They worked through the mountains of southern Oregon to Klamath Lake, across the northeastern tip of California, and on through the deserts of northern Nevada to the Humboldt River and the California Trail. The emigrants who used the South Road in 1846 suffered dreadfully from thirst, Indian alarms and, later, from drenching downpours in the Oregon timberlands. Rescuers—Harris was with them—prevented serious loss of life and during subsequent years the so-called Applegate (South) Road, like the Barlow Trail, spared many the travail of the Columbia's gorge.

The knowledge dismayed him not one bit, however. He liked Oregon, and he was sure his wife and children would also like it well enough not to mind the effort of getting there. So in the spring of 1846, joining an eastbound party of seventeen other men, he rode home to Indiana to fetch them.

On July 7 the travelers, carrying with them 700 letters for mailing in the States, reached St. Joseph, Missouri. Because of threats of war against both England and Mexico, westbound emigration was much lighter than it had been during the preceding year. Even so, Palmer's group had passed fifteen companies strung out at short distances—word was getting around that small groups fared better than large ones. In spite of the conflict that developed with Mexico, almost half of these travelers were aimed toward California.

The other possible war, with Great Britain, had not materialized. Before Palmer reached home (newspapers as far away as Washington carried accounts of his trip), he learned that the United States and England had compromised their differences. The Northwest as far as the 49th parallel, including Puget Sound but not Vancouver Island, was now American territory. The accord intensified interest in Oregon. To take advantage of the trend, Palmer immediately wrote so detailed a journal of his adventures that the volume was used as a guidebook for later travel to the West.

Before more than a few copies of the journal were off the press, Palmer was in Independence again, this time with his family. Ironically enough, Congress, floundering through furious debates over the extension of slavery, had done nothing to organize the new territory which its expansionists had been so eager to acquire. Oregon, possessing neither a proper governor, legislature, nor territorial laws, existed in a legal vacuum. Nevertheless people poured in. One estimate says that in 1847 4500 people journeyed into the Northwest, only 1000 into war-torn California. Even more significantly, perhaps, 1847 was also the year when an advance party of Mormons, led by Brigham Young, left their winter quarters near Council Bluffs and moved up the north bank of the Platte, hunting new homes beyond the Rocky Mountains for their displaced fellows. It was the beginning of one of the most astounding folk movements in history, surpassed only by the frenzied Gold Rush that flooded along much of the same trail two years later.

Of the 4500 persons bound for Oregon in 1847, a sizable portion went down the Humboldt River and followed the Applegate (South) Road through southern Oregon into the upper Willamette. Palmer, however, elected captain of a train of 99 wagons, clung with the majority of the travelers to the familiar way by the Snake, through Grande Ronde, and over the Blue Mountains toward the Umatilla and the Dalles. In Palmer's caravan, as in the others, several travelers fell ill with measles. Some of the worst of the sufferers were taken (as sufferers had been taken every year) to Marcus and Narcissa Whitman's mission at Waiilatpu for nursing. There they came into contact with Cayuse Indians. Other Cayuses, trading game and dried fish and bits of corn to the passing wagons in the Blue Mountains, also picked up the disease.

Unlike the whites, the Indians of a hundred or more years ago were blessed with no partial immunity to measles. Before the harried Whitmans had fully grasped the horrors latent in the situation, more than half the Cayuse tribe had perished under unspeakable conditions.

The epidemic topped years of growing ill will, most of it springing from causes outside the province of this book. Because of that animosity, agitators among the surviving Indians found ready listeners when they charged that Marcus Whitman was deliberately poisoning the tribe so that this influx of white men could seize the Cayuse lands. Besides, Indian tradition allowed members of a bereaved family to kill a medicine man who failed to cure one of their members—and Whitman was currently failing with dozens.

The massacre came on the morning of November 29, 1847. Narcissa, Marcus, and eleven more men were brutally slain. Forty-seven other persons, thirty-four of them children, were held captive for weeks. Two additional children who had been adopted by the Whitmans and who were bedridden at the time with measles, died of neglect—Louise Sager and Helen Mar Meek, the latter the abandoned daughter of mountain man Joe Meek.

Most, probably all, of the women and older girls among the captives were raped, including another adopted child of the Whitmans', Mary Ann Bridger, daughter of mountain man Jim Bridger. Finally the terrified prisoners were ransomed by still another mountain man, Peter Skene Ogden of the Hudson's Bay Company. But Mary Ann Bridger shortly thereafter died as a result of her ordeal.

Word of the massacre shook a furious army of volunteer soldiers out of the little towns of the Willamette. As they marched toward Waiilatpu under Cornelius Gilliam, captain of one of the emigrant trains of 1844, the Indians fled. The Oregon Trail was open again. But a general war was feared, and the provisional government of Oregon wanted the government of the United States to pay some heed to the territory's plight. Although winter locked the mountains, Joe Meek (Stephen Meek's brother and Helen Mar's father) was asked whether he could possibly get dispatches through to Washington. Joe said he'd try.

Accompanied by nine men, he made the trip in almost record time. Some of the way the group traveled on snowshoes made from willow twigs. In the valley of the Bear they ate one of their horses to keep from starving. Often they avoided Indians by journeying through the freezing night. They arrived in St. Louis rawskinned, bearded, dirty. Joe, a born showman, decided to stay that way. Wearing his trail-stained buckskins and announcing himself through the fascinated newspapers as "Envoy Extraordinary and Minister Plenipotentiary from the Republic of Oregon to the Court of the United States," he walked straight into the White House itself.

The story of the Whitman massacre shocked the entire country. Congress forgot its dissensions long enough to organize Oregon Territory and appoint Joseph Lane governor. Joe Meek was named United States Marshal and authorized to take the new governor and his entourage back to Oregon.

By now late summer 1848 had arrived. Joe decided against risking his dudes to the rough winters of the Blue Mountains. Instead, they turned their wagons down the Santa Fe trial. At the capital of New Mexico they transferred their gear to packhorses and rode by way of Tucson and the ancient Gila River route to the Colorado, forded it on rafts made of bullrushes, and continued through the grim deserts to Los Angeles. There they heard word of the incredible discovery at Sutter's Mill that would turn the Oregon and California trails into highways beaten so broad and bare that the marveling Indians would name the way the great medicine road of the whites. Gold! Jim Clyman, traveling west once again with a dangerously small party in the summer of 1848, heard the news from eastbound Mormons somewhere on the slopes of the Sierra Nevada. Peter Burnett of the 1843 emigrants heard it in Oregon and joined the throng rushing south. An Arkansas newspaper printed the first story in the States. A shiver ran through the nation, and the frontier vaulted more than a thousand miles westward almost overnight.

Meek did not pause to mine any California gold. By ship and canoe he must get the governor to Oregon as soon as possible. He made it by March 1849. It is appropriate that he, an old mountain man, should have been chosen to do it. Ever since the day Champlain had stood on the shores of Lake Huron and had peered west into mystery, fur-gatherers had been the ones to take civilization just a little farther along the trail, until at last the yearnings came true and men stood beside the sea of their desiring.

BIBLIOGRAPHY AND
ACKNOWLEDGMENTS

Sources for the main divisions of this book are noted below in the general bibliography, which is arranged topically. Additional, more specific references follow, arranged by chapter and topic. There is, of course, some overlapping. The intent is not to furnish data for scholars but to suggest to interested readers avenues to additional information.

The unpublished sources used in preparing this account include a letter, October 7, 1809, of Pierre Menard to Langlois, photostat furnished by the Missouri Historical Society; and Cyrus Shepard's "Journal of a Trip across the Plains in 1834," microfilm furnished through the courtesy of the Coe Collection, Yale University Library.

At the Henry E. Huntington Library, San Marino, California, I was privileged to peruse William Marshall Anderson's "Notes of Remembrance Taken on a Tour of the Rocky Mountains March 11, 1834 to September 29, 1834," and the manuscript diaries of Elkanah Walker and Mary R. Walker. The diaries of Mary Walker were published, with deletions, by the University of Montana in 1932 in the *Sources of Northwest History,* number 15. At the Huntington Library also, I was able to use a typescript, prepared by C. J. Brosnan, of Francis Ermatinger's "Correspondence, 1823–1853," finding especially useful his letters to his brother Edward dated March 11, 1836, March 16 and June 1, 1837, and March 19, 1838.

The Wyles Collection at the library of the University of California at Santa Barbara contains microcards of nearly every item listed in Henry Wagner's and Charles Camp's *The Plains and the Rockies, A Bibliography of Original Narratives of Travel and Adventure, 1800–1865.* These reproductions made readily available many rare accounts I could not otherwise have studied.

I learned of the Menard letter cited above from Richard Oglesby. Its colloquial French and difficult penmanship were deciphered for me by Denise Miller and Andrée Schlemmer. Dale L. Morgan answered various questions with his usual unfailing courtesy and exhaustive care. George R. Stewart and Joe Backus first and later Tom May were delightful traveling companions along various sections of the trail, trips most pleasantly broken by the hospitality of Sue and Charles Beck at their ranch near Dubois, Wyoming. Leith Moreland helped with the maps; the data for those dealing with the Great Lakes and Upper Mississippi were furnished in large part by the Minnesota Historical Society.

My wife Mildred typed the finished copy of the manuscript; more importantly, she regenerated buoyancy when at times I began to sag.

GENERAL BIBLIOGRAPHY

Histories Relating to the Northwest

Bancroft, Hubert H. *History of the Northwest Coast*, 2 vols. San Francisco, 1886.

------. *History of Oregon, 1834–1888* (vol. 1) San Francisco, 1886.

Billington, Ray Allen. *Westward Expansion: A History of the American Frontier*. New York, 1950.

------. *The Far Western Frontier*. New York, 1956.

Carey, Charles H. *A General History of Oregon*, 2 vols. Portland, 1935.

Fuller, George. *A History of the Pacific Northwest*. New York, 1931.

Graebner, Norman A. *Empire on the Pacific*. New York, 1955.

Howay, F. W., W. W. Sage, and H. F. Angus. *British Columbia and the United States*. Toronto, 1942.

Johansen, Dorothy and Charles M. Gates. *Empire on the Columbia*. New York, 1957.

Morton, Arthur S. *A History of the Canadian West*. London, 1939.

Riegel, Robert. *America Moves West*. New York, 1956.

Winther, Oscar Osburn. *The Old Oregon Country*. Stanford, California, 1950.

Extended Accounts of the British and American Fur Trade

Berry, Don. *A Majority of Scoundrels*. New York, 1961.

Chittenden, Hiram M. *The American Fur Trade of the Far West*, 2 vols. Stanford, California, 1954.

DeVoto, Bernard. *Across the Wide Missouri*. Boston, 1947.

Innis, Harold A. *The Fur Trade in Canada* (rev. ed.). Toronto, 1956.

MacKay, Douglas. *The Honourable Company*. Indianapolis, 1936.

Morgan, Dale L. *Jedediah Smith and the Opening of the West*. Indianapolis, 1953.

Phillips, Paul C. *The Fur Trade*, 2 vols. Norman, Oklahoma, 1961.

Rich, E. E. (ed.) *The Letters of John McLoughlin From Fort Vancouver to the Governor and Committee*, 1825 (see especially introduction by W. Kaye Lamb), 3 vols. Toronto, 1941, 1943, 1944.

Sunder, John E. *Bill Sublette, Mountain Man*. Norman, Oklahoma, 1959.

Victor, Francis Fuller. *The River of the West* (Joe Meek's autobiography). Hartford, 1871.

General Accounts of the Westward Migrations

Bell, James Christy, Jr. *Opening A Highway to the Pacific, 1838–46*. New York, 1921.

Ghent, W. J. *The Road to Oregon*. New York, 1929.
Hulbert, Archer B. *Where Rolls the Oregon* and *The Call of the Columbia* (vols. iii and iv of *Overland to the Pacific*). Denver, 1933, 1934.
Monaghan, Jay. *The Overland Trail*. Indianapolis, 1937.
Paden, Irene D. *The Wake of the Prairie Schooner*. New York, 1943.
Dale, Harrison C. "The Organization of the Oregon Emigrating Companies," *Oregon Historical Quarterly*, XVI (Sept. 1915), 205–27.

Missionary Activities

Brosnan, Cornelius. *Jason Lee, Prophet of the New Oregon*. New York, 1932.
Chittenden, H. M. and H. T. Richardson. *Life, Letters, and Travels of Pierre-Jean de Smet, S.J., 1801–1873*, 4 vols. New York, 1905.
Drury, Clifford M. *Henry Harmon Spalding*. Caldwell, Idaho, 1936.
———. *Marcus Whitman, M.D.* Caldwell, Idaho, 1937.
———. *Elkanah and Mary Walker*. Caldwell, Idaho, 1940.
Gray, William H. *A History of Oregon, 1792–1849*. Portland, Oregon, 1870.
Hulbert, Archer B. and Dorothy P. *The Oregon Crusade* (vol. v of *Overland to the Pacific*). Denver, 1935.
———. *Marcus Whitman, Crusader*, 3 vols. Denver, 1936–41.
Jones, Nard. *The Great Command*. Boston, 1959.
Whitman, Marcus and Narcissa. Letters, Journals, miscellany. *Oregon Pioneers Association Transactions, 1891, 1893*.

General Reference Works

Dictionary of American Biography.
Hodge, Frederick W. *Handbook of American Indians North of Mexico*, 2 vols. Reprint, New York, 1959.
Wheat, Carl I. *Mapping the Transmississippi West*, vols. i and ii. San Francisco, 1957, 1958.
Wagner, Henry R. and Charles L. Camp. *The Plains and the Rockies. A Bibliography of Original Narratives . . . 1800–1865* (third ed., revised). Columbus, Ohio, 1953.

BIBLIOGRAPHY OF SPECIFIC TOPICS

CHAPTERS 1–3

EARLY EXPLORATIONS, GENERAL ACCOUNTS
Bakeless, John. *The Eyes of Discovery*. New York, 1950.
Brebner, J. Bartlett. *Canada, A Modern History*. Ann Arbor, 1960.
———. *The Explorers of North America*. New York, 1933.

BIBLIOGRAPHY AND ACKNOWLEDGMENTS

Burpee, Lawrence J. *The Search for the Western Sea*, 2 vols. New York, 1936.
DeVoto, Bernard. *The Course of Empire*. Boston, 1952.
Lamb, Harold. *New Found World*. New York, 1955.
Wrong, George M. *The Conquest of New France*. New Haven, 1921.

SPECIFIC EXPLORATIONS
CHARLEVOIX

Kellogg, Louise P. (ed.) *Father Pierre François Xavier de Charlevoix*, 2 vols. (see esp. vol. ii). Chicago, 1923.

LA SALLE

Parkman, Francis. *La Salle and the Discovery of the Great West*. Various editions.

VÉRENDRYE

Burpee, Lawrence J. (ed.) *Journals and Letters of Pierre Gaultier de Varennes de la Vérendrye* (esp. pages 290–361, 406–32). Toronto, 1927.
Robinson, Doane. "La Vérendrye's Farthest West," *Proceedings of the State Historical Society of Wisconsin, 1913* (pp. 146–50).
Smurr, John W. "A New La Vérendrye Theory," *Pacific Northwest Quarterly*, XLIII (Jan. 1952), 51–64.

CARVER AND ROGERS

Carver, Jonathan. *Travels through the Interior Parts of North America...* (facsimile edition). Minneapolis, 1956.
Cuneo, John R. *Robert Rogers of the Rangers*. New York, 1959.
Elliott, T. C. "The Strange Case of Jonathan Carver and the Name Oregon," *Oregon Historical Quarterly*, XX (Dec. 1920), 341–68.
———. "Jonathan Carver's Source for the Name Oregon," *Oregon Historical Quarterly*, XXIII (March 1922), 52–69.
Kellogg, Louise P. "The Mission of Johathan Carver," *Wisconsin Magazine of History*, XII (Dec. 1928), 127–45.

UPPER MISSOURI RIVER AND MANDAN INDIANS

Catlin, George. *North American Indians* (Letters 10–22). Philadelphia, 1913.
Coues, Elliott (ed.) *New Light on the Early History of the Greater Northwest. The Manuscript Journals of Alexander Henry and David Thompson* (vol. i, 285–405). New York, 1897.
Mackenzie, Charles. "The Mississouri Indians... 1804–06," in L. R. Masson, *Les Bourgeois de la Compagnie du Nord-Ouest*, Vol. I. Quebec, 1889–90.
Thompson, David. *Narrative of His Explorations* (J. B. Tyrrell, ed.), pp. 230–40. Toronto, 1916.

CHAPTER 4

THE NORTHWEST COAST, 1776–1800

Cook, James and James King. *A Voyage to the Pacific Ocean* . . . , 3 vols. (vol. ii). London, 1784.

Howay, F. W. (ed.) *Voyages of the "Columbia" to the North West Coast.* Boston, 1941.

Manning, William R. "The Nootka Sound Controversy," *American Historical Association Annual Report for 1904.*

Meares, John. *Voyages* . . . *to the Northwest Coast of America,* 2 vols. London, 1790.

EXPLORATIONS ACROSS CANADA

Davidson, Gordon C. *The North West Company.* Berkeley, 1918.

Mackenzie, Alexander. *Voyages from Montreal* . . . *to the Frozen and Pacific Oceans.* Toronto, 1927.

Also Brebner, Burpee, DeVoto, and Masson as cited for chapters 1–3.

SPANISH EXPLORATIONS ON THE MISSOURI RIVER

Abel, Annie H. (ed.) *Tabeau's Narrative of Loisel's Expedition to the Upper Missouri.* Norman, Oklahoma, 1939.

Houck, Louis. *The Spanish Regime in Missouri,* Vol. II, 161–92, 247–58. Chicago, 1909.

Nasatir, A. P. *Before Lewis and Clark. Documents Illustrating the History of the Missouri, 1785–1804,* 2 vols. St. Louis, 1952.

———. "An Account of Spanish Louisiana," *Missouri Historical Review,* XXIV (1930), 219–39, 432–60, 585–608.

———. "The Anglo-Spanish Frontier in the Illinois Country . . . ," *Journal of the Illinois State Historical Society,* XXI (October 1928), 291–358.

———. "Anglo-Spanish Rivalry on the Upper Missouri," *Mississippi Valley Historical Review,* XVI (December 1929), 359–82; (March 1930), 507–28.

———. "The Formation of the Missouri Company," *Missouri Historical Review,* XXV (October 1930), 10–22.

———. "Jacques D'Eglise on the Upper Missouri, 1791–95," *Mississippi Valley Historical Review,* XIV (June 1927), 47–71.

———. "John Evans, Explorer and Surveyor," *Missouri Historical Review,* XXV (January, April, July, 1931), 219–39, 432–60, 585–608.

Quaife, Milo (ed.) "Extracts from Captain McKay's Journal," *Proceedings of the State Historical Society of Wisconsin* (1915), pp. 186–210.

Williams, David. "John Evans' Strange Journey," *American Historical Review,* LIV (Jan., April 1949), 277–95, 508–29.

BIBLIOGRAPHY AND ACKNOWLEDGMENTS

CHAPTERS 5–6

LEWIS AND CLARK

Bakeless, John. *Lewis and Clark, Partners in Discovery.* New York, 1947.

DeVoto, Bernard. *The Journals of Lewis and Clark* (see especially the introduction). Boston, 1953.

Thwaites, R. G. (ed.) *The Original Journals of Lewis and Clark,* 7 vols. New York, 1905.

Burpee, L. J. (ed.) *Journal of Francis Antoine Laroque ... to the Yellowstone, 1805.* Ottawa, 1910.

CHAPTER 7

TRADING AND TRAPPING METHODS

McIlvaine, Caroline M. (ed.) *The Autobiography of Gurdon Saltonstall Hubbard* (pp. 51–58, 74–124). Chicago, 1911.

MacKenzie, Charles, as cited in references for chapters 1–3 (see pp. 332–33).

Innis, Harold A. *The Fur Trade of Canada* (pp. 405–6). Toronto, 1956.

Martin, Horace T. *Castorologia* (pp. 121–30). Montreal, 1892.

Morgan, Lewis H. *The American Beaver and His Works* (pp. 223–40). Philadelphia, 1868.

EARLY AMERICAN ADVENTURES ON THE MISSOURI

Harris, Burton. *John Colter, His Years in the Rockies.* New York, 1952.

James, Thomas. *Three Years Among the Mexicans and Indians* (Walter B. Douglas, ed.) (chapters I–II). St. Louis, 1916.

Douglas, Walter B. "Manuel Lisa," *Missouri Historical Collections,* III (1911), 233–68; IV (1911), 367–406.

Holmes, Reuben. "The Five Scalps" (Stella M. Drumm, ed.), *Glimpses of the Past,* V (January–March 1938), Missouri Historical Society.

Pryor, Nathaniel. "Report" on the encounter with the Arikara. *Annals of Iowa,* I (3rd series), 616–19.

LETTERS, REPORTS ABOUT SHE-HE-KE'S RETURN

Carter, Clarence E. (ed.) *Territorial Papers of the United States,* vol. xiv, *The Territory of Louisiana-Missouri, 1806–09* (pp. 108–9, 122, 126, 153–54, 285–86, 343–48). Washington, D.C., 1949.

TROUBLE WITH BLACKFEET (*Miscellaneous*)

Biddle, Thomas to Col. Atkinson, Oct. 29, 1819. *American State Papers, Indian Affairs,* vol. ii, pp. 201–3. Washington, 1834.

Thompson, *Narrative,* as cited, pp. 423–45, 551–52.

BIBLIOGRAPHY AND ACKNOWLEDGMENTS

THOMPSON AND PINCH-PERCH

Barry, J. Nielson. "Lieutenant Jeremy Pinch," *Oregon Historical Quarterly*, XXXVIII (Sept. 1937), 323–27.

Elliott, T. C. "The Strange Case of David Thompson and Jeremy Pinch," *Oregon Historical Quarterly*, XL (Sept. 1939), 188–99.

Ghent, W. J. "Jeremy Pinch Again," *Oregon Historical Quarterly*, XL (December 1939), 308–14.

CHAPTER 8

THE ASTORIAN ADVENTURE

Brackenridge, Henry. *Journal of a Voyage up the River Missouri.* . . . [R. G. Thwaites, *Early Western Travels*, vol. vi, pp. 27–146. Cleveland, 1905.]

Bradbury, John. *Travels in the Interior of North America.* . . . [R. G. Thwaites, *Early Western Travels*, vol. v, pp. 35–183, 224–34]

Franchère, Gabriel. *Narrative of a Voyage to the Northwest Coast.* . . . [R. G. Thwaites, *Early Western Travels*, vol. vi.]

Irving, Washington. *Astoria*, 2 vols. Philadelphia, 1836.

Porter, Kenneth W. *John Jacob Astor, Business Man*, 164–207, Cambridge, Mass., 1931.

Rollins, Philip A. *The Discovery of the Oregon Trail* (contains Robert Stuart's *Journal* and *Travelling Memoranda*, also W. P. Hunt's diary, translated from *Nouvelles Annales des Voyages.* . . .). New York, 1935.

Ross, Alexander. *Adventures of the First Settlers on the Oregon.* . . . London, 1849.

Barry, J. Nielson. "Astorians," *Washington Historical Quarterly*, XXIV (October 1933), 221–31, 282–301.

Bridgwater, Dorothy W. (ed.) "John Jacob Astor Relative to His Settlement on the Columbia River," *The Yale University Library Gazette*, XXIV (Oct. 1949), 47–69.

Drumm, Stella M. "More About Some Astorians," *Oregon Historical Quarterly*, XXIV (Dec. 1923), 335–60.

CHAPTERS 9–11

PROPOSALS TO OCCUPY OREGON

Ambler, Charles. *The Life and Diary of John Floyd* (pp. 52–75). Richmond, Va., 1918.

Benton, Thomas Hart. *Abridgment of the Debates of Congress* (vol. vii, pp. 74–81, 392–405; vol. viii, 195–221). New York, 1858.

———. *Thirty Years' View* (vol. I, pp. 13–14, 50–54, 109–11). New York, 1854–56.

Bourne, Edward G. "Aspects of Oregon History Before 1840," *Oregon Historical Quarterly*, VI (Sept. 1905), 261–70.

BIBLIOGRAPHY AND ACKNOWLEDGMENTS

THE YELLOWSTONE EXPEDITION

American State Papers. Military Affairs, vol. i, pp. 324–25; vol. ii, 33–34. Washington, 1832–34.

Carter, Clarence E. (ed.) Territorial Papers of the United States, vol. xv, The Territory of Missouri. Washington, 1952.

Niles' Register, vols. xiv, xv, xvi, passim. Baltimore, Maryland.

Goodwin, Cardinal. "A Larger View of the Yellowstone Expedition, 1819–20," The Mississippi Valley Historical Review, IV (Dec. 1917), 299–313.

Jameson, J. Franklin. "The Correspondence of John C. Calhoun," Annual Report of the American Historical Association, II (1899), 134–36, 150–70.

Wesley, Edgar. "A Still Larger View of the So-Called Yellowstone Expedition," North Dakota Historical Quarterly, V (July 1931), 219–38.

THE ARIKARA BATTLE AND AFTERMATH

American State Papers. Military Affairs, vol. ii, pp. 578–79, 587–95. Washington, 1832–34.

Benton, Thomas H. Abridgment, as cited above (vol. vii, pp. 543–56).

Camp, Charles L. (ed.). James Clyman, Frontiersman (pp. 7–25). Portland, Oregon. 1960.

Dale, Harrison C. The Ashley-Smith Explorations. . . . 1822–29. Glendale, Calif., 1941.

Frost, Donald McKay. Notes of General Ashley, The Overland Trail, and South Pass. Worcester, Mass., 1945.

Robinson, Doane. (ed.). "Official Correspondence Pertaining to the Leavenworth Expedition of 1823," South Dakota Historical Collections, I (1907), 179–256.

United States Government, 18th Congress, First Session, Senate Document 1, Serial 89.

———, 18th Congress, First Session, Senate Document 56, Serial 91.

OPENING OF ROCKY MOUNTAIN FUR TRADE

Camp, Charles L., as cited above (pp. 26–29, 35–38).

Dale, Harrison C., as cited above. Ashley's "Narrative," pp. 115–58.

Ferris, Warren A. Life in the Rocky Mountains (pp. 1–22). Denver, 1940.

Frost, Donald McKay, as cited above (passim).

Morgan, Dale L. and Carl I. Wheat. Jedediah Smith and His Maps of the American West. San Francisco, 1954.

United States Government, 21st Congress, Second Session, Senate Document 31, Serial 203.

———. 22nd Congress, First Session. Senate Document 90, Serial 213.

Mattes, Merrill J. "Hiram Scott, Fur Trader," Nebraska History, XXVI (July–September 1945), 127–62.

BIBLIOGRAPHY AND ACKNOWLEDGMENTS

————. "Jackson Hole, Crossroads of the Western Fur Trade, 1807–1840." *Pacific Northwest Quarterly*, XXXVIII (April 1946).

Morgan, Dale L. (ed.). "The Diary of William L. Ashley," Missouri Historical Society *Bulletin*, XI (Oct. 1954; Feb., April 1955).

Reid, Russell and C. G. Gannon. (eds.) "Journal of the Atkinson-O'Fallon Expedition," *North Dakota Historical Quarterly*, IV (October, 1929), 5–56.

BRITISH-AMERICAN FUR TRADE CONFLICT

Merk, Frederick. (ed.). *Fur Trade and Empire: George Simpson's Journal, 1824–25* (see especially Introduction and Letters in Appendix A, Cambridge, Mass., 1931. pp. 257–77, 281–85).

————. "The Snake Country Expedition. . . . 1824–25," *Mississippi Valley Historical Review*, XXI (June 1934).

Rich, E. E. (ed.). *Peter Skene Ogden's Snake Country Journals, 1824–25 and 1825–26*. London, 1950.

Ross, Alexander. *Fur Hunters of the Far West*, 2 vols. London, 1855.

Simpson, George. *Part of a Dispatch . . . to the . . . Hudson's Bay Company*. (E. E. Rich, ed.) (pp. 49–75). London and Toronto, 1947.

United States Government. 21st Congress, 2nd Session, *Senate Document 39*, Serial 203.

CHAPTERS 12–13

HALL J. KELLEY

Hall J. Kelley on Oregon (F. W. Powell, ed.) Princeton, 1932. A collection of five of Kelley's published works.

Powell, Fred W. "Hall Jackson Kelley, Prophet of Oregon," *Oregon Historical Quarterly*, XVIII (1917).

Snelling, W. J. Attacks on Kelley in *The New England Magazine*, II (February and April, 1832), 123–32, 320–26.

Woodall, Allen E. "William Joseph Snelling: A Review of His Life and Writings," abstract in University of Pittsburgh *Bulletin*, XXIX (Jan. 1933), 281–86.

BONNEVILLE, WYETH AND JASON LEE

Ball, John. *Autobiography* (compiled by Kate Ball Powers, Flora Ball Hopkins, Lucy Ball) (pp. 59–98). Grand Rapids, Michigan, 1925.

Irving, Washington. *The Adventures of Captain Bonneville* (Edgeley W. Todd, ed.) Norman, Oklahoma, 1961.

Russell, Osborne. *Journal of a Trapper* (Aubrey L. Haynes, ed.) (pp. 1–5). Portland, Oregon, 1957.

Townsend, John K. *Narrative of a Journey . . . to the Columbia River*, in R. G. Thwaites' *Early Western Travels*, vol. xxi. Cleveland, 1905.

Wyeth, John B. *Oregon. Or, a Short History of a Long Journey*, in R. G. Thwaites' *Early Western Travels*, vol. xxi. Cleveland, 1905.

Wyeth, Nathaniel. *Correspondence and Journals, 1831–36* (F. G. Young, ed.) Eugene, Oregon, 1899.

Ball, John. "Across the Continent Seventy Years Ago," *Oregon Historical Quarterly*, III (March 1902).

Eaton, W. Clement. "Nathaniel Wyeth's Oregon Expeditions," *Pacific Historical Review*, IV (1935), 101–13.

Lee, Jason. "Diary," *Oregon Historical Quarterly*, XVII (June, Sept., Dec., 1916), 116–46, 297–430.

CHAPTERS 14–16

THE MISSIONARIES

(See also this heading under Manuscripts and General Bibliography)

Chambers, J. S. *The Conquest of Cholera, America's Greatest Scourge.* New York, 1938.

Palladino, J. B. *Indian and White in the Northwest* (chaps. I–IV). Lancaster, Pennsylvania, 1922.

Parker, Samuel. *Journal of an Exploring Tour . . .* (pp. 1–148). Ithaca, New York, 1838.

Brown, David L. "Three Years in the Rocky Mountains," by a Trapper. *Cincinnati Daily Morning Atlas*, Sept. 8, 10, 11, 12, 13, 1845.

Eells, Myra F. "Diary," *Transactions of the Oregon Pioneer Association* (pp. 54–88a). Portland, 1889.

Gray, William H. "Journal, December 28, 1836–October 15, 1837, *The Whitman College Quarterly*, XVI (June 1913).

Rogers, Cornelius. "The Journey to the Rocky Mountains," *Oregonian and Indians Advocate*, I (December 1838).

Walker, Mary R. "Diary," *Sources of Northwest History*, No. 15. Missoula, Montana, 1932.

CHAPTERS 17–18

EMIGRATIONS OF 1839–40

Hafen, LeRoy R. and Ann W. Hafen (eds.). *To the Rockies and Oregon.* Glendale, California, 1955. Contains diaries and reminiscences by members of the Peoria party—Cook, Holman, Oakley, Smith, Shortess.

Farnham, Thomas Jefferson. *Travels in the Great Western Prairies.* In R. G. Thwaites', *Early Western Travels*, vols. xxviii–xxix. Cleveland, 1906.

Newell, Robert. "Memorandum" (Dorothy Johansen, ed.) Portland, Oregon, 1959.

Wislizenus, F. A. *A Journey to the Rocky Mountains in the Year 1839.* St. Louis, 1912.

Lee, Jason. "Peoria Speech" (Stuart Mackford, ed.) *Oregon Historical Quarterly*, LIX (March 1958), 19–26.

Munger, Asahel. "Diary," *Oregon Historical Quarterly*, VIII (Dec. 1907), 387–405.

Shippee, Lester Burrell. "Federal Relations of Oregon," *Oregon Historical Quarterly*, XXIX (Dec. 1918), 283–305.

Tarascon, Lewis A. "To the People of the United States ... on ... a Wagon Road ... to the River Columbia" (broadside), Huntington Library, San Marino, California.

————. Western proposals in *Magazine of History*, Extra Number 148. Tarrytown, New York, 1929.

EMIGRATIONS OF 1840, 1841, 1842

Allen, A. J. *Ten Years in Oregon. Travels and Adventures of Dr. E. White and Lady* ... Ithaca, New York, 1848.

Bidwell, John. *A Journey to California*. San Francisco, 1937.

Chittenden, Hiram M. and Alfred T. Richardson. *Life, Letters, and Travels of Father Pierre-Jean De Smet, S.J. 1801–1873*. New York, 1905. (The Indian delegations, pp. 19–43; the 1840 trip, pp. 198–304; the 1841 trip, pp. 272–314.)

Crawford, Medorem. *Journal, 1842* (F. G. Young, ed.). Eugene, Oregon, 1897.

Frémont, John Charles. *Narratives of Exploration and Adventure* (Allan Nevins, ed.) New York, 1956. (First expedition, pp. 86–118.)

Hastings, Lansford. *The Emigrants' Guide to Oregon and California* (pp. 1–33). Princeton, 1932.

Williams, Joseph. *Narrative of a Tour to the Oregon Territory*, in Hafen and Hafen, *op. cit.*, pp. 199–287.

Tobie, H. E. "From the Missouri to the Columbia, 1841," *Oregon Historical Quarterly*, XXXVIII (June 1937), 135–59.

CHAPTER 19

EMIGRATION OF 1843

Applegate, Jesse A. *Recollections of My Boyhood*. Chicago, 1934.

Burnett, Peter. *Recollections and Opinions of an Old Pioneer* (chap. iii). New York, 1880.

Edwards, Philip L. *Sketch of Oregon Territory*. Liberty, Missouri, 1842.

Field, Matthew C. *Prairie and Mountain Sketches* (Kate Gregg and John F. McDermott, eds.) Norman, Oklahoma, 1957.

Frémont, John C. *Op. cit.*, pp. 182–307.

Johnson, Overton and William H. Winter. *Route Across the Rocky Mountains.* ... Princeton, 1932.

Wilkes, George. *A History of Oregon.* ... New York, 1845.

Applegate, Jesse. "A Day with the Cow Column in 1843," *Oregon Historical Quarterly*, I (December 1900).

Burnett, Peter. "Letters," *Oregon Historical Quarterly*, III (1902), 398–426.

BIBLIOGRAPHY AND ACKNOWLEDGMENTS

Nesmith, James W. "Diary," *Oregon Historical Quarterly*, VII (Dec. 1906), 329–59.

Newby, William T. "Diary," *Oregon Historical Quarterly*, XL (Sept. 1939), 219–42.

CHAPTER 20

EMIGRATIONS OF 1844

Camp, Charles L. (ed.) *James Clyman, Frontiersman* (pp. 59–136, 267–77, 317–27). Portland, Oregon, 1960.

Parrish, Edward Evans. Journal, *Oregon Pioneer Association Transactions* (1888), pp. 82–122.

Minto, John. "Reminiscenses . . . in 1844," *Oregon Historical Society Quarterly*, II (June, Sept. 1901), 119–67, 209–54.

EMIGRATIONS OF 1845

Palmer, Joel. *Journal of Travels . . . to the Mouth of the Columbia River.* In R. G. Thwaites', *Early Western Travels*, vol. xxx. Cleveland, 1906.

Hancock, Samuel. *Narrative.* New York, 1927.

Barley, Walter. "The Barlow Road," *Oregon Historical Quarterly*, XIII (Sept. 1912), 287–96.

Barlow, Mary S. "History of the Barlow Road," *Oregon Historical Quarterly*, III (March 1902), 71–81.

EMIGRATIONS OF 1846

Bryant, Edwin. *What I Saw in California* (chaps. I–X). New York, 1848.

DeVoto, Bernard. *The Year of Decision: 1846.* Boston, 1943.

Parkman, Francis. *The California and Oregon Trail* (chaps. I–IX). Various editions.

Thornton, J. Quinn. *Oregon and California in 1848.* New York, 1849.

Applegate, Lindsay. "The Applegate Route in the Year 1846," *Oregon Historical Quarterly*, XXII (March 1921), 12–45.

INDEX

A

Acadia, 5, 9, 23
Adams, John Quincy, 175
Adams, Thomas (Indian), 331–332
Alaska, 54, 147
Albany traders, 57
Aleutian Peninsula, 54
Alleghenies, 5
Allis, Samuel, 270, 287, 289–290
American Board of Foreign Missions,
    269–271, 280, 310–311, 316, 344,
    359, 362
American Fur Company, 48n, 174, 232–
    233, 242, 246, 253
    caravans, 272, 280, 289–298, 318
American Philosophical Society, 65, 90
American Revolution, 61, 65
American Society for Encouraging the
    Settlement of the Oregon Territory,
    227–229, 327
Anza, Juan Bautista de, 66
Applegate, Jesse, 365, 368, 370, 373,
    375, 385–386
Arapaho Indians, 162, 165
Arikara Indians, 39, 48, 79n, 101, 134–
    136, 141, 179–180
Arkansas, 15
Arkansas River, 334
Armstrong, John, 65
Ashburton-Webster negotiations, 345,
    363
Ashley, William, 176–182, 189, 192–
    204, 206, 208, 211, 214–215, 224
Ashley Creek, 197
Assiniboine Indians, 17, 36, 42–43
Assiniboine River, 35–36
Astor, John Jacob, 146–148, 166–167,
    197
    expedition to Columbia River, 146–
    167
Astoria, 156–157, 159–160, 197
Astorians, 146–167
Athabaska Pass, 144
Atkinson, General Henry, 172, 207
Aztecs, 11

B

Badlands, 183
Ball, John, 231, 234, 243
Bancroft, Hubert Howe, 247
Banque Générale in Paris, 9–10
Barlow, Samuel, 396
Barlow Trail, 396n
Barnett, Joseph, 390–391
Bear Lake, 198, 210–211
Bear River, 208–209, 256, 300, 378
Beaux Hommes, Indian village, 45
Beauharnois, Governor, 28, 33, 44
Beaver, trapping, 119–124, 133, 185,
    192, 205, 210
Bella Coola, 71
Bent, Charles and George, 361
Benton, Thomas Hart, 145, 174–176,
    182, 207, 214
Bering, Vitus, 54
Bidwell-Bartelson party, 350–352
Bienville, Sieur de, 19–22
Big Hole Valley, 114
Big Horn country, 47, 182, 243
Big Horn River, 206
Biloxi, Mississippi, 19
Bismark, South Dakota, 37
Bitterroot Valley, 110–111, 366
Black Hills of South Dakota, 47, 219,
    235
Black's Fork, 377
Blackbird, Chief, 81–82
Blackfeet Indians, 109, 139–140, 143,
    179, 198–199
Bobé, Father, 20, 23
Boise River, 161, 260, 262, 303, 380
Bonneville, Benjamin Louis, 228–230,
    232–233, 236, 242–243, 245–247,
    257–264
Boston groups bound for Oregon, 226–
    227, 244, 246, 362
Bourgmont, Etienne de, 21–22, 25
Bozeman Pass, 114
Braddock, General, 51
Bridger, Jim, 315, 320, 340, 377–378
Bridger, Mary Ann, 399

413

INDEX

INDEX

INDEX

INDEX

INDEX

Books by David Lavender published by the UNP

Bent's Fort (BB 545)

Land of Giants: The Drive to the Pacific Northwest, 1750–1950 (Cloth and BB 679)

One Man's West (Cloth and BB 633)

The Rockies (Cloth and BB 763)

Westward Vision: The Story of the Oregon Trail (Cloth and BB 905)